Faces of War

Researching Your Adopted Soldier

Jennifer Holik

Also By Jennifer Holik

Stories from the World War II Battlefield
World War II Writing Prompts

Stories from the World War II Battlefield Volume 3
Writing the Stories of War

Stories from the World War II Battlefield Volume 2
Navigating the Service Records for the Navy, Coast Guard, Marine Corps, and Merchant Marines

Stories from the World War II Battlefield Volume 1
Reconstructing Army, Air Corps, and National Guard Service

Stories from the Battlefield: A Beginning Guide to World War II Research

The Tiger's Widow

Stories of the Lost

Engaging the Next Generation: A Guide for Genealogy Societies and Libraries

Branching Out: Genealogy for Adults

Branching Out: Genealogy for High School Students

Branching Out: Genealogy for 4th-8th Grades Students

Branching Out: Genealogy for 1st-3rd Grade Students

To Soar with the Tigers

Copyright Information

Copyright © 2016 Jennifer Holik
Publisher: Generations, Woodridge, Illinois

Editor: Logan Ausmus.
Cover Designer: Sarah Sucansky.

Holik, Jennifer, 1973 –
    Faces of War: Researching Your Adopted Soldier / Jennifer Holik. Includes bibliographical references and indexes.

ISBN: 1-938226-39-9
ISBN: 978-1-938226-39-7

Printed in the United States of America

Dedication

To all those who look after our soldiers overseas. Thank you for your dedication to honoring their service and memories.

Table of Contents

Purpose of this Book

Toni Morrison said, "If there's a book that you want to read, but it hasn't been written yet, then you must write it."

In 2015, I wrote and published two books in a new series, *Stories from the World War II Battlefield*. I wrote these books because nothing existed in the market, to help people research their World War II civilian, soldier, sailor, or Marine's service. I found only one book which barely assisted those researching Army service, updated in 2013. The two other military service books I found were six to ten years out of date. I found nothing to help families of Navy, Marine Corps, Merchant Marines, Air Corps/Army Air Forces, National Guard, and Coast Guard personnel with their research.

Volume 1 of this book series helps researchers move step-by-step through Army, Air Corps/Air Forces, and National Guard research, in over 300 pages. Volume 2 helps researchers with their Navy, Coast Guard, Marine Corps, and Merchant Marines research, in over 400 pages. Both volumes contain many examples of records.

After assisting men and women overseas who adopt graves officially through an Adoption Foundation program, or unofficially by just visiting the grave often, at any American Battle Monuments Commission (ABMC) World War I and World War II cemetery, I realized a book focused on the unique way overseas researchers conduct American military research, was needed. Thus, this book was born.

Please note the American Battle Monuments Commission (ABMC) does not offer a grave adoption program. These programs are created by private groups.

The documents contained and discussed in this book, and Volumes 1 and 2 of the *Stories from the World War II Battlefield*, are by no means the end of what is available. The records shown are commonly used to start research. There are thousands more available at different locations in the United States and Europe. It would be impossible to provide information on all records in these volumes.

Rather than create an ever changing printed appendix of additional resources and bibliographies, I gathered the most important together online. You can find these resources in my World War II Toolbox, located on my website, **The World War II Research and Writing Center**. The website contains full-length files you can view at your leisure.

Want to know more and keep up with my work, research, and U.S. and European speaking engagements? Please visit my website and subscribe to my quarterly newsletter.

Websites

World War II Research and Writing Center
http://wwiiresearchandwritingcenter.com

Introduction

Note: Instead of repeatedly naming each branch of the service when I talk about a serviceman or woman, throughout the book I use the term "soldier" to refer to anyone who fought during the war, despite their official title of Soldier (Army), Airman (Air Corps/Army Air Forces), Sailor (Navy, Merchant Marine, Coast Guard), or Marine (Marine Corps.)

World War I was fought between 1914 and 1918. This Great War laid the foundation for what would be World War II, a conflict that ravaged much of the globe between the years 1939 and 1945. Both wars affected generations of people who witnessed and experienced extreme danger on the front lines. It changed technology, the roles of men and women at home, and created a new way of living for many around the world.

During World War II, in the United States, this generation of soldiers and home front supporters were dubbed "The Greatest Generation." It is important to realize that, while the Greatest Generation suffered many losses and their lives were drastically changed, those changes trickled down to future generations. The men and women who lived through the hell of war changed and shaped the way we view war today. Their actions and work laid the foundation for those in subsequent generations to have more choices, especially women. Have you ever stopped to consider how the results of both wars affect your generation? Do we really need to understand the service and sacrifice of those who fought and died, to live today? Yes, we do, and to discover the answer we need to ask ourselves, "What can we learn by studying the past?"

Research and Write the Story

Have you ever attempted World War I or World War II research on your adopted soldier and hit a brick wall because of the lack of records available online? Did you get stuck because all the records burned? Researchers have been conditioned through many books and websites to believe there is no way to research a soldier's service if the records burned in the 1973 fire at the National Personnel Records Center in St. Louis, Missouri. However, researching military service can take many winding paths. There are many starting points from which the research can begin.

Researching a soldier's service is not a "one size fits all" approach and there is a process. If you adopted the graves of multiple soldiers across different branches, you will discover that the records are similar, yet different. Some branches provide more information on certain types of records than others.

Military research usually does not happen in chronological order of the soldier's service life. Often we find a piece here and a piece there, each from different time periods. We then have to locate records to fill in the gaps as much as possible. Because research does not happen in chronological order, creating a timeline of service is helpful. You will learn how in this book.

Finally, I feel the most important part of the research process is writing and sharing the information we locate on soldiers. Throughout the research process, I am constantly writing notes and pieces of biographies. Writing during the research process allows you to locate gaps, inconsistencies, and errors in the research. This provides an opportunity to seek new resources and information, which help to make the story as complete as possible. As you continue researching and writing, eventually you will find a story about the soldier's service you can share with others.

My Challenge to You

I believe everyone has a story that should be told. I also believe it is our duty to preserve the past so the memories of those who fought to preserve our freedoms are not lost in time. We have an obligation to pass these stories and lessons to the world so the history can be carried forward.

Do you need help writing the story? My book *Stories from the World War II Battlefield Volume 3: Writing the Stories of War* is available on my website. It contains tips on preparing to write the story and over 500 writing prompts to get the creative juices flowing.

To see finished examples of soldier stories, please read my books *Stories of the Lost* and *The Tiger's Widow,* available on my website. The stories contained in these volumes are vastly different due to the records and information available when I wrote them. The fact each story is different is good, because each story provides concrete examples of how you can begin the research and writing process with varying amounts of information.

My challenge to you after reading this volume is to begin researching and writing your soldier's story. Are you ready to accept the challenge?

Books

Holik, Jennifer. *Stories of the Lost.* Generations, Woodridge, IL: 2014.
Holik, Jennifer. *The Tiger's Widow.* Generations, Woodridge, IL: 2014.

Basics of Research

Throughout the course of my research, I have been honored to meet many individuals in Europe who have an interest in World War I and II. Their interests range from adopting graves, participating in re-enactments, providing tours, running museums, planning Liberation ceremonies, conducting research on specific units or battles, and researching the history of the area in which they live as it pertains to both World Wars. Each of these individuals taught me something about war from a records and a research standpoint. This includes how challenging it can be to obtain records from Europe, because many of the records needed are held in the United States.

The process for someone living overseas to begin research is slightly different from where an American would begin. Typically, an American researcher is investigating a family member. More often than not, there will be a family story, photographs, letters, records, and other materials the family holds which can be used to start the research. Local archives and museums may have information which can be obtained to piece together more of the soldier's story. The next step is investigating federal archives like the National Personnel Records Center (NPRC) in St. Louis, Missouri and National Archives in College Park, MD.

A European researcher may begin a soldier's research with limited information because they adopted a grave, are planning a ceremony, work in a museum, heard a story from a family member about soldiers who was in their country, or they are researching a unit or battle. While this list may appear lengthy, there are many other reasons why people research American soldiers. The ease of accessing materials available to an American researcher will not be, in most cases, easy to access for a European researcher due to their storage location. Therefore, many begin their work with online sources because they are the easiest to obtain. To help you navigate the research process, this chapter will explore many options where you can obtain information.

Starting The Process

The best place to begin is the same place an American would begin. Review the checklist on the next page and then complete the "Adopted Soldier Military Service Questionnaire." Write down everything you know about the soldier. It is ok not to have an answer to every question posed on the questionnaire. Start with what you know and work from there. Be sure to document each fact with the source of your information. This makes it easier to return to the original information if discrepancies appear in the research.

Research Checklist

____ Adopted Soldier Military Service Questionnaire

____ Establish Facts and Create a Timeline of Service
    ____ Locate Family Members

    ____ Local Archives

    ____ Researchers
        ____ Unit Specialists
        ____ Branch Specialists
        ____ Reunion Associations

    ____ Historical and Genealogical Societies in the U.S.

____ Online Research and Online Research Summary Form
    ____ Ancestry.com
    ____ Fold3.com
    ____ NARA
    ____ FamilySearch.org
    ____ WWII Toolbox
    ____ ABMC
    ____ Fields of Honor Database

____ Home Sources
    ____ Family stories
    ____ Correspondence from soldiers or families
    ____ Photographs
    ____ Newspaper articles
    ____ Grave adoption paperwork

____ Start Military Records Requests
    ____ OMPF
    ____ Morning Reports
    ____ Unit Records
    ____ IDPF

Adopted Soldier Military Service Questionnaire

Basic Information

Name of Soldier _____

Service Number _____

Branch of the service _____

Unit(s) and dates of service _____

_____

Date of and Place of Birth _____

Names of parents _____

Name of spouse (if applicable) _____

Service Information

Date and place of enlistment _____

Address at enlistment _____

Date and Place of Death _____

Temporary burial location: _____

_____

Permanent burial date and place: _____

_____

Was soldier ever declared Missing in Action? Please provide details.

_____

Was soldier ever a Prisoner of War? Please provide details.

_____

Battles _____

Service outside continental U.S. _____

_____

Ships on which the soldier served or was transported, with dates _____

_____

Decorations and Citations. Please provide the battles, reason(s), and dates for each decoration or citation received.

_____

_____

Wounds received _____

Prior Service _____

Training

Military Occupational Specialty (MOS)/Job _____

Service Schools Attended _____

_____

Discuss what you know about this soldier's service and what questions you have in the space below. Please list all the documents you have obtained and major resources searched. (American Battle Monuments Commission website, Unit Histories, Morning Reports, After Action Reports, S-Journals, Maps, IDPFs, X-Files).

_____

_____

_____

_____

_____

_____

Establish the Facts and Create a Timeline of Service

One of the most important things you can do when you start researching is create a timeline of service. A timeline organizes the multiple dates, places, and service information you find in service records, records created in the field, and at the higher unit and division level. Timelines also more easily show you where your errors are or gaps in service occur. Errors occur because of input error on our part or from conflicting records.

Start with a simple table that shows the Date, Unit/Event, Location, and Source of the information. The Date is the date of the record. Unit/Event is the unit in which the soldier served at that time and what transpired. The Location is where this event happened. The Source is where you obtained the information. It can be as simple as the File name and the document on which you located the information. The point of having a source is so you know exactly where you found the information in the first place so you can refer to it when you have conflicting dates and events.

It is also good to note if a document does not have a date, but has a date/time stamp on it. Some Navy records come undated but with date/time stamps, which show a date after the original document was sent. Keep in mind, in those days, communication was not fast as it is today with instant messages, Twitter, and Facebook. Often orders and communiques crossed in the "mail." Let's look at two examples of timelines. The first is a brief list of dates for World War I soldier Private Michael Kokoska.

Private Michael Kokoska

Date	Unit/Event	Location	Source
28 September 1891	Birth	Chicago	WWI Draft Card
March 1918	32nd Division over-seas	France	The 32nd Division History
June 1918	32nd Division stationed in "Quiet Sector"	Alsace	The 32nd Division History
27 June 1918	Death	Near Manspach, France	WWI Burial File
June 1918	Temporary Burial	Near Manspach, France	WWI Burial File
19 January 1920	Parents notified of temporary burial location		WWI Burial File
29 May 1921	Permanent Burial	Bohemian National Cemetery, Chicago	WWI Burial File

The second timeline for World War II Lt. Commander George Tyler Howe, was created in Word. Excel would work equally as well. Using the information in the table, I can begin to create a timeline of his service, see gaps in the research, and ask questions that might not have readily appeared as I perused the paperwork.

Note: The information provided here came from his summary of service, which was 10 pages long. Notes were made on the summary, items crossed out, or the word REVOKED appeared on some lines. My initial outline was created from this source, but as I moved through the records I had some "errors" to correct, which made sense based on the actual record versus the summary. Names of ships are typed as they appeared on the summary of service.[1]

Lt. Commander George Tyler Howe

1910

16 June 1910   Appointed midshipman from Michigan, 4th District

1911

3 June 1911   Joined "Indiana"

23 August 1911   Service completed. "On Football Squad."

1912

15 June 1912   Joined "New Hampshire"

25 July 1912   Joined "Alabama"

23 August 1912   Cruise completed. "On football squad."

1913

7 June 1913   Joined "New Hampshire"

22 June 1913   Joined "Idaho"

25 August 1913   Cruise completed

1914

28 May 1914   Detached Naval Academy June 5 and wait orders. On July 6, to the "Prairie" to other vessel (Det. 5 June) under orders to Mexican waters. Relieved upon arrival and to "Nebraska". Rep 6 July.

6 June 1914   Promoted to Ensign #93

Basics of Research

20 June 1914	Commissioned, regular, from June 6, 1914
26 June 1914	Uncompleted portion of orders of May 28 revoked. To the "Nebraska" 6 July.
8 July 1914	Accepted appointment and executed oath of office this date

1915

1 May 1915	Leave extended until May 18. Total leave days April 27 to May17.
3 December 1915	Admitted treatment, Naval Hospital Boston, Mass this date

1916

12 May 1916	Leave 2 days, May 15 and 16
18 May 1916	Detached "Nebraska" and to the Receiving ship at Boston, Mass
2 June 1916	Detached 15 June and to the "Montana" 15 July for torpedo instruction
21 July 1916	Leave 2 days July 22 and 23
13 October 1916	Leave for 2 days October 14 to 15
21 November 1916	Detached and to the "Fulton" 9 January 1917 for sub instruction

1917

26 February 1917	To exam for promotion on board "Fulton"
6 June1917	Lieutenant (JG) Commissioned from 6 June 1917
3 July 1917	Detached "Fulton" and to Norfolk, VA Fifth Naval District for duty in connection with the training of personnel from the Naval Reserve Force 8 August 1917. To ad ditional temporary duty on the Montgomery Connection summary court martial and return
22 August 1917	Det. End for the Fifth Naval District
1 October 1917	Admitted for treatment Naval Hospital at Norfolk, Virginia
15 October 1917	Lieutenant (JG) #13
8 December 1917	Detached and to the K-7
24 December 1917	Temporarily appointed from the 15th day of October 1917.

Add Historical Context When You Write the Story

After completing an outline of the service of a soldier, it is important to add vital information from the soldier's life and that of his family. This means adding births, marriages, deaths, census residences, and other details. Doing this places the life of the soldier and his service in historical context and creates a fuller story. This is especially important if the soldier was a career military man and his family traveled from base to base with him.

To illustrate historical context, let's return to George Tyler Howe's service timeline and see what it looks like in a first draft written format with context. Several pieces of George's family history have been added to his timeline, which is now in paragraph format as if we were writing his biography. As you read this section, note there are pieces missing or unknown, such as his marriage date and place. This example demonstrates the fact you do not need to have all the answers to write a soldier's story.

A note on dates: In my timelines, I used a military date format which is day-month-year. In my narrative I switched to a format used more regularly by civilians the month-day-year format. You can write timelines and narrative any way you feel comfortable.

George Tyler Howe

Our Howe Family story continues with the family of George Tyler Howe, Sr. and his three sons, George Tyler Howe, Jr., Edgar Bocock Howe, and John William Howe.

George Tyler Howe, Sr., was born December 23, 1889, in Chicago, Cook, Illinois, to Harry Tyler Howe and Rosella Jones Howe.[2] Harry had been married previously to Emma Glidden, who died in Fernwood, Illinois in April 1886.[3] The couple had three children, George's step-siblings, Grace, Arthur, and Herbert. After Emma's death, Harry remarried to a woman named Rosella Jones. Together they had six children, William, Charles, George, Mary, Horace, and Florence.

On May 7, 1910, the U.S. Census showed George Sr. living with his family in Paw Paw, Michigan. He was 21 years old and had applied to the Annapolis Naval Academy.[4] On June 16, 1910, George was admitted to Annapolis and appointed midshipman third class from the Michigan, 4th District.[5]

Throughout his instruction at Annapolis, George learned many military skills and participated in mandatory cruises. These cruises were on U.S. Naval Ships and Midshipmen traveled to many locations around the world learning the skills of sailors. George first cruised on June 3, 1911, on the *"Indiana."* This cruise lasted until August 23, 1911.[6]

In his second year at Annapolis, on June 15, 1912, George was detached to the *"New Hampshire"* for a few weeks before joining the *"Alabama"* on July 25, 1912. His cruise was completed on August 23, 1912.[7]

The third year at Annapolis sent George on two ships, the *"New Hampshire"* on June 7, 1913, and the "Idaho" on June 22, 1913. His cruises were completed August 25, 1913.[8]

In George's final year at Annapolis was detached from the Naval Academy on May 28, 1914, through June 5 to await orders. George graduated from Annapolis on June 6, 1914 and was promoted from Midshipman to Ensign #93. He was commissioned as a regular on June 20, 1914 with a start date of June 6. On July 6,

George was detached to the *"Prairie"* under orders to Mexican waters. Relieved upon arrival and detached to the *"Nebraska"* on July 8, 1914. [9]

George remained stationed on the *"Nebraska"* until May 18, 1916. In late December 1915, he was admitted for medical treatment at the Naval Hospital in Boston, Massachusetts. This was the first of many Naval Hospital admissions George would have over his career. At the time of this writing, the reasons for each medical admission are unknown.

May 18, 1916, George was detached from the *"Nebraska"* and sent to the Receiving Ship in Boston. On June 2 he was ordered to the "Montana" effective June 15 for torpedo instruction. Then on November 21, 1916, he was detached from the "Montana" and sent to the "Fulton" for submarine instruction.

George married Mercedes Wilson sometime before 1918 when their first child was born. The 1930 census shows George was 26 when he married, which puts the year about 1915-1916 depending on when the census was taken versus his birthday. Mercedes is currently a mystery. Depending on which record you look at, she has been reported to have been born in Mexico, Illinois, New Jersey, and New Mexico. It is also unknown who her parents are, so at this time, she is difficult to trace prior to her marriage to George.

1917 was a busy year for George, as he was detached to several stations, again treated in the hospital, and was up for promotion to Lieutenant Junior Grade (Lt. jg). On February 26, 1917, George took an examination for possible promotion while aboard the "Fulton." He passed and was commissioned as a Lieutenant Junior Grade on June 6, 1917. Then on July 3, 1917, he was detached from the "Fulton" and sent to the Fifth Naval District in Norfolk, Virginia for duty in connection with the training of personnel from the Naval Reserve Force. On August 8, he was sent on temporary duty on the Montgomery Connection summary court martial and then return when finished. His detachment with the Fifth Naval District ended August 22, 1917, and on October 1 he was again admitted for treatment at the Naval Hospital at Norfolk, Virginia. December 8, George was detached to the K-7.[10]

List The Facts and Document the Sources

For each record, digital or paper you locate, you need a way to track the source. This is extremely important, even if you never intend to publish or share the history with anyone else. At some point in the future you may want to refer to the information again. Knowing exactly where you found the information for each fact will help you more easily pick the research up and move forward. Should you intend to publish, citing your sources provides credibility to the research and writing.

Three main texts exist to help people in documenting sources. In the genealogy field, the best source is Elizabeth Shown Mills' *Evidence Explained!* In the history field, the University of Chicago Press' *Turabian Citation Guide* and *The Chicago Manual of Style*. You can also use Bibme which helps you format source citations in the styles of MLA, ALA, Chicago, and Turabian.

Citing sources, particularly for online documents or clues, is imperative. In your citation, include the File Name, Date of Access, Website title, Website URL, and notes on the file or website. The Date of Access is important because the online world changes all the time. The file you find today and download may not exist a week from now. When you cite your sources and include the date of access, as it provides more credibility to the online source.

How do you keep track of the sources you use? You can use the Master Source Summary, shown after this section, to document every source you examine for information. A couple of examples of sources have been entered to show you how to complete the form.

The next step is to evaluate the information contained in each source you list on your Master Source Summary. You can use the Research Summary, shown after this section, to document the information you locate in each record, book, website, or other source you review.

Both of these summary sheets can be created in Word or Excel and modified to your specific research purposes. In Excel, use Word Wrap to enlarge the cells as you insert information.

Create a Research Plan

Creating a plan for military research is another important piece of the research process. A plan documents the sources you wish to examine and repositories, libraries, and archives you wish to visit or contact to explore their resources. It also helps keep you on track with your research.

For example, as I continue the research for Private Michael Kokoska, my research plan might look like the following. The repository could be an actual location or a website. The source to search can be a book, archival file, website, or other set of records. Notes can be the date you plan to visit the repository or date you sent in an inquiry. It may also contain notes on the unit or other details you need to remember when searching that specific resource. Create your plan in a way that makes sense for you to use.

Repository	Source to Search	Notes
NPRC	OMPF and Payroll Records	
Illinois State Archives	World War I Bonus Applications	
Historical Chicago Tribune (ProQuest)	Newspaper articles about Michael, photographs of him or the 32nd Division and his obituary.	Available through the library
NARA College Park, MD	32nd Division Unit Records	Look for his Infantry Regiment and any mention of him or his death and burial

Master Source Summary

Date	Repository Name and Location	Name of Website with URL or other Source with Author and Publishing Date

Research Summary

Date	Name of Source	Specific Record, Book Page, Website Reviewed	Notes

Attempt to Locate the Veteran or Family Members

Locating veterans who served with your adopted soldier, or family members of your soldier is another way to gather information. If you can locate veterans or family, explain why you are researching the soldier and ask if they are willing to share information, paperwork, and photographs. How can you find veterans and family members? There are many online resources you can search.

Ancestry.com or FamilySearch.org

Many researchers begin with Ancestry.com or FamilySearch.org to look for a family tree. If a public tree is located, examine the information provided. See if the sources are cited. Are there any photographs? Then contact the tree owner to ask questions and permission to use any photographs or images you find connected to the tree. If you find a possible private tree, contact the tree owner and explain your search. Perhaps they will grant you access to their tree or provide information.

Social Media

Social media is a popular way people connect today. Facebook, Twitter, and Google+ allow users to join groups and connect with family and friends. Facebook has a large number of unit pages and groups dedicated to preserving the memories of specific units. Start by searching these and posting questions about the soldier. Often, these pages and groups are run by members of a reunion group or unit association.

Use Twitter to search for tweets for or about specific groups. A tweet is a status update by a user in 140 characters or less. You can search two ways: using hashtags or a general user search. A hashtag is a keyword preceded by the # sign. For example, look for tweets about the 100th Bomb Group. First, try searching for #WWII. Many tweets will appear to choose from, so let's narrow it down and try #100 and see what appears. Does anything resembling #100thbg or #100thbombgroup or similar appear? If not, try a user search without the hashtag.

To search for a user, enter 100th in the search box. What appears? 100th Bomb Group @100thBG, 100th Bomb Group @100thBombGroup, etc. Explore those users to see who they are. You will find a couple are restaurants and at least one is actually tweeting about the 100th Bomb Group during the war. You can converse with users on Twitter by replying to a tweet. Just remember to keep it 140 characters or less or break your question into multiple tweets.

Google+ is another way to connect with people on social media. Google+ is similar to Facebook in that you can connect with people around the world by adding them to your circles. Google+ also has groups you can join to discuss specific topics.

There are many other options for social media available, and it is user preference as to which one(s) you prefer to work with. Always check privacy policies and settings before signing up for any to ensure your information is secure.

Reunion Groups or Unit Associations

Reunion Groups and Unit Associations often have a historian who maintains lists of original unit members who served in the war. Many of these organizations were started after World War I. Often the lists of association members who joined the group are also kept. These lists usually contain name, address, phone number, email, unit, and death date.

Reunion Groups and Unit Associations may have policies regarding privacy, and therefore not release information to you about a veteran or the family. You can request to have your information forwarded on in the hope that the veteran or family member contacts you. Also check the association website to see if any newsletters or booklets have been published which might contain the information.

Historical and Genealogical Societies in the U.S.

Historical and genealogical societies in the U.S. can be an incredible resource because they often hold local and genealogical records. These records may be in the form of vital records, census, land records, newspapers, photographs, letters, and diaries. Often you can learn about your soldier, his life and family, and the area in which he grew up.

To locate a historical society in the state in which your soldier lived, visit the Preservation Directory website and search by state. All Historical Societies in that state will appear in a list with a website and email address, where available. http://bit.ly/1he1Xpn To search for a genealogical society, search for the name of the town from which your soldier came plus 'genealogy society' and see what results emerge.

Newspapers

Search historical newspapers for lists of soldiers going to war, lists of wounded, prisoners, missing and the dead. Families often places memorial notices or obituaries for soldier after they were notified of the death or when the remains were returned to the U.S. Newspapers during both World Wars printed photographs of soldiers and letters they sent home. It was also common to provide the name of the next-of-kin and their address with these notices.

Using these resources, you may learn the names of next-of-kin or the funeral home which handled the arrangements. This information allows you to search White Pages or other online phone directories for family. You can also contact the funeral home to ask if they will pass on your contact information to the family.

Online Databases

Online databases, of which there are many, can provide many small clues to help you along the research path. Remember that many company databases which provide digitized copies of records, are subscription-based.

Explore Local Archive, Museum and Library Holdings

Europe has countless military museums, libraries, and archives which may hold World War II research materials. There are numerous ways to discover which repository may hold information you can use to write your soldier's story. Try a variety of searches to learn where records may be held.

- **Search for a unit plus the country.** For example, 8th Air Force Holland or 101st Airborne Holland. ***Note:** for Holland, also try Netherlands. During World War II, reports and maps indicated Holland, but websites and archives today may have things listed under both.

- **Search for a unit or battle and specific area of a country or city.** For example, 82nd Airborne, Arnhem, Holland or 1st Division Normandy.

- **Unsure which museums or repositories exist in a country?** Search for World War II museums and the country. New museums and repositories are created all the time so search often and ask other researchers if they know of repositories.

- **Visit the website for a specific museum and search their holdings.** If an online Finding Aid or Database of holdings does not exist, email the museum curator or other staff to inquire about holdings.

- **Search local and university library collections to see what books or archival materials they hold.** If your local library does not carry a specific book, see if you can borrow it through Inter-Library Loan from another library in your country.

- **Look for online history or military journals.** Many sites may require a subscription to a specific organization which produces the journal, while other sites may be free. Libraries and museums may subscribe to journals and offer this as a service to their visitors.

Visit military museums to view exhibits. There might not be a paper or digital collection you can view to use for research purposes, but the exhibit may provide historical context to help you make sense of your research. Pay attention to the books, documents, and other paper materials within exhibits for clues to look for in other collections.

Contact Researchers

There are many World War I and World War II researchers around the world. The problem sometimes, is finding them. Locating a researcher can be a challenging task if a researcher's website is not properly tagged and does not rank high in Google search results. It is a good idea to examine several pages of search results to see if you can find someone to help you. One place to start your search before Google is Facebook Groups.

Facebook Groups

You can often find a Facebook group for a specific unit, battle, or branch of the military for both wars. Within those groups which apply to the unit you are researching, ask questions to learn more about your soldier or his unit. You can also ask specifically for someone who specializes in the unit or a professional researcher.

One thing to watch for in these groups is the differing responses you may receive for a question. Always explore all record options and compare stories, or "facts," you read in responses to official records. Each person has a different experience with research and therefore, has a different opinion of how it should or can be done.

Unit Specialists

Search online for unit or branch specialists and veteran or reunion associations. Each of these groups or individuals will have specialized information for a particular unit or division. Sometimes the information will be digitized and placed on their website. Other times it will not, and you will need to ask the website owner or researcher questions about the records. The individuals who do specific unit research will often have a wide network of colleagues (professional and hobbyist) who may be able to assist you. It never hurts to ask about other researchers or resources.

Military Research Online

In this digital age, when more books, photographs, maps, and documents appear online daily, many assume everything available to researchers is online. This is not true. One example of a record you will almost never find online is a soldier's Official Military Service File (OMPF,) unless someone has digitized and placed it on a website. The only copy of these records is held at the National Personnel Records Center (NPRC.) Most, if not all, of the records you need to more fully tell your soldier's story will be found in archives, libraries, and personal collections. Does this mean you should not attempt research online? No. It means you should not expect everything to be available online.

Why should you research online?

You will gain an education.

Many websites, blogs, and expert forums, provide information on World War II research, discuss the process, brick walls, and tell the stories of soldiers. No one site or book can provide all the answers. It is important to explore as many as possible.

You may discover digitized records.

Many units formed reunion or association groups after the war to stay connected. In recent years, the unit historians have digitized materials for their unit and placed them on their websites. Some units may not have placed their records online. If the website does not have records, ask the historian about the group's archival holdings. You can also visit my World War II Toolbox and go to Division and Unit Resources. Look at the 90th Division Association's website for examples of digitized records.

You will often add facts to your timeline.

As you search online and locate information, add this to your timeline. Record where you found the information and proceed with additional research on and offline.

Books have been digitized.

Many of the unit histories written by the units after the war have been digitized and made available on sites like GoogleBooks and Internet Archive. Sites like these are one of the first places you should look for information.

Connect with other researchers and veterans.

You may connect with other researchers investigating the same unit or battle. You may also connect with veterans who can provide more information on the war and the overall experience.

Connect with family.

Online family trees abound, some of which do not have accurate information, so check your facts! Examining online trees is a good way to locate additional records or facts you may not have known about your soldier.

Search the collaterals.

Using online resources, you can search for the collaterals, those individuals who served with your soldier. Uncovering pieces of their stories may help you tell yours. It may be unreasonable to search for every infantryman who served with your soldier, so look for the men who ran the unit or company. If your soldier was part of a bomber crew, the list of those he served with will be much shorter.

Starting Your Online Research

After exhausting the home and public sources, ordering the OMPF, and writing down everything that is known about the soldier, I suggest going online to discover additional details and research leads. As with offline research, cite your sources, and track website on which you located information. To help you track where you have been online, download my Online Research Summary form at http://bit.ly/1dZafj7. And always remember there are errors in online and offline records. Check and double check your facts.

Check the date of information.

When using online records or websites, be sure to check the date the site or information was posted. World War II records access changes often, and you could be looking at out of date, incorrect information. For instance, any site that tells you to write to College Park, MD for an IDPF is out of date. The same applies to any site that tells you only next-of-kin can access World War II personnel files. It is likely that they are out of date. The rules have changed in the last few years.

Use indexes and understand the limitations.

Indexes for online records will only get you so far. Often, errors happen when records are created, which then creates errors in the indexes. Some records are difficult to read, which makes indexing difficult. Keep in mind the way one person deciphers writing may be different from the way another does. This leads to errors in the creation of indexes for handwritten records. Also, indexing may not capture every record. This requires us to conduct page by page searches of records if we suspect our individual is listed within the record.

Lack of an index entry was the case with Pvt. William F. Cowart of the Marine Corps, who appears on the USMC Muster Rolls on Ancestry.com in January, April, and October 1943. However, he does not appear in the Ancestry.com index in November, the month he was killed on Tarawa. Knowing his unit, I was able to narrow down the roll number and search the November 1943 Muster Rolls page by page to locate his KIA entry. All months of the Muster Rolls are available on Ancestry.com, but you have to dig for them. They will not automatically show up in the index.

Online Research Summary

Date	Name of Website with URL or other Source with Author and Publishing Date	Notes

Navigating the Spider Web

Searching the internet for World War II resources is comparable to navigating a spider web. Everything is connected, but you can quickly lose your way. Sometimes losing your way is beneficial because you discover resources you might not have otherwise. To help you navigate the spider web, track where you have been, and what you discovered use the Online Research Sheet on the following page.

Locating Information Using a Search Engine

To locate information on a specific individual or unit, try the following suggestions in your favorite search engine. Each engine will return slightly different results based on how that engine categorizes links. We will use Pvt. James Privoznik as an example for our search.

U.S. Army
Pvt. James Privoznik, 36640529 from Illinois
Final unit: "F" Company, 358th Infantry Regiment, 90th Infantry Division
KIA 11 January 1945

• Try using quotes around exact phrases you wish to search. "James Privoznik" is an example.

• Search by name and serial/service number. Try James Privoznik 36640529, or just the number. Usually the results will come from the NARA Enlistment Database, if the soldier was in the Army and enlisted. Sometimes it will come from articles or blog posts, unless records have been indexed.

• Use specific and unique terms. Try 90th Infantry Division, 358th Infantry WWII, 90th Division WWII, or any combination.

• Capitalization usually doesn't matter when searching.

• Try the wildcard using the * symbol. WWII* or Privoznik*

• Change your search preferences to search a specific date range of items posted online. For example, maybe you are looking for a person and only articles posted this year or a specific date range of 2012-2014.

• Try using advanced searches to add more criteria to the search. ProQuest newspaper search is one engine that uses this function.

Additional Search Techniques

• Search for the name of a group. For example, the 100th Bomb Group was called the Bloody Hundredth or Bloody 100th.

• For Air Corps, try searching for the name of the plane, a pilot, or bomb crew flew.

• Search for names of bridges taken, battles fought, cities bombed, specific Hills (and their numbers).

• Try a specific group and the name of a military report you wish to locate. For example, 100th Bomb Group Mission Report, 90th Division After Action Report, or 327 Engineer Morning Reports.

A question I am often asked is how to find the unit(s) in which a soldier served, online, if the researcher has no idea which unit to search. This is a hit or miss search. If documents with the soldier's name have been digitized or written about in an article or blog post, you may locate them through a search.

A Sample of Websites with World War II Record Collections or Information

There are too many websites for military research to list them all, but I will touch on a few of the major players with digitized records. Each site continually updates databases and image files of military records, so it is a good idea to visit them often or subscribe to their newsletters to know when updates are made. Examples of records on each site are mentioned here, and are not a complete listing. The links to these sites are listed in the resource section for this book on my website. For additional World War II related websites, visit the World War II Toolbox on my website.

Searching these websites, and others like them, you will generally search by surname or a combination of surname plus given name. Depending on the search criteria available, adding date of birth, death, or date of service may narrow down search results.

General Resources

American Battle Monuments Commission (ABMC)
http://abmc.gov

This is a free site created by the federal government to honor all our soldiers buried in the American Battle Monument Commission American Military Cemeteries overseas or listed on the Tablets of the Missing. The site also includes histories of the cemeteries, teaching resources, and interactive timelines.

Search Tips: From the main page, you can search by surname. When the results appear, especially if you have a common surname, filter them by war, cemetery (if known), or branch of the service. Army and Air Corps will have the soldier's serial number with the entry. Navy, Marine Corps, and Coast Guard do not show this information.

Ancestry.com
http://ancestry.com

Ancestry.com is a subscription based website to help researchers create online family trees and locate information. Many libraries offer a free library version of Ancestry.com on-site at the library. Ancestry.com has numerous World War II related databases.

Search Tips: Begin your search with the soldier's name and date of birth. Explore the military resources which appear to see if there is a match. Explore the online family trees to see if your soldier has been entered and if there is additional information you do not have. Contact the tree owner if you believe there is a match within a private tree. You can also try searching the card catalog for specific military databases and searching within those.

Digital Public Library of America
http://dp.la

The Digital Public Library of America brings together media resources from libraries across the country in one place.

Search Tips: Search by general keywords like "World War II," or be more specific with "82nd Airborne" and see what results appear. The results screen allows you to filter the results by media type, along the left side of the screen. Books may take you to the Hathi Trust website, where you can view the books, but not download unless you have a partner login. Even if you cannot download the book, if you have enough interest in it, obtain it through interlibrary loan, or see if Internet Archive has a copy.

FamilySearch
http://familysearch.org

FamilySearch is a free website run by the Mormon Church. You can create free family trees, search for records, read books, and order records on microfilm to be shipped and viewed at a local Family History Center. The main record source is the World War II Draft Registration Cards, but there are a few state-level record groups.

Search Tips: I always find it easier to search by area in the world and within that area, a specific record set. This focuses my search and does not bring up every possible record within FamilySearch's enormous database of records. How do you search like this?

From the main page click the SEARCH icon. When the map appears, select your location by continent. Then choose the state you wish to view, and the record set within the state. Not all FamilySearch images have been indexed. There is a good chance you will need to sort through many images of records to locate an index, which may exist, within a record set.

FamilySearch Digitized Books
http://bit.ly/1xGAnrl

FamilySearch has not only digitized genealogical records from all over the world, but also has access to more than 150,000 books through its own library and partner libraries.

Search Tips: Use the Search function to locate books with the subject World War II. The book results can be sorted by material type, collection, language, and author/creator. The search results also provide additional subject related to World War II you can view along the left sidebar.

Fields of Honor Database
http://fieldsofhonor-database.com/

The Fields of Honor Database is a compilation of all the names of soldiers buried and listed on the Walls of the Missing at three cemeteries in Belgium and Holland. These are The Netherlands American Cemetery (Margraten), Henri-Chapelle, and Ardennes. The database contains information on service and when available, photographs of the soldiers. Sources of all the information provided are cited at the bottom of the entry.

The Fields of Honor volunteers are happy to respond to questions and accept photographs and information on soldiers in the database.

Search Tips: Start by searching for the soldier by name. The database can be a little finicky so be sure to capitalize the surname and name. Rosenkrantz, David. You can also select a specific cemetery and go to the letter of the surname to view all those in the database.

FindAGrave
http://findagrave.com

FindAGrave is a free, volunteer run site containing grave listings, often with photos. One issue with this site is if there are multiple entries for the same individual at the same cemetery, they may be linked as siblings rather than stand-alone.

Search Tips: Start by searching the 132+ million grave records with the link on the right side of the page. This link brings up a page with many search options from name, dates of birth and death, grave location, and filters. Please remember the ABMC created a memorial for each individual buried at their cemeteries or listed on the Tablets of the Missing. Others may have also created memorials for these same people. Use caution when gathering this information and pay attention to IF or WHERE the individual is actually buried. It could be they are still Missing In Action or just have a Memorial Stone.

Fold3.com
http://fold3.com

Fold3.com is a paid subscription site offering military records from U.S. conflicts. Many libraries offer this as a free version on-site. Fold3.com has numerous World War II related databases. The databases can be a little difficult to navigate though. OCR picks up approximately 80% of the words in a scanned document, which leaves a lot of room for researchers to miss key records.

Search Tips: Start by searching for the soldier's name in the WWII Record collections from the main search screen. For an example, let's look for records for Staff Sergeant David Rosenkrantz of I Company, 504th PIR, 82nd Airborne. PIR stands for Parachute Infantry Regiment, a phrase which may or may not be spelled out in records. Searching for David's name does not bring up many results, although we see many of the same records as can be found on Ancestry.com.

Since we know David was in the 504th PIR, we can go directly to specific record sets to search. Go into Modify Search and remove David's name, but enter 504th into the Keyword box. This is where searching takes on a whole new dimension. You have to play with 504th versus 504 and look for records that show 504th PIR or 82nd Airborne. When we search for 504th, we are hoping to stumble upon an entry about David, but also looking for historical context and battle information.

Two specific record sets to search, in which you can usually find a lot of information, are WWII European Theater Army Records and WWII Foreign Military Studies, 1945-1954. Searching within these sets for units or battles often brings great results.

The key to locating information in Fold3.com is to be patient and try every possibility from keywords, names, and searching within record sets.

Google Books
http://books.google.com/

Google Books is a collection of digitized public domain books and book previews. It is a great resource for out of print books or discovering a source to research.

Search Tips: Search by book title or author or general keywords to see what books are available. If a book you suspect should be in the public domain appears on the list, but not in full text availability, see if it exists on Internet Archive.

Historical Newspaper Archives

There are several historical newspaper archives available in the U.S. I will not attempt to list them all in this chapter, but will provide a few sites where you can begin a search. Also check ProQuest, Ancestry.com, and Fold3.com, which are discussed in this chapter.

Chronicling America
http://chroniclingamerica.loc.gov/

The Library of Congress newspaper archives.

Genealogy Bank
http://www.genealogybank.com/

A subscription site with more than 7,000 newspapers.

Newspaper Archive
http://newspaperarchive.com/

A subscription site with more than 400 years of newspapers for all 50 U.S. states and 22 other countries.

Search Tip: Search for newspapers within the locale your soldier lived or where he trained. You may find free online newspapers or libraries which offer free look-ups. Check local archives in Europe for newspapers which may provide historical context and photographs for the unit in which your soldier served.

Internet Archive
https://archive.org/

Internet Archive is a digital library which houses public domain books, manuscripts, music, videos, and photographs.

Search Tips: Search Internet Archive for media specific items. For example, start by choosing books and search within that only for 82nd Airborne. What books do you discover? Now try the same search in all media. What appears?

Military Research Online

Library of Congress

http://loc.gov

The Library of Congress is a free resource which covers many topics of interest to the people of the United States. Veterans Oral Histories can be searched here, and you can learn how to submit your own. There are resources for newspapers, maps, and other digitized materials related to World War II.

Search Tips: The Library of Congress (LOC) website has an easy to use search function which allows you to conduct a general search or a specific media search. On the results page, along the left side of the screen, are several categories by which you can filter the results.

National Archives

http://archives.gov

The National Archives is a repository for federal records. Online databases include:

- Electronic Army Serial Number Merged File, ca. 1938 - 1946 (Enlistment Records)
- Electronic Army Serial Number Merged File, ca. 1938 - 1946 (Reserve Corps Records)
- World War II Prisoners of War Data File, 12/7/1941 - 11/19/1946
- World War II Prisoners of the Japanese File, 2007 Update, ca. 1941 - ca. 1945
- Japanese-American Internee Data File, 1942 - 1946
- Naval Group China Muster Roll and Report of Change Punch Cards, 1942 – 1945

Search Tips: Search the NARA databases by surname, given name. If you have a common surname and the search form allows for an advanced search, try different variables in the search. Most of the database you find on NARA's website are also on Ancestry.com and Fold3.com.

Pritzker Military Museum and Library

http://pritzkermilitary.org

The Pritzker Military Museum and Library is a non-partisan research library focusing primarily on the stories of the Citizen Soldier through all wars. The library houses books on many military topics including conflicts, histories, equipment, and individual soldier stories. Books are available in English and several other languages, which allow researchers to learn different views of a war or the outcome.

Search Tips: The library website is easy to navigate. When searching for books which you can request through interlibrary loan, search by author, keyword, or title. Other media options are available on the results screen along the right side of the screen.

ProQuest

http://proquest.com/

ProQuest is a subscription based service offered through most libraries, and is usually accessible from home using your library card. Newspapers and databases vary based on location and what databases the library subscribes to each year. For example, in Chicago libraries, most ProQuest services include the Historical Chicago Tribune, Historical New York Times, and a variety of database.

Search Tips: I use ProQuest a lot for newspaper research. It is, again, a resource which has OCR and only 80% of the text appears in search results. There are times when you need to do a page by page or day by day search for specific articles if you cannot find them through search.

For example, during World War II, the newspaper printed articles, often titled, "Army Dead," on average, three times a week. Those articles contained the names of soldiers Missing, Wounded, Prisoner, or Killed In Action with the name of their next-of-kin and home address. These lists were printed 30-90 days, usually, after the War Department notified the family of the loss or change in status. I have had to use the search daily approach to find the names of cousins who were labeled KIA during the war. It requires a bit of patience.

White Pages – Online Phone Directories
http://www.whitepages.com/

Several online phone directories exist, and White Pages is only one option. These directories can be used to locate next-of-kin if you have a location nailed down where they possibly live.

Search Tip: Google "White Pages" or "Phone Directory" for a general search, or add the locale to the search to narrow down your options.

Wikipedia
http://wikipedia.org

Wikipedia is an online encyclopedia of information created by various contributors. It almost always appears on the first page of search engine results. While Wikipedia can provide some background information, and may provide a source or two for you to investigate, it should be used with caution.

Example: 35th Infantry Division (United States)
https://en.wikipedia.org/wiki/35th_Infantry_Division_(United_States)

This article contains a lot of useful information to be used as background information. Much of it is sourced if you look at the bottom of the page. This allows you to locate and review the sources used. The article could benefit from improvements, which would fill out all the units attached or which belonged to the 35th so you could learn more about them.

Example: 129th Infantry Regiment (United States)
https://en.wikipedia.org/wiki/129th_Infantry_Regiment_(United_States)

This article only lists books for further reading. Note there are no other sources included which would be useful to a researcher. The article is tagged at the top indicating citations and other information would be appreciated if a volunteer would like to add them to the article.

WorldCat
https://worldcat.org/

WorldCat is a searchable database of books, videos, films, and magazines for the entire world. Using World-Cat, often through your local library on-site or at home, you can search for books to request through inter-library loan if your library system does not have a specific book, magazine, or other media.

Search Tips: WorldCat is easy to use, and the entry form is straightforward. If a book does not appear, which you believe should appear, try adding or removing search terms until it is found.

World War II History Network

http://wwiihistorynetwork.com

The World War II History Network is a member network of authors, educators, historians, genealogists, and those with an interest in research World War II. There are numerous groups covering most aspects of war, member blogs, and book giveaways.

Search Tips: The World War II History Network does not contain online books or documents. There are many forums where people exchange information and "how-to" advice. You can use the search form at the top of the website to locate specific topics.

Military Branch-Specific Resources

Air Force Historical Research Agency (AFHRA)

http://afhra.af.mil/index.asp

The Air Force Historical Research Agency maintains records for the Army Air Corps activities during the war. Records include Missing Air Crew Reports, Accident Reports, unit histories, and mission reports.

Naval History and Heritage Command

http://history.navy.mil/index.html

The research center and website have been undergoing renovation, but are due to be open and full of information in 2015.

U.S. Army Center of Military History

http://history.army.mil/

The resources on this website are vast and include the Army Green Books, which detail the war and all the working parts; histories, research resources, and digitized materials.

United States Marine Corps History Division

https://mcu.usmc.mil/historydivision/SitePages/Home.aspx

Visit their Frequently Requested page for information on records and resources. There is also information for units, digitized books, and research assistance.

Social Media Options

Facebook

http://facebook.com

Social media options abound for World War II research. Facebook hosts many groups and pages dedicated to units, divisions, reenactment groups, all service branches, and cemeteries. Use the search box to look for a specific group. For example, try 100th on its own. The search results appear for 100th Bomb Group, 100th Infantry Division, and so forth. Each page or group is named differently, so you need to explore to see if they are really what you seek.

Individuals on Facebook are also a great resource. As you interact with people in the World War II groups, friend some and share information. In Europe, the World War II historians, re-enactors, collectors, grave adopters, authors, and others have a great network. I have never encountered anyone who wasn't willing to offer some sort of help in the last several years when I have asked questions.

LinkedIn
http://linkedin.com

LinkedIn has professional groups for aspects of World War II and you can locate professionals doing specific research there. Just as on Facebook, try to connect with other professionals researching or writing about the unit you are interested in learning more about.

Twitter
http://twitter.com

Information and discussions are seen on Twitter through tweets. A tweet is a status update by a user in 140 characters or less. You can search two ways, using hashtags or a general user search. A hashtag is a keyword preceded by the # sign. For example, look for tweets about the 100th Bomb Group. First, try searching for #WWII. Many tweets will appear to choose from, so let's narrow it down and try #100 and see what appears. Does anything resembling #100thbg or #100thbombgroup or similar appear? If not, try a user search without the hashtag.

To search for a user, enter 100th in the search box. What appears? 100th Bomb Group @100thBG, 100th Bomb Group @100thBombGroup, etc. Explore those users to see who they are. You will find a couple are restaurants, and at least one is actually tweeting about the 100th Bomb Group during the war. You can converse with users on Twitter by replying to a tweet. Just remember to keep it 140 characters or less or break your question into multiple tweets.

Blogs

Blogs written by those researching the war or writing about it can be found. Search for "WWII Blogs," "100th Bomb Group Blog," "World War II Blogs" or specific branches plus the word blog. Try a combination of things to locate what you are looking for. Search results will include any website or social media site with those keywords, not just blogs.

Pinterest
http://pinterest.com/

Finally, Pinterest is another popular social media site which functions as a bulletin board on which you can "pin" photos linked to articles or blog posts. The member boards are searchable, in the same ways you would search for blogs or specific units on Facebook. You can create your own boards, follow members who have boards in which you are interested, and pin things from other websites.

Final Suggestions for Online Research

Each time you come upon an unfamiliar phrase, unit, battle, name, or location of battle, go online and see what you can discover. Track where you have been using the Online Source Summary sheet and keep good notes. Return to sites you visited in the past, as they often change over time. A site which provided very little information six months ago may have many divisional reports online today. And finally, use caution with the information you discover and check it against paper record sources

Starting Military Research

Starting military research should not be a daunting task. Instead it should be viewed as an adventurous journey through which you will likely travel to different countries to connect to the story of your soldier. Typically, there are three common starting points for military research: hearing a military story, finding or receiving pieces of a serviceman's file, letters, uniform, or other pieces that contain clues or spark interest, and death information for your soldier.

To help you navigate this journey, we first must identify common roadblocks to research and then explore resources to help you locate basic information before starting military records research. Then we can begin to address the clues found within the first two starting points.

The Roadblocks and Common Questions

Roadblocks should be viewed as stepping stones and learning experiences in our military research. They can be overcome with some creativity and the exploration of alternate records and resources.

I'm not next of kin.

I'm not next of kin is also a common roadblock that many researchers have been conditioned to accept. However, records access regarding service records has changed in the last several years. Official Military Personnel Files (OMPF) are available if a soldier was discharged or died by 1954.

If your soldier stayed in the military after and served post-1954, those records are still only available by the veteran or next-of-kin. Who is considered a next-of-kin if the veteran is deceased? The next-of-kin can be any of the following: Surviving spouse that has not remarried. Father. Mother. Son. Daughter. Sister. Brother. As next-of-kin, you must provide proof of death in the form of a death certificate, obituary, funeral cards or other documentation.

Medical records are a different story. To access medical records for Navy and Marine Corps personnel, you must be the veteran or next-of-kin and provide proof of death. This holds true even if the sailor or Marine has been dead 100 years. This access is unlikely to change anytime soon. There are no restrictions for medical records for those who served in the Army, Army Air Forces, or National Guard at the time of this writing.

All the record burned! How can I reconstruct a service file?

There was a massive fire in 1973 at the National Personnel Records Center (NPRC) in St. Louis, Missouri. Approximately 80% of the Army and Army Air Forces/Air Corps records were destroyed. These records were never duplicated or microfilmed, nor were they indexed. Additionally, many records were loaned to the Department of Veterans Affairs (VA) prior to the fire. Because of these factors, the NPRC had no way to know exactly which records were affected, until a request is made. Today the NPRC works to preserve any burned files that are salvageable and pull information from alternate record sources to document service.

When the fire was extinguished, the NPRC began removing fire and water damaged documents that could possibly be saved. They sent vital records out of the facility to a safe location in case the fire rekindled. One of these valuable record sets was the Army and Air Corps Morning Reports. These reports help track service and are especially important because so many of the Army and Air Corps records burned.

In an effort to preserve the burned records, a separate storage area at the NPRC was established for what staffers now called the burned records or "B" files. As some of these files were reconstructed, another locate was established to store the "R" files or reconstructed files. At the same time, alternate sources for service information were accessed. There are many alternate sources used, but a few include: Veterans Administration (VA) Claim files, military hospital medical records, Selective Service System (SSS) files, and various pay records. These alternate sources will never provide the complete picture of your soldier's service if his file burned, but will provide enough information with other sources to document service and tell the story.

I think my soldier changed units.

When you examine the Separation Papers for a soldier or the World War I Burial File or World War II Individual Deceased Personnel File, the unit listed could be the first or the final unit in which the soldier served. This is usually not the only unit. Using Morning Reports, Marine Corps Muster Rolls, Naval Deck Logs, as well as Unit Journals and Histories, you can usually trace the movements of a soldier and unit changes.

The records are not online.

Many people say, *"I know this soldier served in the Army but I cannot find his enlistment record online."* First, only the men who enlisted in the Army will be in the World War II National Archives Enlistment Database. Most of the men who served were drafted, and their records will not be listed in the Army Enlistment Database. If a soldier re-enlisted after World War II, it is possible the second enlistment will be shown in the National Archives database rather than the first.

In today's digital age it is assumed that everything of importance has been digitized and is available somewhere online. This is absolutely not true. Only a small percentage of available records housed around the world have been digitized and made available online.

While many World War I and World War II records have been digitized by Division or Unit Associations, or companies like Fold3.com or Ancestry.com, the paper records available still far outnumber what is available online. And, Official Military Personnel Files (OMPFs,) have never been online likely due to privacy restrictions and the amount of time it would take to digitize them.

I live in Europe and records are not easily accessible.

European researchers approach the research of American soldiers a bit differently because of location. Quite often, they begin the search with online sources like Fold3.com, Ancestry.com, FindAGrave, Fields of Honor Database, and National Archives Databases. There are many ways a European researcher can obtain information beyond the online resources.

The cost of obtaining service files is large because I have many to request. Is there a less expensive alternative?

Unfortunately, no. The NPRC charges photocopy fees. If you have a Navy, Coast Guard, or Marine Corps file, those are potentially large files because they were not affected by the fire. Army, Air Corps, and National Guard records were affected and may either be much smaller or not exist. There lies the difference in photocopy fees. In my opinion, if you have to choose which files to order and pay for first, choose the files that are intact.

I cannot find my soldier!

One common reason you may not locate a soldier in some records, particularly if you are using indexes to search, is the way the name is spelled. Errors in spelling did occur as records were created which then carries over into record indexes. You may need to search various spellings of a name to locate your soldier. One example I found recently was Richard PARROW appeared as Richard PERROW on a few records. **Hint:** Try using the phonetic spelling as you search.

Home Sources

After completing the Adopted Soldier Military Service Questionnaire and exploring online resources, it is time to look for home sources. A home source is a document, photograph, piece of memorabilia, or ephemera that provides clues to the puzzle you are attempting to solve. You may ask what sources could you have if you have adopted this soldier and he is not of your family. You might have information obtained from other sources or the family members of the soldier. It is worth reviewing what you have.

If you are in touch with the soldier's relatives, ask them to search their homes for clues. Search for information to help you complete the adopted soldier military service questionnaire or add structure and details to your soldier's story. Home sources include, but are not limited to, the following list. A more complete list is available after this section as a checklist.

Bibles. Within family Bibles, we often find names of family members with dates of birth, marriage, death, and other significant dates like military service.

Burial Flags. Burial flags were presented to the family after their soldier was buried. Often, a family received two: one when the War Department notified them of their soldier's death and burial overseas, and a second when the soldier was buried permanently after the war. Flags may not provide information on their own, but if the original box or packaging they arrived in is available, dates taken from those items can help narrow down a date of death if the date is unknown.

Church and School Records. Both churches and schools printed information in church bulletins or school newsletters. Investigate the high school and colleges your soldier attended. See what courses they took or activities in which they participated. Ask the school if they have an archive of military letters sent to the school by the troops.

Company Records. Check with the businesses and companies for which the soldiers worked prior to the war. The Hawthorne Works Western Electric Company in Cicero, Illinois published photos and the "doings" of military personnel who had worked for the company in their monthly newsletter and magazine. Companies often published obituaries or notices of change in status from active to Missing In Action, Prisoner of War, or Killed In Action. Company records also provide a glimpse into the life of the soldier prior to the war. If the soldier returned to the company after the war, see what other records exist in Human Resources.

Country Guides. Guides to European countries were printed during the war and sold to soldiers. These guides contained the history of the "must see" tourist sites. These will not contain information about your soldier but they will provide a clue as to where the soldier had been. If the soldier wrote in the books, those notes may lead to additional research.

Diaries, Letters and Postcards. Did the soldier keep a diary or send letters and V-Mail home? Were postcards sent home? The military censored a lot of material in letters and postcards sent home. For instance, the soldier could not say specifically where he was and letters sent home might read Somewhere in New Guinea or Somewhere in Europe. He also could not say specifically what he was doing. While these letters will not have some key information we would wish they would, they give us an idea of life as a soldier. The constant fighting, health risks, food situation, weather, and loneliness. Again, they provide context for the soldier's story and may provide clues. Check the envelopes of letters for service numbers and unit information.

Employment Records. Researchers can use employment records for pre and post-World War II research. These records may provide information that suggests why a soldier was placed in a specific role during the war. You may also find information for addresses, next of kin, educational, and military histories.

Family Genealogies. Many people have compiled family trees, which you can find online, in books, or on pieces of paper in someone's home. These can be good starting points, but you should verify the facts found in these genealogies. Humans do make mistakes, and we do not always catch those mistakes before we pass the information on to someone else. Also, new records may surface which change some of the facts.

Family stories and memories. Write down every family story you hear, even if the versions differ; there is a grain of truth within every family story. It is up to you to sort the story out through the records. In some cases this will be easy, while in others it will prove more difficult.

Fraternal & Military Organization Records. The VFW and American Legion are two organizations that support veterans and their families. While some posts may no longer exist, it is worth checking newspapers and family files for this kind of information. Also check with the national level organization about records and resources. Also investigate other organizations to which your soldier may have belonged, like the Elk or Moose. Often you will find people who knew the soldier or can direct you to records or resources.

Headgear. Pieces of the soldier's uniform, including headgear may provide clues as to the type of service or rank.

Home Movies. Did your family take home movies? Do you have any with your soldier in uniform? Are there any taken of parades or war gatherings in the U.S.? What clues do these movies provide?

Identification Tags. Dog tags or identification tags are one of the best resources because they provide the service number of the soldier. Depending on when they were issued, tags may also contain the next of kin's name and address.

Insignia. The insignia or patches on a soldier's uniform represent the division he was in during the war.

Insurance Records. When we think about insurance records, we are not only looking at the end of life records. Check previous employers for insurance paperwork and check the military service records or Veterans Administration files. Every soldier was supposed to complete a life insurance policy before going to war. These records will contain home address and next of kin or beneficiaries names and addresses. Sometimes ages will be included, which can be helpful with genealogy.

Letters. See Diaries, Letters, and Postcards.

Medals. Medals provide the basics of stories on theaters of war, battles fought, wounds received, and honors received. Use the medals to search for further records of engagements with the enemy and the historical context surrounding that engagement.

Memorial Notices. When a family received the telegram that their soldier had been killed (this applies to World War I as well), some families would place a Memorial Notice in the newspaper. Memorial Notices may contain the unit to which the soldier belonged, dates and places of training and service, educational information, and next of kin information. If the remains were repatriated, an obituary would be placed in the newspaper providing funeral details. Obituaries often provided next of kin, funeral information, and a full reference to military service or a mention.

Military Citations. Military citations will not always be found within a family's files or a service file. Some citations were issued after the war and soldier's discharge and become part of the unit files. However, if you find a military citation, you will know what award your soldier received which can lead you into further research about his service.

Military Equipment. Many soldiers returned from war with military equipment. Some of these may have been souvenirs or training weapons. Each tells a story.

Military Paperwork (discharge papers, enlistment papers, medical records). Look for the Separation and Discharge Papers from the military. Some soldiers may also have enlistment papers, old basic training booklets, competency paperwork, or notes he took while in training or at the front. Each of these sources will provide clues to service.

Military Pocket Guides. Small stapled books containing combat information, lists of officers, and other information may be among a soldier's belongings. These items may not tell you where a soldier fought, but they will provide information on what skills they needed to serve or with whom they served.

Military Uniforms. Uniforms provide visual clues to a soldier's service. Look for pins indicating expertise in certain areas, like rifleman. Look for patches that indicate unit or rank. The uniform type also provides the branch of service in which the soldier served.

Military Unit Newsletters or Newspapers. Some units created newsletters or newspapers while overseas as a way to keep the company updated on events or news from home. Often these will provide a date and general location of service which can help you complete a timeline of service.

Navy Cruise Books. Navy Cruise Books are like school yearbooks. They provide photographs of the sailors on a ship during a specific time period (cruise) and information about the cruise. Sailors often autographed each other's books before being detached to another station.

Newspaper Articles. Go beyond the obituaries when you search the newspaper. Look for articles that describe the war in the theater of operations in which your soldier served because they may name your soldier. Look for write-ups about soldiers preparing to ship out or those who received promotions or accomplished a huge feat.

Families placed memorial notices in newspapers on the anniversary of their soldier's death. These often provide unit information. Keep in mind that the last unit to be shown on a discharge paper, Burial File or Individual Deceased Personnel File, obituary, or memorial notice, may not be the only unit in which a soldier served. It does, however, give you a starting point for research.

Also, once the war department notified the family of the change in status of a soldier, those lists were published in major newspapers. During World War II, the Historical *Chicago Tribune* published lists of "Army Dead" or "Missing in Action" on average, three times a week. Search for lists that show a status change to Missing in Action (MIA), Killed in Action (KIA), Prisoner of War (POW), and those who were wounded. These lists appeared 30-90 days, on average, after the War Department notified the family of the change of status. In some cases, the delay was even longer than 90 days, so keep looking.

Obituaries and Memorial Notices. See Memorial Notices.

Photographs of the soldier. Photographs also provide visual clues to a soldier's service. Use these clues just as you would use uniform insignia and badges, to piece together the puzzle. Do the photos show a beach or jungle scene indicating war in the Pacific, or the wooded forests of northern Europe? This information helps put your soldier in a specific place at a specific time, around which you can build a story and look for more information.

Postcards. See Diaries, Letters, and Postcards.

Scrapbook. Family scrapbooks can be an excellent source of information. Many families kept photographs, letters, postcards, newspaper clippings, and other memorabilia in scrapbooks. In the 1940s scrapbook pages were made of heavy black paper, which tends to crumble after many years. If the photos and other memorabilia can be safely removed from these crumbling books and stored in an archival sleeve, folder, or box, you have a better chance of preserving the materials.

Souvenirs. Soldiers often brought home souvenirs from service. With each item there is a story you can hopefully capture before it is too late. My grandfather brought home a silver bracelet with links. The largest link says ROME Italy 1944 with an etching of the coliseum. There are links for Africa, Cassino, Firenzi, and Sicily. I know one of the Liberty Ships he was on stopped in Italy, but since I never had the opportunity to speak with my grandfather, I have no idea if he saw all these places.

State-Level War Participation Certificate. It was common for a soldier to return to his home after the war ended before possibly moving elsewhere. If you have a State-Level War Participation Certificate, it provides proof your ancestor lived in that state during his service. For researchers who may not have known the original state of service, this can lead to additional state and county level records. These certificates were issued by the state. You can check state archives to see if any copies were retained, beyond the original sent to the family.

Uniform Buttons. Uniform buttons differed between military branches. Buttons can be helpful if you are unsure exactly in which branch your soldier served.

Uniform Patches. Patches are also helpful in determining Division in which a soldier served. They will not tell you specifically what Unit or Company within the Division your soldier served, but it provides a starting point.

Unit Association Websites (Reunion materials). Many veterans joined Associations or Reunion groups after the war or later in life. You might find correspondence from the group to the veteran in the form of letters, newsletters, or magazines. Use these to pull clues about the battles in which this unit fought, the men with whom your soldier served, and memories about the war. Placed into context or a research plan, these clues can unlock many doors.

Unit Awards. Within the unit records, and sometimes the soldier's service file, you will find unit commendations or award memos. These too provide context for service and battles fought.

Unit Histories. Unit histories were created after the war by both the unit themselves and official military histories. Both are valuable in research as they provide context to the overall service of a unit. These histories may not list your soldier by name unless he was an officer, but the clues and context they provide may help you move down additional research paths.

Unit Newsletters Created Overseas. See Military Unit Newsletters or Newspapers.

Unit Photographs. Unit photographs, particularly the very long narrow photos taken at training camps of units prior to shipping out or upon completion of training, can provide clues. When I was researching the Army service of Private James Privoznik, I was able to trace his service back to February 1944 through Morning Reports and other documents. His service file burned, but I knew he had joined the Army at least a year prior. Within his belongings was a unit photograph, in which I could not identify him out of all the men pictured, but the bottom said, "Camp Butner, NC 126th MM Co. January 1944." This was exactly the clue I needed to have Morning Reports checked. Morning Reports are discussed later in this book, but track the entry, exit, and status changes of a soldier in a Company.

When I received the Morning Reports, they showed James had been part of the 126th MM Company (Medium Maintenance Company) from February 1944 back to February 1943 when he was inducted into the Army. Never rule out photos found within your soldier's collection. Treat them just as you would a document, to which you refer to often for additional clues.

Veterans Affairs Files. After the war, veterans often filed claims through the Veterans Affairs (VA) office for medical and other reasons. The VA holds these files which may contain some basic service and health history. These are among the first files you should request, because it takes months for the VA to respond.

Wartime Telegrams. Wartime telegrams held by the family may also provide clues as to the service number, unit, and important events in the life of the soldier. Telegrams were sent from soldiers to the family to pass news. They were also sent by the War Department to families to notify them of a soldier's change in status to Missing, Prisoner, Wounded, or Killed in Action. These telegrams are sometimes found within service files, Individual Deceased Personnel Files, and Insurance files.

World War I and World War II Bonus Applications. After both World Wars, the government provided a bonus payment for service overseas. These bonus applications are often found within state archival holdings. Some, for states like Pennsylvania, have been digitized and placed online. The Bonus Application would have been filed in the state in which the soldier lived after service. Check with the State Archives regarding holdings and access. In some states, these records are open and available. In other states, like Illinois, laws restrict access for many more years.

Interview a veteran

Finally, one of the most important things you can do to move your research along is to interview a veteran. who served with your adopted soldier. Unfortunately, hundreds of World War II veterans die each day around the world. The veterans who served with your adopted soldier may have already passed away. If this is the case, you have other options to learn what it was like to serve. Keep in mind the memories and recollections are 70+ years old and may not be quite accurate.

Locate and speak to a veteran who served in the same Division or unit in which your soldier served during the time period in which your soldier was in that Division or unit. The veteran may have never known your soldier, but can provide context as to what it was like fighting in that unit. This context will help you shape the story of your soldier and may trigger ideas on other resources to search in your quest to document your soldier's service.

Another option is to locate and listen to an oral history. Oral histories can be found in many libraries, archives, and online. One of the most well-known oral history projects is the Library of Congress Veterans Oral History Project. To locate oral histories, some which may be digitized, search the database

```
Websites

Library of Congress Veterans Oral History Project
http://loc.gov/vets/
```

and request copies of histories or visit the Library of Congress to use the materials. The Library also has a program for the general public to conduct interviews and submit them to the collection. Details on accessing oral histories and participating in the program can be found on the Library's website.

Public Records

The next place to look for information after home sources are publicly available records.

Separation Papers. Many soldiers filed their discharge papers with the County Clerk's office or the Recorder's Office after the war. Some counties may have these records on file and available for use.

Draft Registration Records. During World War II there was a draft, and each man had to register. Only the records for the "Old Man's Draft" are available online through Ancestry.com and Fold3.com. These draft cards are for those too old to serve unless it was absolutely necessary.

Local Histories. Local histories written in a rural area may provide more information on soldiers than one written in an urban area. Fewer soldiers existed in the rural areas and were therefore easier to chronicle. While the local histories of an urban area may not provide information on specific soldiers, it will provide context and clues to use in research.

Local Libraries and University Collections. Many local libraries and university libraries and special collections have newspapers, photographs, movies, ephemera, letters, diaries, and unit histories.

Search the Collaterals. Attempt to contact others who served with your military ancestor. While many World War II veterans have passed away, many still live. Search for those who served with your ancestor, or even who served in the same unit. Hearing their stories will provide context for your soldier story. It will also give you a better feel for what life was like for that soldier.

Military Home Source Checklist

_____ Bibles
_____ Burial Flags
_____ Church Records
_____ Company Newsletters
_____ Country Guides
_____ Diaries & Journals
_____ Employment Records
_____ Family Genealogies
_____ Fraternal Organization Records
_____ Headgear
_____ Home Movies
_____ Identification Tags
_____ Insignia
_____ Insurance Records
_____ Letters
_____ Maps
_____ Memorial Notices
_____ Military Citations
_____ Military Equipment
_____ Military Medals & Ribbons
_____ Military Medical Records
_____ Military Pocket Guides
_____ Military Separation Papers
_____ Military Uniforms
_____ Military Unit Newsletters or
        Newspapers
_____ Navy Cruise Books

_____ Newspaper Articles
_____ Obituaries
_____ Pension Records
_____ Photographs
_____ Postcards
_____ School Records
_____ Scrapbook
_____ Souvenirs
_____ State-Level War Participation
_____ Uniform Buttons
_____ Uniform Patches
_____ Unit Association Websites (Reunion
        materials)
_____ Unit Awards
_____ Unit Histories
_____ Unit Newsletters Created Overseas
_____ Unit Photographs
_____ V-Mail
_____ VFW and Other Veteran Group
        Records (see Fraternal & Military
        Organizations)
_____ Wartime Telegrams
_____ World War I and II Bonus Applications

Offline Military Research

The next step in researching your adopted soldier's service, is looking for records and understanding what you find in those records. Throughout this chapter, we will explore where to request records, what the information on the records mean, and how to decipher soldier statuses.

Reasons the Records May Not Exist

World War I and World War II records may not exist for several reasons. We have already discussed the fire at the National Personnel Records Center in 1973, which destroyed roughly 80% of the Army, Army Air Corps and National Guard Records. There are other reasons records other than service files do not exist. Here are a few scenarios to consider.

The ship was sunk or the plane went down. The Coast Guard and Navy maintained Deck Logs and Muster Rolls on paper on the ships or stations. Army, Air Corps, and National Guard soldiers may have been on ships, even if they are not listed on Muster Rolls. If those ships or stations were bombed or the ship sunk, the records were likely lost. The same applies for the Marine Corps, which was under the authority of the Navy. Some of their records may have been located on ships.

Fire was another factor in the destruction of records, as seen in a Marine Corps Marine Air Group 21 Unit History supplement.[1]

```
Enclosure:          (a) Unit History, Marine Aircraft Group Twenty-One.
                    (b) Deficiencies in Enclosure (a), listing of.

     1.             Unit History, Marine Aircraft Group Twenty-One,
covering period 1 August, 1941, to 1 January, 1945, forwarded.

     2.             Subject History is deficient in some respects
because the copies of MAG-21 War Diary for the period 7 December, 1941
to 11 February, 1943 (when the Group left Ewa for the Russell Islands)
were destroyed by fire. Wherever possible these deficiencies have
been supplied by information obtained from personal interviews and
research work in checking muster rolls and other available documents
in the forward area.
```

Source: USMC Intelligence Letter dated 22 January 1945. World War II War Diaries, Other Operational Records and Histories, compiled ca. 01/01/1942 - ca. 06/01/1946, documenting the period ca. 09/01/1939 - ca. 05/30/1946; Records of the Naval Operating Forces, Record Group 313; National Archives, College Park, MD.

Pilots and Bomber Crews likely had some of their records with them as they flew overseas or base to base. If the plane crashed and burned, the records would have been destroyed. For the Army, if the company records for the Division were being transported on a truck which was hit and destroyed, it is possible those records were lost.

Errors in the creation of records. The individuals handling the records also made mistakes. Pieces of one soldier's file may have ended up in another, whether it was a family member with the same name or someone completely different, due to the chaos and confusion of war. An example is a Marine named William F. Cowart. Cowart was Killed in Action on the island of Tarawa on 20 November 1943.[2] His Individual Deceased Personnel File (IDPF) contains a photo of a different man. It is not uncommon for Marine Corps, Navy, and Coast Guard IDPFs to have photos of the soldiers. The photos are usually headshots taken after enlistment with the service number at the bottom. The photos are included in the service file. The service number on the photo in Cowart's file did not match his. The photo was actually for a Marine killed the following day named Richard Courtleigh.[3]

As you consider the reasons records may no longer exist, understand many of these reasons are also reasons service men's personal effects were never returned to the family when they were declared Missing in Action, Prisoner of War, or Killed in Action.

World War I Military Service

Before we look at World War II records, it is worth mentioning the fact that some soldiers served prior to World War II. There may be records you can obtain to learn about prior service that will impact your research in World War II.

The steps in this chapter regarding locating service files and other information on a soldier apply to those who served in World War I or World War II. The records created in World War I have the same or similar record in World War II.

World War I Discharge Papers

After both World Wars, veterans were encouraged to file their Discharge or Separation papers with the County Recorder or Clerk for safe keeping. This is one of the first places you should check for either war's service.

Repository: National Personnel Records Center, St. Louis, MO.

Veterans Administration (VA)

The VA is another place to request a search for records, and was briefly touched upon in the previous chapter. A search should be initiated early for VA records because of the length of time it takes to receive a response.

Repository: U.S. Department of Veterans Affairs

WWI Draft Registration Cards

World War I Draft Registration cards have been digitized, and are available online through Ancestry.com, Fold3.com, and FamilySearch.org. Draft Cards provide a snapshot in time of a soldier's life providing details on address, date of birth, occupation and employer, physical description, next of kin, and most importantly, the draft board number. The draft board number is important because it allows you to search newspapers for lists of men declared physically fit for duty and troop lists. The cards also help you place your soldier in a specific place in 1917 or 1918.

Repository: National Personnel Records Center, St. Louis, MO.

Statement of Service Cards

The Statement of Service Cards were created by the military, and in 1922, sent to State Adjutant General's Offices. Unfortunately, not all states possess these valuable cards. The cards contain name, service number, units, locations of training and overseas service, awards earned, wounds received, next-of-kin information, and death information if they died in service.

Repository: Check the State Archives where your soldier lived when he entered service.

World War I Bonus Applications

After both world wars, states issued bonus payments to soldiers, or their beneficiary if they died in service. This bonus payment was calculated for each branch based on days served stateside and overseas. World War I Bonus Applications are usually held within a state's archival holdings and may contain discharge or separation papers as part of the application. These applications often contain next-of-kin information, service information, and affidavits from friends and family.

Repository: Check the State Archives where your soldier lived when he entered service. Some of these records were digitized on Ancestry.com.

National Guard Units

National Guard records are held in each state's archives, or Adjutant General's Office if the unit was not federalized. If your soldier served in the National Guard at any time prior to World War II, check with your state. During World War II, many National Guard units were federalized and placed under the control of the Army. Therefore, the records for Army and National Guard are the same, and will be held not with the state, but with the NPRC.

Repository: If the unit was not federalized, check the State Archives or the State National Guard Office where your soldier lived when he entered service. If the unit was federalized, the records are at the NPRC.

Foreign Service Records

Prior to the United States' entry into World War II, many young men felt compelled to take up the fight with foreign countries on behalf of the Allies. Canada and Britain are two countries which men fought for. Investigate the records in those countries if you believe your soldier fought for another prior to our entry in the war.

The World War II Draft

The Selective Service System was established by President Roosevelt in 1940. This act created the first peacetime draft. After its establishment, there were six separate draft registrations between 1940 and 1946.

#1	16 October 1940	Men born on or after October 17, 1904 and on or before October 16, 1919.
#2	1 July 1941	Men born on or after October 17, 1919 and on or before July 12, 1920 and those from Registration no. 1 who failed to register.
#3	16 February 1942	Men born on or after February 17, 1897 and on or before December 31, 1921.
#4	27 April 1942	Men born on or before April 28, 1877 and on or before February 16, 1897.
#5	30 June 1942	Men born on or after January 1, 1922 and on or before June 30, 1924.
#6	11-31 December 1942	Men born on or after July 1, 1924 and on or before December 31, 1942. Also for men who reach their 18th birthday on or after January 1, 1943.

There was a special draft registration between November 16 and December 31, 1943, for men born after December 31, 1898 and before January 1, 1926, as well as men born after January 1, 1926, when they turned 18.

The NPRC in St. Louis holds the Selective Service Records. There are two main groups of these records. One group consists of the fourth registration cards. These draft registration cards are considered the "Old Man's Draft" and have been digitized. Researchers can search and view them on paid websites, such as Ancestry.com and Fold3.com, which many libraries provide free access to for patrons. The second group consists of all other registrations of men born between February 17, 1897, and July 31, 1927. There are two options for ordering Selective Service Records. One is only the Draft registration card. The other is the Classification History, which includes the Draft Registration Card. *See David Lardner's Civilian Selective Service Data Card in previous chapter for a Classification History example.*

Repository: National Personnel Records Center, St. Louis, MO.

The quality of the World War II Draft Registration Cards was not great when I received them. This is a good example of the quality of records sometimes received from the WWII-era.

I did find it interesting for two of my soldiers who were Killed In Action, that their cards indicated this.

In addition, the date my grandfather was discharged from the Navy was written across the top of his card.

Source: Selective Service Draft Registration Card. Frank J. Winkler. National Personnel Records Center, St. Louis, Missouri.

Serial/Service Numbers

The primary piece of information you need to search military records, beyond the soldier's name, is his service number, which, depending on the branch they served in, can also be referred to as a Serial Number. Within this volume, I will refer to this number as the service number. Service numbers were issued to help identify the soldier as he moved from unit to unit. A service number is similar to a Social Security Number. Both help identify individuals. Service numbers were issued by each branch of the service to officers and enlisted men. Social Security Numbers were **not** used by the military for identification until after World War II.

Identification Tags

Each soldier was given two identification tags, also known as dog tags. These contained the name of the soldier, service number, year of tetanus inoculation, blood type, and next of kin with address and religion code. By 1943, the tag was modified to only show the name, service number, tetanus inoculation, blood type and religion. These provide valuable information when starting your research.

Locating a Service Number

What happens when you do not have a Soldier's Discharge Papers, know his service number, or unit? You can contact the NPRC in St. Louis by letter and ask them to search the VA Index. (Form 180 will not work for this request.) The VA Index is an index of all service members. The cards will provide the following information on a soldier:

- Name.
- Address upon discharge or death.
- Service Number.
- Rank.
- Birth date.
- Enlistment, Discharge, and/or death date.
- First unit in which he/she served.

Repository: National Personnel Records Center, St. Louis, MO.

Obtaining Military Service Records

National Archives is made up of several facilities. The main facility is in Washington, D.C. The facility that holds personnel records (OMPFs) and other individual and unit records is the National Personnel Records Center in St. Louis, Missouri. There are many other Federal Records Centers across the United States called Regional Centers. It can be confusing to figure out which facility holds the records you wish to see. The easiest way to determine if a Regional Center has records you seek is to use the Finding Aid for Regional Centers, which you can find in the Additional Resources section for my books, on my website.

Requesting the Service File

The Official Military Personnel File (OMPF) for the Army, Army Air Corps (current day Air Force), Navy (including Armed Guard,) Coast Guard, Marine Corps, and federalized National Guard records are held at the NPRC in St. Louis. There are three ways to access these records.

Mail in Form 180

The least expensive way to begin a search is to fill out and mail Form 180 on the NPRC website and see if the file survived. If records are discovered, NPRC will send you a letter indicating such, as well as your fee for copies. Form 180 will ONLY search personnel and medical records.

> NPRC Form 180
> http://www.archives.gov/research/order/standard-form-180.pdf

Visit NPRC In-Person

You can visit the NPRC in-person, but there is a procedure for doing so. Visit their website for current rules regarding making an appointment, what is allowed in the research room, and how to request files and microfilm.

Hire a Researcher

Another option is to hire an independent researcher who knows their way around the NPRC records. There are many more valuable records at the NPRC besides the service files, such as Morning Reports, that Form 180 will not search for you. NARA does have a researcher's list you can check.

> I highly recommend Norm Richards, a researcher on NARA's NPRC list, with whom I have personally worked with for several years. Mr. Richards is also one of the historians for the 90th Division and is very knowledgeable.
>
> AAA Military Research
> Email: normrichards9@gmail.com
> Please tell him I referred you.

Non-Federalized National Guard Records

Non-Federalized National Guard records are held at the state level in a state archive, state military museum, or state VA administration office. Check with your state to find out if they hold any records.

Merchant Marines Records

The Merchant Marines were a civilian organization, except during wartime, when they fell under the Department of the Navy. Service members *who survived the war* have records available with discharges from the U.S. Coast Guard. You can write to the following address providing the information requested to request a search. Include the name, date of birth, copy of death certificate if deceased, social security number, address, and Z or service number.

Repository for Merchant Marines who survived the war:

Commanding Officer
USCG-National Maritime Center (NMC-421)
ATTN: Correspondence Section
100 Forbes Drive
Martinsburg, WV 25404

Repository for Merchant Marines who were killed during the war: National Personnel Records Center, St. Louis, MO. Provide the name, date of birth, date of death, social security number, address, and Z or service number.

Contents of a Military Service File

The contents of a Military Service File are similar across branches, yet different based on the needs and requirements of a specific branch. The contents often include the following items. This list is by no means complete, but it is meant to provide a sample of contents. The following chapters will provide more in-depth examples for each branch of the military.

Qualification card

A Qualification Card required the potential service man or woman to list vital information, address, education and work history, additional training and talents, hobbies, sports, and languages spoken.

Letters of recommendation if the soldier enlisted prior to the war

In addition to letters of recommendation, there may also be an application for service.

Physical Examination record

These pages contained information on vaccines given, physicals, and dental work and records. The physical and dental records were important should a soldier need to be identified at any time.

Enlistment record or contract

This record provides vital information, date of entry into the service, and the soldier's signature.

Insurance information

Each soldier was required to take out an insurance policy and list beneficiaries which were often next-of-kin and their addresses.

Pay records

Each man carried a "Soldier's Individual Pay Record" book with him or with the unit. In this was a record of the pay he received during enlistment. This information may be found in a service record.

Training Information

Information on dates and places of training, type of training, and scores received.

Medical Information

There may be medical information and notes prior to a soldier going overseas, while he was overseas, and when he returned and was examined prior to discharge.

Station, Ship, or any other Location of Service

Documentation on where a soldier was stationed on board a ship, training base, or theater of war can be found either as separate documents or within other records in the file.

Discharge Paper or Separation Papers

The discharge paper contained the soldier's name, rank, last unit in which he served (this does not mean the only unit), awards received, training received, and location of discharge. These records also contained the length of time served overseas, including which theater.

Prior Military Service

As you navigate various military records, you may encounter dates of service which do not coincide with other records you may have regarding your soldier. The IDPF for 2nd Lt. Fred A. Davis, Army Air Corps stated his entry into current service (note that it says current) was in 1943.[4] However, Fred was originally part of a National Guard Unit the 106th Cavalry until he transferred into the Air Corps in 1940, according to a newspaper article concerning his death and Missing in Action status.[5] He began his current and final service with the Air Corps in 1943 after earning his wings and becoming an officer.[6] Fred's service file burned, but the information was obtained through newspaper articles and his IDPF.

Rank and Unit

As stated above, the unit that appears on the final paperwork, whether a Discharge Certificate, World War I Burial File, or World War II IDPF, may not be the only unit in which that soldier served. Using that unit as a starting point, additional records can be searched backward to get a clearer picture of that soldier's service.

Example:
James Privoznik
11 January 1945
PFC F Company 358th Infantry Regiment 90th Division

This means James served as a Private First Class under Patton's Third Army in the 90th Division. He was part of the 358th Infantry, F Company. This is stated on his Report of Burial dated 17 January 1945.[7] However, he was part of this unit for only the last 14 days of his life. Using this information, I had Army Morning Reports searched backward to trace his entry into the 358th Infantry from a prior unit. Using Morning Reports, I was able to trace his entire service start to finish.

MOS (Military Occupational Specialty)

Reviewing military paperwork from the service record, Morning Reports and discharge papers, you will see something called MOS. This is the Military Occupational Specialty, or job the soldier held. Commonly held jobs included infantry, pilot, armored, clerk, sailor, and medic. For a detailed description of all the MOS available, please see the *Technical Manual – Military Occupational Classification of Enlisted Personnel PDF*. This manual is available in my World War II Toolbox on my website.

James Privoznik, who was discussed in the Rank and Unit section, had upon his death, the MOS 745. This was a rifleman. He held that MOS for approximately 14 days, given to him about 27 December 1944.[8] Prior to that, he was in the 90th Division, 790th Ordnance Company in which he held the MOS of 189, which was given to him 18 December 1944.[9] That position was Rigger. Prior to this, he held a different MOS. Unfortunately no record exists (at this point) to say what that MOS was within the Ordnance Company. As you can see from this example, sometimes we get most of the information we seek, but not all.

Education – From High School to College and Specialized Training

As the war effort ramped up during the 1940s, with the participation of both military and civilians, new programs and systems of education were put in place. This ensured everyone was able to give 100% to winning the war. Across the country, high schools, colleges, and universities took up the call to arms. They armed their faculty with expertise to assist the military in training men and women for various duties. Grade school and high schools implemented programs to educate students about rationing, improving patriotic spirit, and military service. During the 1940s not every man or woman attended college as is common today. College was more of an option for men, as it was still a man's world.

Not every soldier was automatically sent to a training camp. In 1942, the Army created the Army Specialized Training Program (ASTP) to educate intellectually and academically talented enlisted men. One idea behind the program was to keep these intellectuals off the front lines as long as possible. These would be the men who would help win the war.

The military used the colleges and universities across the country as the base for this training. Through the ASTP, more than 140,000 men were provided with a college education and military technical training. Upon completion of training, these enlisted men and officers were promoted. These new officers facilitated the end of the war.

The ASTP lasted less than two years. In April 1944, the military knew the demand for front-line soldiers would be needed for Operation Overlord (D-Day) on June 6th. The men were released from academic duty and placed into units still stationed state-side. These did not go overseas until late 1944.

There was somewhat of a stigma attached to the men who were in the ASTP. These men were more educated than the average soldier and were not accepted into the ranks without some issues. In some ways, the men were seen as cowards because they attended school rather than immediately joining the fight. Some of the enlisted men viewed them as mightier than God because of their education. Not only did the ASTPers have an issue, but also the academics who taught them. These professors were seen as a threat, someone who would enter a unit and immediately earn stripes, thereby stripping another soldier of his. Usually the AST-Pers were not promoted until they had combat experience and the rank opened up due to casualties.

Records at Educational Facilities

Educational facilities are another place to locate military information. Contact the libraries and archives of the schools your ancestor attended for high school, college (pre-military service) and any college training they received once they joined the military. If you are unsure where your ancestor attended, search the newspapers for information on graduation, awards, and military service. These articles often have school information. You can also make a list of the schools that were in existence at the time your soldier may have attended and contact them to inquire about a search for your ancestor. Check the local public library where you soldier lived, because many have local history rooms or genealogy sections with war memorial type information. If the locale also has a historical society or museum, that is another resource to check.

Educational records may include the following:

Academic Records. If you want to know what kind of student your soldier was, seek academic records. Depending on the school rules or local or state laws, there may be restrictions on accessing the records.

Alumni Organizations. Check with the school alumni department or group. You may discover reunion information, lists of class members' names and current addresses, and photographs.

Letters, Postcards, Photographs, and Film. Military personnel may have sent postcards, photographs, letters, and film to their schools and may be housed in the library's special collections department. In addition, colleges and universities which held military classes may have photographed or filmed their students.

Oral Histories. Check the special collections departments at colleges and universities that trained soldiers during the war. Their collections may contain oral histories and donated documentation regarding service. You can also search the Library of Congress' Veterans Oral History Project.

School Newspapers. Many high schools and colleges produced newspapers. These papers may not be indexed, but if they exist and you have a narrow time frame to search, you may discover clues about the life of your soldier.

Yearbooks. Yearbooks usually include photos and other interesting information about the students. These are often held within a school archive or local library. Some yearbooks have been digitized and placed online.

Communication During World War II

As we explore the historical context in which our ancestor lived during both World Wars, we need to remember that communication was not as it is today. During both wars, there was no texting, cell phones, social media, or faxing. Communication was much slower than today. Word traveled through a unit or Division by word of mouth, written reports, and radio. From the theaters of war to the home front, word traveled by military ships, telegram, phone, and mail. Be mindful of this as you explore records and histories of the war. It helps explain gaps in records, length of time the family was notified of an event with their soldier, and record inconsistencies.

One very important thing to keep in mind as you research is the fact that you will not always find the information on a report or record the day you think it should be listed. It took time for word to reach the company clerk or go up the lines to the division level. If your soldier was wounded, missing, taken prisoner, or killed in action, it may have been a day, several days, or more before that information was listed in a report. You must check the date you believe an event occurred and many days after.

The same concept applies for newspaper articles. Lists of soldiers were placed in the newspapers for wounds, missing, prisoner, and killed in action statuses. These lists appeared 30-90 days after the War Department notified the family of the change in status.

When to Hire a Researcher

Anyone can conduct military research and write their soldier's story, but not everyone has the time, ability to travel to repositories, or desire to do so. This is when hiring a researcher or writer is helpful.

Finding Researchers

Where can you find researchers? My World War II Research and Writing Center offers many researcher options including myself. Many repositories and libraries have researcher lists on their websites. The individuals on these lists are usually not endorsed by the organization, but add people as they request to be added. Check each researcher's qualifications and contact several before initiating a project.

Tip! Finding a researcher on an "expert" website/forum may not be the best option. Read through each expert's profile to see their experience and skill areas. Read through the questions asked of them, as well as the answers provided. If a researcher is giving the same answers over and over, regardless of the question, it is likely they are unaware of additional records which actually exist.

Military Death Records

Many records were created across the branches during the war to document Missing in Action and Killed in Action statuses of soldiers. During World War I this file was called a Burial File. During World War II, it was called the Individual Deceased Personnel File (IDPF.)

Death information is also captured in Morning Reports, Missing Air Crew Reports (MACRs) (Army, Air Corps, and National Guard) and Crew Lists and Muster Rolls (Navy, Marines, Coast Guard, and Merchant Marines.)

The American Battle Monuments Commission

Upon conclusion of both World Wars, the U.S. government began bringing home the soldiers who survived and handling the final disposition of those who did not. Due to high numbers of Soldier Dead buried overseas, the government established permanent American Military Cemeteries overseas. Families had the choice to permanently bury their soldier who was killed overseas in an American Military Cemetery or have the soldier's remains repatriated and buried in a cemetery in the United States. The government covered the expenses for both options.

After World War II, for the families who chose to leave their Soldier Dead overseas, and for the unknown soldiers, re-interment in permanent American Military Cemeteries took place after all the dead who needed to be repatriated were returned home. The 209 temporary cemeteries across Europe, North Africa, and the Pacific were condensed to 14 cemeteries in foreign countries.[1]

Soldier Dead is a term used by the military to describe those valiant men and women who gave the ultimate sacrifice during military service. This term will be used throughout this chapter to refer to our honored war dead.

The American Battle Monuments Commission (ABMC) oversees the cemeteries which hold our American military dead around the world. ABMC was established in 1923 by Congress to honor our Great War dead.[2] These cemeteries were granted in perpetuity to our government and remain tax free. Burial in these cemeteries was not just of our male G.I.'s but also Red Cross workers, USO entertainers, and others seen as military personnel during World War I and II.

The cemeteries were laid out to be green, expansive, beautiful, and full of peace. Each headstone is made of marble in the shape of a cross or Star of David, depending on the religion of the soldier. Visitor's centers were erected which depict battles fought nearby. Memorials were built listing the names of the missing and to honor all who fought and died.

The cemeteries are groomed and cared for by AMBC staff and decorated with flags and flowers for ceremonies throughout the year. The ABMC offers photography services for families who wish to have a photograph of their Soldier Dead's grave and the cemetery. They also offer floral services if you wish to have flowers placed on a soldier's grave.

To fully appreciate how these cemeteries came into existence and honor those buried beneath the foreign soil, we must discuss the men who helped build the cemeteries. Who were they? What kind of job did they have during and after the wars? How did they care for our most honored dead? And how did they shape the cemeteries we visit today?

These men were from the Quartermaster Graves Registration Service. What follows is not an exhaustive history of this unit because many books have been written on the subject. The purpose is to provide an overview to help put each soldier's life and death into greater context.

Graves Registration Service History

The Graves Registration Service (GRS) has a long history dating back to 1862 when Congress gave the President authorization to create permanent American military cemeteries. This act gave the President the ability to seek and purchase land for these cemeteries.[3] In 1867 Congress gave the Quartermaster General in the U.S. Army the responsibility to establish military cemeteries, handle burials, keep records, and handle ongoing maintenance of these cemeteries.[4] The Quartermaster handled the burials of our soldiers from the Civil War, Spanish-American War and World War I.

During World War I, the number of dead was in approximately 77,000 scattered over many battlefields and buried within 2,400 cemeteries in England and Europe.[5] Eventually roughly ¾ of these Soldier Dead were either repatriated to the U.S. or interred in one of the eight permanent military cemeteries in England or Europe. When World War I ended, the Graves Registration Service worked to consolidate these cemeteries and recover remains buried in enemy lands.

When the U.S. entered World War II, one thing the Army was determined to do was not established thousands of small cemeteries. Instead, they planned to establish several cemeteries near the fighting and bring Soldier Dead to these cemeteries. Collection points were established so the combat units could assist in the collection and identification of the deceased. The GRS men found if identification could take place near the battlefield with information from the combat unit there was a higher chance of positively identifying the deceased. When the unit had moved on and no one was available to help identify the dead, many were brought to the collection points and cemeteries as unknowns.

The Job

When we think of a cemetery in the U.S. or one of the ABMC cemeteries, we picture a beautiful, expansive, quiet, peaceful, rolling green, lush, and clean cemetery. Just as we are conditioned to think of our World War II veterans as older men and women, we are conditioned to see military cemeteries as beautiful. This was not always the case.

As the U.S. prepared for war, the men of the Graves Registration Service was trained and prepared to go with the troops and handle the casualties. GRS workers were responsible for locating suitable cemetery sites overseas. Once selected after examining the terrain, soil quality, and distance to enemy lines, they began plotting the cemetery. Maps were drawn, processing tents were set up and the men assigned tasks. Local civilian workers were called in to help dig graves and bury the dead.

The job of a Graves Registration Service man was not glamorous. Nor was it discussed and publicized very often. As unsung heroes, these men worked tirelessly to care for the remains of not only our U.S. Soldier Dead but also enemy dead. Within practically every U.S. established cemetery, there was a section for German dead. Our GRS men worked to identify every casualty they buried. This was not always possible. When information was gathered about the unidentified soldiers, it was placed in a canister or bottle and buried in the grave.

GRS collecting remains and documenting personal effects and identification. Photo courtesy the American Battle Monuments Commission.

Both U.S. and enemy dead were buried in these temporary cemeteries. Why? It was important to bury all the dead for several reasons. The primary reason was health concerns. Decomposing bodies out in the open would spread disease and lower troop morale. It was better the troops did not encounter the remains of their comrades, lest the fear and panic they already felt increase, making them unable to do their job effectively.

There was also the respect for the fallen and families back home. Our men and women made the ultimate sacrifice for their country. They deserved respect from those who cared for them after death since their families could not.

Also, soldiers were buried for forensic reasons. Information was gathered to not only identify them but also on how they were killed. Furthermore, GRS buried for political reasons which showed both allies and enemies we have a heart, are human and care for others with compassion.

The GRS in World War II was not only responsible for collecting, identifying, and burying the Soldier Dead, but also handling personal effects. The men had a system by which they worked on the stripping line to handle personal effects which would be returned to the owner's family.

There are many people who make up the Quartermaster Graves Registration (QMGR) Unit. The individuals who primarily handled the Soldier Dead are described here. The description which follows is not meant to be an exhaustive look at the make-up of the QMGR Unit, but to give you an idea of some components. GRS personnel duties varied by person. Each was trained for a specific job during and after basic training.

GRS Platoon Headquarters

Platoon Leader. The Platoon Leader's duties varied depending on whether or not the platoon was part of the company at the time of operation. Overall the Platoon Leader selected a cemetery site and was responsible for training, discipline, supplies, and transportation. When the platoon was part of the company, other miscellaneous duties were assigned.[7]

Platoon Sergeant. The Platoon Sergeant assisted the Platoon Leader in his duties.[8]

Surveyor. The Surveyor supervised the layout of the cemeteries. He usually trained a team to work with him to clear a space for use.[9]

Other Positions. The Liaison Agent served as a replacement for the Platoon Leader at various meetings. A Supply Specialist requisitioned and maintained stock for the unit. And a Light Truck Driver was the messenger for the Platoon and had miscellaneous duties as assigned.[10]

GRS Collection and Evacuation Section

Section Chief. The Section Chief was the supervisor of all the GRS specialists. In certain situations when the combat troops are unable to help evacuate the Soldier Dead, the Section Chief assumes this responsibility.[11]

Graves Registration Specialists. Graves Registration Specialists were specifically trained in receiving Soldier Dead, identification procedures, record keeping, effects collection and distribution, and burial. These men worked with Assistant Graves Registration Specialists who had many of the same tasks.[12]

Graves Registration Clerk. The duties of the Graves Registration Clerk were to prepare all the reports on the Soldier Dead which became part of the Individual Deceased Personnel File (IDPF) and were sent to Headquarters in weekly reports.[13]

Still Photographer. A Still Photographer was used in cases where remains could not be identified. The photographer took photographs of the face and torso, tattoos, other identifying markings on the body and fingers in case prints could be identified.[14]

Technical Operations Personnel

Graves Registration Chief. The Graves Registration Chief supervised the Technical Operations Personnel under his command. He also oversaw four platoons and planned personnel jobs and in some cases, the cemeteries.[15]

Identification Chief. The Identification Chief worked with the Graves Registration Chief to supervise all the teams who worked with the Soldier Dead. He ensured the effects were transferred appropriately, records were completed, and as often as possible, each soldier was identified. He was also responsible for, "taking of fingerprints, preparation of tooth charts, …..and recording of accurate physical descriptions on appropriate forms."[16]

Draftsman. The Draftsman planned the cemetery layout and plotted it on a map.[17]

Fluoroscope Operator. The Fluoroscope Operator had an important job within the Technical Operations Personnel group. He was responsible for scanning the body to identify the location of identification tags which may have become embedded in the body. He also looked for possible foreign bodies such as shrapnel, unexploded devices, and other objects. When needed, the Fluoroscope Operator ran a chemical laboratory.[18]

Carpenter. The Carpenter handled all the usual carpentry duties within a GRS unit including creating crosses for the grave markers, building fences around the cemeteries, constructing signs to direct Collection Units and others to the GRS collecting points or cemeteries, and other miscellaneous duties as required.[19]

Obstacles for the Graves Registration Service

Pacific Theater of War

Graves Registration Units were not always present at battles in the Pacific Theater of War therefore, the burial of Soldier Dead was left primarily to the Marines and Navy units on the islands of battle. Temporary cemeteries were established, often using the trench burial system, to bury soldiers. The burial party would erect some sort of marker or cross over the grave before departing. The temporary cemeteries established were not always plotted, charted, or properly documented as to who was buried in them, as was done in the European Theater. This led to major identification and recovery issues after the war.

GRS preparing crosses for graves in a temporary cemetery. Photo courtesy the American Battle Monuments Commission.

Record keeping was sparse, and for many of the soldiers killed, you will not find complete IDPFs with Reports of Burial like you might in the European Theater. Notations may have been made in a personnel file or the file contains telegrams or letters sent to the family of the deceased.

A primary example of the lack of records is the Battle of Tarawa in the Gilbert Islands in November 1943. The Marines took the island of Tarawa, and many lost their lives. Trench burial was utilized and families were notified, based on limited records, that their Marine had died and was buried on Tarawa. After hostilities ceased on the island, the Navy Seabees came in to take care of the cemeteries. Not being trained in GRS procedures, many of the remains were disinterred without proper documentation. Also, in an attempt to clean up the cemeteries, markers were moved, but the remains were not. This led to great confusion as to who was actually buried there when the war ended. Families later received a letter stating the remains of their Marine could not be located or repatriated. Today, efforts are ongoing by many organizations to identify and repatriate these valiant men.

An example of these letters follows in regards to Marine Pvt. William F. Cowart who was killed on Tarawa 20 November 1943. The first letter is from the military to his mother regarding his temporary burial. The second letter is from 1947 when the GRS was attempting to identify and repatriate remains. It states that they are unable to identify William's remains.

Letter to Mrs. Cowart

471443
DGU-MM-sem

29 February, 1944.

My dear Mrs. Cowart:

Receipt is acknowledged of your letter regarding your son, the late Private William F. Cowart, U. S. Marine Corps Reserve.

I regret that the brief report received in this Headquarters states only that your son lost his life in action at Tarawa, Gilbert Islands, on November 29, 1943, and that his remains were temporarily interred on that Island.

Upon cessation of hostilities, it is the present intention of the Navy Department to return to this country the remains of Naval and Marine Corps personnel who lost their lives in the service of their country, if the next of kin so desire.

With renewed assurances of sympathy, I am

Sincerely yours,

JOSEPHUS DANIELS, JR.,
Captain, U. S. Marine Corps.

Mrs. Alice Cowart,
Route #3,
Millport, Alabama.

Source: Official Military Personnel File for William F. Cowart, serial no. 417443, Letter to Mrs. Cowart (mother) dated 29 Feb 1944 from Captain Marine Corps. National Personnel Records Center, St. Louis, MO.

Letter to Mrs. Cowart

471443
DGU-1159-rft

10 February, 1947.

My dear Mrs. Cowart:

  I wish to supplement previous correspondence regarding the disposition of the remains of your son, the late Private
William F. Cowart, U. S. Marine Corps Reserve, who lost his life
in the conquest of Tarawa.

  During the intense four-day battle to wrest this
strategically important island from the Japanese, approximately one thousand Marines made the supreme sacrifice. While
that critical operation was being fought, it was essential that
the remains of the dead be interred immediately in order to
safeguard the health of the living and to facilitate rendering
aid to the wounded. Under the fierce stress of battle on this
small island, hasty burial methods could not be avoided, and,
consequently, we were unable to survey and to chart the burial
places with full accuracy or to record all the details of
burial information.

  As soon as Tarawa was captured, our battle-scarred
Marine Corps units were relieved by garrison forces and were
sent to other Pacific islands for recuperation. Having been
supplied with all available information concerning the Marine
Corps dead, these forces arranged, charted and beautified the
cemeteries and furnished this Headquarters with reports of the
names and grave locations of the Marines buried there. Among
these reports was one stating that your son's remains were
buried on Tarawa, and this information was furnished you.

  Recently the American Graves Registration Service,
under direction of the Quartermaster General of the U. S. Army,
has been disinterring the bodies of the dead buried in various
isolated plots and reburying them in a centrally located cemetery preparatory to transporting the remains to a final resting
place selected by the next of kin.

  I regret extremely that I must inform you that the
remains of your son were not found to be beneath the marker
previously reported. Subsequent investigation has revealed
that in some instances well-meaning persons had erected individual commemorative markers in memory of our heroic dead.

- 1 -

*Source: Individual Deceased Personnel File for William F. Cowart, serial no. 417443, Letter to Mrs. Cowart (mother) dated 10
Nov 1947 from General USMC Commandant of the Marine Corps. Army Human Resource Command, Ft. Knox, KY.*

471443
DGU-1159-rft   10 February, 1947.

Since the Graves Registration Service has been unable to locate
the remains of Private Cowart, it must be assumed that his body
was among the unidentified dead and that the cross was erected in
his honored memory rather than actually as a marker identifying
the location of his grave.

Continued efforts are being made to locate unmarked
graves and every scientific means known is being employed to
establish the identity of our unidentified dead.

I am deeply grieved that there must now be added to
your sorrow this most distressing information. It is earnestly hoped that the continuing and unremitting efforts which
will be made may yet lead to the location and identification
of your son's remains, in which event you will be notified
immediately.

Sincerely yours,

A. A. VANDEGRIPT,
General, U.S.M.C.,
Commandant of the Marine Corps.

Mrs. Alice Cowart,
    Route #3,
        Millport, Alabama.

- 2 -

*Source: Individual Deceased Personnel File for William F. Cowart, serial no. 417443, Letter to Mrs. Cowart (mother) dated 10
Nov 1947 from General USMC Commandant of the Mariter of the Marine Corps. Army Human Resource Command, Ft. Knox, KY.*

European Theater of War

As well-prepared and trained as GRS men were, nothing could have prepared them for the onslaught of dead, which would appear when the Allies invaded the beaches of Normandy on 6 June 1944.

The GRS men participating in the Normandy Invasion were underprepared for the number of soldiers who would be killed during the invasion. Improvising along the way, these GRS men established ways to track both the identification of Soldier Dead and their belongings. It was not, however, a perfect system. Not only were the dead brought to each collecting station, but the GRS men were given maps and coordinates of temporary graves or downed planes and gliders which needed to be cleared.

Colonel Elbert E. Legg, a GRS Sergeant in the 603rd Quartermaster Graves Registration Company, stated they used parachutes as a burial shroud since they had landed without mattress covers.[20] The number of dead arriving daily, even before the cemetery could be marked out, exceeded their supplies and manpower. Until more manpower was brought in, the bare minimum was done in tracking personal effects. At one point, Colonel Legg was required to move to a new sector due to heavy enemy fighting. He tied up the personal effects bags in a parachute and hid it in a hedgerow until he could return to the area.[21]

We must always keep in mind, especially when discussing any facet of war, the fact that the men did the best they could at the time with the resources and knowledge they had. It was war. War is hell, full of chaos and confusion. Bullets flew and guns boomed, which made it difficult for the GRS men to do their jobs perfectly when they received each new dead soldier.

Establishing Temporary Cemeteries

Before a cemetery could be established and Soldier Dead collected and buried, sites had to be examined. GRS men looked for good terrain, sites close to main roads, and with natural protection in the form of trees or hedges. These trees or hedges would grow over time and offer more privacy to the cemetery grounds. They also checked soil conditions, evaluated drainage, looked for potential mines, and the destruction which surrounded the potential cemetery area. In some cases, GRS men looked for areas near combat zones where they knew heavy fighting would occur. This made it somewhat easier to transport and collect the Soldier Dead.

When a cemetery was laid out, there were certain guidelines to be followed.[22] These included:

• Graves were to be at least five feet in depth.

• When soldiers were interred, the head of each should face the same direction.

• A marker was to be placed at the head of each grave.

• Graves were to be numbered consecutively.

• If a trench burial system had to be implemented, the same procedure for laying out Soldier Dead was followed.

• Graves should align horizontally and vertically with other graves.

• A cemetery map should be drawn for indicating north. Separate plans should be drawn for each cemetery or burial plot if it is a trench burial.

A bivouac site, or camping area, was selected near the cemetery site which provided shelter from the weather, water, good drainage, and was free of disease. When possible, GRS men selected towns which provided undamaged homes, hospitals, schools, and other buildings to house the men.

In some cases, the dead would not be buried in temporary cemeteries, but temporary graves on the battlefield. The combat units were instructed to create a burial duty of at least two soldiers to bury the dead as quickly as possible. Due to combat conditions, there was not enough time to fill out paperwork or pull identification tags or personal effects. The Soldier Dead were buried and some marker was placed at their grave and notes written to indicate where the remains were located. The GRS men would later sweep the battlefields and disinter these hastily buried men.[23]

The Collection Point - Remains Recovery Process

A Collection Point was established on a main road and was used as the location the Soldier Dead were brought, usually by units in combat or GRS men. Collection Points contained an administrative tent, examination tent, examination area, and a screen to shelter passing troops from the view of their dead comrades.

The GRS men at Collection Points identified when possible, collected personal effects, and transported the Soldier Dead to the nearest American cemetery for burial. When they arrived at a cemetery, GRS workers again checked identification, effects, and rechecked records before temporary burial occurred.

GRS claimed the remains of a soldier from a unit, along the road side or battle ground. Men worked in the mud, rain, deep snow, jungles and on beaches in their recovery efforts. During December and January 1945, when the Battle of the Bulge raged, the weather was bitter cold and snow packed the ground for weeks. This made the job of grave digging and handling the dead ever more difficult.[25] These men also crossed back and forth over enemy lines putting their own lives in danger.

The recovery process was meant to collect both complete bodies and scattered remains. Consider the soldier who received a gunshot wound to the head. That most likely constituted a complete body or set of remains. Now, think about the men hit by shells. These bodies would have been in all sorts of condition, and may have been scattered around the area in which they were killed. GRS could not always attend to the dead immediately after they were killed, so these men encountered all stages of decomposition.

GRS collecting remains along the road and battlefield. Photo courtesy the American Battle Monuments Commission.

What Soldiers Carried

A common question families would ask when they received word their Soldier was dead was, "Where are his personal effects?" Families wanted every piece of their soldier they could get, both as a way to remember them and to grieve for them.

First, it is important to note that all usable clothing, shoes and equipment were stripped off and sent to the Quartermaster Supply Depots to be reused. What families were not told is that the soldiers carried very little of what was theirs on their person. The Army issued their clothing, bags, and equipment. They did wear identification tags, and may have carried wallets, rings, insignia, letters, photos, and money; but little else was theirs.

What happened to the things they carried? The enemy may have picked items off the dead. The soldier may have sold or given away watches and such. Friends may have taken an item off their dead buddy for safekeeping. Or it may have been destroyed when the soldier was killed.[26] There were other reasons personal effects may have been missing. Duffle bags were usually on a truck

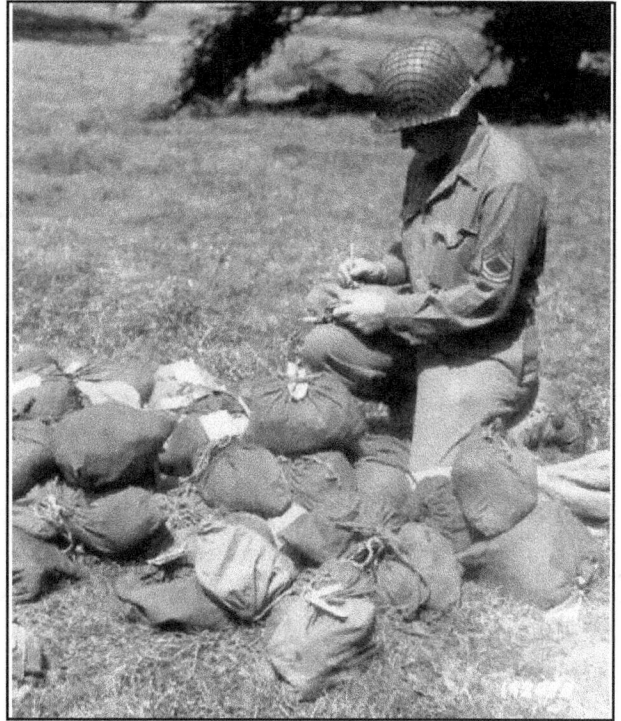

GRS bagging personal effects after processing remains. Photo courtesy the American Battle Monuments Commission.

or ship, and not always near the troops. In cases where the truck or ship was bombed or hit a mine and blew up, the personal effects were likely lost.

Effects collected were bagged and sent to the Effects Bureau in Kansas City, Missouri. Here, effects were cleaned of blood and grime. It was then determined if the effect should be returned to the family. In some cases, things were not sent to the family.

For instance, if letters from a girlfriend were found on a soldier, and he was married, based on the service records, those letters would have been destroyed. If an item was destroyed or badly damaged as a result of the cause of death, those items were described to the family in a letter. The family was then given the choice as to whether or not they wanted the item.

Most families were happy to receive anything from their soldier, and sent letters to the Quartermaster thanking them for sending the effects. In other cases, the Quartermaster received letters from family members accusing them of being thieves and the lowest men on earth for "stealing" money or other items from their Soldier Dead. The government did not educate the public about the chaos overseas or the work of the GRS men and the conditions under which they worked. Combine this with the pain and grief of a family member, and anger and hate was directed at the only place they could think of, the Quartermaster General in the Effects Bureau.

Identification Process

When a soldier's remains, either U.S. or German, were recovered, every attempt at identification took place.

The procedure for processing remains and identification began at the stripping line, where troops initially removed explosives and equipment. Another soldier would take these items to a nearby ammo and equipment area so they could be inventoried and reissued.

The next step was when medical sergeants came in with a clerk. The sergeants cut pockets and other pieces of clothing in order to locate identification tags and remove personal effects. Typically, these men worked without gloves in destroyed and decomposed remains. Identification tags were sought as part of this process, even when the remains were in bad condition.

To identify a Soldier Dead, identification tags were sought first. If those could not be recovered, then a soldier's comrades were consulted, if they were available, to help identify the soldier. Rings, insignia, pay records, letters and photographs that may have been carried were also used in the process. In some cases, dental records and laundry marks were used.

Upon first issue of clothing in the Army, a soldier would put a laundry mark in his clothing to show that it was his. This mark was the first letter of his surname plus the last four digits of his serial number. However, when serving on the front lines, when a soldier entered a wash-up station, he may or may not have had his duffle bag with his clothing available. In those cases, the men stripped, left their clothing, went into the wash station on one end, came out the other and were given new clothes. It was the hope that the clothes were the size they needed, but this was not always the case. Because clothes were reissued over and over, there may have been several different laundry marks, which would have made it very difficult to positively identify the Soldier Dead.

Positive Identification

When a Soldier Dead was identified, a mattress cover which, was used as a shroud, was prepared for him by painting his name, rank, and serial number on it. Then his remains were arranged and closed in the shroud. One identification tag was inserted into deceased's mouth before he was placed in a grave. The other identification tag was attached to the cross on the grave. Next, paperwork would be sent to the War Department in order to notify the next of kin. The bags of personal effects from the Army, Air Corps, and National Guard were shipped to Kansas City, MO.

Unknown Identification

Not all Soldier Dead were identified because of the condition of the body when it was received by the GRS. Other factors included advanced decomposition, as well as none of the soldier's comrades being available to help identify him.

To assist in identification, a still photographer was brought in to photograph the face, torso and other identifying marks on the body when the remains were in a condition this would be helpful. Photos were also taken of the fingers and hands in case prints could not be obtained. A fluoroscope was used to see if the identification tags were embedded in the body or if other foreign matter resided there.

When all available identification options were exhausted and remains could not be identified, they were assigned an X number since there was no serial number by which to identify them. This X number was placed on reports. Duplicate reports were created for the unknown soldiers. When possible, fingerprints of all 10 fingers were taken and put into the Report of Death.[27] Unknown remains were placed into a mattress cover and X number was painted on the bag. The personal effects for the Army, Air Corps, and National Guard were shipped to Kansas City, MO.

Two metallic tags with the X number were made. One was inserted into deceased's mouth and the other was attached to the cross on the grave. The duplicate copy of records was placed in a bottle and buried with Soldier Dead. This allowed for possible identification at a later time when the remains were disinterred.

In cases where bodies were mangled or adhered together due to a plane crash or other disaster, if the GRS men were unable to disentangle the remains, a group burial would have been conducted. In these cases most were unidentified because the remains were destroyed beyond recognition.[28]

The Individual Deceased Personnel File

This section is comprised of two parts. First, I will explain the common contents of an IDPF. Second, I will explain how the IDPF can be used to start research and reconstruct details of a burned personnel file. In World War I, this file was called a Burial File. It contained similar documents to what was created during World War II.

One of the <u>most</u> important things you can do to ease the analysis of an IDPF is to print it and put the documents in date order. Most IDPFs are now emailed out as a PDF download. The records are never in date order, which can make analysis even more confusing. Print the file, no matter how lengthy, and place it in date order.

When a soldier was declared Missing in Action (MIA) or Killed in Action (KIA), an IDPF was created. Why was a death file created when a soldier was declared missing? It was rare someone who was declared missing ever returned alive, unless they were declared a Prisoner of War (POW). The file would be started, and it would include a Battle Casualty Report that listed the soldier as MIA. If the soldier was recovered later, his status would be changed to KIA. If he was never recovered, he would receive a Finding Of Death (FOD) and his death date would be at least one year plus one day after his MIA status began.

The IDPF was created for soldiers who could be identified, and each record will contain at least the soldier's name and service number. If the remains of a soldier were brought to the Graves Registration Service or a cemetery and could not be identified, a file with the same contents as the IDPF was created, but it was called an X-File.

The X-File used an X-number in place of a service number. The X-number was assigned from number one, moving forward based on the next burial of an unknown soldier in a temporary cemetery. Each temporary cemetery had its own X-numbering system. Details on the soldier would be recorded in the X-File just as it would have the IDPF. A match to a soldier would be attempted. In cases where an unknown soldier with an X-File was identified, the X-File was merged into the IDPF. Therefore, the IDPF will have both soldier with his service number pages and X-File pages.

Soldier Statuses

Missing in Action (MIA)

The MIA status was given to any soldier if he did not return to his unit within 24 hours of being listed on the previous day's report. For Army or National Guard soldiers, the change may not be shown on a report the following day, but several days later as information reached the clerk. An Air Corps airman would likely show a status change the following day after a mission. Airmen were easier to track and report because they either returned from a mission or they did not.

Prisoner of War (POW)

The POW status was given to a soldier declared MIA if word reached the military through the enemy or Red Cross.

Killed in Action (KIA)

The KIA status was given to a soldier who was KIA and his body was recovered soon after the death, or his death was verified by at least one other soldier. What does this mean? An example of a verified death is one in which several men were seen getting in a boat to cross a river. Men from the shore witnessed the men crossing and drowning. Even if their remains were not recovered, they are given a KIA status because other soldiers confirmed their deaths. This is the official date of death.

Finding Of Death (FOD)

The FOD status was given to a soldier when he had been MIA for a year plus one day if his remains had not been recovered. This was done according to the provisions of Section 5 of Public Law 490, 77th Congress, 7 March 1942.[29] When a soldier was officially declared deceased, the family could claim the insurance benefits, any pay due the soldier, and begin closing the estate.

The FOD would be a year plus one day after the date of the MIA status. The MIA status may be indicated as the Presumed Date of Death in official reports within the personnel file and IDPF. The FOD or Presumed Date of Death is the official date of death, even though it is likely the soldier died before the year plus one day.

The Marine Corps is one branch with an exception to this rule. Marines lost in enemy territory and declared MIA were left on the Muster Rolls for the year of MIA status. At the end of one year, the MIA cases were reviewed and a determination was made as to a FOD status or continued MIA status. The reason given for a continued MIA status was the possibility the Marine was a POW.

This was the case for USMC Pilot 1st Lt. Robert E. Bishop and his gunner, Pfc. Richard L. Parrow, who was declared MIA 17 January 1944. Their cases were reviewed in 1945, and a determination of continued MIA status was made.[30] The case was reviewed again in January 1946 after the cessation of hostilities with Japan. The military had emptied the POW camps in the Pacific and interviewed detainees. No information on Bishop or Parrow was discovered, and the men were given a FOD on 15 January 1946. Paperwork in

Bishop's service file provided detailed documentation of the findings. A letter explaining the findings was sent to Bishop's parents.[31]

Unrecoverable Status A status of Unrecoverable was given to a soldier in his IDPF, in most cases, if the remains could not be recovered due to the circumstances surrounding their death, the location of death, and they were lost and unable to be found. For example, many of the sailors and Marines aboard the *USS Oklahoma* were deemed unrecoverable after the ship sunk. According to the IDPF for Fireman 1st Class Samuel W. Crowder, a report by a Graves Registration Board stated the following regarding the recoverability of the personnel on that ship.

> *"Information in this headquarters indicates that the above-named personnel, consisting of eleven (11) marines, seven (7) Navy officers and there hundred fifty (350) Navy enlisted men, were aboard the USS OKLAHOMA when that vessel was sunk during the Japanese bombing raid on Pearl Harbor, Oahu, Territory of Hawaii on 7 December 1941. Available records also show that 25 persons were recovered and interred as known burials at the time of the incident and an additional (34) remains have been identified by the AGRS-PAZ Board of Review. No further information is available. (Exhibit B.)"[32]*

A soldier unrecoverable due to location could be a bombing crew who crashed into the ocean. If the plane did not sink in shallow water, the likelihood of the remains being recovered was slim. Another example is a POW who died in a camp and was buried in the camp's cemetery. In one case, the Soviet Army took over a POW camp's grounds and turned it into a Soviet Army Training Base. When the war ended, Graves Registration Service members were not allowed to recover the remains of possible U.S. servicemen buried there.

A soldier unrecoverable due to not being found could be a Marine on Tarawa. Many men were lost when the fighting occurred, and Graves Registration was unable to properly account for the remains and bury them until months later. The destruction of the graves and bodies due to shelling, shore erosion, and lack of proper burial made it nearly impossible for many of those Marines to be identified.

If you would like to learn more information about the process of recovery from a U.S. Navy Diver who attempted to recover remains after the bombing, please read Edward C. Raymer's book , *"Descent into Darkness: Pearl Harbor, 1941: A Navy Diver's Memoir."* The book provides a very graphic explanation of the circumstances in which the divers and personnel assigned to attempt to recover the men who died in the ships at Pearl Harbor. It answers a lot of questions as to why the men, overall, were never recovered, or were unable to be identified.

Contents of an IDPF

The main components of an IDPF are generally the same across all branches of the military during World War II. The contents of each file will vary based on the circumstances of the MIA status or death.

Report of Burial

A Report of Burial contained the soldier's name, date of death, place of death, and a copy of his identification tag, if located, stamped onto the form using an addressograph machine. The report also contained the grave location of the soldier with the names of the men buried on either side of him, to help with identification purposes. At the time the report was created, if the emergency contact and religious information was available, it was also added. A list of personal effects was included if any were found on the body. Personal effects for the soldier not located on his person at death or recovery were inventoried separately.

A Report of Burial will be in a file created during the war by the Graves Registration Service. You may not encounter this form in every IDPF. If the soldier was recovered after the war, it is possible the Graves Registration Service or other unit used a Report of Interment.

Report of Interment

The Report of Interment was used for several reasons by the Graves Registration Service. The report was used when remains of an unknown solider were disinterred after the war ended to attempt identification. It was also used when the Graves Registration Service disinterred soldiers to move them to a permanent cemetery from a temporary cemetery and when laying out a permanent cemetery.

Casualty Report

The Battle Casualty Report (Army, Air Corps, National Guard) or the Casualty Report (Navy and Marine Corps) had the usual service information in addition to the date of casualty, which could have been designated as MIA or KIA, name of the next of kin and relationship to the deceased as well as the date notified of the casualty.

Report of Death

The Report of Death listed the deceased's usual information, branch of service, date of birth and death, date of active entry in service, where he was killed, emergency contact and beneficiary information. There was a section at the bottom of the form which allowed for additional information about the deceased. Usually some statement about when the evidence of death was received by the war department was included in this section.

Telegrams

Telegrams or letters sent to the next-of-kin regarding MIA and KIA statuses may be found within the IDPF.

Inventory of Effects

The Inventory of Effects form described the items collected to be sent to the family. It was broken out by package number in case there were multiple packages to send to a next of kin. These were accompanied by a letter to the family regarding the remains. There was a duplicate letter sent which had to be signed by the next of kin acknowledging the receipt of effects. In the case of officers, there may have been multiple Inventory of Effect forms created from the officer's remains and his personal belongings in camp or held somewhere other than where he died.

Prisoner of War Cards or Information

If a soldier was taken as a German POW, their IDPF may contain the POW cards and information from captured German records or the Red Cross. These cards may include photos of the soldier. Those taken as a POW by the Japanese often do not have the card in their IDPF. They must be requested separately from NARA in College Park, MD.

Report of Investigation Area Search

Searches for soldiers who were MIA or buried in isolated graves were conducted after the war ended. Graves Registration Service visited locations provided by units who had provided coordinates or locations of isolated graves. GRS also visited towns near battles and known plane crash sites to interview town and church officials and the townspeople regarding isolated graves. Included with this report are often pages from the Missing Air Crew Report (MACR). The MACR will be explained in the chapter on Records Created in the Field.

Checklist of Unknowns

Included with the Report of Investigation Area Search, if remains were recovered, is the Checklist of Unknowns. When a soldier was recovered from an isolated grave, he was given an X-number in place of a service number. All identifying information obtainable at that moment was documented, and the remains, plus any personal effects, were transported to a temporary cemetery. At the cemetery, an attempt at identification would be made. If this was accomplished, the X-file documentation was incorporated into the IDPF for the identified soldier. Often included with these reports are testimony from officials and townspeople, maps, a Notice of Disinterment, and additional details about the Soldier Dead.

Disinterment Directive

The Disinterment Directive form contained the basic identifying information on the Soldier Dead: Name, rank, service number, date of death, cemetery name and location of grave, name and address of next of kin, condition of remains, date disinterred, and remains prepared.

Receipt of Remains

The form was used for Soldier Dead repatriated, not buried in overseas cemeteries. This form was signed by the next of kin or funeral home receiving the remains when they arrived in the hometown.

Family Correspondence

IDPFs often contain correspondence from family members asking about personal effects, the circumstances of their soldier's death, or location and repatriation of the remains. The correspondence can be heartbreaking or graphic, depending on the nature of the letter.

If Deceased was Unidentified

If the deceased was unable to be identified, a form which allowed for fingerprinting was used and inserted into the file. This form contained space to list a physical description and information on personal effects or other things which might help identify the deceased.

The next step in attempting to identify a soldier was contacting St. Louis or Washington, D.C. to obtain the dental records and fingerprints for soldiers who may be the unidentified soldier. Lists of soldiers who were MIA and unrecovered in the location of the unidentified soldier were compiled based on battle maps and plans. The units that had been in the area were narrowed down and those who were still unaccounted for would have records requested.

In some cases, when the information was received by the Graves Registration Service, it would contain basic training information with locations and dates as detailed. More extensive details from a service file are usually not found in the IDPF. Pages from the IDPF may be found within a service file.

IDPF Record Examples - Report of Burial

GRAVES REGISTRATION
Form No. 1
(Revised 1 Sept. 1943)

RESTRICTED
REPORT OF BURIAL
TM 10-630 AND AR 30-1815

2 July, 1944
Date

243

Winkler, Frank J.
Last Name   First   Initial

Pvt
Rank

36695605
Serial No.

243

115 Inf Reg
Organization

OCT 1 0 1944

29th Combat Area	1 July 1944	GSW- Right Lobe
Place of Death	Date of Death	Cause of Death
2 July	La Cambe Cem	La Cambe, Fr.
Time and Date of Burial	Name of Cemetery	Name or Coordinates of Location
146	8	F	Stake
Grave Number	Row Number	Plot Number	Type of Marker

Disposition of Identification Tags: Buried with body Yes ☒ No ☐   Attached to Marker Yes ☒ No ☐

If No Identification Tags
        How were remains identified?

What means of identification were buried with the body?

        Identification Tag

To determine Right or Left use Deceased's Right and Left.
Who is buried on:

Deceased's Right: Cenar, M.J.   33009558   147
                  Name   Serial No.   Rank   Organization   Grave No.

Deceased's Left: Van-Loon, J   36116571   145
                  Name   Serial No.   Rank   Organization   Grave No.

Signature or Name, Rank and if possible Organization of person furnishing above Data when other than officer reporting burial.

If print of identification tag is not affixed fill in below:

FRANK J WINKLER
36695605 T43-: B

Emergency Addressee ___ Frank Winkler
                                Name

____ 4134 W. 31st St., Chicago, Ill
                     Address

Religion ___ Protestant

List only Personal Effects **Found on Body** and disposition of same:

        ring
        papers
        4 souvenir coins

                    620 Francs
                    2 cents- U.S.

Signature of Officer or other person reporting burial
E. H. HOSFORD
1st LT. Q.M.C.
Verified by G.R.S. Officer

HQ. FOR. 22/0/43. 380M/S/15219

Report of Interment

RESTRICTED

Corrected Copy

REPORT OF INTERMENT
(AR 30-1810 and AR 30-1815)

WD QMC FORM 1042
(Rev. 1 Apr. 1945)
(Supersedes GRS Form 1)

DATE OF REPORT

Section 1.—IDENTIFICATION.

Imprint Identification Tag If Possible
DO NOT TYPE

NAME (*Last, first, middle initial*) ALEXANDER, Henry R.

UNKNOWN-X-102-A

SERIAL No. 839 31 38
Unknown

GRADE SF2c / Unknown

ORGANIZATION USNAAB Navy 415 / Unknown

BRANCH OF SERVICE USNR
A.O.P.

RACE White / Unknown

RELIGION Protestant / Unknown

IF OTHER THAN U.S. DEAD, GIVE NAME OF COUNTRY

PLACE OF DEATH
Normandy, France

CAUSE OF DEATH
K.I.A.

DATE OF DEATH
6 June 1944

EMERGENCY ADDRESSEE (*Name, relationship, and address*)
NOK: (Mother) Mabel Alice Alexander UNKNOWN
2112 5th   Fort Worth, Texas

IDENTIFICATION TAGS FOUND ON BODY (U.S. or none)
NONE

IF NO TAGS FOUND ON BODY, DESCRIBE MEANS OF IDENTIFICATION (*If unidentified, fill in section 5 on reverse*)
Identified by comparison of physical and dental characteristic circumstances of death and recovery. Approved by the Bureau of Medicine and Surgery, Department of the Navy.

WERE SUBSTITUTE TAGS PROVIDED? (*Yes or no*)
YES

LIST PERSONAL EFFECTS FOUND ON BODY AND DISPOSITION OF SAME
NONE

Section 2.—BURIAL. *If other than in established cemetery, furnish sketch and map coordinates on reverse.*

NAME, NUMBER, COORDINATES, AND LOCATION OF CEMETERY.
U.S. Military Cemetery St. Laurent s/Mer No 1, France (675896)

DATE OF BURIAL	HOUR	BURIED IN (Shroud, blanket, or name of other)	TYPE OF GRAVE MARKER	PLOT NO.	ROW NO.	GRAVE No.
		Casket	temp. wooden cross	B	9	162

WAS THIS A REBURIAL? (*Yes or no*)
No

IF A REBURIAL, INDICATE NAME, NUMBER, COORDINATES OF PREVIOUS CEMETERY, AND LOCATION OF GRAVE

PLOT NO.	ROW NO.	GRAVE NO.

TYPE OF RELIGIOUS CEREMONY

PERSON CONDUCTING BURIAL RITES

IF IDENTIFICATION TAGS NOT USED, DESCRIBE IDENTIFICATION DATA AND CONTAINERS BURIED WITH BODY
One copy of WD. QMC Form No 1042 placed in burial bottle and buried with remains.

IDENTIFICATION TAG BURIED WITH BODY (*Yes or no*)
No

IDENTIFICATION TAG ATTACHED TO MARKER (*Yes or no*)
Yes, embossed plate

BODY BURIED ON DECEASED LEFT, NAME (*Last, first, middle initial*)	RANK	SERIAL NO.	ORGANIZATION	GRAVE NO.
LEWIS, Leonard L.	Lt jg	276-816	USNR	161

BODY BURIED ON DECEASED RIGHT, NAME (*Last, first, middle initial*)	RANK	SERIAL NO.	ORGANIZATION	GRAVE NO.
MARCH, Robert M.		32524489	—	163

SIGNATURE OF PERSON PREPARING REPORT
ERNEST C. GADDY
CWO USA C.I.P.

SIGNATURE OF GRS OFFICER VERIFYING REPORT
ELLSWORTH T. MAC INTYRE
CAPTAIN QMC C.I.P.

DISTRIBUTION OF REPORT: Signed original for U.S. and allied dead, signed original and one copy for enemy dead, to the Quartermaster General through Headquarters GRS Officer. Copies for retention in theater as prescribed by theater commander.

RESTRICTED

Source: Individual Deceased Personnel File for Henry R. Alexander, serial no. 8393138, Report of Interment page 1. Army Human Resource Command, Ft. Knox, KY.

Report of Interment

Declassified in accordance with E.O. 13526, dated 5 January 2010

RESTRICTED

Section 3.— UNIDENTIFIED REMAINS.

INSTRUCTIONS:
(a) Great care will be taken to record the most minute clues for the future identity of unidentified remains. Fill in anatomical characteristics below, and any other clues under "Other," such as shoe size, social security number; position of body found in airplanes, vehicles, and tanks; and serial numbers of airplanes, vehicles, and tanks.
(b) A fingerprint, or prints, are the most valuable of all clues. Imprint all fingers and thumbs in the chart at left, or as many as possible. If no fingerprint or prints can be secured, the condition of each and every tooth will be indicated on the tooth chart in accordance with diagram below. Tooth chart will not be accomplished if one or more fingerprints are secured.

HEIGHT	WEIGHT	COLOR OF EYES	COLOR OF HAIR	BIRTHMARKS, SCARS, OR TATTOOS
Est. 5'10 3/8"	UTD	UTD	UTD	UTD

WEAPON AND SERIAL No.	LAUNDRY MARKS	WHERE BODY WAS BURIED OR FOUND
NONE	See below	Normandy, France

OTHER IDENTIFICATION CLUES. Original report of burial states: clothing marking "B.2220" found at time of burial" Chemical laboratory Examination revealed the following markings on remnants of GI service shoes:

CONT 40 W1 550 M 5?5
209 TOM DEPOT JAN 30-1943 (This marking is evidently a manufacturer's stamp

FILLINGS — SILVER FILLING / GOLD FILLING

CAVITIES — CAVITY / DECAYED

MISSING TEETH — TOOTH MISSING

CROWNED TEETH — PORCELAIN CROWN / GOLD CROWN

BRIDGE WORK — GOLD BRIDGE

DIAGRAM REPRESENTS THE MOUTH WIDE OPEN

UPPER

LOWER

FURNISH SKETCH AND MAP REFERENCE AND COORDINATES FOR BURIAL IN OTHER THAN ESTABLISHED CEMETERY

REMARKS: Form 11 Identification Check List and Form 1 A Tooth Chart accomplished.
Unable to obtain fingerprints because of missing and decomposed portions.
Estimated weight of remains processed: 28 Lbs.

RESTRICTED

G.H. - 2-46 - 90,000 - 79,783

Source: Individual Deceased Personnel File for Henry R. Alexander, serial no. 8393138, Report of Interment page 2. Army Human Resource Command, Ft. Knox, KY.

SKELETAL CHART

ALEXANDER, Henry R.
==X-102=(A)=B==
St. Laurent s/Mer France

(BLACK OUT PARTS OF BODY NOT RECEIVED AT CEMETERY)

Plot B, Row 9, Grave 162

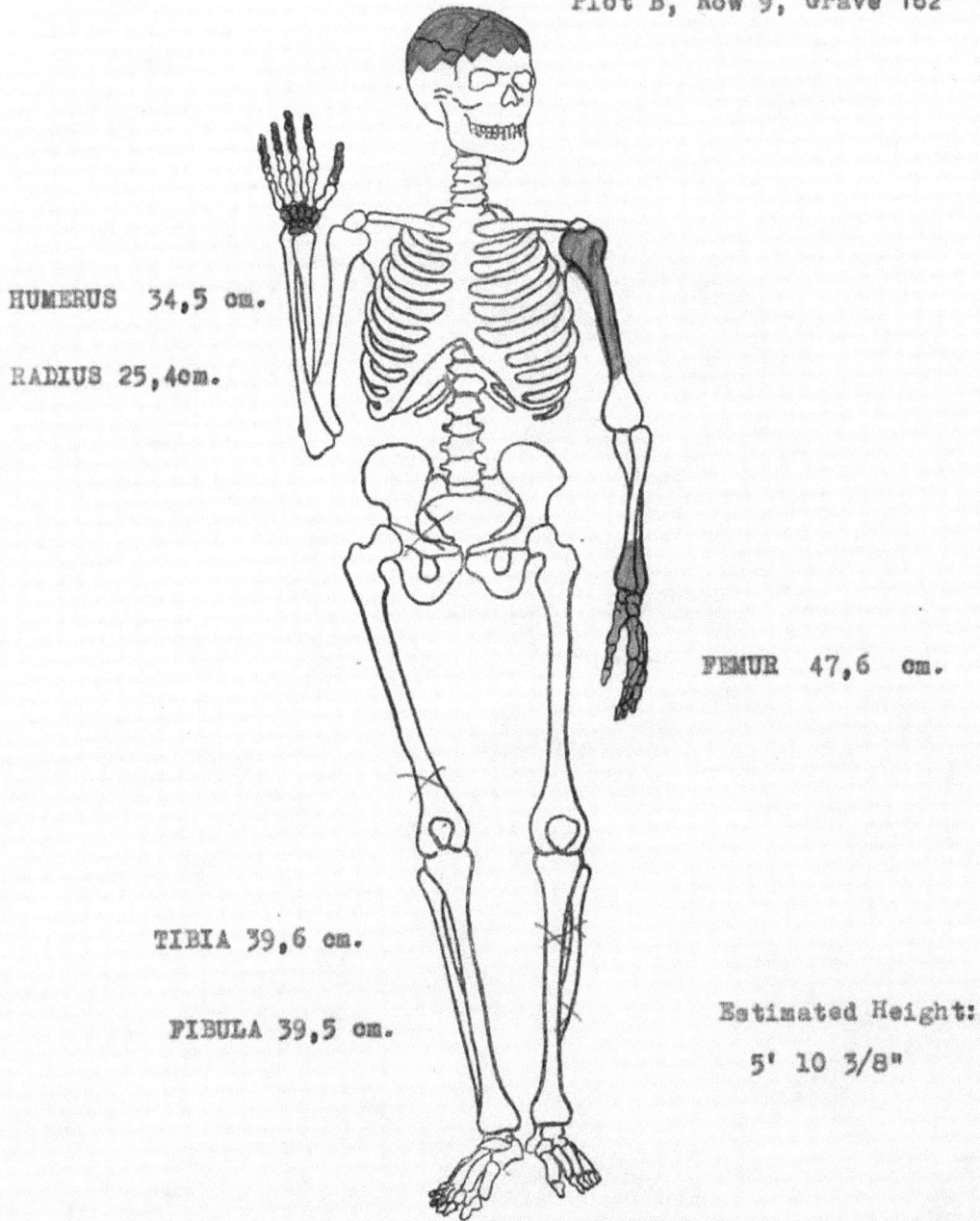

HUMERUS 34,5 cm.

RADIUS 25,4cm.

FEMUR 47,6 cm.

TIBIA 39,6 cm.

FIBULA 39,5 cm.

Estimated Height:

5' 10 3/8"

CHART "A"

Source: Individual Deceased Personnel File for Henry R. Alexander, serial no. 8393138, Skeletal Chart. Army Human Resource Command, Ft. Knox, KY.

Casualty Report

U S M C CASUALTY REPORT   DATE 18Jan46   CARD Y   CAS. NO. 077420

NAME		RANK	CLASS	IDENT. NO.
PARROW, Richard Leonard		PFC	USMCR	487825

ORGANIZATION POW&P Det Hq USMC		TYPE OF CASUALTY	AREA	DATE OF CASUALTY
Washington, D.C.		MIA-KIA	Pac	15Jan46

DATE APPT./ENLIST	PLACE OF APPT./ENLIST	DATE ACTIVE DUTY	PRIOR SER.	MISC. STA.	MARITAL	RACE
10Nov42	Boston, Mass.		No	NRON	S	

DATE OF BIRTH	PLACE OF BIRTH	LEGAL RESIDENCE	AVCAD
15Jan20	Cambridge, Mass.	Cambridge, Mass.	

NEXT OF KIN	RELATION	ADDRESS OF KIN
Mr. &Mrs. Richard Parrow	Prnt	214 Chestnut Street, Cambridge, Mass.

BENEFICIARY (Name and Address)

DGB: Mrs. Catherine Parrow(Mother)Address same as above

PLACE OF CASUALTY	NATURE OF WOUND	PRESENT STATUS
Rabaul, New Britain		NO FA.

REMARKS (Additional Information - Disposition of Remains) Prev reported MIA 17Jan44.

DATE AND SOURCE OF REPORT FINDING OF DEATH BY SECNAV DTD 15Jan46   CHECKER   lh

NAME		RANK	CLASS	IDENT. NO.
PARROW, Richard Leonard		PFC	USMCR	487825

LT (JG) W. E. MARSDEN, MSC, USN

NOV 8 1949

Source: Individual Deceased Personnel File for Richard Parrow, serial no. 487825, USMC Casualty Report. Army Human Resource Command, Ft. Knox, KY.

Report of Death

THE ADJUTANT GENERAL'S OFFICE

WASHINGTON 25, D. C.

REPORT OF DEATH   25 Aug 1944

DATE MLD/ELC/4024

FULL NAME	ARMY SERIAL NUMBER	GRADE
Winkler, Frank J.	36 695 605	Pvt.

HOME ADDRESS	ARM OR SERVICE	DATE OF BIRTH
Chicago, Ill.	Inf.	1 Nov 24

PLACE OF DEATH	CAUSE OF DEATH	DATE OF DEATH
European Area	Killed in action	24 Jun 44

STATION OF DECEASED	DATE OF ENTRY ON CURRENT ACTIVE SERVICE	LENGTH OF SERVICE FOR PAY PURPOSES		
		YEARS	MONTHS	DAYS
European Area	29 Sep 43			

EMERGENCY ADDRESSEE (NAME, RELATIONSHIP & ADDRESS)

Mrs. Jennie K. Winkler, mother, 4134 West 31st St., Chicago, Ill.

BENEFICIARY (NAME, RELATIONSHIP & ADDRESS)

Mrs. Jennie K. Winkler, mother, same as above
Mr. Fran Winkler, father, same as above

INVESTIGATION MADE?		IN LINE OF DUTY		OWN MISCONDUCT		WAS DECEASED ON DUTY STATUS		AUTHORIZED ABSENCE		IN FLYING PAY STATUS		OTHER PAY STATUS (SPECIFY BELOW)	
YES	NO	YES	NO	YES	NO	YES	NO	YES	NO	YES	NO	YES	NO
											X		

ADDITIONAL DATA AND/OR STATEMENT

The individual named in this report of death is held by the War Department to have been in a missing in action status from 24 Jun 44 until such absence was terminated on 7 Aug 44, when evidence considered sufficient to establish the fact of death was received by the Secretary of War from a commander in the European Area.

COPIES FURNISHED:

S. G. O.   F. D. I.   F. O., U. S. A.
S. O. Q. M. G.   O. F. C.   ARMY EFFECTS BUREAU CASUALTY BRANCH FILE
Q. A. O.   VET. ADMIN.   A. G. 201 FILE

☒ BATTLE
☐ NON-BATTLE

BY ORDER OF THE SECRETARY OF WAR:

ADJUTANT GENERAL

WD. AGO. FORM NO. 52-1, 29 MAY 1944

Source: Individual Deceased Personnel File for Frank Winkler, serial no. 36695605, Report of Death dated 25 Aug 1944 . Army Human Resource Command, Ft. Knox, KY.

Telegram or Letter Regarding Death

Declassified in accordance with Executive Order 13526

AMERICAN-HAWAIIAN STEAMSHIP COMPANY
OPERATING DEPARTMENT

CABLE AND RADIO
ADDRESS
AMHAWAII

S. S. CAP ____ VOY. ___ W. B.
                                    E. B.
WRITTEN AT Tarawa, Gilbert Islands

DATE February 23, 1944

(IN REPLY TO OPERATING
DEPT. LETTER, FILE NO.) _____

SUBJECT _____

Mr. & Mrs. D. W. Spotts,
1223 Corona St.,
Denver, Colorado.

Dear Mr. & Mrs. D.W. Spotts:

It is with profound sadness, and with heartfelt sympathy that I am writing this letter to you. Your son, Elvis M. Spotts died on board this ship, February 22, 1944, in the line of duty, apparently from an electric shock. Everything that was humanely possible to revive him was tried. A Doctor, Lieut. E.C. Potter, U.S.N.R., was called aboard ship, and was in attendance for over a hour without getting any signs of life.

Your sons body was removed from the ship on the evening of February 22, 1944, by orders of authorities ashore. On the morning of February 23, 1944, at 11:00 A.M., funeral services were held with military honors and the reading of a Protestant Service by Francis T. Cooke, Chaplain, U.S.N.R. Burial was in the U.S. Marine Cemetery, Tarawa, Gilbert Islands. A white cross will be erected over his grave by the Chaplain.

All your son's personal belongings have been inventoried and packed and will be forwarded to you upon our arrival at a United States Port.

Respectfully yours,

L A Carlisle

L. A. CARLISLE
Master

Source: Individual Deceased Personnel File for Elvis Spotts, serial no. Z-394396, Letter to family regarding death. Army Human Resource Command, Ft. Knox, KY.

Telegram Regarding MIA Status

STANDARD FORM No. 14A
Approved by the President
MARCH 10, 1926

TELEGRAM

~~IAL~~ BUSINESS—GOVERNMENT RATES

FROM **WAR DEPARTMENT**

BUREAU

JON 3838

AG 201 DAVIS, FRED A (25 NOV 43) SPXPC-N 329127-1 (1) 27 NOVEMBER 1943
ASN O-683416

MRS FRED A DAVIS
1038 LOYALA AVENUE
CHICAGO ILLINOIS

THE SECRETARY OF WAR DESIRES ME TO EXPRESS HIS REGRET THAT YOUR

HUSBAND SECOND LIEUTENANT FRED A DAVIS HAS BEEN REPORTED MISSING

IN ACTION SINCE TWO NOVEMBER OVER AUSTRIA IF FURTHER DETAILS OR

OTHER INFORMATION ARE RECEIVED YOU WILL BE PROMPTLY NOTIFIED

ULIO
THE ADJUTANT GENERAL

BATTLE

OFFICIAL:

ADJUTANT GENERAL.

Source: Individual Deceased Personnel File for Fred A. Davis, serial no. O-683416, Telegram to wife regarding MIA status dated 1 Dec 1943. Army Human Resource Command, Ft. Knox, KY.

Personal Effects

Sheet ___ of ___ Sheets   ARMY EFFECTS BUREAU   _G_   Deceased _____
Box No. _____

INVENTORY   _Box 64_   Missing _____
P.O.W. _____
Abandoned _____

SHOWN ON TALLY-IN AS _Fred A. Davis_   ORIGINAL NO. OF PKGS. _____

TALLY-IN NO. _5152_   INVENTORY DATE _10/14/44_   CASE NO. _39,668_

EFFECTS OF _Fred A. Davis_   RANK _Lt._

A.S.N. _O-683416_   ORG. _Unknown_

PACKAGE DESCRIPTION: _#1 carton_

ARTICLE DESCRIPTION

1 Barrack Bag ✓	
1 towel ✓	
1 tie ✓	
1 shirt ✓	
1 pr swim trunks ✓	
1 pr tennis shoes ✓	
1 pr socks ✓	
1 sweat suit ✓	

REMARKS: _Rechecked_
No Information
O.A.I. not available
No correspondence
Shortage on reverse ✓

ATTACHMENTS: ✓
2 inventory ✓

NO CORRESPONDENCE

SHORTAGE ON REVERSE

G. I. ON REVERSE

STORAGE SPACE) _548_   SAFE STORAGE _____ VAULT STORAGE _____   WEIGHT SHIPPED _NOV 1 1944_

Source: Individual Deceased Personnel File for Fred A. Davis, serial no. O-683416, List of Personal Effects. Army Human Resource Command, Ft. Knox, KY.

Prisoner of War Card

Source: Individual Deceased Personnel File for Clarkson Russell, serial no. 31241290, German POW Card. Army Human Resource Command, Ft. Knox, KY.

Prisoner of War Card

Declassified in accordance with Executive Order 13526

Lager:

	Datum	Grund der Bestrafung	Strafmaß	Verbüßt, Datum
Strafen im Kr.-Gef.-Lager				

Schutzimpfungen während der Gefangenschaft gegen			Erkrankungen				
Pocken		Sonstige Impfungen (Th.-Parath., Ruhr, Cholera usw.)	Krankheit	Revier		Lazarett — Krankenhaus	
				von	bis	von	bis
am	am	am					
Erfolg	gegen	gegen					
am	am	am					
Erfolg	gegen	gegen					
am	am	am					
Erfolg	gegen	gegen					
	am	am					
	gegen	gegen					

	Datum	Grund der Versetzung	Neues Kr.-Gef.-Lager		Datum	Grund der Versetzung	Neues Kr.-Gef.-Lager
Versetzungen	7.1.43 von St. XII A			Versetzungen			
	22.1.45 von St. IV B an STl. VIII A						

Kommandos

Datum	Art des Kommandos	Rückkehrdatum
30.I.45	Im Krankenrevier d. Schloss VII † verstorben, Lung.-Oedem.)	
30 Jan 45	died in Sick Bay g Stalag VIII A — (Lung-Edema)	

⊙ 9656 42 5 D

Source: Individual Deceased Personnel File for Clarkson Russell, serial no. 31241290, German POW Card. Army Human Resource Command, Ft. Knox, KY.

Checklist of Unknowns

AGRC
FORM No. 11
Revised 5 January 1946

1 F - 7020 E

CHECK LIST OF UNKNOWNS

(to be completely filled out and attached to each copy of Report of Interment
WD QMC Form 1042)

Unknown X - 7704
Cemetery U.S.Mil.Cem.St.Avold,France
Plot _____ Row _____ Grave _____

1. Arrived at cemetery _____
   (hour)   (date)

2. Place of death Poettsching, Austria P-48 X 4649
   (name of closest town)   (coordinates and letter Prefex, maps)

   (Sheet, scale and serials used)

3. Remains recovered or disinterred by 612 Gr. Co.
                                         (name and organization)

4. Evacuated to Cemetery by C.I.P.
                            (name and organization)

5. **Description of clothing and equipment : (if clothes do not fit, obtain size from body measurements).**

	Clothing Markings	Sizes	Indicate unusual markings Color wear, tear, repairs, etc.

Item

*Headgear none
           (type)

Raincoat none

Overcoat none

Jacket, Field none

Jacket, Combat none

Mackinaw none

Sweater none

Jacket, HBT none

*Shirt, Wool OD none

Undershirt, Wool none

Undershirt, Cotton Remnants of

Trousers HBT none

*Trousers, Wool OD Remnants of

— 1 —

Source: Individual Deceased Personnel File for Fred A. Davis, serial no. O-683416, Checklist of Unknowns. Army Human Resource Command, Ft. Knox, KY.

Belt, Web none

Drawers, Wool none

Drawers, Cotton Remnants of marked : twice FAD, 3416

Leggins, Wool none   (Note unusual lacing)

Socks, Cotton Remnants of wool

*Shoes none (type)

Overshoes none

Web Equipment none(Type)

(Other item) none

(Other item) none
*If body is nude, sizes of these items should be computed by measuring the remains.

6. Chevrons or
    Insignia none
                              (type & location : shirt, jacket, coat, helmet)

    Shoulder Patch none

7. Does clothing indicate that deceased was a member of the Air, Ground or Naval Forces

                              Air Force

8. Description of Remains :
                    Est   Est
    Age UTD Height 5'9" Weight 160 lbs Description of wounds   UTD

    Bandages or dressings UTD   Scars UTD
                                                        (length, width, location)

                              Tattoos UTD
                              (Number, location — illustrate on sep. page)
    Outstanding miles, warts or birthmarks UTD
                              (yes-no ; description, location)

    Sunburn or tan, other than hands & face   UTD

    Complexion UTD
                              (light, med. dark, clear, pimples, pocks, freckles)

    Build UTD
                              (large, fat, thin, muscular)

    Hair dark brown, 1½ " long shlightly wavy
                              (color, length, quantity, curly, wavy, straight, whorls, or definite parting).

— 2 —

Source: Individual Deceased Personnel File for Fred A. Davis, serial no. O-683416, Checklist of Unknowns. Army Human Resource Command, Ft. Knox, KY.

Hair ___UTD___
(baldness, widows peak, distinctive cutting or other characteristics).

Sideburns __UTD__   Mustache __UTD__   Board or __UTD__
(color, setting, shape)   (color, size, shape)   (length, heavy)

Goatee __UTD__
(light, color, extent)

Eyes __UTD__   Eyebrows __UTD__
(color, setting, shape)   (color, bushiness, extent across nose)

Nose __UTD__   Ears __UTD__
(size, shape, straight)   (size, set close to or far from head)

Mouth __UTD__   Lips __UTD__
(large, medium, small)   (small large, full)

Teeth __See tooth chart__
(white, size, unevenness, spacing, noticeable crowns, fillings, extract).

Chin __UTD__
(prominent, receding, pointed, dimple, double)

Jaw __UTD__   Circumference of head in inches __skull fractured__
(large, small, normal)   (hat band)

Neck __UTD__   Larynx __UTD__
(size, length, short, normal, wrinkled)   (prominent, normal)

Shoulders __UTD__   Arms __UTD__
(broad, straight, small, rounded)   (length, muscular, color)

(extent and quantity of hair)

Hands __UTD__

Fingers __UTD__
(short, thick, long, slender, size of knuckles, missing fingers or joints)

(Unusual characteristics of fingernails)

Chest __UTD__
(size of nipples, color, quantity & extent of hair, large, small normal)

Back __UTD__   aist __UTD__
(quantity & extent of hair)   (size of navel, appendectomy, amount)

Circumcision __UTD__   Pubic hair __light brown__
(quantity & color of hair)   (yes-no)   (color)

Herniaplasty __UTD__
(yes-no ; location)

Legs __UTD__
(inseam, muscular, knock-kneed, bowed, normal, quantity, color & extent of hair)

— 3 —

Source: Individual Deceased Personnel File for Fred A. Davis, serial no. O-683416, Checklist of Unknowns. Army Human Resource Command, Ft. Knox, KY.

90

Hair   UTD
(baldness, widows peak, distinctive cutting or other characteristics).

Sideburns UTD   Mustache UTD   Board or UTD
(color, setting, shape)   (color, size, shape)   (length, heavy)

Goatee UTD
(light, color, extent)

Eyes UTD   Eyebrows UTD
(color, setting, shape)   (color, bushiness, extent across nose)

Nose UTD   Ears UTD
(size, shape, straight)   (size, set close to or far from head)

Mouth UTD   Lips UTD
(large, medium, small)   (small large, full)

Teeth See tooth chart
(white, size, unevenness, spacing, noticeable crowns, fillings, extract).

Chin UTD
(prominent, receding, pointed, dimple, double)

Jaw UTD   Circumference of head in inches skull fractured
(large, small, normal)   (hat band)

Neck UTD   Larynx UTD
(size, length, short, normal, wrinkled)   (prominent, normal)

Shoulders UTD   Arms UTD
(broad, straight, small, rounded)   (length, muscular, color)

(extent and quantity of hair)

Hands UTD

Fingers UTD
(short, thick, long, slender, size of knuckles, missing fingers or joints)

(Unusual characteristics of fingernails)

Chest UTD
(size of nipples, color, quantity & extent of hair, large, small normal)

Back UTD   aist UTD
(quantity & extent of hair)   (size of navel, appendectomy. amount)

Circumcision UTD   Pubic hair light brown
(quantity & color of hair)   (yes-no)   (color)

Herniaplasty UTD
(yes-no ; location)

Legs UTD
(inseam, muscular, knock-kneed, bowed, normal, quantity, color & extent of hair)

— 3 —

Source: Individual Deceased Personnel File for Fred A. Davis, serial no. O-683416, Checklist of Unknowns. Army Human Resource Command, Ft. Knox, KY.

Feet _____ UTD _____   Toes _____ UTD _____
       (size, corns, callouses, flat)   (slender, straight, crooked, overlap)

Evidence of healed factures _____ UTD _____
                                   (nose, arms, legs, etc.)

9. Black out parts of body not received at cemetery :

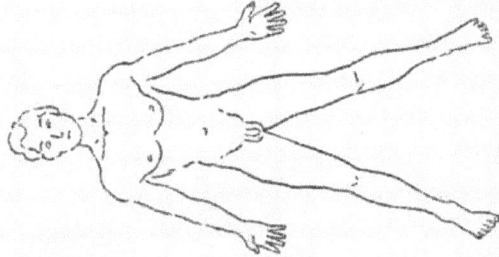

10. Have fingerprints been placed on Report of Interment _____ No _____
                                             (yes-no)

    If not, explain _____

11. Has tooth chart been prepared _____ yes _____ If not, explain _____
                                   (yes-no)

12. Remarks : Entire remains revovered in final stage of decomposition.

                Weight of remains 70 lbs.

I certify that I have personally viewed the remains of subject deceased and all resulting information has been recorded to the best of my knowledge.

                               R.G. JOHNSON
                                Officer's Name

                               2nd Lt. Inf.
                                Rank   Service

                               LAB. Off. C.I.P.
                                  Organization

— 4 —

Mod. 79790 - 35 M - 1-46 - Pap. du Sentier, Imp., Paris - O.P.L. 31.3134

Source: Individual Deceased Personnel File for Fred A. Davis, serial no. O-683416, Checklist of Unknowns. Army Human Resource Command, Ft. Knox, KY.

Lichtenweg 52.   Pöttsching,den 22.8.46.

Erklärung

    Es war Ende M i 1944 den genauen Tag weiss ich nicht mehr. Ich fuhr mit meinem Pferd aufs Feld um zu arbeiten,kurz nach Beginn der Arbeit erfolgte F..........rm. Wahrend des Alarms hielt ich mit dem Pferd in einer Hutte auf, wo auch s schon die Nachbarn von meinem Arbeitsfeld Zuflucht vor den Flaksplittern der Flakbatterie aus Wr.Neustadt nahmen. Da das Pferd sehr unruhig war bedurfte es meiner Aufmerksamkeit und hinderte mich der Beobachtung der Vorgange in der Luft.

    Auf einmal horten wir laut s Motoren.erausch und kurze Feuerstosse. Wie mir mein Nachbar dann erzahlte soll ein deutsches Jagdflugzeug eine amerikanische, vom Verband abgedrangte Maschine angegriffen und in Brand geschossen haben.

    Nach Beendigung des Alarms wurde ich von Ang.origen des deutschen Militars, einer Scheinwerferbatterie die etwa 800 meter von meinem Feld entfernt ihre Stellung hatte und ehrend des Alarms das Feld kontrollierten, aufgefordert, zwei Verwundete und einen Toten amerikanischen Flieger die von ihnen gefunden wurden, mit meinem Fuhrwerk zur Ortsgendarmeriestelle zu bringen.

    Nachdem ich zuerst die zwei Verwu deten hinein gefuhrt hatte, naturlich unter Bewachung, denn zwei Angehörige des deutschen Militars fuhren mit, holte ich dann den Toten bei dem wieder ein Posten stand. Diesen musste zuerst zur Gendarmerie und von dort in den Firedhof bringen. Es handelte sich um einenSoldaten von 17 bis 18 Jahren, blondes Haar und mittlere Grosse.

                        unterschrieben:Pankl Johann

Translation

Pankl Johann, Farmer
Pottsching, Lichtenweg 52.   22.8.1946

Statement

    It was at the end of May 1944, I don't remember the exact day. I was working in the field with my horse when the alarm started. I took my horse to a shed nearby, other neighbours had already taken refuge there. The horse was very restless, which requested my attention, therefore I could not see what was going on in the air. Suddenly we heard a loud motor noise and machine guns. My neighbour told me afterwards that a German plane had hit an American plane so badly that it started burning in the air. After the alarmwas over, members of the German Army, belonging to a search light battery at about 800 m distance from my field, came to me to bring two wounded and one deceased American flyer,which they had found,with my carriage to the Gendarmerie.

    First I brought the wounded soldiers there,guarded by two members of the German Army,then I went to get the deceased, who was also guarded by a post. This one I took first to the Gendarmerie and then to the cemetery. It was a soldier about 17 or 18 years old, blond hair and middle sized.

                        signed: Pankl Johann

Source: Individual Deceased Personnel File for Fred A. Davis, serial no. O-683416, Checklist of Unknowns, Testimony. Army Human Resource Command, Ft. Knox, KY.

Schuldeiterin, Pottsching   Pottsching,22.8.46

    itragung in der Ortschroni von
Pottsching im November 1943.

        Ein angeschossener Flieger wurde nach Pottsching
abgedrängt. Ich sah, wie sich ein abgeloster Flugel tanzend
zur Erde bewegte, zahlreiche hellglanzende Metallspitter
aren in der Hone sichtbar. Ein Pilot sprang it einem Fallschirm ab. Der Hinterteil des Luftschiffes lag verbeult auf
der Langenoden. Nu mer auf diesem Wrack: 2 7 2 8 9 1 L
und die Farben blau-weiss-rot.
        Zwei amerikanische tote Flieger habe ich am
selben Tage noch im Totenhauschen besichtigt. Durch die
Glasfenster.
        Der Angriff erfolgte in drei Wellen und dauerte
bis gegen 44 Uhr nachmittags.
        Das Wrack und die beiden Toten besichtigt von der
Lehrerin Elisabeth Witzani und ihren damaligen Ferien-
kind Lothar Endemann aus Oberhausen, Rheinland, damals
10 Jahre alt.

                        unterschrieben:Elisabeth Witzani

Translation

Elisabeth Witzani
School teacher   Pottschinh,22.8.1946

            Report of community records
            Pottsching in November 1943.

        A Bomber, hit by anti-aircraft, flew over Pottsching.
I saw a broken wing and lots of metal splinters in the air.
One pilot bailed out by parachute. The back part of the
plane was lying on the field of Langenoden. Number of the
wreckage: 2 7 2 8 9 1 L the colors were blue-white and red.
                            dead
        The same day I saw two/American flyers in the morgue
through a glass window.

        The raid was in three waves and lasted until approx.
1530 hours.

        The wreckage and the two deceased seen by school-
teacher Elisabeth Witzani and the child Lothar Endemann
from Oberhausen, Rhineland, at that time 10 years old.

                        signed: Elisabeth Witzani

Source: Individual Deceased Personnel File for Fred A. Davis, serial no. O-683416, Checklist of Unknowns, Testimony. Army Human Resource Command, Ft. Knox, KY.

Hermine Noss
Pottsching
Wiener Neustadt Strasse 48   Pottsching, 22.8.46

S t a t e m e n t

Ich habe gesehen wie Ende Mai 1944, den genau-
en Tag kann ich nicht angeben, der Landwirt Johann Pankl,
Pottsching Lichtenweg 24 zuerst zwei Verwundete amerikani-
sche Flieger dann einen toten amerikanischen Flieger, zur
Gendarmerie gefahren hat, die aus funfzig Meter hohe aus
der Maschine absprangen wobei sich der Fallschirm nicht
offnete.
        Der tote amerikanische Flieger musste inner-
liche Verletzungen davon getragen haben, da er ausserlich
nur wenig angeschlagen war. Nach meiner Ansicht handelt
es sich um einen Soldaten im Alter von etwa 18 Jahren handelt
blondes Harr und mittlere Grosse.

                        unterschrieben:

                        Hermine Noss

Translation

Hermine Noss
Pottsching
Wiener Neustadtstrasse 48   Pottsching 22.8.46

S t a t e m e n t

        At the end of May 1944, I don't know the exact date,
I saw the farmer Johann Pankl, Pottsching Lichtenweg 24
drive, first two wounded American flyers and then one
American flyer, to the Gendarmerie. They had jumped
at approx. 50 m height from the plane but their parachutes did not open.

        The deceased American flyer showed only little out-
wardappearing injuries. It must have been a soldier
around 18 years old, blond hair and middle sized.

                        signed: Hermine Noss

Source: Individual Deceased Personnel File for Fred A. Davis, serial no. O-683416, Checklist of Unknowns, Testimony. Army Human Resource Command, Ft. Knox, KY.

Checklist of Unknowns - Map

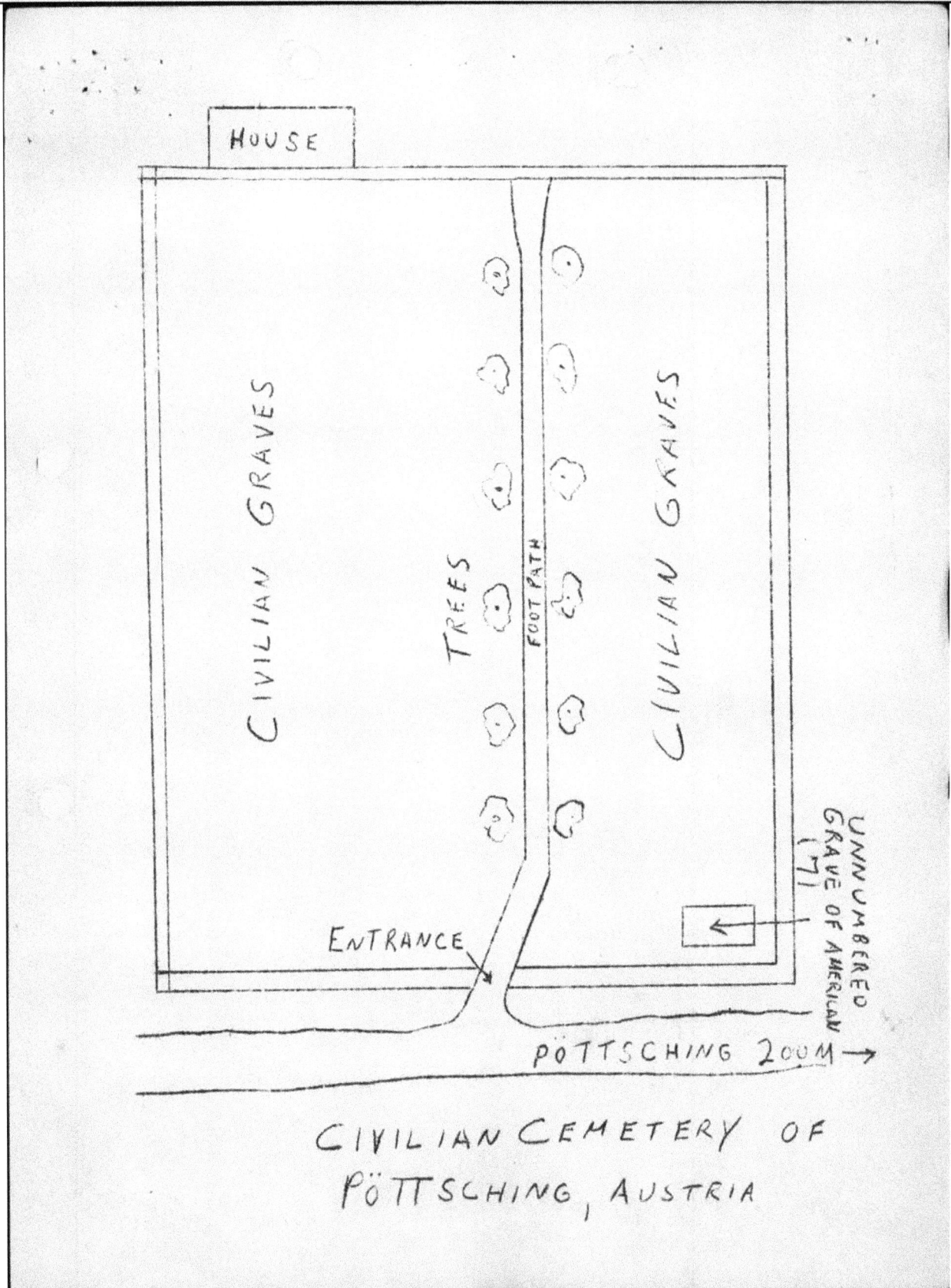

HOUSE

CIVILIAN GRAVES

CIVILIAN GRAVES

TREES

FOOT PATH

ENTRANCE

UNNUMBERED GRAVE OF AMERICAN (7)

PÖTTSCHING 200M →

CIVILIAN CEMETERY OF PÖTTSCHING, AUSTRIA

Source: Individual Deceased Personnel File for Fred A. Davis, serial no. O-683416, Checklist of Unknowns, Map. Army Human Resource Command, Ft. Knox, KY.

Report of Disinterment

DMS

USMC ST. AVOLD, NCE
Plot K, Row 40, Grave 22
Date reburied: 24 May 49

DISINTERMENT DIRECTIVE

M.R. SWART
CAPT., QMC

SECTION A—
NAME AND BURIAL LOCATION OF DECEASED

DIRECTIVE NUMBER	DATE		
3574 16033	15	03	49
	DAY	MONTH	YEAR

NAME	SERIAL NUMBER	GRADE	ARM	RACE	RELIGION
DAVIS FRED A	O-6834162	LT	1	1	1

CEMETERY	PLOT	ROW	GRAVE	DISPOSITION OF REMAINS	
ST AVOLD FRANCE	4 M	3	68	3503	80
				CODE	DIST. CTR.

SECTION B — CONSIGNEE AND NEXT OF KIN

NAME AND ADDRESS OF CONSIGNEE	NAME AND ADDRESS OF NEXT OF KIN
ST. AVOLD, FRANCE	MAY 27 1949
	ELSIE J. SHERRILL (MOTHER)
	532 WEST 66TH STREET
	CHICAGO, ILLINOIS (Flag sent)

SECTION C — DISINTERMENT AND IDENTIFICATION

NAME	SERIAL NUMBER	GRADE	DATE OF DEATH	DATE DISINTERRED

IDENTIFICATION TAG ON	ORGANIZATION	RELIGION	IDENTIFICATION VERIFIED BY
☐ REMAINS ☐ MARKER	USAAF		NAME AND TITLE

SECTION D — PREPARATION OF REMAINS FOR SHIPMENT

NATURE OF BURIAL	CONDITION OF REMAINS

OTHER MEANS OF IDENTIFICATION

SEE ATTACHED WORK SHEET

MINOR DISCREPANCIES (*Prepare Discrepancy Report QMC Form 1194a for major discrepancies.*)

REMAINS PREPARED AND PLACED IN CASKET

DATE   BY

CASKET SEALED BY   EMBALMER (*Signature*)

Karl K Kasca, Embalmer   Karl K Kasca

CASKET BOXED AND MARKED   SHIPPING CONTAINER All markings, tags
27 Apr 49   Karl K Kasca   and bottles verified by
DATE   BY   Frank B Callaghan, 1st Lt FA

I hereby certify that all the foregoing operations were conducted and accomplished under my immediate supervision and that the report above is correct.

Frank B Callaghan, 1st Lt FA 7857 AGRC Zone 3 Hq

SIGNATURE OF AGRS INSPECTOR

REMARKS AND SPECIAL INSTRUCTIONS

FILE
29 JUN 1949
REPATRIATION
BRANCH
MEM. DIV.

QMC FORM 1194
REV 11 FEB 48

FINAL LETTER SENT   24 JUN 1949

Source: Individual Deceased Personnel File for Fred A. Davis, serial no. O-683416, Disinterment Directive. Army Human Resource Command, Ft. Knox, KY.

RECEIPT OF REMAINS
DAY LETTER

| DISTRIBUTION CENTER | AGR DIV., CHICAGO QUARTERMASTER DEPOT
1819 W. PERSHING RD., CHICAGO, ILLINOIS |

A. LINHART & SONS
5318 WEST 25TH ST.
CICERO, ILLINOIS

ROUTINE

REMAINS CONSIGNED TO:

293

REMAINS OF THE LATE   PVT FRANK J. WINKLER

WILL BE DELIVERED TO YOU ON   MON. 3 MAY 1948   AT APPROXIMATELY 1:30 PM
                                                              C.S.T.

ACCOMPANIED BY MILITARY ESCORT.   REQUEST YOU IMMEDIATELY INFORM THE NEXT OF

KIN AND THAT YOU MAKE ARRANGEMENTS TO ACCEPT REMAINS UPON DELIVERY.   REFER

TO CONTROL NUMBER   2379

CARROLL J. GRINNELL
LT. COL. Q.M.C.

RECORDS BRANCH
MAY 17 12 48 PM '48
MEMORIAL DIVISION

I, THE UNDERSIGNED, DO HEREBY ACKNOWLEDGE RECEIPT OF THE REMAINS OF THE ABOVE-NAMED DECEASED

THIS ___3___ DAY OF ___MAY___, 19_48_
     DAY   MONTH

T/5 Charles J. Shepherd
WITNESS (Escort)

A Linhart & Sons
By James J Linhart
CONSIGNEE

REV. 18A

EB

QMC FORM **1193**
15 NOV 44

10—40973-1   U. S. GOVERNMENT PRINTING OFFICE

Source: Individual Deceased Personnel File for Frank Winkler, serial no. 36695605, Receipt of Remains dated 3 May 1948. Army Human Resource Command, Ft. Knox, KY.

Family Correspondence - Fred A. Davis

39668th Ch-i-c-go-ell
7/14/44

IMMEDIATE ACTION

Dear 2nd. Lt. Rodgers.

I received your letter of april. 11-
in regards to my. Son. 2nd Lt. Fred. a Davis
that you have Received some of his
Personal belongings. which was his request
for me to have. Well I would appreciate
you sending them to me. Every little thing
of his is Very Dear to me. I have some Very
Dear keep sakes here at home. I have his
silver wings he gave me. and his Diploma
when he Graduated. at Eagle Pass. Texas
June. th 26-1943. I'm Very proud of him. I also
have two other sons in Service. which
Enlisted in. 1941- one is in Africa For the past
ninteen months. his name. is Sgt. Harry E. Davis
and the other one was in Hawaii For 10½ months
he is now in the states. he is m/sgt. Geo. E. Davis
of Camp. Hood Texas. in regards to Fred.
I trust he may be a Prisoner of war some
place. I'll never loose faith. Naturally I do
worry. I would be more then greatful to have
any thing belonging to him. yes. my son is
Married. he got Married on a Very short notice
a girl he meet on furlough. her name is
Patricia. Davis. 1038. Loyola. ave Chicago. my
other two sons are married Harry has been
Married four years this coming June. and
in regards to their Father. I havent seen

over

Source: *Individual Deceased Personnel File for Fred A. Davis, serial no. O-683416, Letter from mom to Lt. Rodgers dated 14 April 1944. Army Human Resource Command, Ft. Knox, KY.*

or heard of him for seventeen years. so
I wouldn't know. if he is dead or alive
I will be more then glad to furnish you
with any information which you would
care to know. I have received several
letters. from a captain that was in the
same Bombardment with my son. Fred.
he said he would be more then glad to
let me know if any news. which he
might received of my son. I hope I have
told you. what you wanted to know. I just
can't seem to write as I want to my mind
seems to be a blank.

yours. Very Truely

Elsie J. Sherill

532. W. 66. St

Chicago. Ill.

Source: Individual Deceased Personnel File for Fred A. Davis, serial no. O-683416, Letter from mom to Lt. Rodgers dated 14 April 1944. Army Human Resource Command, Ft. Knox, KY.

Records Created by the Graves Registration Service

The GRS created records which were occasionally included in a soldier's IDPF. These included the following forms.[33]

Collecting Point Register

The Collecting Point Register was created at a collection site, and was not a standard form. It included name, rank, serial number, evacuation number and other pieces of information relevant to the death and location of the remains.

Certificate of Identity

The Certificate of Identity was Form DD 565, which was signed by the person identifying the remains in the field. It may have been a comrade in arms, or anyone who could present evidence as to the identity of the Soldier Dead.

Report of Recovery of Unknown

The Report of Recovery of Unknown contained information regarding the unknown Soldier Dead, where he was recovered, the condition of the remains, and anything that might identify him in the future.

Grave Plot Chart

The Grave Plot Chart was a standard form DD 568, created for every plot in a cemetery. Names and grave numbers of all deceased were listed here.

Historical File

The file was a register of interments and additional records held by the GRS to identify both cemetery burials and isolated burials.

Burial Overseas

Each temporary cemetery had different policies, but ceremonies were held to honor the dead daily, or as often as a military chaplain could be spared. In Margraten, Holland, burial services were held daily by the military chaplain sent from headquarters. The company of GRS men at Margraten performed their own small ceremony with the village priest after the official one to honor the dead they had buried that day. Upon conclusion of the ceremony, a firing squad shot their volleys, Taps was played and the flag was lowered from the flag pole with great reverence.[34]

Notification of Family

The family was notified of Missing in Action and Killed in Action statuses within a couple of months of the event. When the family was notified, they were done so through the War Department. The War Department then published lists of the Missing in Action, Killed in Action, or Prisoner of War soldiers and their next of kin in the newspapers. Usually the next of kin's address was included in these lists. These notices appeared as soon as a month after the status changes, but could take three months or more before the names would appear in the paper.

What was not usually explained to the family was exactly how their soldier died. They were not told about the condition of the body at death or upon locating the remains. The family was not told if there were personal effects on the body. This made it difficult for the family who not only was grieving for their soldier but could not understand why no effects were coming back.

Final Disposition of War Dead

After the war ended, the U.S. government began working with overseas officials to secure the authorization to use ports, disinter remains in private cemeteries, and authorization to use rail and waterways to transport remains to major sea ports.[35] Once this was in place, the government was able to contact families of the Soldier Dead to inquire about their wishes for the final burial of their Soldier Dead.

There were four major areas of concentration during the repatriation process. These were: to locate isolated graves and identify the remains buried within these graves, condense the cemeteries into as few as possible across Europe and Asia, and return Soldier Dead to the U.S., if requested by the family.[36] GRS went in search of unfound remains and began disinterring remains from temporary cemeteries in enemy lands. Every effort was made to find all MIA and those killed in action.

The government began notifying families of the location of their Soldier Dead beginning in late 1946, and continued for several years afterward. Depending on when the soldier died, it is possible he had been buried overseas two or more years before the family was notified of the location.

The GRS men stationed overseas after the war ended had the duty to now disinter and prepare our country's Soldier Dead for final burial at home or overseas. Civilians in the areas where the temporary cemeteries had been built were hired to help with disinterment. What they uncovered were remains in all states of decomposition. Disinfectants were used to help mask the odor, but did little good.

At Margraten, the procedure was to take disinterred remains to the morgue where "all clothing and flesh were removed, then burned" before the remaining skeleton was cleaned and sterilized for final placement in the hermetically sealed casket.[37] During the entire disinterment process, identities were checked, double checked, and triple checked before they were finally laid to rest in their caskets and boxed for shipping. It was a job few would want to do, but the GRS men carried it out with great dignity and decorum for the soldiers who gave the ultimate sacrifice.

Repatriation

Shortly after, the government gave the families the option to have the remains disinterred, at government expense, and returned to a U.S. cemetery for burial. The other option was reburial in a permanent American cemetery overseas. The disinterment and repatriation process took several years after the war ended, partly due to a shortage of materials for cases for the caskets, and a shortage of metal for the caskets themselves.

Final burial at Hamm (Luxembourg) Cemetery about 1949. Photo courtesy the American Battle Monuments Commission.

One of the first shipments to Europe took place in May 1947, when the Liberty Ship *Joseph V. Connolly* was sent to deliver steel coffins. The coffins were "made of steel with bronze finish" and "were seamless, a cover set on a rubber gasket is sealed with thirty-two lugs."[38] These coffins were placed into a wooden shipping case after the Soldier Dead was placed inside and the lid sealed. The shipping cases had the name, rank, and serial number of the soldier inscribed on the case. The shipping cases were stored in warehouses, when possible, or stacked in fields and covered with tarps until they were ready for transport by rail or water to the ports. Upon transport to the ports, each shipping case was covered with an American Flag. The flag remained on the case until it was delivered to a home or funeral home in the U.S.

Once the Soldier Dead were returned to the U.S., they were sent to one of fifty receiving stations set up in to receive the casketed remains. The caskets were transported to these receiving stations on converted Army and Navy train cars which held 66 shipping cases per car. Each funeral train held an honor guard which traveled with the Soldier Dead.[39]

The soldiers who remained behind at the request of their families, or who were unknowns, were interred in a permanent American Military Cemetery, which became part of the American Battle Monuments Commission. For those who remained, burial services were held for each Soldier Dead at the permanent cemetery. Burial flags were then sent to the next-of-kin.

Identification and Repatriation of War Dead Today

At the time of this writing, the Joint POW/MIA Accounting Command deactivated and merged with the Defense Prisoners of War Missing Personnel Office and Life Sciences Equipment Laboratory. Today the new organization is the Defense POW/MIA Accounting Agency (DPAA.) It is unclear what changes will officially be made and how that will impact the identification process. What is known, is that the media has portrayed the process as "dysfunctional" and time-consuming, however the media has not satisfactorily explained the process and the reasons why the scientific process takes so long.

Currently the process to identify remains and create casualty profiles of missing personnel is lengthy. It is not just a matter of obtaining a next-of-kin's DNA and testing. A lot of research goes into the battles and areas where soldiers fell or were buried to narrow down a list of possible unresolved casualties. These possible unresolved casualties are researched in depth through the OMPFs, IDPFs, casualty cards, morning reports, muster rolls, etc. and reports created throughout the war on all levels from upper command units down to company level reports in addition to Graves Registration documents. Obtaining these records and then beginning the research to bring possible identification of Unknown remains down to one or two individuals takes time as the records are not always available on-site. In some cases, even the governmental agencies often have to wait for other governmental agencies to locate, copy, and deliver records, just like the general public.

Consider also the records themselves. They were created during the chaos of war. Records were lost due to fire or other destruction during war time. Errors occurred within the records because humans make mistakes, especially under extremely stressful conditions. And, as you read earlier in this chapter, the treatment of the remains upon final burial make the task more time consuming as every piece of evidence must be evaluated against other pieces of evidence.

The U.S. government needs your help if you have a family member who was Missing In Action or unrecoverable during any war. You can help by submitting DNA samples for use in identification efforts as remains are recovered. To learn more, visit the Army's Past Conflict Repatriations Branch PCRB website listed in the resource section for this book on my website.

Complexities of the IDPF and Research

Uncovering the death story of your ancestor is not always as clear cut and easy as people may believe. The information contained within an IDPF can be confusing and conflicting. Whether you are using this file at the beginning of your research or acquire it along the way, it can be used to reconstruct some service history, and help make sense of the death and burial of your soldier.

You can use the questions at the end of this chapter to create a service timeline, locate information, and piece together your soldier's story.

Requesting Burial File or IDPF

World War I Burial Files are held at the National Personnel Records Center in St. Louis, Missouri. To obtain a copy of this record, write to them at the address available on their website. Form 180 will not fulfill this request. There will be a charge for copies and postage.

IDPFs are free files as of the date of this writing and take on average nine to fifteen plus months to receive. If the file was previously requested and scanned at Ft. Knox, then you may receive it in less time. To request an IDPF email your request to: USARMY.KNOX.HRC.MBX.FOIA@MAIL.MIL. Cite the Freedom of Information Action (FOIA) in your request and provide as many details about the soldier as possible including his or her name, service number, date of death, and unit.

Researching Women

At the beginning of the war, the culture and mindset of the country was primarily that women stayed home to fulfill their roles as homemakers and daughters. A college education was almost unheard of then.

The branches of the military soon learned, as more men filled combat roles, the jobs they vacated had to be filled by someone. The military, somewhat reluctantly, began recruiting women to serve. Women were recruited by the Army initially as Women's Army Auxiliary Corps (WAACs). By 1943, the Auxiliary was dropped, and they were officially inducted as part of the Army and became the Women's Army Corps (WACs.) WACs served both the Army and Air Corps.

Thousands of women took up the call to serve for a variety of reasons. Some felt a patriotic duty to their country, while other women took up the fight for a loved one who had been killed. Some women sought adventure and a release from their "boring" lives. The military provided an opportunity to see the world, even if that meant only new parts of the United States.

The Navy recruited female volunteers for the Women Accepted for Volunteer Emergency Service (WAVES.) The Coast Guard recruited volunteers for the Semper Paratus Always Ready (SPAR.) The Marine Corps sought recruits for the Marine Corps Women's Reserve (MCWR) and the Women Airforce Service Pilots (WASPs.) Women were also recruited by the military to serve as nurses. The National Guard, if federalized for service, was under the authority of the Army during the war. This was the only branch not to recruit women for service.

The idea behind recruiting a woman to serve was to replace a man who could be sent off to fight. Women in all branches trained, often on college campuses, for jobs in the medical and mechanical fields, parachute rigging, clerical jobs, intelligence work, weather forecasting, and flying. The education and experience gained in the military provided women more options than being a housewife after the war ended.

Women who served in the military laid the foundation for women in future generations to have the opportunity to serve in the military. Their service provided the option to work outside the home in jobs that were more technical than clerical. Colleges and universities also saw an increase in the number of women attending. The amazing women of World War II proved marriage was not the only option available. Finally, these women provided the inspiration for all women to dream big, do the impossible, and have a richer life with fewer societal restrictions.

Minority Women in the Military

Minority women, such as Japanese Americans or African Americans, were not immediately accepted into the military. African-American women due to discrimination of their skin color. Japanese American women due to the possibility they were Japanese spies. Studies were done to see if either minority group would fit into the military structure and function well. In the end, both were admitted to the Women's Army Corps.

OMPFs for Women

Records for women, in any branch of the service, are held at the National Personnel Records Center (NPRC) in St. Louis, Missouri. You request women's records the same way in which you request men's records. Keep in mind the records that burned also included women's files if the women served in a branch where they were integrated with the military, not serving as a volunteer.

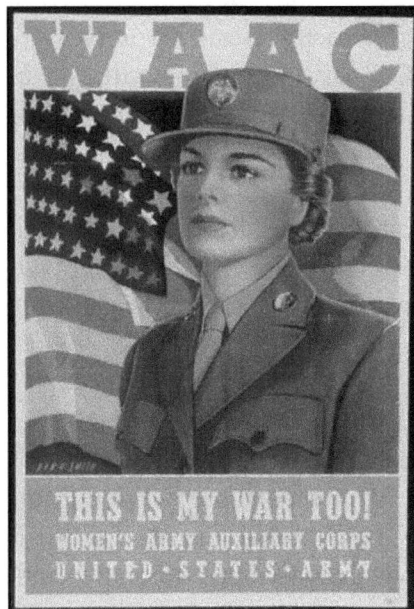

Source: National Archives and Records Administration.

The Army - Women's Army Corps (WACs)

The Women's Army Auxiliary Corps (WAAC) was formed on May 14, 1942, when Congress passed a bill to create a new section of the Army, which would be led by Oveta Culp Hobby. The original plan was to recruit 150,000 women into service, but Congress adopted a limit of 25,000. This limit was met very quickly and the goal was raised to the original 150,000 by the end of 1942.[2]

Requirements were placed on who could be recruited. WAACs had to be between the ages of 21 and 45 with no dependents. They were to be at least 5' tall and weigh at least 100 pounds. Recruits were required to have short, neat haircuts above the collar, and could wear subtle make-up and nail polish. Uniforms had to be neat and pressed, and the only allowable jewelry was watches, signet, and wedding rings.[3] Many benefits were offered the WAACs, such as medical and dental benefits, furlough, free mail, and use of the Army Exchange as part of their service.[4]

After completing all the official paperwork, undergoing physical examinations, and receiving all clothing and supplies, women were sent to training camps, just as the men were. The first WAAC training camp was established at Fort Des Moines, Iowa. Training was similar to that of an Army man, as women attended indoor classroom training and outdoor physical training. Women also practiced and marched close order drills. An important difference between men and women in the military was women were not officially trained in the use of weapons. Women were not allowed on the battlefield, with the exception of serving as nurses or essential personnel.

Once trained, enlisted personnel were placed into one of three units; the Army Air Forces (AAF,) Army Ground Forces (AGF,) or the Army Service Forces (ASF). Contingents of WAACs were formed with roughly 150 women. The makeup of a unit was three commissioned officers, 22 noncommissioned officers, and the rest enlisted personnel.

In the field on duty, WAACs initially filled many vacant office jobs. As the war progressed, the women were trained to take over jobs as engineers, photographers, medics, control tower operators, broadcasters, and weather observers.

A major change occurred in 1943 for the WAACs, as the Army wanted them as an official part of the Army, not as volunteers working alongside the Army. On July 3, 1943, a bill was passed and the WAAC was dissolved. Women were given the option to join the newly established Women's Army Corp (WAC) and enjoy the benefits and protection of all those serving in the Army.[5] Shortly after the bill went into effect, women who re-enlisted were given the option to serve overseas in combat areas in North Africa, Europe, the Pacific,

China, India, Burma, and the Middle East.

Repository: National Personnel Records Center, St. Louis, MO

The Army Air Corps – Women Air Force Service Pilots (WASPs) and Women's Auxiliary Ferrying Squadron (WAFS)

During World War II, the Army Air Corps fell under the authority of the Army as the Air Force, as we know it today, was not yet established. In late 1942, Nancy Harkness Love established the Women's Auxiliary Ferrying Squadron (WAFS) with the intent to teach women to fly planes. Women, rather than men, would then ferry planes between factories and military bases, thereby releasing a male pilot for combat.

Originally 25 women were accepted into this program. They had to be between the ages of 21 and 35, possess a commercial pilot's license, have flown at least 500 hours, and have no less than a 250 horsepower rating.[6] The women were then sent through training with the U.S. Air Transport Command and learned code, military courtesy and procedures, military law, instrument training, meteorology, and weather forecasting. The recruits also learned to fly many types of planes.

A month later, Jacqueline Cochran formed the Women's Flying Training Detachment (WFTD) in Texas. It was her intent to train female pilots to go to England to ferry planes. Less than a year after the WFTD was formed, the WAFS and WFTD were combined to form the Women's Air Force Service Pilots, or WASPs. Unfortunately, the WASPs did not become an official part of the Army Air Corps, and always remained outside of it, like the WAAC did until it was absorbed into the Army.

The WASPs were seen as Civil Service Employees, according to the military, and you will find their personnel files at the NPRC in the Civilian Employee record group. It wasn't until 1977 that the House passed a bill giving World War II WASPs full veterans benefits and recognition.[7]

WASP training included military training in customs, duties, procedures, law, Articles of War, drill and ceremonies, information, Tables of Order, and basic training topics. Training was 23 weeks in length and included 115 hours of flying time and 180 hours of ground school. Ground school consisted of education on navigation, Morse code, maps, weather, communications, math and physics, and first aid training. Recruits underwent intensive training in pilot procedures. Flight school consisted of flying over 200 different types of planes. Recruits learned how to use the controls and fly each type of plane.

After training, WASPs tested planes coming off the factory floor. When approved for combat, the WASPs flew the planes so as to put some flying time on the engines before they ferried the planes from factories to training bases. WASPs also trained male pilots, in addition to flying planes with gunnery targets to train gunners.

Repository: National Personnel Records Center, St. Louis, MO -Civilian Employee Records. Also NARA College Park, MD. Record Group: 160 (1936-1946) Records of Headquarters Army Service Forces [ASF]. Record Group: 337 (1916-1954) Records of Headquarters Army Ground Forces [AGF]. Record Group: 407 (1905-1981) Records of the Adjutant General's Office, 1917- [AGO].

Army Nurse Corps

The Army Nurse Corps (ANC) has roots in the American Revolution, when women were called to duty. During World War I, Army Nurses were in great demand, both state-side and overseas. Enrollment in the Army Nurse Corps was high during the war and many training hospitals were established. After the war, enrollment numbers dwindled, as the need for nurses fell and women resumed their usual roles. Only two training hospitals remained; Walter Reed and Letterman.

By 1920, the Army Reorganization Act allowed Army Nurses to have the same rank as officers, and allowed them to wear the insignia. The Act provided specialized training for nurses, such as anesthesia. This change promoted the need for nurses in the Army, and an increase in the number of women interested in nursing as a career rose.

During the 1930s, the country suffered a Great Depression, and all branches of the military cut back on recruitment and training. The demand for nurses fell once again, until the beginning of the 1940s, when the rest of the world was at war. The U.S. military saw a need, once again, to recruit and train nurses for possible service.

Source: National Archives and Records Administration.

Nurses who served in the U.S. Army Nurse Corps were either already in the service of the Army in 1940, or were sworn in from the private sector and the Red Cross Nurses Reserves. Many Red Cross nurses chose to move from reserve to active duty in late 1940 and looked for professional advancement, travel, adventure, and additional nursing experience. As the war gained strength the need for nurses grew as enrollment fell, President Roosevelt initiated a draft for nurses.

Early in the war, only white female nurses were recruited. No attempt was made to recruit men or African-American nurses, even though many were qualified. By 1941, after studying the effects of using African-American nurses and doctors, the Army began employing both in segregated facilities. Segregation of African-Americans and whites did not occur until much later in the war.

Army Nurses served in stateside training camps, veterans homes, POW camps, on Navy ships and in overseas hospitals. Nurses were also aboard aircraft that transported the wounded from the front to hospitals. If your nurse was ever declared MIA, and there is a chance she was onboard an aircraft, look for a Missing Air Crew Report with her name as a passenger.

After hostilities ceased, many Army Nurses returned to civilian life, while others continued their service in the Army. In 1947, a permanent Army Nurse Corps was established by Congress. This measure allowed equal pay, rank, and status for Nurses with their male counterparts in the service. A year later, all the service branches integrated, made permanent the Nurse Corps, and began allowing female physicians to practice within the various branches of service.

Red Cross and the USO

Women also served in the Red Cross and USO. Both organizations served the troops and helped raise morale. The Red Cross was founded by Clara Barton on May 21, 1881.[8] The Red Cross was established to protect and assist military injured personnel and provide relief to servicemen. During World War I, the Red Cross focused more on both national and international relief and assistance. On the home front, it provided safety training programs, nutrition education, and home care for the sick.

During World War II, the Red Cross was called upon to create care packages for POWs in both the European and Pacific Theaters of War. Sadly, many of the prisoners never received the packages created and sent by the Red Cross and the families of the prisoners. Prison guards kept much of what was sent for themselves.

When prisoners were taken to POW camps, the Red Cross was notified, and did their best to provide information to the U.S. government and families. Not every prisoner was reported, as was the case for Louis Zamperini, who was used for propaganda purposes. His identity was not released until the end of the war. The Red Cross' job was to notify families their soldier was alive and being held as a prisoner. Through the Red Cross, families and prisoners were usually allowed to send letters.

On the home front, the Red Cross held blood drives and donated blood for use by the armed forces, both overseas and at home. This program continued after the war into the present day. The Red Cross assisted families in tracing Jewish individuals both during and after the war. The Red Cross utilized, and still utilizes, international databases and organizations to help U.S. citizens trace their Jewish ancestors who may have perished in the Holocaust. The Red Cross has access to databases, lists of internments, and deaths.

Repository: Contact the Red Cross first, then search educational facilities, newspapers, newsletters, company records, home sources, and the National Archives.

United Service Organization (USO)

The United Service Organization (USO) was founded by President Franklin D. Roosevelt in 1941 after several organizations joined forces to support the war effort. He felt one organization to handle this task was appropriate. These organizations were the Salvation Army, Young Men's Christian Association, Young Women's Christian Association, National Catholic Community Services, National Travelers Aid Association and the National Jewish Welfare Board.[9]

The purpose of the USO was to provide emotional support to the troops, which was accomplished through the creation of traveling shows in all theaters of war. USO Canteens were built where officers and enlisted men could visit while off duty. At the Canteens, the men received refreshments, entertainment, girls to talk to or dance with, and quiet time to write letters, read, or relax and forget the war for a little while.

Repository: USO Records are scattered. Check the following resources to begin your search. The New York Public Library has a collection, donated by the USO Camp Shows, which contains history of the USO, photographs, and show information.

Army, Air Corps, and National Guard Service Records

Throughout this volume, I describe many resources and records which can help you trace or reconstruct the service of your Army, Air Corps, or National Guard soldier, particularly if their records burned. In this chapter we will examine the Official Military Personnel File (OMPF), also known as the service record. During World War II the Air Corps (now known as the Air Force) and federalized National Guard units fell under the authority of the Army. Therefore, the records are very similar, yet different. Please visit my website for full file examples of records.

Prior Service History

Soldiers did not always serve just once. There are many who served prior to the mid-1930s when the military was cutting back. Many of these men rejoined the service when the war broke out. If they remained in the same military branch, their service number will likely be the same. If they moved branches, their service number will be different. Look for prior service information within the OMPF for dates and branch. You can use this information to pull prior service records.

There are a few cases in which a soldier may not be considered prior service. For example, when a man joined the Army and later applied to be a pilot for the Air Corps. If he succeeded and became an officer, his service number will change. It is important to look for records under both branches and service numbers.

This was often the case with the Navy and Marine Corps. Men joined the Navy, went through basic training, and then applied to for aviation school. Once they passed all the requirements and became an officer, some chose to move to the Marine Corps to serve. This information will be contained within the Marine Corps file under prior service. An example of the Navy and Marine Corps is discussed in Volume 2 of this series.

The Official Military Personnel File

The OMPF can be a large and descriptive file if the soldier had served many years, or a smaller file if he was only in during part of the war. The main documents often found in an OMPF are described here. After I describe each section of the file, I will provide document examples so you can see what the record usually looks like.

In addition to the documents described in this chapter, files may contain letters for information requests from relatives and others conducting research. The original request will be included in the file, which means you may discover a relative you did not know existed.

For these examples, I will be using the several pages from the 112 page OMPF for Captain Paul White, 90th Division. Paul White enlisted in the Army after attending college. While attending college at Oregon State, Paul was a member of the ROTC.

One of the most important things you should do when you receive the OMPF is sort it in chronological order, that way the reports and events make sense.

Enlistment Information

Captain Paul White. Photo courtesy: Sophy Lyndon and Vincent Orrière.

Enlistment information was contained in several documents including applications, qualification cards, and medical information.

Application for Reserves if not drafted. The Application was a standard form across all branches, and required a potential serviceman to provide information about his life, education, job history, prior service history, and family information. Often, the man had to write a letter explaining why he wished to join the service, as well as providing proof of birth, high school or college transcripts, and letters of recommendation.

Service Qualification Card or Report. The Service Qualification Card contained much of the information on the service application, with the inclusion of more information on hobbies and sports participation. This card may have also contained information on service.

Next-of-Kin and Insurance Information. Each reservist had to complete next-of-kin contact information in case of wounds, Missing In Action, Prisoner of War, or Killed In Action status changes. Connected to this information was insurance beneficiary information.

Medical information. Some medical information will be included in an OMPF, usually regarding the physical and dental exams conducted upon induction or change in rank. When soldiers were treated in stateside hospitals, sometimes those records will be included.

It is important to note that not all medical information is contained in the OMPF. There are usually separate medical files. These files can only be requested by the veteran or his next-of-kin, even if the soldier has been dead 100 years. It is important if you are the veteran or next-of-kin, you request these records. If the veteran is deceased, you must provide proof of death in the form of a death certificate, obituary, or funeral paperwork.

When a soldier had been declared Killed In Action or given a Finding Of Death, documents making this official were sent to the family and the insurance carrier when needed.

Appointments for Rank and Promotions

If an enlisted man rose in rank to officer status, the commission certificate will be included in the OMPF. This record provides information on the new rank and date it was official. An Oath of Office for the Officer may also be included, which contains the date of change in rank and his signature.

Temporary appointments in rank were also given when needed. This usually appears in the file as a letter or memo explaining the temporary change and duties required of the serviceman.

Training and Educational Information

The training information and any special training courses completed will be included in the OMPF. The Certificate of Completion of a course provides information on specific training, location, and date your soldier received. If a man was going through flight school, those records would also be a part of his file. The documents may appear as official certificates of completion, or as a letter or memo to be sent to Headquarters and placed in the man's file.

Army men who wished to attempt pilot training completed applications, which were then sent to the Army Air Forces. The Commanding Officer of the unit in which the soldier was serving had the option to suggest the applicant not be recommended for pilot training. When this occurs, a brief explanation of why the soldier is valuable to his current unit is included.

Travel Orders

Travel orders were included in the file to document every move a soldier made off base. The orders often included the name, rank, and service number of several men being transferred from one unit to another. An explanation of when to depart, how to travel, and when to arrive was included.

Awards and Citations Earned

The OMPF contains letters or memos providing citations to a unit and awards issued. Sometimes, the award issued was done so on an official form for that specific award. Paul White earned the Combat Infantry Badge, effective 10 June 1944, after the 90th Division entered France during the several day long D-day invasion.

Paul was recommended for the Bronze Star and was awarded this medal in the fall of 1944. The documents included in his file include the Recommendation for Award and letter of award.
Finally, Paul was awarded the Purple Heart, posthumously, as of 24 August 1945.

Casualty Telegrams or Notices (MIA, POW, KIA)

Each time a solider has a change in status, meaning he goes from being a healthy, active soldier to wounded, missing, prisoner, or killed, a telegram is sent to the next-of-kin and included in his file. Often, there will also be a Battle Casualty Report explaining the change in status. Paul White's file contains the Casualty Message and Battle Casualty Report declaring him Missing In Action as of 6 August 1944.

Included with his report is a Missing Report explaining the circumstances surrounding his disappearance. Following this is a letter to his wife.

In June of 1945, a letter was received from William H. Bell, who was involved in the event which caused the disappearance of Captain White. His letter described what took place and any knowledge he has of the location of Captain White.

On 7 August 1945, Captain Paul White was given a Finding Of Death because he had not yet been recovered. The Finding Of Death is his official date of death and allowed his wife to collect insurance and other benefits. An explanation of the case and the Finding Of Death is usually included. If not, this will be found in the IDPF for the soldier.

Pieces of a soldier's IDPF may be contained within the OMPF. In the case of Paul White, the Casualty Clearance Plan created by the Graves Registration Service was included in his file. This document provides his name, rank, service number, date of MIA status, physical description, and summary of events surrounding his MIA status.

Discharge or Separation Information

Captain Paul White was officially declared Missing In Action and given a Finding Of Death a year plus one day later. His file does not contain a Discharge paper. The Separation and Discharge papers contain the name, rank, service number, final unit, and MOS (Job) for the soldier. The place of entry & discharge are listed with the theaters of war, in which soldier served and dates of service. Dates the soldier sailed overseas, arrived, then departed overseas to return to the U.S. are also included. The example shown at the end of this section is for another soldier, Martin DeLeonardis from Chicago, Illinois.

OMPF - Paul White Application for Reserves

APPLICATION FOR APPOINTMENT AND STATEMENT OF PREFERENCES FOR RESERVE OFFICERS
(SEE INSTRUCTIONS ON BACK)

From: White,   Paul   (none)   Date January 10-, 19 40
    (Last name)   (First name)   (Middle name)

To: The Adjutant General, Washington, D. C.
        (Through Corps Area or Department Commander)

I hereby make application for appointment as ___Second Lieutenant, Infantry___
                               (Grade)   (Section)
in the Officers' Reserve Corps.

In connection with the application I submit the following information, which I certify to be correct to the best of my knowledge:

1. Permanent address 1317 No. Wallace St.
Indianapolis, Indiana

2. Date of birth May 7-1918 White or colored white
    (Month) (Day) (Year)

3. Place of birth Indianapolis, Ind.

4. State whether or not you are a citizen of the United States and whether by birth or naturalization. (If the latter, append evidence of naturalization, or if evidence not available, state on what date and in what court naturalized.)

    Citizen by birth

5. Married or single single

6. Number of minor children none

7. Name of nearest relative, giving relationship and address, including street and number:

    John Ervin White   Father
    1317 No. Wallace St., Indianapolis, Ind.

8. Father's name * White, John Ervin
             (Last name) (First name) (Middle name)
    Father's address 1317 No. Wallace St.
             (Number and street, or rural route)
    Indianapolis, Ind.
    (City, town, or post office)   (State or country)
    Father's birthplace Indiana

If of foreign birth, state whether or not naturalized. (If naturalized, state on what date and in what court.)

Mother's name † White, Joan   --
        (Present last name) (First name) (Middle name)
Mother's address ‡ same as father's
           (Number and street, or rural route)

    (City, town, or post office)   (State or country)
Mother's birthplace Indiana

9. Marksmanship, giving year of qualification:
    Rifle SS 1939
    Pistol MM 1939

* In giving the names of the father or mother, if either is deceased it will be noted following the name.
† In giving the mother's last name, that which she bears at present will be given.
‡ If the mother's address is the same as the father's, it will be so noted and not repeated.

W. D., A. G. O. Form No. 170
January 1, 1935

10. Languages:

	French	Spanish	German	Other	Other
Speaks fluently					
Speaks fairly	None				
Translates					
Reads					

11. Special knowledge, professional or other
    Forestry

12. Present occupation, years of experience in same and name and address of employer, if any.
    Student about 9 yrs.

13. Experience in other lines and years of same
    Farming and truck driver during vacation

14. Schools attended, other than graded schools, including service schools:

Name of school	Number of years attended	Graduated? Yes or No	Graduated? Year	Degrees
Arsenal HS Indianapolis, Ind.	4	yes	1935	
Butler Univ.	2	no		
O.S.A.C.	3	no	Will grad. June 1940. BS in For.	

Subjects specialized in
    Wood Products

15. Campaigns and battles participated in (give dates)
    None

16. Decorations, citations, and commendations (attach copies)
    None

17. Wounds, giving date and place of occurrence
    None

18. State membership in professional societies
    None

19. Are you at present a member of the Regular Army, Enlisted Reserve Corps, or federally recognized in the National Guard? If so, state which, giving grade and organization or arm or service and date of expiration of enlistment:
    No

3—7585

115

REPORT OF PHYSICAL EXAMINATION

(See AR 40-100 and AR 40-105)

INSTRUCTIONS.—Unless otherwise prescribed, this form will be used for all physical examinations of officers, nurses, or warrant officers; applicants for appointment as such in the Regular Army (R. A.), National Guard (N. G.), or Organized Reserves (O. R.); and enrollment in the Reserve Officers' Training Corps (R. O. T. C.). Indicate nature of examination and component of Army by underlining appropriate terms below. Nature of examination: Appointment, Promotion, Retirement, Annual, Active Duty, Special. Component of Army: R. A., N. G., O. R., R. O. T. C. Use typewriter if practicable. Attach additional sheets if required.

R.O.T.C.

1. White _____ Paul _____ _____ OSAC
   (Last name) (First name) (Middle initial) (Serial No.)

2. Cadet _____ Age 20 _____ Years of service --
   (Grade) (Organization and arm or service) (Nearest birthday) (Whole number only)

3. Typhoid-paratyphoid vaccination: No. series completed 1 Last series April 22/39 19

4. Date of last smallpox vaccination April 6/39 Type of reaction Immune

5. Other vaccinations or immunity tests None

6. Medical history Tonsillectomy 1922. No serious illness since last active duty

7. Eyes Normal
   Distant vision: Right 20/20 correctible to _____ by¹
   (Snellen type) Left 20/20 correctible to _____ by¹
   Near vision: Right J-1 correctible to _____ by¹
   (Jaeger type) Left J-1 correctible to _____ by¹

8. Color perception (red, green, and violet)² Normal

9. Ears Normal
   Hearing, low conversational voice: Right 20/20 left 20/20 Audiometer: Right -- left --

10. Nose and throat Normal

11. Teeth³: Right (Examinee's) Left   Indicate: Restorable carious teeth by ○; nonrestorable cari-
    U. 8 7 6 5 4 3 2 1 1 2 3 4 5 6 7 8   ous teeth by /; missing natural teeth by ×.
    L. 8 7 6 5 4 3 2 1 1 2 3 4 5 6 7 8

12. Remarks, including other defects None
                                                    Classification IV

13. Prosthetic dental appliances None

14. Cardio-vascular system Normal

15. Blood pressure: S. 136 , D 84 Pulse rate: Sitting 78 Immediately after exercise 114
    Two minutes after exercise 84 Character Regular

16. Heart Normal

17. Respiratory system Normal

18. Posture Good Figure Medium Frame Medium
    (Excellent, good, fair, bad) (Slender, medium, stocky, obese) (Light, medium, heavy)

19. Height 71 inches. Weight 133 pounds. Chest: Inspiration 35 inches;
    expiration 32½ inches; rest 34 inches. Abdomen 27½ inches.

20. Bones, joints, and muscles Normal

21. Feet Pes Planus 1st deg. bilat Skin Clear

22. Abdominal viscera Normal

23. Hernia None

24. Hemorrhoids None Varicose veins None

25. Genito-urinary system Normal

¹ If annual physical examination, record only distant and near vision, and state whether defect is properly corrected.
² Not required for annual physical examination.
³ If rejected for appointment in Regular Army because of malocclusion, send plaster models to The Surgeon General.

W. D., A. G. O. Form No. 63
May 15, 1929   3—8237

Offical Military Personnel File. Paul White, serial no. O-391998. Report of Physical Examination. National Personnel Records Center, St. Louis, MO.

Reproduced at the National Archives STL

REPORT OF PHYSICAL EXAMINATION
(See AR 40-100 and AR 40-105)

INSTRUCTIONS.—Unless otherwise prescribed, this form will be used for all physical examinations of officers, nurses, or warrant officers; applicants for appointment as such in the Regular Army (R. A.), National Guard (N. G.), or Organized Reserves (O. R.) and enrollment in the Reserve Officers' Training Corps (R. O. T. C.). Indicate nature of examination and component of Army by underlining appropriate terms below. Nature of examination: Appointment, Promotion, Retirement, Annual, Active Duty, Special. Component of Army: R. A., N. G., O. R., R. O. T. C. Use typewriter if practicable. Attach additional sheets if required.

1. White, Paul J.
    (Last name)   (First name)   (Middle initial)   (Serial No.)

2. _____ _____ Age _21_ Years of service _____
    (Grade)   (Organization and arm or service)   (Nearest birthday)   (Whole number only)

3. Typhoid-paratyphoid vaccination: No. series completed __1__ Last series __Apr.__, 19_39_
4. Date of last smallpox vaccination __Apr. 1939__ Type of reaction __Immune__
5. Other vaccinations or immunity tests __none__
6. Medical history _____
   __no serious illness.__
   __Tonsillectomy 1922__

7. Eyes __normal__
   Distant vision: Right __20/20__ correctible to _____ by¹
   (Snellen type)   Left __20/20__ correctible to _____ by¹
   Near vision: Right __J.1__ correctible to _____ by¹
   (Jaeger type) Left __J.1__ correctible to _____ by¹
8. Color perception (red, green, and violet)² __normal__
9. Ears __normal__
   Hearing, low conversational voice: Right __20/20__ left __20/20__ Audiometer: Right __not taken__ left
10. Nose and throat __normal__
11. Teeth³: Right   (Examinee's)   Left
    U. 8 7 6 5 4 3 2 1 1 2 3 4 5 6 7 8   Indicate: Restorable carious teeth by ○; nonrestorable cari-
    L. 8 7 6 5 4 3 2 1 1 2 3 4 5 6 7 8   ous teeth by /; missing natural teeth by ✕.
12. Remarks, including other defects __none__
                                                Classification __IV__
13. Prosthetic dental appliances __none__
14. Cardio-vascular system __normal__
15. Blood pressure: S. __118__, D. __78__ Pulse rate: Sitting __76__ Immediately after exercise __110__
    Two minutes after exercise __78__ Character __Regular__
16. Heart __normal__
17. Respiratory system __normal__
18. Posture __Good__ Figure __Medium__ Frame __Medium__
    (Excellent, good, fair, bad)   (Slender, medium, stocky, obese)   (Light, medium, heavy)
19. Height __71__ inches. Weight __134__ pounds. Chest: Inspiration __35__ inches;
    expiration __32__ inches; rest __33½__ inches. Abdomen __28__ inches.
20. Bones, joints, and muscles __normal__
21. Feet __normal__ Skin __normal__
22. Abdominal viscera __normal__
23. Hernia __none__
24. Hemorrhoids __none__ Varicose veins __none__
25. Genito-urinary system __normal__

MAR 12 1940
PHYSICALLY QUALIFIED

¹ If annual physical examination, record only distant and near vision, and state whether defect is properly corrected.
² Not required for annual physical examination.
³ If rejected for appointment in Regular Army because of malocclusion, send plaster models to The Surgeon General.

W. D., A. G. O. Form No. 63
May 15, 1929

63—8237

Offical Military Personnel File. Paul White, serial no. O-391998. Report of Physical Examination. National Personnel Records Center, St. Louis, MO.

26. Endocrine system *Normal*
27. Nervous system *normal*

28. Laboratory procedures: Wassermann test *not indicated* Kahn test *not taken*
   Urinalysis: Sp. gr. *1.020* Albumin *none* Sugar *none*
   Microscopical (if indicated) *not indicated*
   Other laboratory procedures *none.*

29. Remarks on defects not sufficiently described above *Health is very good. Firm muscle tone. An active individual who has a lower caloric intake than that required for the energy expended. Gains weight when not in school. X-ray of chest reveals no pathology of heart or lungs. BP on Jan 31, 1940 = 118/78 + 114/78. pm*

30. Corrective measures, or other action recommended *[Feb 1, " = 114/80 + 116/74 "*
   Recommend: *" 2 " = 112/70 + 118/76 "*
   More rest. Higher caloric diet. Improve general hygiene.

31. Is the individual permanently incapacitated for active service? *No*
   If yes, specify defect _____

32. If applicant for appointment: Does he meet physical requirements? *no* Do you recommend
   acceptance with minor physical defects? *yes* If rejection is recommended, specify cause _____

Student Health Service OSC.   N.J. Stone   M.D.,   Corps.
Corvallis, Oregon (Place)   (Name and grade)
Feb. 2 _____, 19*40*.   _____,   Corps.
(Date)   (Name and grade)
          _____,   Corps,
          (Name and grade)

          1st Ind.[1]

Headquarters, _____, 19___
To the Commanding General, _____
   Remarks and recommendations _____

_____ (Name)
_____
(Grade)   (Organization and arm or service)
          Commanding.

          2d Ind.[1]

_____, 19___, To The Adjutant General.
_____
_____
_____

          3d Ind.[1]

War Department, S. G. O., _____, 19___   To The Adjutant General.

   Noted.   See ___ Ind.   Recommend

[1] State action taken on recommendations of the board. If incapacitated for active service, state whether action by retiring board is recommended.

U. S. GOVERNMENT PRINTING OFFICE   c3—6237

RESERVE OFFICER'S QUALIFICATION CARD

NAME (LAST)	WHITE
(FIRST)	PAUL
(MIDDLE)	
(HOME)	
GRADE	2nd Lt.
SECTION	Inf-Res
ASSIGNMENT GROUP	CAAC
ELIGIBILITY	Yes
RACE	W
SERIAL NO.	O-391988
MARITAL STATUS	Single
DEPENDENTS	None

1. DATE OF BIRTH: 5/7/18
   COUNTRY OF BIRTH—OFFICER: USA
   FATHER: USA MOTHER: USA
2. HOME ADDRESS: 922 B St. Springfield, Oregon
3. BUSINESS ADDRESS: Springfield, Plywood Corp. Springfield, Oregon. (EAD Ft. Ord, Calif.)
5. PERSON TO BE NOTIFIED IN AN EMERGENCY: NAME: John E. White, 1317 N. Wallace St., Indianapolis, Indiana
   ADDRESS: 1317 N. Wallace St., Indianapolis, Indiana.
   RELATIONSHIP: Father

BUSINESS IN ORDER OF EXPERIENCE

FIRM NAME	NATURE OF BUSINESS	POSITION HELD	NATURE OF WORK	YEARS EMPLOYED
Indiana National Bank	Banking	Ass.Cashier	Passenger & Transit Clerk	1936-1936 3 mos.
Springfield Plywood Corp.	Douglas Fir Plywood Mill	Freshman	Operator of hot press	1940 2 mos.

7. OTHER EXPERIENCE: Living group pres. at college for 1 yr. Member of Independent Student Council, Living group council & Chairman as member of numerous campus committee at College.

EDUCATION

SCHOOL	DATES	DEGREE—YEAR	GRADUATE?	NAME OF INSTITUTION	SUBJECT MAJORED IN
HIGH SCHOOL	4 yrs.	1935	Yes	Arsenal Technical Schools	Science
COLLEGE	4 yrs.	BS 1940	Yes	Butler University 1 yr. OSC 3 yrs.	Wood Prod.
POST GRADUATE					

9. EXTRA CURRICULAR ACTIVITIES:
10. MEMBERSHIP IN PROFESSIONAL SOCIETIES: None
11. ATHLETIC ABILITY: Track, basketball, Mbr.Sen.Life Sav.Am.Red Cross. INSTRUCTOR: trnd.basic stud.in ROTC dur.sr.yr.at OSC in close ext. ENTERTAINER: Song leader (drill
12. HOBBIES: Fishing, hunting, sports, music

LANGUAGES

	FRENCH	GERMAN	SPANISH
SPEAKS			Slightly
READS			Slightly
TRANSLATES			Slightly

4. MILITARY SPECIALTIES: Co. Officer. 4/8 Troops
5. RECOMMENDED MOBILIZATION ASSIGNMENT—1: Troops 2 Troops 3 Troops
6. ADDITIONAL TRAINING REQUIRED:

PRIOR MILITARY TRAINING

DATES	DUTIES	GRADE	UNIT	GRADE	UNIT

8. WOUNDS, CITATIONS, DECORATIONS:

W. D., A. G. O. Form No.177
August 26, 1940

INACTIVE STATUS CREDITS

DATE	TYPE	HOURS	DATE	TYPE	HOURS	DATE	TYPE	HOURS	DATE	TYPE	DUTIES	GRADE	UNIT	DUTIES

16—10768

Offiical Military Personnel File. Paul White, serial no. O-391998. Classification Questionnaire of Reserve Officers. National Personnel Records Center, St. Louis, MO.

OMPF - Paul White 2nd Lt. Certificate

THE UNITED STATES OF AMERICA

duced at the National Archives- STL

To all who shall see these presents, greeting:

Know Ye, that reposing special trust and confidence in the patriotism, valor, fidelity and abilities of **Paul White**

I do appoint him **Second Lieutenant, Infantry** *in the*

Army of the United States

such appointment to date from the **twenty-fourth** *day of* **May** *nineteen hundred and* **forty** *He is therefore carefully and diligently to discharge the duty of the office to which he is appointed by doing and performing all manner of things thereunto belonging.*

He will enter upon active duty under this commission only when specifically ordered to such active duty by competent authority.

And I do strictly charge and require all Officers and Soldiers under his command when he shall be employed on active duty, to be obedient to his orders as an officer of his grade and position. And he is to observe and follow such orders and directions, from time to time, as he shall receive from me, or the future President of the United States of America, or the General or other Superior Officers set over him, according to the rules and discipline of War.

This Commission evidences an appointment in the Army of the United States, under the provisions of section 37, National Defense Act, as amended, and is to continue in force for a period of five years from the date above specified, and during the pleasure of the President of the United States, for the time being.

Done at the City of Washington, this **twenty-fourth** *day of* **May** *in the year of our Lord one thousand and nine hundred and* **forty** *, and of the Independence of the United States of America the one hundred and* **sixty-fourth** *.*

By the President:

File
4-15-40
LEV-1512

G. E. Isaacs
Adjutant General.

W. D., A. G. O. FORM No. 0650 C.
AUGUST 1, 1938

Offical Military Personnel File. Paul White, serial no. O-391998. Second Lieutenant, Infantry Certificate dated 24 May 1940. National Personnel Records Center, St. Louis, MO.

OMPF - Paul White Promotion to Captain (Temporary)

HEADQUARTERS 357TH INFANTRY
Camp Barkeley, Texas
/ceh

In reply
refer to: 13 August 1943
  201 - White, Paul 8/13/43

SUBJECT: Promotion of Officer.

THRU   : Commanding General, 90th Infantry Division, Camp Barkeley, Texas.

TO   : Commanding General, Third Army, Fort Sam Houston, Texas.

    1. Recommend that PAUL WHITE, 1st Lieutenant, 0-391998, Infantry,
be promoted to the temporary grade of Captain to fill an existing vacancy.

    2.

		GRADE	DATE	COMPONENT
a.	This officer was originally appointed	2d Lt	24 May 40	O R C

    b. This officer was last promoted to 1st Lieutenant, Infantry,
with rank from 4 August 1942, by Par. 21, Special Orders No. 203, War
Department, Washington, D. C., dated 4 August 1942.

    3. a. (1) Position now occupied is Regimental Transportation
Officer, 357th Infantry, Camp Barkeley, Texas.
        (2) T/O authorization for position is Captain, Infantry.

    b. (1) T/O position vacancy to be filled is Regimental Trans-
portation Officer, 357th Infantry, Camp Barkeley, Texas.
        (2) T/O authorization for position is Captain, Infantry.

    4. The officer mentioned above has, for a period of at least six
months, clearly demonstrated his fitness for the responsibilities and duties
of the position and grade for which recommended by the manner in which he
performed the following duties:

Inclusive Dates	Position Held	Unit and Station	Manner of Performance of Duty
26 Jan 43 to 30 Mar 43	Regimental Transportation Officer	357th Infantry La. Maneuver Area	Excellent
31 Mar 43 to present	Regimental Transportation Officer	357th Infantry Camp Barkeley, Texas	Excellent

    5. There is no surplus officer of appropriate grade and branch avail-
able for assignment to the vacancy which promotion is intended to fill.

- 1 -

(201 - White, Paul, 8/13/43, contd)

6. Favorable action on this recommendation and on those submitted previously, upon which final report of action has not been received, will not result in exceeding the number of officers in grade and branch currently authorized by table of organization or table of allotment applicable.

JOHN W. SHEELY,
Colonel, 357th Infantry,
Commanding.

AG 210.2 - Promotion of Officer   1st Ind.
GNMHR-E (13 Aug 43)
HEADQUARTERS 90TH INFANTRY DIVISION, APO 90, Camp Barkeley, Texas, 14 August 1943.

TO : Commanding General, Third Army, Fort Sam Houston, Texas.

THRU: Commanding General, VIII Corps, Brownwood, Texas.

1. Approved. Vacancy exists.

2. There is no surplus officer of appropriate grade and branch available for assignment to the vacancy which promotion is intended to fill.

3. Favorable action on this recommendation and on those submitted previously, upon which final report of action has not been received, will not result in exceeding the number of officers in grade and branch currently authorized by Tables of Organization or table of allotment applicable.

HENRY TERRELL, Jr.,
Major General, U. S. Army,
Commanding.

Offiical Military Personnel File. Paul White, serial no. O-391998. Temporary Duty dated 13 Aug 1943. National Personnel Records Center, St. Louis, MO.

NOTED

Reproduced at the National Archives

12

ARMY EXTENSION COURSES

JUN 24 1940

HEADQUARTERS NINTH CORPS AREA

Certificate of Completion of Subcourse

This is to certify, That ___Mister Paul K. White,___ ___Infantry___

___271 No. Encinitas, Monrovia, Calif.___ .... has successfully
(Address)

completed Subcourse No. ___10-7___, ___Map and Aerial Photograph Reading___
(Title of Subcourse)

Extension Course of the ___Infantry___ {*School
*Department

(19_39_-19_40_ Announcement) with a rating of _83_ % Hours of credit ___15___

Date ___June 17,___ 19_40_.

H. T. Aplington,
Lt. Col., Cavalry
(Name)

Unit Instructor
(Grade, Organization, etc.)

[SEAL]

APPROVED:

By command of Lieutenant General DEWITT:

F. ROSS,
Major, Infantry,

Adjutant General.

W. D., A. G. O. Form No. 152
July 1, 1933

*Strike out word not applicable.

U. S. GOVERNMENT PRINTING OFFICE 3—10173

Offical Military Personnel File. Paul White, serial no. O-391998. Army Extension Course Certificate dated 17 June 1940. National Personnel Records Center, St. Louis, MO.

OMPF - Paul White Combat Infantryman Badge

Last Name — First Name — Middle Initial	Serial Number	Grade	Organization				
				Rescinded	Revoked	Amended	Corrected Copy
WHITE, PAUL	0391998	Capt					

Headquarters Issuing Orders	Order Number		Date of Orders
	General	Special	
357th Inf	6		20 Jul 44

Type of Badge (Strike out one)

COMBAT INFANTRYMAN BADGE
EXPERT

Remarks:

eff: 10 Jun 44

THE ADJUTANT GENERAL'S OFFICE, DECORATIONS AND AWARDS BRANCH, WASHINGTON, D. C.

RECORD OF AWARD OF INFANTRYMAN BADGE

FILE IN ENLISTED BRANCH [ ]   OFFICER'S BRANCH [ ]

WD AGO Form 0706
1 December 1944

Offiical Military Personnel File. Paul White, serial no. O-391998. Combat Infantryman Badge eff 10 Jun 1944. National Personnel Records Center, St. Louis, MO.

OMPF - *Paul White Bronze Star*

SERVICE COMPANY
357TH INFANTRY
APO 90, U. S. Army

201- White, Paul (O) 11 Sep 44.   11 September 1944
            (Name)   (Date)

SUBJECT: Recommendation for Award.

THRU   : Commanding Officer, 357th Infantry.

TO   : Commanding General, 90th Infantry Division.

        Under the provisions of AR 600-45, Cir 1, Hq, ETOUSA, dtd 3 Jan 44, and Cir
                                                  (AR and Circulars)
66, Hq, FUSA, dtd 18 May 44 , it is recommended that the Bronze Star   be
                                                              (Decoration)
awarded the following officer   for conspicuous courage and initiative
                        (O,EM)   (Distinguishing characteristics of
in combat against the enemy.
deed for which award is recommended)

        1. Personal Data:

            a. Paul (NMI) White   Captain   O-391998
                  (Name)   (Rank)   (ASN)
                  Infantry   Service Company, 357th Inf.
                (Arm or service)   (Organization)

            b. Grade, ASN, assignment, and capacity at time of act or service for
which award is recommended Grade-Capt.; ASN—O-391998; assignment-Regimental
Motor Officer; capacity-supply officer.

            c. Decorations previously awarded _____None_____
                                                (General order, number, Headquarters
and date)

            d. No decoration has previously been awarded for this act or service.
(Capt. White   (has) (has not) previously been recommended
            (Name)
for an award on the basis of this or related acts. _____
                                                   (If previously recommended
_____)
give details including action taken by each headquarters to which sent.)

            e. The entire service of ____Capt. White____ since
                                            (Name)
the rendition of the deed or service upon which this recommendation is based has
been honorable.

            f. Entered military service from Tulare, California
                                              (City and State)

                                - 1 -

Rec for Award, 1-White, Paul (NMI) (O)   September 1944

g. Nearest relative <u>Mrs. Paul White</u>   <u>P. O. Box 252</u>
                        (Name)   (Street & No. or RFD)

<u>Tulare</u>   <u>California</u>
   (City)   (State)

2. General Data:

a. Does the officer recommending this award have personal knowledge or was he an eye-witness of the act or service upon which the recommendation is based? _____**Yes**_____. (If "no", testimony in form of certificate or affidavits of at least two persons who have personal knowledge, or were witnesses, must accompany the recommendation) - (In form of enclosure)

b. Is recommendation supported by official records? _____**No**_____
(If "yes", give details _____

3. Specific Data:

a. Exact date of act or period during which service was rendered _____
_____**8 July 1944 to 12 July 1944**_____

b. Location at which act was rendered **Vicinity of Beau Coudray,** **France.**

c. Character of terrain, of hostile observation and of enemy fire_____ **Terrain--rolling small fields with hedgerows; hostile observation good; enemy artillery fire.**

d. Visibility, time of day, and atmospheric conditions **Visibility good; atmospheric conditions generally clear.**

e. Location of enemy **Six hundred yards to the immediate front.**

f. Morale - that of our forces and of the enemy **Our morale good; enemy morale good.**

g. Casualties sustained **Two killed, eleven wounded.**

h. Effect or result of deed in question **Supplied unit with water, food, and ammunition; aided in its organization and direction; secured valuable information of the enemy.**

i. Detailed resume (Using operations maps, and narrative statement), giving complete description of action **Captain Paul White, Regimental Motor Officer, when it was necessary for flank protection at Beau Coudray**

- 2 -

(Ltr,Rec for Award, 201-White, Paul (NMI) (O) 11 September 1944)

France, to organize a provisional company, insisted on accompanying the unit to be of what assistance he could. During all the time that the company was in line Captain White, of his own volition, ran supplies and water through intense artillery fire directly to the men; and of choice, remained with the company at all times to aid in its organization and direction. On July 10, again at his own insistence he personally patrolled well to the front of the company with complete disregard for his own safety, to investigate reports of an enemy strong point, and secured valuable information of enemy positions.

> MARTIN J. MANHOFF,
> Capt., 357th Infantry,
> Commanding.

201-White, Paul ,(NMI) (O)   1st Ind.   GBB/cfg
   (11 Sep 44)

HEADQUARTERS 357TH INFANTRY, APO 90, U. S. Army, 8 October 1944.

TO: Commanding General, 90th Infantry Division, APO 90, U. S. Army.

   Approved.

> G. B. BARTH,
> Colonel, 357th Infantry,
> Commanding.

C.O.N.F.I.D.E.N.T.I.A.L

HEADQUARTERS 90TH INFANTRY DIVISION
APO 90, U. S. Army

13 November 1944

Subject: Award of Bronze Star.

To   : Captain Paul White, O-391998, Infantry, Service Company, 357th
Infantry, APO 90, United States Army.

Under the provisions of AR 600-45 and Section I, Circular 6, Headquarters Third United States Army, 26 April 1944, a Bronze Star is awarded
to:

Captain Paul White, O-391998, Infantry, United States Army, for
heroic service in support of operations against the enemy in France. During
the period 8 July to 12 July 1944, Captain White distinguished himself in
the performance of heroic service. When it became necessary to organize a
provisional rifle company and position it for protection of the exposed flank,
Captain White, Regimental Motor Officer, voluntarily and without regard for
his personal safety, aided in establishing and directing ... ammunition ... directly ... while exposed to hostile enemy
artillery fire. ... Division Commander ... to investigate
and report upon enemy ... activity. His heroic service was in accordance
with military traditions. Entered service from California.

By command of Brigadier General McFarland.

LESLIE V. DIX,
Major ..., G.S.C.,
Adjutant General.

125

C.O.N.F.I.D.E.N.T.I.A.L

Offical Military Personnel File. Paul White, serial no. O-391998. Recommendation for Award dated 11 Sept 1944. National Personnel Records Center, St. Louis, MO.

OMPF - Paul White Purple Heart

Last Name — First N — Middle Initial		Serial Number	Grade	Organization
White, Paul		O391998	Capt.	Infantry

Location or Area

European

of Death

1 August 45 (presumed)

of Award

PURPLE HEART
(POSTHUMOUS)
AND COMBAT INFANTRYMAN BADGE

arks:

Philadelphia QM Depot Engrave and Ship to Next of Kin

PAUL WHITE

GO 24 Aug 45

THE ADJUTANT GENERAL'S OFFICE
DECORATIONS AND AWARDS BRANCH.
WASHINGTON. D. C.

RECORD OF POSTHUMOUS AWARD

OF

PURPLE HEART
AND COMBAT INFANTRYMAN BADGE

Relationship

Wife

Name and Address of Next of Kin

Mrs. Virginia E. White
P. O. Box 1452
Tulare, California

FILE IN ENLISTED BRANCH ☐

OFFICER'S BRANCH ☑

WD AGO Form 0709   1 December 1944

Offiical Military Personnel File. Paul White, serial no. O-391998. Purple Heart Award. National Personnel Records Center, St. Louis, MO.

OMPF - Paul White Casualty Telegram Form

N ~~ be delivered by phone except when authorized by the sender.
Not to be delivered between the hours of 10 PM and 7 AM.

CASUALTY MESSAGE
TELEGRAM

OFFICIAL BUSINESS—GOVERNMENT RATES

WAR DEPARTMENT
BUREAU A. G. D.
CHG. APPROPRIATION
EMR 3814

AG 201 WHITE PAUL 23 AUG 44
ASN O-391 990

SPXPC-N ETO 164 25 AUGUST 1944
DATE

MRS VIRGINIA E WHITE
POST OFFICE BOX 1252
TULARE CALIFORNIA

THE SECRETARY OF WAR DESIRES ME TO EXPRESS HIS DEEP REGRET THAT YOUR

| HUSBAND | CAPTAIN | PAUL WHITE |
| (RELATIONSHIP) | (GRADE) | (NAME) |

HAS BEEN REPORTED MISSING IN ACTION SINCE

| SIX AUGUST | IN FRANCE |
| (DATE) | (LOCALITY) |

DETAILS OR OTHER INFORMATION ARE RECEIVED YOU WILL BE PROMPTLY NOTIFIED

IF FURTHER

OFFICIAL: EWH Van Horn   J A ULIO

ADJUTANT GENERAL   THE ADJUTANT GENERAL

AG 704.1(   )   BATTLE

(Initials & Date)

FRAGILE - HANDLE WITH CARE

74

WAR DEPARTMENT
THE ADJUTANT GENERAL'S OFFICE
WASHINGTON 25, D. C.

—BATTLE CASUALTY REPORT—

NAME	SERIAL NUMBER	GRADE	ARM OR SERVICE	REPORTING THEATRE
WHITE PAUL NMI	O-391998	CAPT	INF	ETO

| PLACE OF CASUALTY | DATE OF CASUALTY | | | FLYING OR JUMPING STAT | TYPE OF CASUALTY | SHIPMENT NUMBER |
	DAY	MONTH	YEAR			
FRANCE	06	AUG	44		MIA	164

NAME AND ADDRESS OF EMERGENCY ADDRESSEE

THE INDIVIDUAL NAMED ABOVE DESIGNATED THE FOLLOWING PERSON AS THE ONE TO BE NOTIFIED IN CASE OF EMERGENCY, AND THE OFFICIAL TELEGRAPHIC AND LETTER NOTIFICATIONS WILL BE SENT TO THIS PERSON. THE RELATIONSHIP, IF ANY, IS SHOWN BELOW. IT SHOULD BE NOTED THAT THIS PERSON IS NOT NECESSARILY THE NEXT-OF-KIN OR RELATIVE DESIGNATED TO BE PAID SIX MONTHS' PAY GRATUITY IN CASE OF DEATH

MR.-MRS.-MISS—FIRST NAME—MIDDLE INITIAL—LAST NAME	RELATIONSHIP	DATE NOTIFIED

NO. AND NAME OF STREET—CITY—STATE

REMARKS: ☐ CORRECTED COPY

Offical Military Personnel File. Paul White, serial no. O-391998. Casualty Telegram and Battle Casualty Report of 6 Aug 1944. National Personnel Records Center, St. Louis, MO.

OMPF - Paul White Missing In Action Form

24 Oct 1944

MISSING REPORT*

75

To accompany WD AGO Forms 66-1 or 24 of Missing or Missing in

Action Personnel (other than those covered by Missing Air Crew Report).

NAME ___ WHITE ___ O-391998 GRADE CAPT Arm or Service INF

ORG ___ 359TH INF APO 90 Date Reported MIA 6 AUG. 44

MISSION ___ ?

POINT OF DEPARTURE M___ DATE ___ 44

INTENDED DESTINATION ___

LAST KNOWN WHEREABOUTS ___

BRIEF RESUME OF CIRCUMSTANCES SURROUNDING DISAPPEARANCE:

On way to ___ fired upon, ___ wounded and Capt. White ___ missing - no trace of ___ being found.

STATEMENTS OF WITNESSES, IF ANY:

___

REMARKS: (Any information not covered above, including details and results of search, if any, conducted)

Date of report _____

(Signature of preparing officer)

WAR DEPT., A.G.O.
CASUALTY STATUS VERIFIED

_____Group_____

_____Date

~~should be~~ classified "Confidential", when submitted.

Offical Military Personnel File. Paul White, serial no. O-391998. Missing Report dated 24 Oct 1944. National Personnel Records Center, St. Louis, MO.

AG 201 White, Paul
PC-N ETO164

26 August 1944

Mrs. Virginia E. White
Post Office Box 1252
Tulare, California

Dear Mrs. White:

This letter is to confirm my recent telegram in which you were regretfully informed that your husband, Captain Paul White, O-391998, Infantry, has been reported missing in action in France since 6 August 1944.

I know that added distress is caused by failure to receive more information or details. Therefore, I wish to assure you that at any time additional information is received it will be transmitted to you without delay, and, if in the meantime no additional information is received, I will again communicate with you at the expiration of three months.

The term "missing in action" is used only to indicate that the whereabouts or status of an individual is not immediately known. It is not intended to convey the impression that the case is closed. I wish to emphasize that every effort is exerted continuously to clear up the status of our personnel. Under war conditions this is a difficult task as you must readily realize. Experience has shown that many persons reported missing in action are subsequently reported as prisoners of war, but as this information is furnished by countries with which we are at war, the War Department is helpless to expedite such reports. However, in order to relieve financial worry, Congress has enacted legislation which continues in force the pay, allowances and allotments to dependents of personnel being carried in a missing status.

Permit me to extend to you my heartfelt sympathy during this period of uncertainty.

Sincerely yours,

J. A. ULIO
Major General,
The Adjutant General.

Offical Military Personnel File. Paul White, serial no. O-391998. Letter to Mrs. Wite from Adjutant General dated 26 Aug 1944. National Personnel Records Center, St. Louis, MO.

OMPF - *Paul White Letter from William Bell Re: Ambush*

CONFIDENTIAL

Reproduced at the National A[...]

13 June, 1945

Subject: Information Concerning
Missing Personnel.

TO: Major John T. Burns AGD
Ass't Chief of Staff, G-2

1. In regards to your letter of June 5th. concerning Captain Paul White O-391998 whom you have listed as missing in action.

2. On August 6,1944 near Mayenne, France time about 2130, the Capt. was driving our Jeep, our regular T4 driver was riding in the right front seat an I was riding in the rear seat. Our Regiment hadd been formed into a task force. The first Bn. was leading it. We had started forward to the first Bn., when we were ambushed at a cross road by a small German patrol. We were fired on with a machine gun an bazooka. The first bu burst killed the T4 an hit me in 4 places, an at the same time knocked the T4 an I out of the Jeep into the ditch by the side of the road. The Capt. was still in the vehicle an finally stopped at the edge of the road. The German's were firing all the time. When the vehicle stopped the Capt. made no attemp to get out of the vehicle. The German's quit firing an after waiting a while came up to the Jeep an pulled the Capt. out an took him away with them. I'm sure that he must have been wounded, but how bad I don't know. I was told later in a letter from Lt. Martin J. Manhoff of the same Regiment an Company that his helmet was found near the Jeep with blood on it. They searched all around the area for any sign's of him or his body, but none could be found. That was the last time that I had any kind of contact with Capt. White.

William A. Bell
W-2105527
William A. Bell
WOJG NMB
Pat. Wakeman Conval. Hos.

NOTED IN
SRAD SECTION

CONFIDENTIAL

3786

Offical Military Personnel File. Paul White, serial no. O-391998. Letter from William Bell describing ambush, dated 13 June 1945. National Personnel Records Center, St. Louis, MO.

7 aug 1945

Form prescribed by
Comptroller General, U.S.
7 October 1944

WAR DEPARTMENT
THE ADJUTANT GENERAL'S OFFICE
WASHINGTON 25, D. C.

Reproduced at the National Archives

3786

FINDING OF DEATH OF MISSING PERSON

Pursuant to the provisions of Section 5 of the Act of 7 March 1942 (Public Law 490 77th Cong.) as amended, upon direction and delegation by The Secretary of War, The Chief, Casualty Branch, The Adjutant General's Office, finds Captain Paul White, Army Serial Number O391998, Infantry to be dead. He was officially reported as missing in action as of the 6th day of August 1944. For the purposes stated in said Act, death is presumed to have occurred on the 7th day of August, 1945.

BY ORDER OF THE SECRETARY OF WAR

ADJUTANT GENERAL
CHIEF, CASUALTY BRANCH

SUMMARY OF INFORMATION

AREA					FLYING STATUS	JUMP STATUS	LINE OF DUTY	OWN MIS-CONDUCT	ON DUTY STATUS	ABSENCE AUTH'D
European					No	No	Yes	No	Yes	

PREVIOUS REVIEWS
None

DATE OF BIRTH	HOME ADDRESS		DATE OF ENTRY ON CURRENT ACTIVE SERVICE	LENGTH OF SERVICE YEARS	MONTH	DAYS
7 May 1918	Indianapolis, Indiana		1 Apr 1941			

EMERGENCY ADDRESSEE

NAME	RELATIONSHIP	ADDRESS
Mrs. Virginia E. White	Wife	P. O. Box 1252 Tulare, California

BENEFICIARIES

NAME	RELATIONSHIP	ADDRESS
Mrs. Virginia E. White	Wife	P. O. Box 1252 Tulare, California
Mrs. John E. White	Mother	1317 No. Wallace Street Indianapolis, Indiana

REMARKS

Distribution 56

Circumstances of Disappearance: Officer was occupant of a jeep which was fired upon by ambushed enemy patrol at Montours, near Mayenne in northwestern France.

FILE AG 201 FILE
Status Review and
Determination Section
Casualty Branch

136

WD AGO FORM 0353
1 FEBRUARY 1945 — THIS FORM SUPERSEDES WD AGO FORM 0353, 1 NOVEMBER 1944, WHICH MAY BE USED UNTIL EXISTING STOCKS ARE EXHAUSTED.

Offical Military Personnel File. Paul White, serial no. O-391998. Finding Of Death dated 7 Aug 1945. National Personnel Records Center, St. Louis, MO.

AG 704 - Dead (7 Aug 45) ~~CONFIDENTIAL~~
S. R. & D. No. 3786

7 August 1945

MEMORANDUM FOR: Chief, Casualty Branch

SUBJECT: Review and Determination of Status
Under the Missing Persons Act.

CLASSIFICATION REMOVED
By Authority of T. A.
Date: 8 - AUG 1948
Initials: ____

SANFORD COFFIN
Captain, A. G. D.

I. - FACTS

1. The following-named officer of Service Company, 357th Infantry, has been carried on War Department records as missing in action, since 6 August 1944 in France, as reported by ETO Shipment No. 164:

Name	ASN	Grade
White, Paul	O391998	Captain

2. This officer's AG 201 file contains a "Missing Report", dated 9 August 1944, prepared by Captain Thomas E. Wilson, Infantry. It states that on 6 August 1944, Captain White departed from Mayenne; that his intended destination was the Regimental Command Post in the vicinity of St. Suzzanne; and that his last known whereabouts was Montsurs. The resume of circumstances surrounding his disappearance follows:

"On way to Regt. C. P. when jeep was fired upon. Driver was killed, W. O. J. G. Bell, a passenger, wounded and Capt. White is missing--no trace of him being found."

Under "Statements of Witnesses, if Any" this notation appears: "W. O. J. G. William Bell (Wounded - Evacuated)."

3. A confidential letter, dated 5 June 1945, (File: AG 201, White, Paul, O391998 (5 Jun 45)) was dispatched from this office to Warrant Officer (jg) William H. Bell requesting information concerning Captain White. His reply, dated 13 June 1945, reveals the following information:

"2. On August 6, 1944 near Mayenne, France time about 2130, the Capt. was driving our Jeep, our regular T4 driver was riding in the right front seat and I was riding in the rear seat. Our Regiment had been formed into a task force. The first Bn. was leading it. We had started forward to the first Bn. when we were ambushed at a cross road by a small German patrol. We

~~CONFIDENTIAL~~

182

Offical Military Personnel File. Paul White, serial no. O-391998. Explanation of Finding Of Death. National Personnel Records Center, St. Louis, MO.

S. R. & D. No. 3786   CONFIDENTIAL

were fired on with a machine gun and bazooka. The
first burst killed the T4 and hit me in 4 places,
and at the same time knocked the T4 and I out of the
Jeep into the ditch by the side of the road. The
Capt. was still in the vehicle and finally stopped
at the edge of the road. The Germans were firing all
the time. When the vehicle stopped the Capt. made
no attempt to get out of the vehicle. The Germans
quit firing and after waiting awhile came up to the
Jeep and pulled the Capt. out and took him away with
them. I'm sure that he must have been wounded, but
how bad I don't know. I was told later in a letter
from Lt. Martin J. Manhoff of the same Regiment and
Company that his helmet was found near the Jeep with
blood on it. They searched all around the area for
any signs of him or his body, but none could be found.
That was the last time that I had any kind of contact
with Capt. White."

4. The AG 201 file also contains a letter from Captain White's wife to
this office, dated 3 December 1944, in which she states that her husband had
mentioned Harry Wright as his driver.

(War Department records show that Technician Fourth Grade Harry Wright,
18,071,010 was reported as killed in action 6 August 1944, by ETO Shipment
No. 171.)

5. Mayenne is located in northwestern France at approximately 48° 18' N -
0° 36' W. Montsurs is about twelve miles southeast of Mayenne.

6. An examination of the files of this person in Casualty Branch and
Officers' Branch, AGO, and of the Index in Prisoner of War Information Bureau,
PMGO, does not reveal any further information relevant to this review.

II. - CONCLUSIONS

1. Captain White and two others occupied a jeep which, on 6 August 1944,
departed from Mayenne, in northwestern France. In the vicinity of Montsurs

CONFIDENTIAL

2

Offiical Military Personnel File. Paul White, serial no. O-391998. Explanation of Finding Of Death. National Personnel Records Center, St. Louis, MO.

S. R. & D. No. 3786

CONFIDENTIAL

(approximately twelve miles southeast of Mayenne), at about 2130 hours, an embushed enemy patrol fired upon the jeep, killing the driver, and wounding a passenger, Warrant Officer Junior Grade William H. Bell. According to Mr. Bell's statement, the Germans pulled Captain White, who was wounded, out of the jeep, and took him away with them. Later, his bloody helmet was found near the jeep; however, a search of the area revealed no other trace of Captain White.

2. Although it is twelve months since Captain White became missing in action, and approximately three months since the cessation of hostilities in Europe, no report has been received in the War Department to indicate that he is alive.

3. In view of the foregoing facts and circumstances, it is concluded that this person may not reasonably be presumed to be living.

III. - RECOMMENDATION

It is recommended that a finding of death be made under the provisions of Section 5 of the Missing Persons Act in the case of Captain Paul White, 0391998, Infantry, and that this finding show the presumed date of death to be 7 August 1945.

Lillian M. Farmley
Investigator

Theodore G. Weinberger
First Lieutenant, AGD

CONCURRED IN:

APPROVED:

JOHN T. BURNS
Lieutenant Colonel, AGD
Officer in Charge
Status Review and
Determination Section

GEORGE F. HERBERT
Colonel, AGD
Chief, Casualty Branch

CONFIDENTIAL

S

Offical Military Personnel File. Paul White, serial no. O-391998. Explanation of Finding Of Death. National Personnel Records Center, St. Louis, MO.

TGW/IMP/ml/4616

AGPC-S 201 White, Paul
(7 Aug 45)   0391998

7 August 1945

Mrs. Virginia E. White
P. O. Box 1252
Tulare, California

Dear Mrs. White:

Since your husband, Captain Paul White, 0391998, Infantry, was reported
missing in action 6 August 1944, the War Department has entertained the
hope that he survived and that information would be revealed dispelling the
uncertainty surrounding his absence. However, as in many cases, the conditions of warfare deny us such information. The record concerning your
husband shows that on 6 August 1944, he and two others occupied a jeep which
departed from Mayenne, in northwestern France. In the vicinity of Montsurs
(approximately twelve miles southeast of Mayenne), at about 9:30 p.m., an
ambushed enemy patrol fired upon the jeep, killing the driver, and wounding
the passenger. The Germans were seen to remove Captain White, who was
wounded, from the jeep, and take him away with them. Later, a search of the
area was conducted, but no trace of your husband was found.

Full consideration has recently been given to all available information bearing on the absence of your husband, including all records, reports
and circumstances. These have been carefully reviewed and considered. In
view of the fact that twelve months have now expired without the receipt
of evidence to support a continued presumption of survival, the War Department must terminate such absence by a presumptive finding of death. Accordingly, an official finding of death has been recorded under the provisions
of Public Law 490, 77th Congress, approved March 7, 1942, as amended.

The finding does not establish an actual or probable date of death;
however, as required by law, it includes a presumptive date of death for
the termination of pay and allowances, settlement of accounts and payment
of death gratuities. In the case of your husband this date has been set as
7 August 1945, the day following the expiration of twelve months' absence.

I regret the necessity for this message but trust that the ending of
a long period of uncertainty may give at least some small measure of con-
solation. I hope you may find sustaining comfort in the thought that the
uncertainty with which war has surrounded the absence of your husband has
enhanced the honor of his service to his country and of his sacrifice.

Sincerely yours,

T. G. Weinberger
1st Lt. A. G. D.

Copies Furnished:
AG 201
Cas. Br.

1 Incl.

FILE AG 201 FILE
Status Review and
Determination Section
Casualty Branch

EDWARD F. WITSELL
Major General
Acting The Adjutant General of the Army

*Offical Military Personnel File. Paul White, serial no. O-391998. Explanation of Finding Of Death. National Personnel Re-
cords Center, St. Louis, MO.*

Enlisted Record & Report of Separation - DeLeonardis

ENLISTED RECORD AND REPORT OF SEPARATION
BOOK570   PAGE598   HONORABLE DISCHARGE

1. LAST NAME - FIRST NAME - MIDDLE INITIAL	2. ARMY SERIAL NO.	3. GRADE	4. ARM OR SERVICE	5. COMPONENT
DE LEONARDIS MARTIN	16 144 977	Tec 4	Sig C	AUS

6. ORGANIZATION	7. DATE OF SEPARATION	8. PLACE OF SEPARATION
Hq Co 52nd Sig Bn	1 Nov 45	Separation CEnter Fort Sheridan Illinois

9. PERMANENT ADDRESS FOR MAILING PURPOSES	10. DATE OF BIRTH	11. PLACE OF BIRTH
1252 Lexington St Chicago Ill	30 Nov 06	Italy

12. ADDRESS FROM WHICH EMPLOYMENT WILL BE SOUGHT	13. COLOR EYES	14. COLOR HAIR	15. HEIGHT	16. WEIGHT	17. NO. DEPEND.
See 9	Brown	Black	5 7	158 LBS.	0

18. RACE	19. MARITAL STATUS	20. U.S. CITIZEN	21. CIVILIAN OCCUPATION AND NO.
WHITE X NEGRO OTHER (specify)	SINGLE X MARRIED OTHER (specify)	YES X NO	Concession Attendant

MILITARY HISTORY

22. DATE OF INDUCTION	23. DATE OF ENLISTMENT	24. DATE OF ENTRY INTO ACTIVE SERVICE	25. PLACE OF ENTRY INTO SERVICE
	27 Oct 42	22 Jul 43	Cp Grant Ill

SELECTIVE SERVICE DATA	26. REGISTERED YES NO X	27. LOCAL S.S. BOARD NO.	28. COUNTY AND STATE	29. HOME ADDRESS AT TIME OF ENTRY INTO SERVICE
				See 9

30. MILITARY OCCUPATIONAL SPECIALTY AND NO.	31. MILITARY QUALIFICATION AND DATE (i.e. infantry, aviation and marksmanship badges, etc.)
Clerk General 055	None

32. BATTLES AND CAMPAIGNS

New Guinea   Southern Philippines   Luzon

33. DECORATIONS AND CITATIONS Victory Medal   American Theater Ribbon   Asiatic Pacific Theater Ribbon with 3 Bronze Battle Stars   Philippines Liberation Ribbon with 1 Bronze Star   3 Overseas Service Bars   1 Service Stripe   Good *

34. WOUNDS RECEIVED IN ACTION

None

35. LATEST IMMUNIZATION DATES				36. SERVICE OUTSIDE CONTINENTAL U. S. AND RETURN		
SMALLPOX Im	TYPHOID St	TETANUS St	OTHER (specify)	DATE OF DEPARTURE	DESTINATION	DATE OF ARRIVAL
Jul 43	Aug 44	Aug 44		14 Jan 44	PTO	4 Feb 44
				26 Sep 45	USA	15 Oct 45

37. TOTAL LENGTH OF SERVICE						38. HIGHEST GRADE HELD
CONTINENTAL SERVICE			FOREIGN SERVICE			
YEARS	MONTHS	DAYS	YEARS	MONTHS	DAYS	
0	6	8	1	9	2	Tec 4

39. PRIOR SERVICE

None

40. REASON AND AUTHORITY FOR SEPARATION

Conv of Govt AR 615-365   Sec V WD Cir 269   7 Sep 45

41. SERVICE SCHOOLS ATTENDED	42. EDUCATION (Years)		
None	Grammar 8	High School 4	College 1½

PAY DATA   vou 14411

43. LONGEVITY FOR PAY PURPOSES			44. MUSTERING OUT PAY		45. SOLDIER DEPOSITS	46. TRAVEL PAY	47. TOTAL AMOUNT, NAME OF DISBURSING OFFICER
YEARS 3	MONTHS 0	DAYS 5	TOTAL $ 300	THIS PAYMENT $ 100		$ 1.30	249.55 LELAND E RICE CAPT FD

INSURANCE NOTICE

IMPORTANT IF PREMIUM IS NOT PAID WHEN DUE OR WITHIN THIRTY-ONE DAYS THEREAFTER, INSURANCE WILL LAPSE. MAKE CHECKS OR MONEY ORDERS PAYABLE TO THE TREASURER OF THE U. S. AND FORWARD TO COLLECTIONS SUBDIVISION, VETERANS ADMINISTRATION, WASHINGTON 25, D. C.

48. KIND OF INSURANCE	49. HOW PAID	50. Effective Date of Allotment Discontinuance	51. Date of Next Premium Due (One month after 50)	52. PREMIUM DUE EACH MONTH	53. INTENTION OF VETERAN TO
Nat. Serv. X U.S. Govt. None	Allotment X Direct to V. A.	Nov 45		$	Continue Continue Only Discontinue X

54.

55. REMARKS (This space for completion of above items or entry of other items specified in W. D. Directives)

RIGHT THUMB PRINT

Lapel Button Issued   ASR Score (2 Sep 45) 61
Inactive status ERC from 27 Oct 42 to 21 Jul 43
*Conduct Medal GO 1 Hq 52nd Sig Bn 45

56. SIGNATURE OF PERSON BEING SEPARATED	57. PERSONNEL OFFICER (Type name, grade and organization - signature)
Martin De Leonardis	R D DICKEY 1st Lt INF

Offiical Military Personnel File. Martin DeLeonardis, serial no. 16144977. Separation Paper dated 1 Nov 1945. National Personnel Records Center, St. Louis, MO.

Reconstructing a Service History

If your soldier's file burned in 1973, there is no way to reconstruct or locate the original documents which were included. However, there are ways to begin the reconstruction of service history. The items described in this section are one place to begin. In the next chapter, I will describe several records created in the field, which will also help you create a timeline of service.

Separation and Discharge Paper

Look for the Separation and Discharge paperwork your soldier brought home from the war. If this paperwork is not in your home, check with the County Recorder or County Clerk in the county where he lived when discharged. Veterans were encouraged to file a copy of their papers with the county for safe keeping.

Newspaper Articles

The newspapers ran articles on soldiers entering service, when they were transferred to a different camp or base, and when they were promoted. Sometimes, the information and photograph for the article came from the family. In other cases, the information was provided by the War Department.

The newspapers also ran short notes or letters from soldiers serving overseas. These may not tell you exactly where the soldier was serving, but they may provide clues and add to your timeline.

Obituaries and Memorial Notices

Obituaries, memorial notices, and funeral information may contain service history or a general overview of where a soldier attended basic training, when they were sent overseas, possibly a unit, and death date and location . If the death occurred while the soldier was in service, you will need to obtain the IDPF and learn as much as you can about his death and service.

Veterans Affairs

Contact the Veterans Affairs (VA) office if your soldier survived the war. Some service history should be included in their files. Note: These files take months to receive. You may need to follow-up a couple of times to ensure your request was received.

Contact Veterans with Whom Your Soldier Served

Try to locate and speak with veterans who served with your soldier. The veterans will not have specific service information from the OMPF, but they may have papers, letters, photographs, and oral history to help provide some context, clues, and a timeline to your soldier's service.

Examine the IDPF

If your soldier was declared Missing In Action or Killed In Action, and you have his IDPF, it may contain bits of service information scattered throughout. Some pages may be obvious they were from the OMPF and other pages may contain pieces of history written onto an identification form or piece of correspondence. Family letters included in the IDPF may contain clues to service.

To illustrate where service information may be included, from all the sources discussed in this section to reconstruct service history, we will examine the IDPF of 2nd Lt. Fred. A. Davis. 2nd Lt. Davis's records were destroyed in the 1973 fire. All that remains are clues from other record sources.

Reconstructing the Service of 2nd Lt. Fred A. Davis

Reconstructing service can begin at any point in the record and home source search. Fred's search began with his name and branch of the service. From there, knowing almost nothing else, I searched for mention of him in the Historical Chicago Tribune newspaper during the war. Not knowing where Fred was buried I searched the American Battle Monuments Commission to see if he appeared in their database. He did.

I then requested his IDPF and his Missing Air Crew Report. Roughly a year later, I connected with a researcher online who had extensively researched and written about the final mission in which Fred flew and was killed. This researcher provided an Air Force Accident Report for Fred's crew in Michigan as they prepared to fly overseas.

Newspaper Research

The Chicago Daily Tribune for December 25, 1943 ran an article called "Soldiers Who Are Missing In Action."[1] Fred is pictured in this article, and listed in the Chicago and Vicinity section by name, rank, and next of kin's name and address. With this information, I know Fred was missing by the end of 1943.

A second article was located in *The Chicago Daily Tribune* dated November 23, 1944 called "Chicago Airmen Die in Action; 1 Man Missing."[2] This article says,

> *"Second Lt. Fred A. Davis, 24, co-pilot of a Liberator bomber, was reported missing after a flight over Austria, Nov. 2, his wife, Patricia, of 1038 Loyola Av., said yesterday. He enlisted in the Black Horse troop, later the 106th cavalry, in 1940, and two years later transferred to the air forces. A son, Fred Jr., and his mother, Mrs. Elsie Sherrill, 532 W. 66th St., also survive."*

Analyzing the Newspaper Articles

Now, looking at both of these articles, written a year apart, it appears Fred went missing twice - once in 1943 and again in 1944. This did not happen. Fred's wife did not specify what year Fred was missing. If she did, the newspaper left that piece of information out of the article. The timeline actually shows that Fred was declared Missing In Action on 3 November 1943 when his plane went down in Austria. A year plus one day later, a Finding Of Death (FOD) was given which was reported in the newspaper even though it does not clearly state this. Now his wife could collect his insurance and final payroll disbursements.

The article also tells us Fred originally enlisted in the Black Horse Troop, 106th Cavalry. This was a National Guard unit which was federalized in late 1940. Roughly two years later, in 1942, Fred transferred into the Army Air Corps. Fred's National Guard records would have been held at the NPRC in St. Louis. Unfortunately they, like his Army Air Corps records, burned. This information does, however, allow me to contact researchers working on the Black Horse Troop to attempt to locate additional information.

American Battle Monuments Commission

The American Battle Monuments Commission (ABMC) had an entry for 2nd Lt. Fred Davis in the Lorraine Cemetery. The information provided in his entry stated the following.[3]

Fred A. Davis
Second Lieutenant, U.S. Army Air Forces
344th Bomber Squadron, 98th Bomber Group, Heavy
Entered the Service From: Illinois
Service #: O-683416
Date of Death: November 02, 1943
Wars or Conflicts: World War II
Buried: Plot K Row 40 Grave 22
Lorraine American Cemetery St. Avold, France
Awards: Purple Heart

At the time I searched the ABMC, I did not have Fred's service number. His entry provided that, along with a date of death and final unit. This information allowed me to conduct a search for his OMPF and Morning Reports.

The Missing Air Crew Report (MACR)

The Missing Air Crew Report (MACR) is a record created for the Army Air Corps when a combat plane did not return after a mission. The crew was declared Missing In Action and a record was created to begin documenting the mission, obtain testimony from those who witnessed the plane going down (if possible), provide a little service information, maps of the area searched, if a bombing mission, plane formation, and possibly German documents and testimony. The MACR will be explored more in-depth in the next chapter.

The MACR for the 1st Lt. Jeffries crew, in which Fred was the 2nd Lt. and co-pilot, was number 1143.[4] His file contains several important documents.

German Reports on Crashed American Aircraft. This report was created by the Germans, and documents the date and place of the crash, type of plane, fate of the crew, serial numbers on the plane, and the cause of the loss. Using this information we can begin to piece together the final mission.

Missing Air Crew Report. This is the official report created for the crew. This report provides the date and location of the mission, base from which the crew took off, the weather, equipment on board by serial number, and the names of three witnesses to the crash. It also provides a complete list of the crew by name, rank, and service number.

Using this information, we can begin to add detail to the final mission. We can also begin searching the collaterals, those in the crew. Start by searching the internet for the collaterals, as it may lead you to resources for those men which may, in turn, provide more information on your man.

Certificate. Several witness statements are provided in the file. Each describes the point in the mission where Davis's plane was hit and disappeared. These documents provide additional context to the crash.

The rest of the MACR contains combat and downing reports, which summarize the mission and plane loss. It also contains German records, which, for the most part, have been transcribed throughout the file.

The Individual Deceased Personnel File

Scattered throughout the Individual Deceased Personnel File (IDPF) may be bits and pieces of service information. These pieces may be included on several different pages or within reports. Sometimes a family letter will be included that contains information, or pages from the OMPF. Several clues were found in Fred's IDPF.

In a letter from Fred's mother to 2nd Lt. Fred Rodgers, dated 14 April 1944, she provides clues, about not only Fred, but his brothers in the service. His mom stated she had Fred's Silver Wings and diploma he earned when he graduated at Eagle Pass, Texas on 26 June 1943. She lists two other sons in the Army, Sgt. Harvy Davis, who enlisted in 1941 and is stationed in North Africa, and M/Sgt G. [George] Davis, who was currently stationed at Camp Hood, Texas. She mentions the marriages of Harvey and Fred, stating Fred would be married four years. The number of years married allows me to search for a marriage license. According to the letter, their father is not in the picture and hasn't been seen in years. We also have his mother's current address.

Request for New Letter of Inquiry. The request form was created to verify the next of kin before final interment. This form, dated 9 December 1948, tells us Fred's widow had remarried by 1948. This means she no longer was the next-of-kin or had a say in Fred's final interment. The information and proof of the remarriage, was on file at the VA. If I request Fred's VA files, I hope to find this information included.

Identification Data Sheet. The Identification Data Sheet, completed after Fred was declared Missing In Action, contains service information requested from his OMPF. It stated his name, rank, service number, and final unit. It also contains two locations where he trained prior to flying overseas: Independence, Kansas from 21 February 1943 to 23 April 1943, and Eagle Pass, Texas from 24 April 1943 to 26 June 1943. Using this information, we can add to his timeline for training then explore resources for those training camps.

Physical Examination for Flying. The Physical Examination for Flying provides additional service and training details. We have Fred's original Army Air Force service number and his Officer's number. We know how many years he has completed in the service and where he is currently stationed. We know the date he qualified as a pilot. The form also tells us a bit about his health history.

Dental Identification. The Dental Identification form was created as part of the OMPF each time the serviceman saw the dentist. The more accurate the dental records were, the better chances of identifying the soldier if he was killed and had no other identification on him. This form is dated, shows the service branch, and his enlisted service number.

Morning Reports

Morning Reports are a record created for each unit by company. To search these, you must know the company in which a soldier was serving. The reports were created daily to document the entry and exit of soldiers in a company, promotions, changes in their job, and changes in status. A more in-depth examination of these records is included in the following chapter.

I obtained a few of Fred's Morning Reports. Records are only as good as the person creating them or providing the information. Fred's did not contain where he was transferred from, and it was difficult to trace him prior to his final mission. The report for 3 November 1943 shows Fred and his crew were Missing In Action.5 The reports provide the name, rank, and service number for all men listed.

Air Force Accident Report

I was able to obtain the Air Force Accident Report for Fred's crew prior to going overseas. The accident occurred at Kellogg Field in Michigan on 8 September 1943. His Accident Report number is 44-09-08-59.6

The "File Code" for the Accident Report is fiscal year - month-day - report number for that day. Fiscal year for the USAAF started in July, so for months July through December, you need to subtract one for calendar year. In Fred's example 44-09-08-059, this is the 59th accident report on 8 September 1943. In late 1944 the USAAF introduced minor accident reports. Stateside accidents started at number 200 and overseas reports started at number 700. In 1948 the USAAF went to calendar year cause some overlap in report number for July thru December 1947 and 1948.

Errors did occur in all types of World War II records, so if you cannot locate the record based on the date you know or believe an event occurred, attempt to search a different way or contact a researcher who specializes in the specific record type, and ask them for a different search. In Fred's case, the company Aviation Archaeology has a database on their website which allows me to search for Fred, the date of his accident, or his pilot's name. When in doubt, I contact Craig Fuller, owner of Aviation Archaeology, and ask for help.

The Accident Report provided one main page, which can help reconstruct service history. This is the Report of Aircraft Accident form. This form provides the name, rank, and service numbers for the crew, the date and location of the accident, and the unit in which the crew currently belonged. Using this information, Morning Reports could be searched to possibly trace Fred forward or backward in time.

2nd Lt. Fred A. Davis's Timeline of Service

Using all of the sources above, I was able to create a timeline of service for Fred. This outline is only the beginning of his research. He likely flew additional missions, for which I can obtain documentation. I can research this history of his unit, the missions he flew, the collaterals, and more on his family to piece together a more complete story.

Abbreviations for sources: MR – Morning Report. MACR – Missing Air Crew Report. IDPF – Individual Deceased Personnel File.

Date	Unit/Event	Location	Source
29 Jul 1920	Birth	New York	
25 Nov 1940	Enlisted in National Guard 106th Black Horse Cavalry	Serial No. 20620161	Newspaper article
29 Sept 1942	Qualified as Pilot		Physical Exam dated 1943
21 Feb 1943-23 Apr 1943	Central Flying Training Command.	Independence, KS	IDPF

24 Apr 1943-26 June 1943	57th Basic Flying Training Group, 33rd Flying Training Wing	Eagle Pass, TX	IDPF
By 26 June 1943	Got his Officer's Silver Wings		Letter from mom in IDPF
2 Jul 1943	Married	Chicago	
by 8 Sept 1943	2nd Air Force 6th Heavy Bomber Processing HQ		
9 Oct 1943	344th BS 98th BG (H) 12th AF	Hergla, Tunisia	MR
By 2 Nov 1943	344th Bomb Squadron, 98th Bomb Group (H) 12th Air Foce	Hergla, Tunisia	IDPF, MACR, MR
3 Nov 1943		Departed Hergla, Tunisia flying North-Northeast to Wiener Neustadt, Austria to hit a Bomb Factor	KIA
3 Nov 1943	Death	Poettsching, Austria	X-File/IDPF Disinterred by 612th GRS Co.
25 Dec 1943	Newspaper article MIA	Chicago Tribune	
23 Nov 1944	Newspaper article KIA	Chicago Tribune	Doesn't provide year of MIA
4 Nov 1944	Finding Of Death	Cairo, Egypt	IDPF
9 Sept 1946	Disinterred communal grave Austria	Poettsching, Austria	IDPF
4 Oct 1946	2nd Burial	St. Avold	IDPF
9 Apr 1947	3rd Burial	St. Avold	IDPF
24 June 1949	4th and final burial Plot 4M Row 3 Grave 68	St. Avold (Lorraine)	IDPF

Records Created in the Field

The creation of a soldier's story is affected by many pieces. Once you have established the basic facts on a soldier's service, it is time to move beyond only researching the individual to his unit, collaterals within his unit, and the overall organizational histories. Looking at the story from several angles will provide a greater picture of service placed in historical context.

Records Created at the Company Level

Morning Reports

A Morning Report was created each day outlining events of the prior day for the events of a Company. To locate information in Morning Reports you must know the Company in which your soldier served. It is not enough to know in which division or regiment. The Company can be found on a discharge paper or IDPF or any other letter or document that has a unit listed on it. Morning Reports can be traced in any direction based on the information you have.

For example, James Privoznik served in the 90th Division, 358th Infantry Regiment, F Company, for the last 14 days of his life. Therefore, the Morning Reports that should list him would be for F Company of the 90th Division, 358th Infantry.

Each company was required to submit a Company Morning Report that ran from midnight to midnight. These reports listed the location of the company for the date of the report. It listed strength of the unit in numbers of men, details of those entering and leaving the company, details of those declared AWOL, missing In Action, Killed In Action, or wounded. The reports also provided information on the day's events. Some clerks reported weather conditions, in addition to the usual information on where the unit was fighting, and other enemy encounters.

The companies were required to report numbers of men at each meal, which provided information to the Army, who then was able to provide food and appropriate supplies for the soldiers. These numbers also alerted headquarters when the ranks were depleted and replacements were needed.

Morning Reports are useful because they can help you track a soldier's service from start to finish, as long as the company clerk included all the details of the entrance and exit of a soldier, showing where he came from, and where he was going. Not all company clerks did this or had the time to do this. Think about D-Day, 6 June 1944, and the days following. Everything was chaotic as men were moving from place to place. Some were separated from their units, and many more had been killed. With this in mind, when you search for your soldier on a Morning Report, you will not always find him, and the event like Missing In Action, on the date you think you will. It could have been reported several days later. Some clerks also reported when a soldier was sent into a unit as a replacement, based on a General or Special Order from Headquarters.

Morning Reports for Pfc. James Privoznik

On the next group of pages, you will find Morning Reports for F Company, 358th Infantry Regiment, 90th Division. These reports are copied from microfilm, which is not always in the best shape to present clear quality. The reports provide an example of how to trace service, location of a company, and the action occurring.

Repository: National Personnel Records Center, St. Louis, MO.

Questions a Morning Report May Answer:

1. Name, rank, service number, and unit in which a soldier was stationed on a particular day.
2. Location of the company each day.
3. Names of personnel moving in and out of the company, along with reason for movement.
4. Record of the day's events, which may include weather, morale, movement, and enemy engagement.
5. For an Air Corps bombing crew, when several other bombers went missing, you have the names of collaterals to research, which may provide additional clues to the mission, losses, and your airman.

Morning Reports for James Privoznik

COMPANY
MORNING REPORT ENDING 2400 28 December 194 4
(DAY) (MONTH) (YEAR)

STATION Elzange. VU 9586 Nord de Guerre
ORGANIZATION 790th Ordnance L.M. Company Ord
(CO. DET. ETC.) (PARENT UNIT) (ARM OR SERVICE)

SERIAL NUMBER	NAME	GRADE	CODE
35300797	Ellis, Ernest E.	Pfc	J
Duty - 014			
38009301	Garner, Virgil E.	Pfc	
Duty - 014			
35040528	Privoznik, James F.	Pfc	
Duty - 189			
12158180	Felton, Sidney NMI	Pvt	
Duty - 521			
32548142	Hosmer, Raymond B.	Pvt	
Duty - 348			
34424995	Taylor, James W.	Pvt	
Duty - 348			
32131451	Townsend, Thomas G.	Pvt	
Duty - 913			

Above 7 EM assgd to 358th Inf per par 9
so #280, Hq 90th Inf Div dtd 27 Dec 44.
Departed.

OFFICER STRENGTH	FLD O & CAPT		1ST LT		2D LT		WO		FLT O	
	PRES	ABS'T	PRES	ABS'T	PRES	ABS'T	PRES	ABS'T	PRES	ABS'T
ASSIGNED										
ATTACHED UNASSIGNED										
ATTACHED FR OTHER ORGN										
TOTAL										

AVN CADET & ENLISTED STRENGTH	AVIATION CADETS		ENLISTED MEN			
	PRESENT	ABSENT	PRESENT FOR DUTY	PRESENT NOT FOR DUTY	ABSENT	PRESENT AND ABSENT
ASSIGNED						
ATTACHED UNASSIGNED						
ATTACHED FR OTHER ORGN						
TOTAL						

R A T I O N S

I ESTIMATED NUMBER OF RATIONS REQUIRED FOR DAY OF WEEK DATE NUMBER
II MESS ATTENDANCE FOR DAY OF THIS REPORT TOTAL ÷ 3 AVERAGE
BREAKFAST DINNER SUPPER
III MEN AUTHORIZED TO MESS SEPARATELY MEN ATCHD FOR RATIONS
MEN ATCHD TO OTHER ORGN FOR RATIONS O & OTHERS MESSED TOTAL
MEN PRESENT LESS RET PLUS

PAGE 1 OF 2 PAGES
I CERTIFY THAT THIS MORNING REPORT IS CORRECT AND
THAT RATION FIGURES IN PART II REPRESENT AN ACTUAL
COUNT AS REPORTED TO ME:

SIGNATURE
W.D., A.G.O. FORM NO. 7
MARCH 15, 1943 (NAME) (GRADE) (ARM OR SERVICE)
WD COPY THRU MRU OR SCU

Morning Report for 790th Ordnance, 90th Division dated 28 Dec 1944. National Personnel Records Center, St. Louis, MO.

Left Form

COMPANY MORNING REPORT — ENDING 2400 29 Dec 1944

STATION Wehingen, Germany WQ 1196 Nord de Guerre
ORGANIZATION Co F 358th Inf Regt Inf

SERIAL NUMBER	NAME	GRADE	CODE
14434093	Taylor, James W	Pvt	B
32508142	Hosmer, Raymond B	Pvt	B

Above 2 EM asgd & jd fr 790th Ord LM 27 Dec 44 per par 9 SO 280 Hq 90th Inf Div Race white MOG 302 MOS 745 — 27/2 — 745

| 34209301 | Garner, Virgil E | Pfc | B |

Asgd & jd fr 790th Ord LM 27 Dec 44 per par 9 SO 280 Hq 90th Inf Div Race white MOG 011 MOS 745 — 27/2 — 745

| 32131151 | Townsend, Thomas Q | Pvt | B |

Asgd & jd fr 790th Ord LM 27 Dec 44 per par 9 SO 280 Hq 90th Inf Div Race white MOG 111 MOS 745 — 27/2 — 745

| 12158160 | Felton, Sidney | Pvt | B |

Asgd & jd fr 790th Ord LM 27 Dec 44 per par 9 SO 280 Hq 90th Inf Div Race white MOG 131 MOS 745 — 27/2 — 745

| 36640529 | Privoznik, James F | Pfc | B |

Asgd & jd fr 790th Ord LM 27 Dec 44 per par 9 SO 280 Hq 90th Inf Div Race white MOG 010 MOS 745 — 27/2 — 745

PAGE 1 OF 2 PAGES

Right Form

COMPANY MORNING REPORT — ENDING 2400 29 Dec 1944

STATION Wehingen, Germany WQ 1196 Nord de Guerre
ORGANIZATION Co F 358th Inf Regt Inf

SERIAL NUMBER	NAME	GRADE	CODE
11083246	Baldwin, Robert E	Pvt	C

Dy to asgd in gr to 315th Engr Combat Bn 29 Dec 44 By 745 Auth: par 1 SO 282 Hq 90th Inf Div

RECORD OF EVENTS

29 Dec 44 Co remained in same defensive location No enemy action No casualties Weather clear & cold Morale good

OFFICERS STRENGTH	FLD O & CAPT PRES	ABS'T	1ST LT PRES	ABS'T	2D LT PRES	ABS'T	WO PRES	ABS'T	FLD'O PRES	ABS'T
ASSIGNED	1		3		1					
ATTACHED										
TOTAL	1		3		1					

AVN CADET & ENLISTED STRENGTH	PRESENT	ABSENT	PRESENT FOR DUTY	PRESENT NOT FOR DY	ABSENT	PRESENT ENL LEAUGE
ASSIGNED			190		13	203
ATTACHED						
TOTAL			190		13	203

ESTIMATED NUMBER OF RATIONS REQUIRED FOR — DAY OF WEEK Wed DATE 3 Jan 45 — NUMBER 195

MESS ATTENDANCE FOR DAY OF THIS REPORT BREAKFAST 195 DINNER 195 SUPPER 195 TOTAL 585 AVERAGE 195

MEN AUTHORIZED TO MESS SEPARATELY — MEN PRESENT 190 LESS 190 PLUS 5 — NET 5 — 195

PAGE 2 OF 2 PAGES

SIGNATURE CHARLES G. BARNDT Capt Inf

Morning Report for F Co, 358th Infantry, 90th Division dated 29 Dec 1944. National Personnel Records Center, St. Louis, MO.

COMPANY MORNING REPORT ENDING 2400 30 Dec 194 4

STATION Wehingen, Germany WQ 1196 Nord de Guarre
ORGANIZATION Co F 358th Inf Regt Inf

SERIAL NUMBER	NAME	GRADE	CODE
35832680	Avery, Melvin D	Pvt	B

Asgd & jd fr Hq Btry 90th Div Arty 27 Dec 44 per par 9 SO 280 Hq 90th Inf Div Rate Wd sta MOS 010 MOS 745

| 36167827 | King, Charles H | S/Sgt | 1-3 |
| 36166276 | Martonosi, Lewis L | S/Sgt | 1-3 |

Above 2 EM promoted to T/Sgt 29 Dec 44 per par 3 SO 149 Hq 358th Inf MOS changed to 651/45

35811152	Branham, Barney D	Sgt	1-4
32957185	Keenan, Arthur	Sgt	
37407258	Krueger, George A	Sgt	

Above 3 EM promoted to S/Sgt 29 Dec 44 per par 3 SO 149 Hq 358th Inf MOS 653 653

| 31405129 | Heller, Karl E | Pfc | |

Dy to SLD 27 Dec 44 315th clr sta (not dropped fr asgnt) to RTD 30 Dec 44

| 31124359 | Hunt, Earl G | Pfc | |

Dy to SLD 29 Dec 44 315th clr sta (not dropped fr asgnt) to RTD 30 Dec 44

PAGE 1 OF 2 PAGES

COMPANY MORNING REPORT ENDING 2400 30 Dec 194 4

STATION Wehingen, Germany WQ 1196 Nord de Guarre
ORGANIZATION Co F 358th Inf Regt Inf

SERIAL NUMBER	NAME	GRADE	CODE

RECORD OF EVENTS

30 Dec 44 Co remained in same position. Some artillery fire falling in our area. No casualties Morale good Weather clear and cold

OFFICER STRENGTH	FLD O & CAPT		1ST LT		2D LT		WO		PLT O	
	PRES	ABS'T	PRES	ABS'T	PRES	ABS'T	PRES	ABS'T	PRES	ABS'T
ASSIGNED	1		3		1					
TOTAL	1		3		1					

AVN CADET & ENLISTED STRENGTH	AVIATION CADETS		ENLISTED MEN			
	PRESENT	ABSENT	PRESENT FOR DUTY	PRESENT NOT FOR DY	ABSENT	TOTAL
ASSIGNED			191		13	204
TOTAL			191		13	204

RATIONS: ESTIMATED NUMBER OF RATIONS REQUIRED FOR DAY OF WEEK Thurs DATE 1 Jan 45 NUMBER 196
MESS ATTENDANCE FOR DAY OF THIS REPORT TOTAL 588 AVERAGE 196
BREAKFAST 196 DINNER 196 SUPPER 196
MEN PRESENT 191 LESS NET 191 MEN ATTCHD FOR RATIONS D & OTHERS MESSED 5 PLUS

PAGE 2 OF 2 PAGES

SIGNATURE

3

Morning Report for F Co, 358th Infantry, 90th Division dated 30 Dec 1944. National Personnel Records Center, St. Louis, MO.

Monthly Personnel Rosters

Monthly Personnel Rosters were created at the beginning of each month at the company level. Similar to a Morning Report, these reports listed every man in that company. Unfortunately many of these records were lost in the 1973 Fire at the NPRC. Some rosters may have found their way into some unit histories or the personal files of soldiers who kept them as souvenirs. You may discover some of these in donated papers to local museums, libraries, and archives.

Repository: National Archives, College Park, MD. Also check the unit files at National Archives, College Park, MD.

Monthly Personnel Roster, B Co 71st QM BN-LM, Camp Livingston, LA. National Personnel Records Center, St. Louis, MO.

Duty Rosters and Company Orders

Another set of records that may no longer exist are Duty Rosters. Duty Rosters were created each evening for the next day, outlining the fatigue duty of non-combat troops. There was a system for rotating jobs in which the man who had not worked a specific job, like Kitchen Police (KP), was next in line. These records typically do not exist within official records because they were used for each day and then destroyed, as there was no further use for them. Once again though, you may find these in personal collections, libraries, museums, and archives.

Looking at Company Orders, we may see something that says General Order Number 1. General Orders were issued at the company level with a '1' for the first order of each year. These often showed promotions at the company level from Private to Private First Class. In some cases these General Orders listed items of clothing or gear that had to be replaced by the soldier and the cost of that item.

Repository: National Archives, College Park, MD.

Army Air Force Accident Reports and Missing Air Crew Reports

Two record sets created specifically for the Army Air Corps are the Army Air Force Accident Reports and the Missing Air Crew Reports (MACRs). Both reports will be discussed and analyzed in detail in this section, and more fully explored in Volume 3 of this series.

These reports may appear to be similar, but they are used for different purposes. People often become confused about which report they need. Army Air Force Accident Reports were created for operational accidents, not aircraft that crashed due to combat damage. The accident did not always result in the death of the pilot or crew. In general, these reports were created for accidents in the United States, although some exist for accidents in England. Air Force Accident Reports will document Army Air Corps personnel onboard the planes.

MACR's were created in mid-1943 and primarily covered combat losses, but sometimes exist for aircraft that went missing on operational flights overseas. These reports were filed within 48 hours of a plane going missing unless the crew made it back to friendly lines before 48 hours had elapsed. MACRs not only document fighter pilots or bombing crews, but also hospital planes or troop transports, which may have carried personnel in other branches of the military. If your soldier was declared MIA due to an air crash, regardless of branch, this is one record you should seek.

There are instances when a combat loss occurred, but no MACR was completed, particularly prior to their inception in mid-1943. In the North African and Pacific Theaters, MACRs are not often found. The reason for this is unknown. Perhaps, due to the timeframe of the North African campaign, the information was recorded elsewhere. The pilots who flew in the Pacific Theater completed missions spanning greater distances from base, and often island hopped. It is unclear if MACRs were not used as extensively, or simply lost. In these instances, you should check Mission/Sortie Reports, Morning Reports, and Unit Histories for additional details. Searching the collaterals in these cases is also a good idea, as it may lead to additional resources.

You will discover throughout these volumes that the different branches of the military created similar records. The Navy used an Accident Report for pilots involved in an accident and who were lost or declared MIA rather than two separate reports. These reports were typically only one to two pages in length prior to 1952. Only the basic facts were listed on the report. Additional details may be found within the IDPF or Deck Logs. This report will be explored more in Volumes 2 and 3.

There are some exceptions to the definitions and use of the records above. In a conversation with Craig Fuller of Aviation Archaeology, when I obtained some of these reports, he provided a few scenarios for these valuable records.

Scenario 1: It is possible to have an accident report for an aircraft that was on a combat mission. For instance, if two bombers took off for a bombing mission and collided midair during the form up over England, this would be an accident report. Now, if that midair occurred over Germany while on a bombing run, this would likely be an MACR because they would not know if it was an operational accident, or if one of the planes had combat damage, causing it to fly into the other aircraft.

Scenario 2: You will also see MACR's with aircraft that took off from the US en-route to a destination overseas, but the airplane never showed up. While it is likely that these airplanes crashed and were not shot down, there is a slight possibility they were shot, and again, the crew is missing, so a MACR is appropriate.

Scenario 3: On occasion, there are both a MACR and an accident report for a loss. The scenario just described where it is not sure whether the plane was shot down or it crashed into the ocean, so it might have both reports, or might only have one. Other cases are when a plane was missing and then, after being found, it was determined it crashed due to an accident rather than combat damage.

Army Air Force Accident Reports

The Army Air Force Accident Reports vary in content and length, but the main components remain the same. Air Force Accident Reports are usually indexed by the pilot's name. Searching for a co-pilot or crew member may not be easy. In those cases, you want to write to the National Archives, Air Force Historical Research Agency, or Aviation Archaeology to ask for a search of your crewmember. Try to provide the date of the accident or date range, location of accident, and any other information, such as service number and rank on that soldier. Let's examine the components of 2nd Lt. Fred Davis' Accident Report throughout this section.

Report of Accident

The Report of Accident document contained the main pieces of information which included:

• Names of all crew on board, along with rank and service number.

• Type of plane flown.

• Mission or training run information.

• Number of hours flown in that type of aircraft or in general.

• Location of crash.

• Location of base from which aircraft departed.

Description of Accident and Witness Reports

Depending on when, where, and how the accident occurred, there may or may not be witnesses. If someone witnessed the accident, a write-up about what was seen will be included in the report. The War Department conducted a full investigation into the crashes, and some reports contain many pages of testimony about the pieces of the crash, secret equipment on the planes, different possibilities for the crash, and the final determination of the cause. In some cases, the cause is undetermined and remains a mystery because no witnesses were available, or the wreckage is such that nothing official can be determined.

Photographs and Maps

Most reports contain photographs of the crash scene. These are not the best photographs, as they have been microfilmed with the report, thus, they appear dark and grainy in many cases. They do, however, give you somewhat of an idea of what the crash scene looked like. Accidents occurring away from an airfield may contain maps with diagrams of the crash scene. Officials study the terrain, elevation, obstacles (buildings, trees, mountains, etc.) that may have contributed to the accident. Diagrams exist, in some cases, for the spread of wreckage.

Description of Accident or Summary of Report

A description of the accident with a summary will be included in these reports. The report will describe the crash, list those involved, when and where it occurred, summarize the information in the entire report, and often provide recommendations for the pilot or crew and Air Corps.

Repository: National Archives, College Park, MD. Air Force Historical Research Agency. Aviation Archaeology website.

Questions an Air Force Accident Report May Answer:

1. What was his service number?
2. When and where did the accident occur?
3. What unit was he in?
4. Was the pilot or crew declared MIA or KIA?
5. If pilot or crew was KIA, what were the circumstances surrounding the deaths and recovery?

WAR DEPARTMENT
A. A. F. Form No. 14
(Revised May 15, 1942)

ACCIDENT No. 110

WAR DEPARTMENT
Kellogg Field, Battle Creek, Michigan
U. S. ARMY AIR FORCES

REPORT OF AIRCRAFT ACCIDENT

(1) Place ... Kellogg Field, Battle Creek, Mich., (2) Date ... 8 Sept. 1943 (3) Time 1515

AIRCRAFT: (4) Type and model ... B-24-D (5) A. F. No. 42-72891 (6) Station Herington, Kansas

Organization: (7) 2nd A.F. (8) 6th H.Proc. (9)

(Command and Air Force)   (Group)   (Squadron)

PERSONNEL

UNIT (10)	NAME (Last name first) (11)	RATING (12)	SERIAL NO. (13)	RANK (14)	PERSONNEL CLASS (15)	BRANCH (16)	AIR FORCE OR COMMAND (17)	RESULT TO PERSONNEL (18)	USE OF PARACHUTE (19)
P	JEFFRIES, F.S.	P	O-671943	2nd Lt.	01	AC	2nd AF	None	None
CP	DAVIS, F.A.	CP	O-683416	"	01	"	"	"	"
N	EGAN, E.F.	N	O-673122	"	01	"	"	"	"
B	MC ATEE, C.G.	B	O-667317	"	01	"	"	"	"
E	FULWILER, H.D.	E	13065667	S/Sgt	30	"	"	"	"
R	KEON, L.F.	R	31081963	Pvt.	30	"	"	"	"
AE	BONNET, F.C.	AE	12080483	Sgt.	30	"	"	"	"
AR	RICKARD, C.J.	AR	32447608	Sgt.	30	"	"	"	"
AG	WOLFE, L.G.	AG	36531556	Sgt.	30	"	"	"	"
G	FLEISCHBEIN, F.A.	G	19088594	Pvt.	30	"	"	"	"

PILOT CHARGED WITH ACCIDENT

(20) JEFFRIES FRENCH S. (21) O-671943 (22) 2nd Lt. (23) A.C. (24) O-R

(Last name) (First name) (Middle initial) (Serial number) (Rank) (Personnel class) (Branch)

Assigned (25) 2nd A.F. (26) 6th Heavy Processing (27) (28) Herington, Kan.

(Command and Air Force)   (Group)   (Squadron)   (Station)

Attached for flying (29) 2nd A.F. (30) 6th H.Proc (31) (32) Herington, Kan.

(Command and Air Force)   (Group)   (Squadron)   (Station)

Original rating (33) Pilot (34) 2/16/43 Present rating (35) Pilot (36) 2/16/43 Instrument rating (37) 8/3/43

(Rating)   (Date)   (Rating)   (Date)   (Date)

FIRST PILOT HOURS:
(at the time of this accident)

(38) This type ... APP 211
(39) This model ... 211
(40) Last 90 days ... 100
(41) Total ...

(42) Instrument time last 6 months ... 50 hrs
(43) Instrument time last 30 days ... 10 "
(44) Night time last 6 months ... 100 "
(45) Night time last 30 days ...

AIRCRAFT DAMAGE

	DAMAGE			(49) LIST OF DAMAGED PARTS
(46) Aircraft	3			Left wing tip "O" Slight damage to hangar door
(47) Engine(s)	4	/	/	Possible damage to No. 1 engine
(48) Propeller(s)	#1 "O"	/	/	Prop on No. 1 Engine

(50) Weather at the time of accident ... Clear

(51) Was the pilot flying on instruments at the time of accident ... No

(52) Cleared from Herington, Kan. (53) To Kellogg (54) Kind of clearance Instrument

(55) Pilot's mission ... Flying to P.O.E., Bangor, Maine

(56) Nature of accident ... Taxi

(57) Cause of accident ... Left brake did not hold and plane swung to right hitting hangar wall prop on No. 1, hit hangar doors ruining prop.

Air Force Accident Report. Report of Aircraft Accident no. 44-9-8-59, dated 8 Sept 1943. Aviation Archaeology.

Accident Report Testimony

HEADQUARTERS ARMY AIR BASE
KELLOGG FIELD, BATTLE CREEK, MICHIGAN
ACCIDENT INVESTIGATION COMMITTEE

8 September 1943

SUBJECT: Statement of Navigator
EGAN, E.F. 2nd Lt., A.C., (AUS)
A.S.N. 0-673122
Home Station - Herington, Kansas

TO   ; Whom it may concern

1. Accident report to Airplane B-24-D Serial #42-72891 at
Kellogg Field, Battle Creek, Michigan, 8 September 1943.   I was
riding in waist of airplane as it was being taxied over to hangar
for repairs to No. 2 engine.   I was changing from flying clothes
to uniform and not observing what was occurring. Didn't realize
anything was amiss until sound of plane's wing striking hangar -
noticed glass flying and then found that our left wing tip had hit
hangar wall and prop of No. 1 engine pushed through the glass in
hangar doors. Only structural damage apparentwas damaged propeller
and slightly damaged wing tip. Faulty brake was answer to accident
given by Co-Pilot and Assistant Engineer.

EDWARD F. EGAN
2nd Lt., Air Corps

CERTIFIED CORRECT:

G. M. Hendricks
G. M. HENDRICKS
1st Lt., A.C.,

Air Force Accident Report. Testimony of Navigator, Accident no. 44-9-8-59, dated 8 Sept 1943. Aviation Archaeology.

157

Accident Report Photos

PROP & HANGAR DOOR DAMAGE

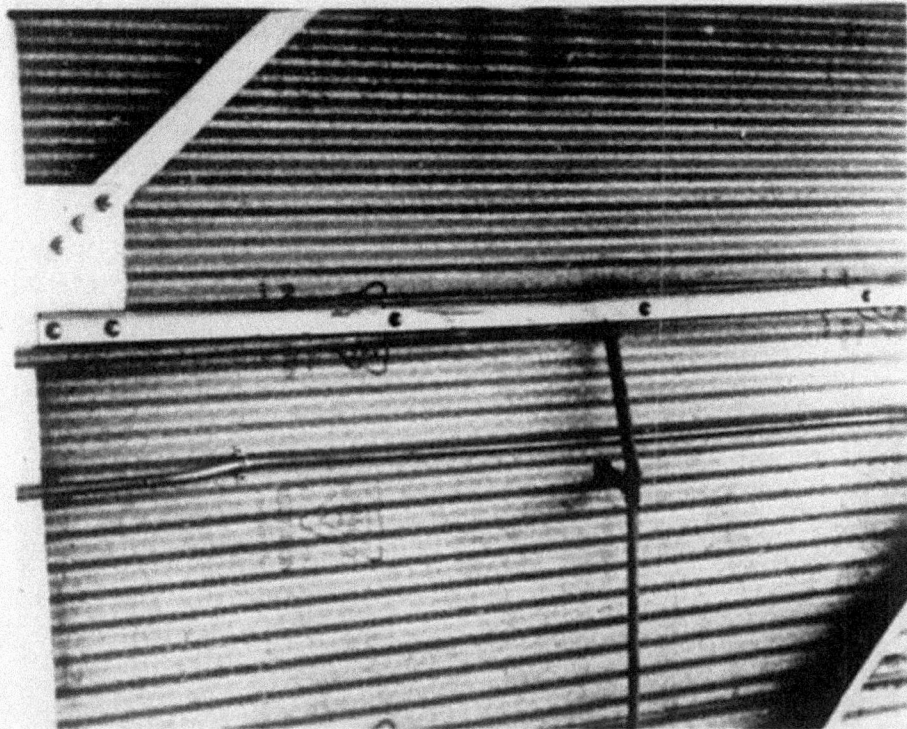

BROKEN WATER PIPE IN HANGAR

Air Force Accident Report. Photographs Accident no. 44-9-8-59, dated 8 Sept 1943. Aviation Archaeology.

Summary of Accident

DESCRIPTION OF ACCIDENT

(Brief narrative of accident. Include statement of responsibility and recommendations for action to prevent repetition)

NARATIVE

A B-24-D airplane A.F. No. 42-72891, pilot Jeffries, F.S., 2nd Lt., A.C., O-671943, arrived at Kellogg Field 8 September 1943 at 1300.

At about 1500 of same date, Co-Pilot Davis, F.A., 2nd Lt., A.C., O-683416, started to taxi the airplane to the transient hangar. As he came into parking position in front of the hangar and attempted the use of brakes, he was confronted by complete braking failure of the left brake. The airplane pivoted to the right, right wheel remaining almost stationary and the left wheel and wing pivoting slightly toward the hangar. The left wing passed through hangar door with the No. 1 outboard propeller striking the side of the hangar and hangar door. The left wing tip was damaged in the contact. No. 1 engine was cut off before hitting the door but was still turning over when it hit, damaging the prop and the door.

Sub-Depot and Base Engineering personnel were immediately called and the airplane removed to Sub-Depot for repairs.

RESPONSIBILITY

As a result of statements of witnesses, it is the Committee's opinion that the accident was a direct result of materiel failure. Experienced Sub-Depot personnel who investigated the hydraulic braking system found that it was completely inoperative.

RECOMMENDATIONS

1. Airplanes bound for overseas shipment should undergo rigorous and thorough inspections before being released to combat crews.

2. Personnel parking airplanes adjacent to buildings should attempt to come to a stop at sufficient distance from such buildings as to enable them, in case of complete braking failure, to turn the airplane by use of throttle and rudder so that it would clear all obstacles.

3. In view of the nature of the accident, no constructive recommendations can be made in regards to personnel.

Signature G. M. Hendricks
Investigating Officer
G.M.HENDRICKS, 1st Lt., AirCorps

8 September 1943

Air Force Accident Report. Summary Accident no. 44-9-8-59, dated 8 Sept 1943. Aviation Archaeology.

Missing Air Crew Reports

Missing Air Crew Reports (MACRs) differ from Accident Reports, because they were created for pilots and crew who either crashed or were lost overseas in combat conditions. Only the Army Air Corps used these reports, and you will not find MACRs for Navy or Marine aviators. Reports of those missing from the Navy and Marine Corps are found in Mission Reports, which will be explored in Volumes 2 and 3. MACRs differ based on the circumstance of the combat loss, but main components include the following.

MACRs often provide many clues to help you continue the research on your pilot or crew member. You can explore the mission they flew, the area over which they crashed, how their remains were recovered (or not), and the unit to which they belonged. Make sure to obtain the IDPF for the crew member if he perished in a crash.

The Missing Air Crew Report

The main document contained in MACR is the Missing Air Crew Report. This document contains the name, rank, unit, and service number of crew members, location within the plane or bomber of each crew member, destination of the plane, and location of the crash or approximate location the plane went missing. The type of aircraft, equipment with service numbers on board, and details about the mission and crash or loss status are also included. Name, rank, and service number of those who witnessed the downing of an aircraft are listed at the bottom of the report.

Downing Report

The Downing Report contains information on the combat loss, including date and location, cause, and the fate of the crew. A combat report, sketch of the area in which the plane was lost, and witness statements are often included.

German Documents

Within European Theater MACRs, there may be German documents and translations of those documents. The Germans documented the planes they shot down, number of crew killed or captured, and credited those losses to a specific unit within the German Army. These reports may provide additional details to assist in locating buried airmen.

Maps/Diagrams

Maps or diagrams may be found within the file, showing the formation of a bomber group in relation to what happened to the lost plane(s). German documents may provide additional details, including coordinates, with a diagram or map.

Testimony on the Combat Loss and Location of Possible Graves or POW Status

Depending on the type and location of the loss, reports may exist within both the European Theater and Pacific Theater as to the fate of the crew. Testimony taken by military units during the war, or the Graves Registration Service during or after the war, may shed light on the fate of the crew.
Examine the MACR located after this section, for the 345th Bomb Group, 500th Bomb Squadron, crew of

160

pilot James C. Buffington, dated 9 January 1945. This plane's crew took off from Tacloban Strip at Leyte, destined for Luzon. The plane was last sighted by Cpl. Myron Mauldin.

The pages following the MACR contain testimony taken after the war, when the soldier was already home in the U.S., dated 24 April 1946. His testimony describes the recovery of some crew members of a B-25 that crashed in the area. In the end, the crew was deemed unrecoverable by Graves Registration.

It is important to understand the information contained in a MACR may not always be for the airmen listed in the report. In the Pacific Theater, when planes went down in remote locations or several were downed in an area, several things could have caused the unrecoverable status of airmen.

Testimonies taken may have been months or years after the plane was lost. Memories fade or become jumbled. Airmen may have been buried, but records were either lost or not kept in the first place. Have you ever played the telephone game where a message was passed, and by the last person it barely resembles the original message? Instead of a record, information passed by word of mouth and was lost. Over time, remains may have been moved or destroyed due to war. There are numerous other reasons for information provided later to be incorrect or insufficient to recover remains. This will be discussed further in Volume 3, when I explore in greater depth, the death and associated records.

Additional Personnel Onboard – Non-Army Air Corps Personnel

Missing planes did not always carry only Air Corps personnel. Hospital planes and troop transport planes were also lost. In the following example, using MACR 13672, you will see not only airmen, but Marines, Army, and Navy personnel or patients onboard the aircraft. This aircraft was going from Mindoro to Leyte. The MACR is shown detailing the mission or flight.

Following the testimony discussed above, the following page lists all the personnel and patients missing due to the aircraft loss. Note at the bottom, the * explaining which patients were not U.S. Army Personnel or Not U.S. Personnel.

The final page shown, is the beginning of a list of each soldier on the aircraft and his next-of-kin to be notified. This page is blurry and difficult to read.

Finally, if members of a crew were captured as POWs, information concerning their capture may be contained within the MACR.

Repository: National Archives, College Park, MD. Air Force Historical Research Agency. Aviation Archaeology website. Fold3.com.

Tip: Fold3.com (a paid site) does have some MACRs available.

Questions a MACR May Answer:

1. For every individual listed in the MACR, what is their name, rank, unit, and service number?
2. Where was the aircraft stationed, and what was its destination?
3. When and where did the accident occur?
4. What was the fate of the crew (MIA, KIA, and POW?)
5. Was there a definitive MIA, KIA, or FOD date?
6. Were the remains buried? Where? Were they recovered?

MACR #1143 2nd Lt. Fred A. Davis

U.S. CONFIDENTIAL EQUALS BRITISH CONFIDENTIAL
XXXXXXXXX

WAR DEPARTMENT
HEADQUARTERS ARMY AIR FORCES
WASHINGTON
MISSING AIR CREW REPORT

Classification changed
to RESTRICTED
by E. A. BRADUNAS, Lt. Col., AC
by F. M. MUENCH, Capt., AC
Date MAR 1 1946

IMPORTANT: This report will be compiled in triplicate by each Army Air
Forces organization within 48 hours of the time an aircraft
is officially reported missing.

1. ORGANIZATION: Location Hergla, Tunisia ; Command or Air Force 12th Air Force
Group 98th Bomb (H) ; Squadron 344th Bomb (H); Detachment
2. SPECIFY: Point of Departure Hergla, Tunisia ; Course North-North East
Intended Destination Wiener Neustadt, Austria Type of Mission Bomb Factory
3. WEATHER CONDITIONS AND VISIBILITY AT TIME OF CRASH OR WHEN LAST REPORTED:
Good
4. GIVE: (a) Date 2/11/43 ; Time 11.30 Gmt ; and Location Wiener Neustadt, Austria
of last known whereabouts of missing aircraft.
(b) Specify whether (x) Last Sighted; ( ) Last Contacted by Radio;
( ) Forced down; ( ) Seen to Crash; or ( ) Information not Available.
5. AIRCRAFT WAS LOST, OR IS BELIEVED TO HAVE BEEN LOST, AS A RESULT OF: (Check only
one ( ) Enemy Aircraft; (X) Enemy Anti-Aircraft; ( ) Other circumstances as
Follows _____
6. AIRCRAFT: Type, Model and Series B-2 ; A.A.F. Serial Number 42-72891
7. ENGINES: Type, Model and Series R-1830-65 A.A.F. Serial Number(a) 42-42150
(a) R-1830-43 (b) 42-90957 ; (c) 42-90956 ; (d) 4291042
8. INSTALLED WEAPONS (Furnish below Make, and Serial Number)
(a) 748714 ; (b) 272891 ; (c) 396277 ; (d) 746691
(e) 748905 ; (f) 375529 ; (g) 382418 ; (h) 396251
9. THE PERSONS LISTED BELOW WERE REPORTED AS: (a) Battle Casualty X
or (b) Non-Battle Casualty
10. NUMBER OF PERSONS ABOARD AIRCRAFT: Crew 10 ; Passengers ; Total 10
(Starting with pilot, furnish the following particulars: If more than 10
persons were aboard aircraft, list similar particulars on separate sheet and
attach original to this form.)

	Crew Position	Name in Full (Last Name First)	Rank	Serial Number
DED 1.	Pilot	Jeffries, French Stewart	2nd Lt.	O-671943
DED 2.	Co-Pilot	Davis, Frederick Allen	2nd Lt.	O-683416
DED 3.	Navigator	Egan, Edward Frederick	2nd Lt.	O-673122
DOD 4.	Bombardier	Chalk, William Raymond, Jr.	2nd Lt.	O-676423
PMC 5.	Engineer	Fulwiler, Harold Dean	T/Sgt.	13066667
EUS 6.	Radio Operator	Rowe, Gordon Allen	T/Sgt.	32143337 RTD
RMC 7.	Asslt Engineer	Bonnet, Fred Charles	S/Sgt.	18080483
DED 8.	Asslt Radio	Rickard, Charles Jenkins	S/Sgt.	32447609
KIA 9.	Armorer Gunner	Fleischbein, Fred Anton	Sgt.	19088594
EUS 10.	Tail Gunner	Wolfe, Lawrence Garnet	S/Sgt.	36531556 RTD

11. IDENTIFY BELOW THE PERSONS WHO ARE BELIEVED TO HAVE LAST KNOWLEDGE OF AIR-
CRAFT AND CHECK APPROPRIATE COLUMN TO INDICATE BASIS FOR SAME:

Check only one Column

Name in Full (Last Name First)	Rank	Serial Number	Contacted By Radio	Last Sighted	Saw Crash	Forced Landing
1. White, James Guy	2nd Lt.	O-671198		X		
2. Syroid, Walter Anthony	2nd Lt.	O-678786		X		
3. Willingham, Nelson Holmes	2nd Lt.	O-680355		X		

12. IF PARACHUTES WERE USED, CHECK THE APPROPRIATE ONE OF THE FOLLOWING
STATEMENTS: (a) Parachutes were used yes; (b) Persons were seen walking away
from scene of crash ; or (c) Any other reason (Specify)
13. ATTACH AERIAL PHOTOGRAPH, MAP, CHART, OR SKETCH, SHOWING APPROXIMATE LOCATION
WHERE AIRCRAFT WAS LAST SEEN.
14. ATTACH EYEWITNESS DESCRIPTION OF CRASH, FORCED LANDING, OR OTHER CIRCUMSTANCES
PERTAINING TO MISSING AIRCRAFT.
15. ATTACH A DESCRIPTION OF THE STATUS OF SPARES IN AIRCRAFT WITH NAME, RANK AND
SERIAL NUMBER None

Date of Report 6 November 1943

Donald [signature]
DONALD [ ], 1st Lt., AC
[ ] of TROUBLE OFFICER.

XXXXXXXXX

U.S. CONFIDENTIAL EQUALS BRITISH CONFIDENTIAL

Missing Air Crew Report #1143, dated 6 Nov 1943. Aviation Archaeology.

163

MACR #1143 Downing Report

In cooperation with: Heavy Home Battery 201/XVII
              & 1st/Heavy AAA Bn 543 (RR)
              & Spec. Batt. 6395 (O)
              & Spec. Batt. 6396 (O)

For Lft R/169/44
Unit: 2d Heavy AAA Bn 290   Observation Post, 4 Nov 43
                                  Place & Date
& 1st/J.G. 27 (Sergeant Schanz)Ri   RED

Downing Report

1. Time (Day, Hour, Minute) of Crash: 2 Nov 43, crashed 1232 Hours
    Exact place of crash, indicate map & coord: Poettsching, r.5602880,
    h/5295150. Map Sheet 4856/57
    Altitude: 7700 meters; alt. of crash: 7200 meters

2. By which unit was downing effected: 2d Heavy AAA Bn 290

3. Type of shot down a/c: Liberator
    Factory No. &/or Markings: Side of tail assembly: L 272891
                               Fuselage: B 24 BCO 166, green "L"

4. Nationality of Enemy: U.S.A.

5. Manner of Destruction and Impact:
    a) flames, with light column of smoke
    b) individual parts flew off, dismantled, exploded
    ....
    e) this side of the front (lines)

6. Fate of Crew: 5 dead; rest bailed out: fate unknown.

7. Why was manner of crash &/or fate of crew not observed: not observed
    because visibility obstructed.

8. Which witnesses
    a) clearly observed crash: Hugo Wenninger, Poettsching
    b) established place of crash: Friedr. Preissegger, Poetsching

Detailed Combat Report of Battery Commander and 2 original witness accounts
are enclosed with the documents.

                                      /s/ (illegible)
CERTIFIED ACCURATE TRANSLATION   Captain & Battery Commander

Carl W. Davis

CARL W. DAVIS, 5 Aug 47

Missing Air Crew Report #1143, Downing Report, dated 5 Aug 1947. Aviation Archaeology.

AA Group, Wiener-Neustadt   Batt. Observation Post, 4 Nov 43
AA Unit, Neudoerfl
2d Heavy AA Unit 290

Combat Report

of Fire of 2/290 on 2 Nov 43, during period 1229-1230 Hours.

a) Date and Time of approaching flight and engagement:
2 Nov 43, 1230 - 1231 Hours. Exploded 1231 Hours.

b) Altitude and estimated speed of target:
Approaching flight 7,700 meters alt., crash alt. 7,200 m., speed 110m/sec.

c) Number of planes and direction of approaching formation; direction of
target: 40-50 craft, approaching 8-9, departing 3-6.

d) Position of Battery, type and number of weapons in action: part
r. 5594.500   h. 528900   Unit Sheet: 4956
8.5/8.8(r)   4 barrels

e) Method of Fire: Destruction fire with Flug-Malsi 43 and Control, target
optically sighted.
Method of fire: Rapid bursts.
Ammo. used: 32 rounds, 8.8 cm

f) Precise data on behavior of formation, particularly the target while under
fire, number of downings in final Combat Report (also by fighters):
In spite of fire, formation kept on course toward objective, a number of
craft trailed white smoke after hits.

g) Participation of other AA units (Army and Navy): Other batteries of the
AA Regt 88(0) fired.

h) Action of own fighter craft (description of attack, number of fighters):
Own fighters engaged the enemy.

i) Weather conditions on target: 0/10 overcast, sunny, hazy.

k) Own losses and damages: none.

l) Other important details for determination of the foregoing: ------

                                        /s/ (illegible)
                                        Captain & Batt. Comdr

CERTIFIED ACCURATE TRANSLATION

Carl W. Davis

CARL W. DAVIS, 5 Aug 47

Missing Air Crew Report #1143, Downing Report, dated 5 Aug 1947. Aviation Archaeology.

Tracing of Course of Target of (Batt.) 2/290, at Downing of Liberator
on 2 Nov 1943.

Place of Crash: Poettsching
Scale: 1:75,000

S K E T C H

Place of Crash: Poettsching
1232 Hours
Battery: 2/290
Shot down from: Wiener-Neustadt
A/C Type: Liberator
Date: 2 Nov 43
Time Shot Down: 1231 Hours
Duration of Fire: 60 seconds
Duration of Action: 80 seconds
Altitude: 7700 meters
Speed: 110 m/sec.
Range: 1/Gp: 5400 m.
Azimuth: 5100 m.
Gun elevation: 65 deg.
Fuse: 315 deg. ∕

Range, last gp: 4800 m.
Azimuth: 1050
Elevation: 65 deg.
No. guns: 4
Station Control: Flug-Malsi-43
w/suppl.
Coord. of place of crash:
r. 5602880
h. 5295150
Coord. of position:
r. 5594,300
h/ 5298,000
Unit sheet: 4856

CERTIFIED ACCURATE TRANSLATION:

Carl W. Davis

CARL W. DAVIS, 5 Aug 47

/s/ illegible
Capt. & Batt. Comdr

Missing Air Crew Report #1143, Downing Report, dated 5 Aug 1947. Aviation Archaeology.

AA Unit, Theresienfeld   Command Post, 27 Nov 43
(Heavy AA 290(0)

Remarks on Downing of a Liberator on 2 Nov 43
Place of Crash: Poettsching

    The action of the craft, after being hit by AA fire, wrapped in
flames, falling out of formation toward the left and loss of altitude,
as well as exploding in the air, was observed by the unit command post,
as well as by the witness Mayor Treuer of Poettsching. Fighters were
not observed in the vicinity of this formation. It is requested that
the participating batteries 6395, 6396 and 1/543 (RR) each be credited
with taking part in a downing (2 points).

                         M.d.W.d.G.b.
                         /s/ Astgauer
                         Major

CERTIFIED ACCURATE TRANSLATION

Carl W. Davis

CARL W. DAVIS, 5 Aug 47

Missing Air Crew Report #1143, Downing Report, dated 5 Aug 1947. Aviation Archaeology.

AA Artillery Group, Wiener-Neustadt   Command Post, 16 Nov 1943
AA Regt 88(C)

<u>Commanding Officer</u>

<u>Remarks on Downing of a Liberator on 2 Nov 43
Place of Crash: Poettsching</u>

        After being hit by a short burst of AA fire, the plane which crashed
at Poettsching was observed enveloped in flames and losing altitude.
Shortly thereafter an explosion occurred and the craft blew apart in the
air. This was observed by the mayor of the community of Poettsching,
district of Eisenstadt. The accounts of the witnesses, Town Inspector
Hugo Wenninger of Poettsching, and the farmer Friedrich Preissegger of
Poettsching, is important in establishing this.

        Documents and sketches submitted by the batteries show no discrep-
ancies. Moreover, the recorded tracing of the target lead only to the
conclusion, that the craft was engaged by the batteries simultaneously,
and was thus brought down.

        It is therefore requested, that the participating batteries,
6395(0), 6396(0), 1/543 (RR), 2/290 and 201/XVII, each be accredited
with taking part in a downing.

                                        Authorized by
                                        /s/ Nicolas
                                        Oberstleutnant (1/Lt)

CERTIFIED ACCURATE TRANSLATION

Carl W. Davis

CARL W. DAVIS, 5 Aug 47

Erratum: Preissegger address is given as Poettsching, Hauptstrasse 13.

Missing Air Crew Report #1143, Downing Report, dated 5 Aug 1947. Aviation Archaeology.

168

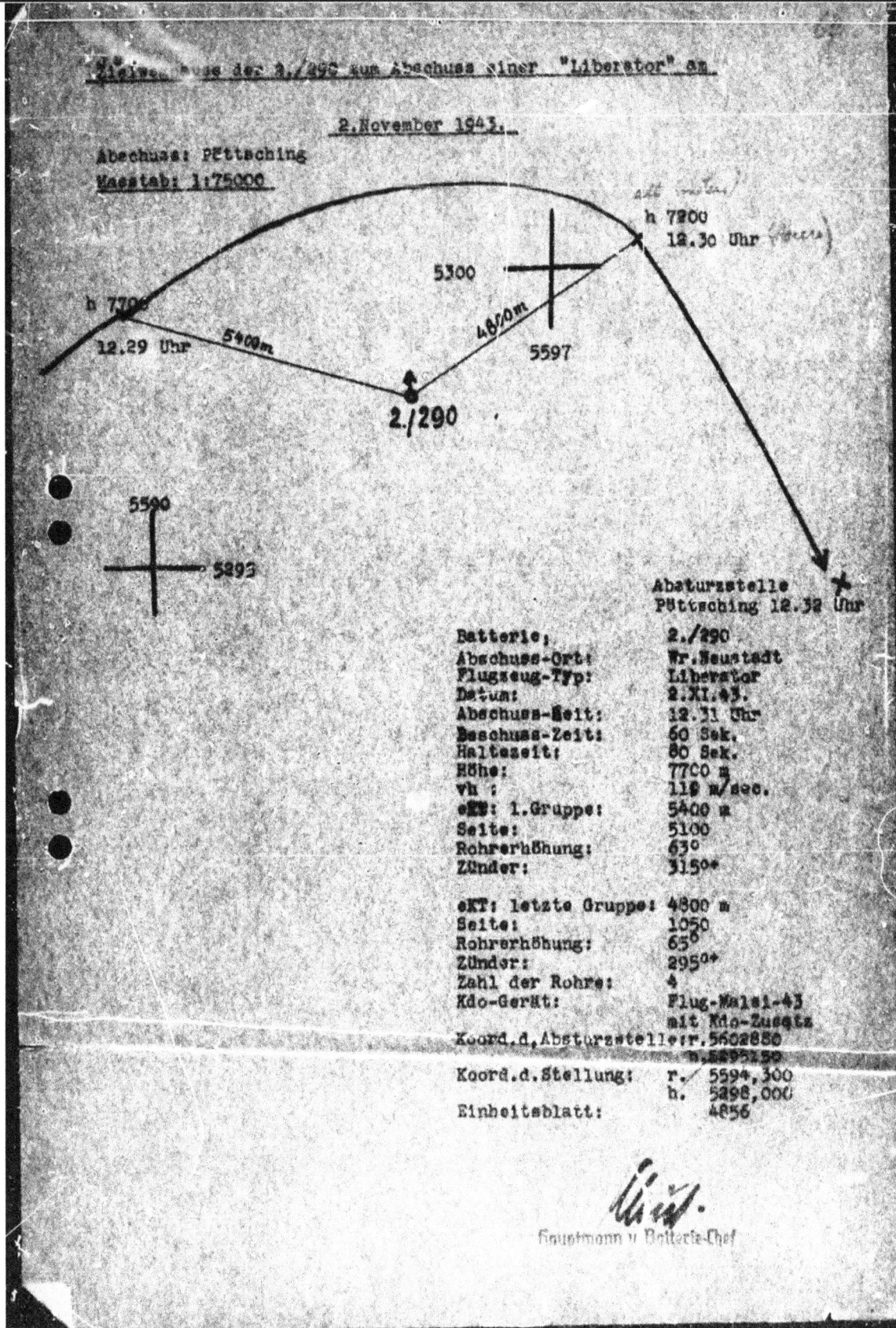

Missing Air Crew Report #1143, German Map. Aviation Archaeology.

MACR #13672 - Hospital Plane

CONFIDENTIAL

WAR DEPARTMENT
HEADQUARTERS ARMY AIR FORCES
WASHINGTON

MISSING AIR CREW REPORT

Classification changed
to RESTRICTED
by _____ Mas. Lt. Col., AC
by R. M. _____ H, Capt., AC
Date _____ MAR _____

1. ORGANIZATION: Location by Name ___Tanauan___ ; Command or Air Force . 5th AF
   Group 433rd T. C. ___ ; Squadron 69th T. C. ; Detachment
2. SPECIFY: Place of Departure ___Elmore (Mindoro)___ ; Course Elmore to Tanauan
   Target or Intended Destination Tanauan (Leyte) ; Type of Mission Air Evac.
3. WEATHER CONDITIONS AND VISIBILITY AT TIME OF CRASH OR WHEN LAST REPORTED: _____
   ___Unknown___
4. GIVE: (a) Day 12 (Month Mar ;Year 1945; Time 1045; and Location Elmore Strip
   of last known whereabouts of missing aircraft.
   (b) Specify whether aircraft was last sighted (X); Last contacted by
   radio ( ); Forced down ( ); Seen to Crash ( ); or Information not Available ( );
5. AIRCRAFT WAS LOST, OR IS BELIEVED TO HAVE BEEN LOST, AS A RESULT OF: (Check
   only one) Enemy Aircraft ( ); Enemy Anti-Aircraft ( ); Other Circumstances as
   follows: ___ Weather
6. AIRCRAFT: Type, Model and Series ___C-46D___ ; AAF Serial Number __44-77373__
7. NICKNAME OF AIRCRAFT, If any ___None___
8. ENGINES: Type, Model and Series P & W R2800-51 : AAF Serial Number
   (a) Left FP-0____89 (b) FP-081985 ; (c) _____ ; (d) _____
9. INSTALLED WEAPONS (Furnish below Make, Type and Serial Number);
   (a) ___2 Thompson Sub-Machine Guns___ ; (b) _____ ; (c) _____
10. THE PERSONS LISTED BELOW WERE REPORTED AS; (a) Battle Casualty _____
    or (b) Non Battle Casualty ___X___
11. NUMBER OF PERSONS ABOARD AIRCRAFT: Crew 4 Passengers Unknown ; Total Unknown
    (Starting with Pilot, furnish the following particulars: If more than 11 persons
    were aboard aircraft, list similar particulars on separate sheet and attach ori-
    ginal to this form.)

	Crew Position	Name in Full (Last Name First)	Grade	Serial Number	Current Status
DED 1.	Pilot	Kelly, Leo J.	2nd Lt.	O-899426	Missing
DED 2.	Co-pilot	Healy, Paul A.	2nd Lt.	O-769437	Missing
DED 3.	Engineer	Oja, Theodore S.	Sgt.	17158005	Missing
DEP 4.	Radio Operator	Kiester, Charles W.	S/Sgt	33080628	Missing
5.	See Attachment No. 4, list of medical attendants and patients.				
6.					
7.					
8.					
9.					
10.					
11.					

Incl 1

-1-

CONFIDENTIAL

Missing Air Crew Report #13672, dated 13 Mar 1945. Aviation Archaeology.

CONFIDENTIAL

12. IDENTIFY BELOW THOSE PERSONS WHO ARE BELIEVED TO HAVE LAST KNOWLEDGE OF AIRCRAFT, AND CHECK APPROPRIATE COLUMN TO INDICATE BASIS FOR SAME:

Check only one Column

Name in Full (Last Name First)	Grade	Serial Number	Contacted by Radio	Last Sighted	Saw Crash	Forced Landing
1. Daugherty, Robert W.	2nd Lt.	O-820962		X		
2. Operations Officer, Elmore Strip.			X			

13. IF PERSONNEL ARE BELIEVED TO HAVE SURVIVED, ANSWER YES TO ONE OF THE FOLLOWING STATEMENTS: (a) Parachutes were used ___; (b) Persons were seen walking away from scene of crash ___; or (c) Any other reason (Specify) Unknown

14. ATTACH AERIAL PHOTOGRAPH, MAP, CHART OR SKETCH, SHOWING APPROXIMATE LOCATION WHERE AIRCRAFT WAS LAST SEEN OR HEARD FROM (Airplane was last seen at Elmore Strip, Mindoro, therefore map, chart, etc. not pertinent.)

15. ATTACH EYEWITNESS DESCRIPTION OF CRASH, FORCED LANDING, OR OTHER CIRCUMSTANCES PERTAINING TO MISSING AIRCRAFT. (See Attachment No. 1)

16. GIVE NAME, GRADE AND SERIAL NUMBER OF OFFICER IN CHARGE OF SEARCH, IF ANY, INCLUDING DESCRIPTION AND EXTENT   No search has been made yet due to weather, but queries have been sent out through AACS, 433rd Troop Carrier Group, and 54th Troop Carrier Wing.

Date of Report 13 March, 1945.

(Signature of Presenting Officer)
RALPH C. ALEXANDER,
Captain, Air Corps,
Commanding.

17. REMARKS OR EYEWITNESS STATEMENTS: (See attachments)

3 ATTACHMENTS:

1. Statement of 2nd Lt. Robert W. Daugherty.
2. Statement of 1st Lt. Bruce L. Marble
3. Message from 69th Sq. to Elmore Strip.
4. List of patients and medical personnel aboard X366.

Incl. 1

-2-

CONFIDENTIAL

Missing Air Crew Report #13672, dated 13 Mar 1945. Aviation Archaeology.

MACR #13672 - Additional Personnel MIA

HEADQUARTERS
54TH TROOP CARRIER WING
APO 248

MEDICAL PERSONNEL ABOARD X366, MISSING 12 MARCH 1945

STATUS	NAME	RANK	ASN	ORGN
	Medical Attendants:			
	Memler, Beatrice H.	2nd Lt.	N-788562	804th MAES
	Hudson, John H.	T/3	18216869	804th MAES
	Patients			
DNB	1. Adamsky, Thomas (NMI)	Pfc	33395514	Hqs 21st Inf Regt
DNB	2. Cots, Fabian T.	T/4	39842703	Hq & Sv 658 Amph Trac Bn
DNB	3. Ingalls, Phillip	Pvt	32472946	13th Sta Hosp
DNB	4. Sintic, Joseph E.	Pvt	35919729	21st Inf Regt
DNB	5. Jahnke, Ray S.	Pfc	36025963	D 186th Inf Regt
DNB	6. Meagher, Harry B.	Pvt	39328703	405 Sig Co Avn
DNB	7. Arel, Gerald P.	Pvt	31383697	3144 Sig Sv Det
DNB	8. Mills, Charles L.	T/4	37158737	1458 ERM
DNB	9. Kvist, Alfred J.	Pfc	36265182	Hqs 34th Inf Regt
DNB	10. Wells, George E.	Sgt	14097552	C 511 Para Inf
DNB	11. Najecki, Edward J.	Pfc	32357358	A 3 Engr Bn (C)
	12. Clarke, Matthew J.	Sgt	20229802	C 19th Inf
DNB	13. Hankerson, John E.	Sgt	34719572	1938 Ordn Co
DNB	14. Howard, Ralph H.	Cpl	14185538	35 Ftr Sq 8 Ftr Gp
DNB	15. Wynn, James L.	T/5	18630578	E 543 EB & SR
DNB	16. Anger, William F.	T/5	39142267	B 658 Amph Trac Bn
**	17. Magboo, Maximo	Pvt		Co B 5th Phil-Amer Army
DNB	18. Johnes, Hurtle	Pfc	34730913	K 162 Inf Regt
DNB	19. Turner, Lytle I.	Pfc	35917725	PCAU 23 USAFFE
*	20. Avers, William H.	Cpl	835152	MAC 32 USMC
DNB	21. Weltick, Harold W.	Pfc	32689091	C 186 Inf Regt
DNB	22. Bishop, Audie H.	Sgt	13036741	303 A D Sq
*	23. Zakrzawski, Rudolph L.	S 1/c	700-92-65	USCG LST #18
DNB	24. Twitchell, James R.	Pfc	39525522	41st Sig Corps
DNB	25. Gilley, Paul M.	Pfc	13117368	543 EB & SR
DNB	26. Collins, Clyde C.	T/5	36264632	Btry B 102 AAA
DNB	27. Fredrickson, Virgil H.	Pvt	37518702	Btry A 102 AAA
DNB	28. White, Clarence H.	Pvt	36218926	5237 Sig Co

    * Not U.S. Army personnel
   ** Not U. S. Personnel

Missing Air Crew Report #13672, Additional Personnel on board aircraft. Aviation Archaeology.

MACR #13672 - Next-of-Kin Sample

1st Lt. Leo J. Kelly   pilot   Mr. Hugh J. Kelly (father)
Rising City, Nebraska

2nd Lt. Paul A. Healy   co-pilot   Mr. Edward C. Healy (father)
Fountain, Minnesota

2nd Lt. Beatrice M. Mealor   Mr. Isidore Makarous (father)
3140 Malcar Street
Los Angeles, California

S/Sgt. John H. Hudson   Mrs. Dorothy K. Hudson (wife)
4310 Mockingbird Lane
Dallas, Texas

S/Sgt. Charles M. Kiester   radio op.   Mr. Paul M. Kiester (father)
547 Hawthorne Avenue
Kittanning, Pennsylvania

Sgt. Theodore S. Oja   engineer   Mrs. Ida Oja (mother)
Box 9
Iron, Minnesota

Sgt. George E. Walls   Mrs. Myrtle Walls (mother)
Edinboro, Mississippi

Sgt. Matthew J. Clarke   Mrs. Winifred Clarke (mother)
288 Riverdale Avenue
Yonkers, New York

Sgt. John E. Hankerson   Mrs. Louise Hankerson (wife)
1341 Kentucky Street
Memphis, Tennessee

Sgt. Fabian T. Cote   Mrs. Donalda Cote (mother)
Island City, Oregon

Sgt. Charles L. Mills   Mrs. Laura Mills (mother)
Route 6
Ft. Wayne, Indiana

Missing Air Crew Report #13672, next-of-kin list, dated 13 Mar 1945. Aviation Archaeology.

Army Air Corps Mission Reports

Mission reports and files contain many pages of documentation to help you understand what occurred each time your airman flew a mission, whether it was for a bombing run or as air support. Reports are organized by Bomb Group or Fighter Group. Within each group, you will find specific squadrons. Within each squadron, you will find crew lists for specific planes. The same crew usually flew together on every mission, unless there was a reason one or more men had to be replaced. Replacement occurred in cases of illness, wounds, or MIA status.

Mission Reports can be several hundred pages long. Documents included in Mission Reports usually include, but are not limited, to the following records:

1. Crew Lists for each plane.
2. Messages regarding the mission, date, time of departure, and formation of planes upon takeoff.
3. Drawings of each squadron's formation in the air.
4. Photographs of bomb sites.
5. Reports of bomb loads, how many bombs were dropped, and success of drop.
6. Reasons for returning planes prior to completing the mission (mechanical issues with the plane).
7. Individual reports by plane on the mission.
8. Call signs and plane markings.
9. Lists and statistics on planes which did not return from the mission, which were seen going down in specific areas, and which returned.
10. Status of each crew member after the mission.
11. Reports on enemy encounters.
12. Intelligence summaries.
13. A recap of the mission, both overall and by plane.

Repository: Air Force Historical Research Agency. NARA College Park. Unit websites.

Questions a Mission Report may answer:

1. Where was the crew headed, and from what station did they leave?
2. How long was the mission supposed to take?
3. What was the target?
4. What kind of planes were involved?
5. How many other planes and crews were involved and what happened to them?
6. What happened to my airman's plane and crew?

View Record Examples

To view examples of Mission Reports transcribed and places online, visit the official website of the 392nd Bomb Group at **http://www.b24.net/**
Scroll down and click "THE MISSIONS."
Each mission link contains the mission summary, aircrew loading lists, and the MACRs.

Organizational Level Records

Moving beyond the company, look for records created at the regimental or division level. These may not name your soldier specifically, but they will provide historical context, as well as what was happening in that unit when your soldier was serving. All of these details add to your soldier's story, and may even lead to new research paths.

After Action Reports

After Action Reports (A/A or AAR) are a compilation of a unit's locations, movements, events, enemy interaction, casualties, and other general details. Individual personnel, other than high ranking officials, were not usually listed in these reports, unless there was an important reason. While you may not find your soldier's name within these reports, you will gain a better understanding of what his service may have been like in a given month.

Repository: National Archives, College Park, MD. Also check online through Internet Archive, Unit Association and Reunion Groups, and Military Research Museums and Libraries.

Questions an After Action Report may answer:

1. Where was the division stationed throughout the month?
2. Who were they fighting?
3. What are the statistics for our wounded, missing, prisoners, and dead?
4. What are the statistics for usage of material?
5. Is there information on weather or other conditions that affected battle?
6. Who is listed in the report, and are there other records for them that may add to the story of my soldier?

View Record Examples

You can view full After Action Reports for the 90th Division at the 90th Division Association's website. Visit: **http://www.90thdivisionassociation.org**
Click "HISTORY" and select "AFTER ACTION REPORTS."

Once there, use the top table and click the "X" in the row that says "SCAN" under Jan 1945. This will open a PDF of the January 1945 After Action Report.

General Orders & Field Orders

General Orders (GO) document policies, procedures, transfers, promotions, awards and citations given to an individual or a unit. They detail key communications to a specific unit. These documents can be helpful when reconstructing a soldier's military career.

If an award or citation was presented to an individual through the parent unit, the information or citation will be included in his unit's General Orders. However, if a Purple Heart or other medal was awarded when the soldier had been transferred from his unit into a Clearing Hospital or other unit, the information will be contained within those Unit Records and General Orders. You can use Morning Reports to trace your soldier and his transfers into other units to gain clues as to which General Orders to search.

Field Orders (FO) were combat orders. These orders directed the action a unit was to take against the enemy. A Field Order had a specific format when it was written. It was comprised of these components.

Paragraph 1: Details about the enemy and allied troops.
Paragraph 2: The who, what, when, where, why, and how of the mission.
Paragraph 3: For each element of the unit, a specific mission was detailed.
Paragraph 4: Administrative details such as medical, evacuation, supply, etc.
Paragraph 5: Information on communication with command posts. Locations of command posts would be included here.

Repository: NARA College Park. Check Division and Reunion Group Websites.

Questions a General Order may answer:

1. Who received an award?
2. Why did the individual(s) receive the award, and when was it issued?

View Record Examples

To view 90th Division General Orders, visit: **http://www.90thdivisionassociation.org**

Click "HISTORY" and select "GENERAL ORDERS."

Staff Reports and Unit Journals

Staff Reports were created by four unit sections, Personnel (S-1), Intelligence (S-2), Operations, (S-3), and Supply (S-4). These records detailed the specific operations carried out by that section or their plans. These sections also kept logs of all correspondence and messages, both incoming and outgoing. Many of these reports no longer exist. The ones that do can paint an excellent picture of what was happening during that moment in the war.

Due to the details of each report, an Operations Periodic Report would be written to summarize the information. Within these reports were maps drawn on translucent paper. This paper, however, has not held up well over the last seventy years, and may no longer exist in many files. For the files that do still have these maps, creating a photocopy of the image, then blowing it up to original size allows a researcher to overlay it on a map to understand the movements of a unit.

A report with a similar format as the Staff Reports are the Unit Journals. These provide messages, orders, and information on the unit each day. In some ways, they are a combination of the Staff Reports.

Records Created in the Field

These reports may not contain the name of your soldier, but they will provide historical context and additional clues to his service.

Repository: National Archives, College Park, MD. Division and Unit websites.

Questions Staff Reports and Unit Journals may answer:

1. What was the weather like? What about battle conditions and terrain?
2. Where were the units and companies within the overall division being sent each day? You can map out your soldier's footsteps.
3. What messages were relayed?
4. What Field Orders were issued, and how did that impact the movement of soldiers?
5. Were the objectives reached for each mission, movement, battle?
6. Was there air support for any enemy encounters, or was it strictly infantry and armor?
7. Were any prisoners captured? Did they have documents?

Unit Journals 357th Infantry Regt, 90th Division

From 6 Jan 45, Date and Hour
To 6 JAN 1945, Date and Hour

JOURNAL OF 357th Infantry

MONNEREN Q0484
Location of Headquarters
NOERDANGE

Time In/Out	Serial No.	Time Dated	Incidents, messages, orders, etc. Action taken
		0500	Message from Division alerts Regt to be ready for movement at 1300 by motor to North.
		0800	Move is to be to III Corps area, north of city of LUXEMBOURG.
		1100	Units ordered, verbally, to proceed North by way of CATTENOM crossing over the MOSELLE. Route from that point through ROUSSY-le-VILLAGE; PRISANGE; HEAPERANGE to LUXEMBOURG; Northwest through to TUNTINGEN to SAUEL, where guides are to be furnished to lead to proper areas. Order of march: 3rd Bn; 1st Bn, Spcl Units, 2nd Bn.
		1300	3rd Bn is en route, 1st preparing to leave.
		1325	Special units leave MONNEREN.
		1530	Special units passing through city of LUXEMBOURG.
		2400	As the column passed north of SAUEL, considerable confusion developed. The 3rd Bn proceeded on to its assembly area at BIGONVILLE. balance of the column reversing itself at the intersection north of RAMBROUGH, the 1st Bn assembling in that area at approximately #### #2000. 2nd Bn assembled in HOSTERT at approximately 2100. Headquarters and special units continued south, finding all towns occupied, finally ending up at NOERDANGE just before the period closed. Units were quartered in the general vicinity of the railroad station.

Unit Journal. 357th Infantry Regiment, 90th Division dated 6 Jan 1945. National Archives, College Park, MD.

JOURNAL OF

357th INFANTRY

NOERDANGE P6929
Location of Headquarters:
USSELDANGE
OSPERN P6834

From 7 JANUARY 45
Date and Hour

To 7 JANUARY 45
Date and Hour

Time In	Out	Serial No.	Time Dated	Incidents, messages, orders, etc.	Action taken
			1045	Headquarters and Special Units leave NOERDANGE to go to USSELDANGE where temporary CP was set up.	
			1400	Hq and Special units leave USSELDANGE.	
			1530	Hq & Spcl units set up at OSPERN; forward CP at HOSTERT, 4 miles North of OSPERN.	
			2400	Continued snow and cold creates quartering problems; no changes in locations of other elements during day. Nothing further at this hour.	

Unit Journal. 357th Infantry Regiment, 90th Division dated 7 Jan 1945. National Archives, College Park, MD.

JOURNAL OF

357th INFANTRY

OSPERN P6834
Location of Headquarters
BA VIGNE P6449

From 8 JANUARY 1945
Date and Hour

To 8 JANUARY 1945
Date and Hour

Time		Serial No.	Time Dated	Incidents, messages, orders, etc.	Action taken
In	Out				
			1200	Rear units moved north out of OSPERN preparatory to assuming positions for attack scheduled for 9th.	
			1900	The following positions have been taken by the regiment: 1st Bn, vicinity WIRZERWEG; 2nd Bn, BAVIGNE, 3rd Bn, LEIFRANGE. Regtl Cp and special units at BAVIGNE; all units in these positions by 1850. Division FO #48, summarized, calls for following action: III Corps attacks at 091000A to eliminate enemy pocket southeast of EASTOGNE. 90th Div attacks through elements of 26th Division, to seize high ground vicinity of BRAS, maintaining contact with the 26th Div on the right and TF SCOTT on the left. Regimental Field Order #22, summarized: Attachments: Co A 773rd TD Bn; Co C 712th Tk Bn; Co C, 3rd Cml Bn; 90th Rcn Troop; Co A (-) 315th Engrs; Co A 315 Med Bn. Attacks two battalions abreast, 1st on right, attacking with A Company; 2nd Bn on left attacking with E and F Cos. 1st Bn to seize initial objective on right, including town of BERLE, ready to continue on order. 2nd Bn, seize initial objective on left and be prepared to advance on order. 3rd Bn to move forward from present area to WILTZERWEG beginning at 0930, being prepared to pass through either of the assault battalions and continue the attk. 90th Rcn to maintain contact between our second battalion and TF SCOTT on the left. The two assaulting battalions have one platoon each of the following: TDs; Tks, Cml Mortars, Engrs. 3rd Bn has same except for Engrs. Objectives set up in the Division overlay were, roughly: Initial, including the towns of BERLE and TRENTHOF (in 359 area), Intermediate objective, the high ground immediately south of the town of DONCOLS and BRAS. Final, oval including the towns DONCOLS and BRAS.	
			2400	Nothing further at this hour.	

Unit Journal. 357th Infantry Regiment, 90th Division dated 8 Jan 1945. National Archives, College Park, MD.

Histories – Unit and Regimental

Unit histories are either written by the men who served or the branch of the service in which that unit existed. It could be said that a history written by the branch of the service makes it an "official" history, and one written by the men make it an "unofficial" history. Why?

It is important to understand that histories written by the men who served may contain some embellishment of service details. They may contain errors in dates and places, names, and events, unless official records were used to compile this history. Additionally, sources of information may not be cited, leaving the reader to wonder from where the information came.

Official military histories, written by the branch historians, typically use official records and cite sources. These sources can be used by individual researchers to locate additional service information about their soldier.

Some of these books may be in your home or the homes of family members. After the war, many divisional books were published and sent to veterans and their families. Sometimes these books were offered for a fee, like the 90th Division history, while others, like Peragamus, the history of the 358th Infantry Regiment, were sent to all soldiers from that Infantry Regiment.

Repository: National Archives, College Park, MD. Online digitized books and division websites.

Questions a Unit History may answer:

1. What did the overall war look like from the perspective of this unit or division?
2. How does this history help tell the story of my individual soldier?
3. What clues can I pull from this overall history to locate additional information about my soldier?
4. Are there details about the wounding, prisoner status, missing status, or death of my soldier?

View Record Examples

Many division and unit groups are digitizing and placing online their histories. To view some of these histories, you can visit the 90th Division Association at **http://www.90thdivisionassociation.org**. Click "HISTORY" and select "UNIT HISTORIES."

Scroll down to WW2 Unit Histories, and look at the 790th Ordnance History. This was written by the Company Commander and is an example of an "unofficial" history. Next, look at the 90th Division Unit History and the 358th Infantry Division booklets. These would be considered more "official" histories.

Air Force Award Cards

The Army Air Corps is the predecessor to today's Air Force. The Army Air Corps was created in 1920 as part of the U.S. Army. The purpose was to have a combatant arm in the skies. By 1941, it was renamed the U.S. Army Air Forces (USAAF.) After the end of World War II, in 1947, it was removed from the umbrella of the Army and placed into its own service branch, the United States Air Force.

The Army Air Force has a record set called the Air Force Award Cards. These records are held at the NPRC in St. Louis, Missouri. Send a request to the same address you sent the Form 180 to request an OMPF search. Provide as much information as you can about your airman.

Each card provides the name and a drawing of the medal and the General Order number, unit, and date the award was issued. Using the information provided on the Award Card, you can write to the Air Force Historical Research Agency and request copies of the citations and orders.

Repository for Air Force Award Cards
National Personnel Records Center
1 Archives Drive
St. Louis, MO 63138

Repository for Citations and General Orders
Air Force Historical Research Agency
600 Chennault Circle
Maxwell AFB, AL
36112

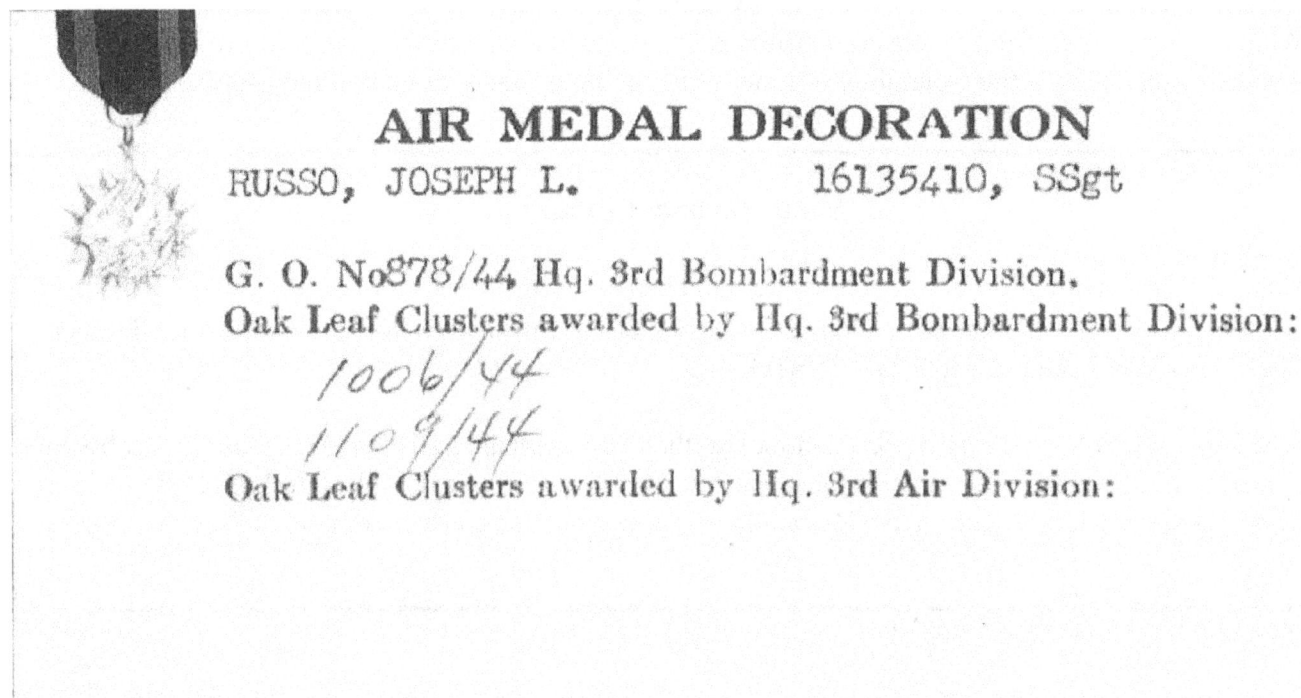

AIR MEDAL DECORATION
RUSSO, JOSEPH L.   16135410, SSgt

G. O. No878/44 Hq. 3rd Bombardment Division.
Oak Leaf Clusters awarded by Hq. 3rd Bombardment Division:
1006/44
1109/44
Oak Leaf Clusters awarded by Hq. 3rd Air Division:

Air Medal Decoration (Air Force Award Card.) Joseph L. Russo, serial no. 16135410. National Personnel Records Center, St. Louis, MO.

Correspondence

Explore the correspondence within unit records. While soldiers could not outline specific things that were happening or exactly where they were, unit correspondence will provide other clues as to what was happening. These clues help provide historical context for your soldier and may lead to new research opportunities.

Repository: National Archives, College Park, MD. Archival collections in libraries and museum. Personal collections.

Questions Correspondence may answer:

1. Reading correspondence from another soldier's perspective, what was the war or battle like for him? How might that affect my soldier's story?
2. If this is an officer within my soldier's unit, is my soldier ever mentioned in official correspondence?
3. Does the correspondence mention other names I should research?

Photographs, Maps, and Aerial Photography

Photographs are another resource which can provide historical context, information on battles and missions, and illustrate what a soldier saw during service. Look for individual soldier photos, miscellaneous photos, battle photos, bombing photos, and maps.

Soldier Photos. Photographs of soldiers can be single person shots or group shots. Pay particular attention to any uniforms, airplanes, vehicles, stripes on the uniform, other clothing, markings on vehicles or aircraft, location of the photograph, or any piece of evidence that might identify the people and what they were doing.

Miscellaneous Photos. Some soldiers carried cameras with them during training and overseas service. Often, these photos will include their buddies, scenery where they were stationed, equipment, and if on leave, tourist sites they may have visited. Even if the photos you discover are undated, comparing them against the service timeline, and possibly the country in which they were, you can piece together additional service history and experiences.

Battle Photos. Photographs which depict the battle, the weapons used, men marching, the prisoners and the dead provide a real glimpse at war. The brutality, hunger, heat or cold, shines through and adds to your soldier's story.

Bombing and Mission Photos. If your soldier was part of an aircrew, look for mission information, photographs of sites to bomb, both prior to and after. Just as men carried cameras into combat, your airman may have photos from the skies.

Maps. Maps are valuable because they help you trace the service locations of your soldier. They provide historical context on both large and small scale maneuvers and missions. Maps illustrate the story of your soldier.

Repository: National Archives, College Park, MD. Air Force Historical Research Agency. Center for Military History. Libraries and archival collections. Personal collections.

Publications - Field Manuals and Training Manuals

If you would like to dig deep and discover what your soldier may have read or learned about as part of his training, look for manuals. The Army created Field Manuals, Technical Manuals, and Training Manuals for everything a soldier needed to learn about weapons, vehicles, and jobs. These books will provide an in-depth examination of aspects of war to provide additional context to your soldier's story.

Repository: Many are digitized online through Internet Archive. Visit my WWII Toolbox for Army manuals. Research libraries. Combined Arms Research Library Digital Library.

Navy Records

The Official Military Personnel File (OMPF) is the official record of service for a sailor. The file can be a large descriptive file if the sailor had served many years or a smaller file if he was only in during part of the war. The main documents often found in an OMPF are described here. Document examples will be provided with each main record description in this chapter.

Files may also contain letters for information requests from relatives and others conducting research. The original request will be included in the file which means you may discover a relative you did not know existed.

One of the most important things you should do when you receive the OMPF is sort it in chronological order so the reports and events make sense. Orders were issued, cancelled, and modified, and the dates of the documents may need to be clarified.

It is important to create a timeline of service based on the records in the file. If the sailor was an officer, there may be pages of only service dates and stations. Use those then go through the file to fill in the blanks.

Because Navy personnel were moved so often, add to the timeline the addresses and stations you find. Include where his family was living, if he was married and they traveled with him. Also add to the timeline main historical events and records like census, vital record information, and other documentation to show a fuller picture of the sailor with his family. This helps put everything into context.

General Contents of a Navy OMPF

Joseph J. Holik, USNR Armed Guard.

The contents of the OMPF were similar, yet varied, depending on the type of service a man sought in the Navy, and when he was inducted. This chapter will provide general summaries of common records found in the OMPF and more specific examples of record images using the OMPFs of Fireman 1st Class Samuel Crowder, who served twice in the Navy and was Killed In Action on the USS Oklahoma on 7 December 1941. Lt(jg) George T. Howe, Jr., a Navy Pilot. Fireman 1st Class Jack Amoroso, a Seabee. And, my grandpa, Seaman 1st Class Naval Armed Guard sailor, Joseph Holik.

Enlistment Information

Applications. Depending on when a sailor joined the Navy, different Applications for Enlistment were used. A man with a college education, applying for Pilot training or officer status, would have completed a slightly different application from a man enlisting or being drafted into service.

Regardless of the type of application, each provided information about the life, education, job history, prior service history, and family information of the applicant. In some cases, such as Pilot training, the man had to write a letter explaining why he wished to join the service and provide proof of birth, college transcripts, and letters of recommendation.

Prior Service History. Sometimes, men will join the Navy and be discharged after their term expires, or in the case when the Navy was cutting personnel in the 1930s, and rejoin during World War II. Prior service history will be included in their OMPF.

Service Qualification Card. The Service Qualification Card contained much of the information on the service application with the inclusion of more information on hobbies and sports participation. This card may have also contained information on service.

Next-of-Kin and Insurance Information. Each reservist had to complete next-of-kin contact information in case of wounds, Missing In Action, Prisoner of War, or Killed In Action status changes. Connected to this information was insurance beneficiary information.

Report of Dependents. The Report of Dependents lists the next-of-kin or dependents of the sailor. This form should be updated if the sailor marries and his dependents change, but this did not always happen.

Medical information. Some medical information will be included in an OMPF, usually regarding the physical and dental exams conducted upon induction or change in rank. Sometimes the records of sailors treated in stateside hospitals were included.

Not all medical information is contained in the OMPF. There are usually separate medical files. These files can only be requested by the veteran or his next-of-kin even if the sailor has been dead 100 years. It is important if you are the veteran or next-of-kin, you request these records. If the veteran is deceased, you must provide proof of death in the form of a death certificate, obituary, or funeral paperwork.

Documentation Slips. There are many slips without a title, contained in Navy files. These slips track changes of station, rank, pay, and provide the name, rank, and serial number of the sailor. Some slips have titles, such as the Change in Rate or Reserve Class slip.

Pay Records. Various pay records, family allowance documents, and insurance paperwork is found within the OMPF. These documents allow a researcher to further piece together the service history with dates, locations, changes in dependents, and status.

Muster Cards. Muster cards outline a specific time period and events which occurred for the sailor. These show name, rank, serial number, and dates of transfers or training.

Summary of Service. Similar to the records in a Marine Corps file, there will be Summary of Service forms which document the Vessel or Station, dates in which the sailor served on that Vessel or Station, and rank. These forms may be lined with a list of dates and locations or in memo format with greater description of service.

Appointments for Rank and Promotions. If an enlisted man rose in rank to Officer, the commission certificate will be included in the OMPF. This record provides information on the new rank and date it is official. An Oath of Office for the Officer may also be included which contains the date of change in rank and his signature.

Temporary appointments in rank were also given when needed. This usually appears in the file as a letter or memo explaining the temporary change and duties required of the serviceman.

Training and Educational Information

The training information and any special training courses completed will be included in the OMPF. The Certificate of Completion of a course provides information on specific training, location and date your sailor received. If a man was going through flight school, those records would also be a part of his file. The documents may appear as official certificates of completion or as a letter or memo to be sent to Headquarters and placed in the man's file.

Travel and Furlough Orders

Travel and furlough documents and orders were included in the file to document every move a sailor made off base. The orders often included the name, rank, and service number of several men being transferred from one unit to another. An explanation of when to depart, how to travel, and when to arrive was included.

Straggler or Deserter Documents. If a sailor was late returning from liberty or furlough, or had disappeared from service, a Straggler or Deserter Form would be included in the file. In the case of my grandfather, Joseph Holik, he was mistakenly listed as a Straggler and soon after, a letter was sent to his wife stating the error.

Awards, Citations, and Commendations

The OMPF contains letters or memos providing citations to an individual or unit, and the awards issued. Sometimes the award issued was done so on an official form for that specific award. These citations and awards may provide clues to service history which includes dates and battle locations.

Miscellaneous Documents

Family Letters. Quite often, the OMPF will contain letters to the military or government, requesting information on the status of their sailor. These often appear after a sailor is declared Missing In Action (MIA) or Killed In Action (KIA.)

Vital Records of Family. Sometimes a sailor had to prove his age or provide proof of his relationship to dependents or next-of-kin. Vital records are often included in the OMPF to prove these relationships.

Death Certificate. Sometimes, but not always, if the sailor was KIA, you will find a death certificate in the OMPF.

References to Other Sources. It is important to read each letter and document carefully within the OMPF. Names and addresses of other sailors with which your sailor fought, may be included.

Letters from Government Officials. Families who needed information from the military and had trouble receiving it, often went to their local VA or County Commissioner for assistance. In other cases, the family approached a higher-level government official such as their Congressman. These government officials acted as a go-between for families and the military to obtain information. This was not only the case during the war, but also up to the current day. You may find in OMPFs received today, the letters and contact information of government officials.

Modern Day Requests for Information. Each time an OMPF is requested, the request form or letter is included with the OMPF. The next person to request the file will receive the OMPF plus the details of all previous requests. This may lead to a new family connection.

Casualty Telegrams or Letters (MIA, POW, KIA)

Every time a sailor had a change in status, meaning he went from being a healthy, active sailor to wounded, missing, prisoner, or killed, a telegram was sent to the next-of-kin and included in his file.

Report of Casualty. The Report of Casualty was completed when a sailor or pilot was KIA or MIA then presumed dead and given a Finding of Death (FOD.) It contains his name, rank, serial number, unit, cause of casualty, next-of-kin, and vital information.

Inventory of Effects. The Inventory of Effects is always found within the IDPF, and sometimes included in the OMPF. This list documents all the personal effects of a sailor who was declared MIA or KIA, and then sent to the effects bureau in Utah for processing.

Discharge or Separation Information

The Separation and Discharge papers contain the name, rank, service number, final unit, MOS (Job) for the sailor, and enlistment and discharge or death information. Theaters of war in which sailor served, dates of service are included. Finally, the dates the man sailed overseas, arrived, then departed overseas to return to the U.S. are also included.

Fireman 1st Class Samuel Crowder

Samuel Warwick Crowder. Photo courtesy of his nephew, Fred Crowder.

N. Nav. 1 (Nov., 1920)

CROWDER 56907
SURNAME

Samuel Warwick
CHRISTIAN NAME

#286-88-01
SERVICE NUMBER

Apprentice Seaman
ENLISTED AS

SERVICE RECORD.

First enlistment

C. S. C. No. _____

Navy Recruiting Station,
Louisville, Ky.   US

ENLISTED AT   CITIZENSHIP

March 3rd 1924.
DATE OF ENLISTMENT

Bugler First Class
DISCHARGED AS

13 June 1927
DATE DISCHARGED

Honorable Discharge
CHARACTER OF DISCHARGE

4—2548

Enlistment Papers 1924

Nav. 351
pr. 1934)

United States { Navy / ~~Naval Reserve, Class~~ }

Fold with this face out

Finished Fi....

LISTMENT of __CROWDER, Samuel Warwick__ ; 286-88-01 ; $54.00
   (Full name, surname to the left)   (Service number)   (Pay per month)

epted for enlistment at __Louisville, Kentucky__ ; __F2c__
                                                        (Rating in which enlisted)

listed at __NRS, Louisville, Kentucky__ Date __26 July 1940__

nsferred to __Receiving Station, NOB, Norfolk, Va.__

upation __Com. Artist and Draftsman__ * Citizenship __U.S.__ Place of birth __Louisville, Ky.__

te of birth __14 June 1906__ Home address __235 E. Jacob__ __Louisville__
                                              (Street and number)   (Town)

__Jefferson__, __Kentucky__
   (County)   (State)

dited to __3rd__ Congressional District, State of __Kentucky__

rried or single __Single__ ; Name and address of next of kin __Mother__
                                                                    (Relation)
__Charlotte B. Cannon__ __235 E. Jacob St., Louisville, Ky.__
        (Name)   (Address)

Continuous Service Certificate ____ Previous service { Navy ~~Reserve~~ } (3 3 11). First enlisted
                                    (Number)   (Years) (Months) (Days)

__March 1924__ at __Louisville, Ky.__ and was last discharged __13 June 1927__
   (Date)   (Place)   (Date)

m the U. S. S. __NAS Hampton Rds,Va.__ with __Honorable__ discharge as __Bugler First Class__
                                              (Character)   (Rate)

vious Coast Guard Service (____). Previous Marine Corps Service (____). Previous
                            (Years) (Months) (Days)   (Years) (Months) (Days)

my Service (____). Age __34__ years __1__ months. Height __5__ feet __8½__ inches. Weight __152__
              (Years) (Months) (Days)

nds. Eyes __Blue 9__ Sex __Male__ Hair __D.Bro.__ Complexion __Ruddy__ Color __W-US__

____ Personal characteristics, ____ marks, etc. ANT: S½"rt.kne;S¼" lt.abd;Sl" rt.ft.

OST: VSLA; S6" btk; S¼" rt.nk; Sl/8" mid. bk.

I CERTIFY that I have carefully examined, agreeably to the Regulations of the Navy, the above-named recruit, and find that, in my opinion, he is free from all bodily defects mental infirmity which would, in any way, disqualify him from performing the duties of his rating, and that he has stated to me that he has no disease concealed or y to be inherited.

F. K. SOUKUP, Lt. Comdr, (MC) USN, Examining Surgeon.

For and in consideration of the pay or wages due to the ratings which may from time to time be assigned me during the continuance of service, I agree to and with ____C. R. WOODSON____ of the United States Navy, as follows:
                                    (Name of commanding officer)

First: To enter the service of the Navy of the United States and to report to such station or vessel of the Navy as I may be ordered to , and to the utmost of my power and ability discharge my several services or duties and be in everything conformable and obedient to the eral requirements and lawful commands of the officers who may be placed over me.

Second: I oblige and subject myself to serve { __4__ years from __26 July__, 1 __940__
                                              { during minority until ____, 1

ess sooner discharged by proper authority, and on the conditions provided by the act of Congress of March 3, 1875, as follows:

SEC. 1422. That it shall be the duty of the commanding officer of any fleet, squadron, or vessel acting singly, when on service, to send to an Atlantic or to a Pacific port of United States as their enlistment may have occurred on either the Atlantic or Pacific Coast of the United States, in some public or other vessel, all petty officers and per- of inferior ratings desiring to go there at the expiration of their terms of enlistment, or as soon thereafter as may be, unless, in his opinion, the detention of such per- for a longer period should be essential to the public interests, in which case he may detain them, or any of them until the vessel to which they belong shall return to Atlantic or Pacific port. All persons enlisted without the limits of the United States may be discharged, on the expiration of their enlistment, either in a foreign port n a port of the United States, or they may be detained as above provided beyond the term of their enlistment; and that all persons sent home or detained by a command- officer, according to the provisions of this act, shall be subject in all respects to the laws and regulations for the government of the Navy until their return to an Atlantic 'acific port and their regular discharge; and all persons so detained by such officer, or reentering to serve until the return to an Atlantic or Pacific port of the vessel to h they belong shall in no case be held in the service more than thirty days after their arrival in said port; and that all persons who shall be so detained beyond their terms nlistment, or who shall after the termination of their enlistment, voluntarily reenter to serve until the return to an Atlantic or Pacific port of the vessel to which belong and their regular discharge therefrom, shall receive for the time during which they are so detained or shall so serve beyond their original terms of enlistment, addition of one-fourth of their former pay: Provided, That the shipping articles shall hereafter contain the substance of this section.

I also oblige myself, during such service, to comply with and be subject to such laws, regulations, and articles for the government of the vy as are or shall be established by the Congress of the United States or other competent authority, and to submit to treatment for the vention of smallpox, typhoid (typhoid prophylaxis), and to such other preventive measures as may be considered necessary by naval horities.

Third: I am of the legal age to enlist; I have never deserted from the United States Navy, Army, Marine Corps, or Coast Guard; I have er been discharged from the United States Service or service on account of disability or through sentence of either civilian or mil- ry court; and I have never been discharged from any service, civil or military, except with good character and for the reasons given by to the recruiting officer prior to enlistment. I am not a member of the National Guard, Naval Reserve, or Marine Corps Reserve.

Fourth: I have had this contract fully explained to me, I understand it, and certify that no promise of any kind has been made to me cerning assignment to duty, or promotion during my enlistment. I understand that if I become a candidate for the Naval Academy and ! to pass the entrance examinations, I will be returned to general service.

Oath of Allegiance: I, ____Samuel Warwick Crowder____

Enlistment Papers 1924

Nav. 351
pr. 1934)

United States { Navy
~~Naval Reserve, Class~~ XX

OVER 8 MONTHS

Finished-File-Layten

Fold with this face out

Finished - Fi Card

ENLISTMENT of __CROWDER, Samuel Warwick__ ; __286-88-01__ ; __$54.00__
(Full name, surname to the left)　　　(Service number)　　　(Pay per month)

accepted for enlistment at __Louisville, Kentucky__ ; __F2c__
(Rating in which enlisted)

enlisted at __NRS, Louisville, Kentucky__ Date __26 July 1940__

transferred to __Receiving Station, NOB, Norfolk, Va.__

occupation __Com.Artist and Draftsman__ * Citizenship __U.S.__ Place of birth __Louisville, Ky.__

date of birth __14 June 1906__ Home address __235 E. Jacob__ __Louisville__
(Street and number)　　　　(Town)

__Jefferson__ , __Kentucky__
(County)　　　(State)

credited to __3rd__ Congressional District, State of __Kentucky__

married or single __Single__ ; Name and address of next of kin __Mother__
(Relation)

__Charlotte B. Cannon__ __235 E. Jacob St., Louisville, Ky.__
(Name)

fail to pass the entrance examinations, I will be returned to general service.

Oath of Allegiance: I, __Samuel Warwick Crowder__

do solemnly swear (or affirm) that I will bear true faith and allegiance to the United States of America, and that I will serve them honestly and faithfully against all their enemies whomsoever, and that I will obey the orders of the President of the United States and the orders of the officers appointed over me, according to the rules and articles for the government of the Navy.

And I do further swear (or affirm) that all statements made by me as now given in this record are correct.

Samuel Warwick Crowder,

SAMUEL WARWICK CROWDER
(Signature in own handwriting, surname to right)

Subscribed and sworn to before me this __26th__ day of __July__ , A. D. __1940__

and contract perfected.

United States citizenship substantiated.

C. R. WOODSON, Lt.-Cdr., USN.,

Commanding, U. S. S. NRS, Louisville, Ky.

* CITIZENSHIP.—Native born, use initials U. S.; Naturalized, N. U. S.; Alien, intention declared, A. D. I.; Alien, A; Guam, Guam; Philippine Islands, P. I.; Samoa, Samoa; and Virgin Islands, V. I.
** For reenlistments with continuous service note Art. D-1002, Bureau of Navigation Manual.

U. S. GOVERNMENT PRINTING OFFICE　4—4790

Official Military Personnel File. Samuel W. Crowder, serial no. 2868801. Enlistment Papers. National Personnel Records Center, St. Louis, Missouri.

Samuel Crowder Honorable Discharge 1927

HONORABLE DISCHARGE,
UNITED STATES NAVY.

SERIES C

C40936

U. S. NAVAL AIR STATION.
NAVAL OPERATING BASE.
HAMPTON ROADS, VA.

U.S. _____
(Name of vessel or station.)

Crowder, Samuel Warwick
(Name of enlisted man.)

3 March 1924
(Date of enlistment.)

Bug 1c   286-88-01
(Rating at date of discharge.)   (Service number.)

13 June 1927
(Date of discharge.)

(Place of discharge.)

Bug 1c
(Rating best qualified to fill.)

G.S.C. No. none   { H.D.Button yes
                    { delivered,   (yes or no.)

1233 Ashland Ave, Louisville, Ky.
(Home address.)

Pay per month at discharge, - - $54.00

Paid in full at discharge, - - - - $57.15

_____ Commanding Officer.

Note.—Stubs to be forwarded, as bound, to the Bureau of
Navigation when the discharges in the book have been issued.

CROWDER, Samuel Warwick, Fireman 1c, USN — PEARL HARBOR.

The claimant, mother of the deceased is a widow and she is fifty-four years of age with no income of her own. She has one son who contributed approximately $600.00 during the year toward the support of his mother. One year prior to his death, the deceased contributed approximately $70.00 to the support of his mother.

(Enlisted July 26, 1940 USN, died December 7, 1941)

Official Military Personnel File. Samuel W. Crowder, serial no. 2868801. Honorable Discharge Certificate. National Personnel Records Center, St. Louis, Missouri.

Application for Enlistment 5 April 1940

APPLICATION FOR ENLISTMENT

Reproduced at the National Archives- STL

-3rd--- Congressional District, County of __Jefferson__ State of __Kentucky__
(This information to be supplied by Recruiter)

Last school grade completed: _5_   _Louisville, Kentucky_
Reason for enlistment: _Career_   (Place)
Language qualifications: _none_   _April 5,_ 19_40_
What is your trade? _Cane artist & Orpheum_   (Date)

I desire to submit my application for an enlistment of _4_ years in the United States Navy, and declare that I am of good habits and character in all respects; that I have never deserted from the U. S. Navy, Marine Corps, Army, Coast Guard or Civilian Conservation Corps. Having been informed that any false statements made by me would bar me from enlisting, I certify that the following statements are correct:

Name in full: _Samuel_ _Warwick_ _Crowder_
                (First)   (Middle)   (Last)

Date of birth: _June 14 1906_ Place of birth: _Louisville, Ky._
            (Month) (Day) (Year)   (City and State)

What is your race? _White_ If you were born in foreign territory, how did you acquire citizenship?
_____ Are you now a U. S. citizen? _yes_

Have you anyone solely or partially dependent upon you for support? _no_

Are you married? _no_ Have you ever been married? _no_
            (Yes or No)   (Yes or no)

Home Address: _235 E Jacob Louisville Ky._
          (Street No.) (Name of Street) (City or Town) (State)

Former address: _U. S. Navy_ Length of time lived at residence _2 yrs 3 mo_

Former address: _____ Length of time lived at residence _____

Where was your father born? _Louisville_ Where was your mother born? _Jeffersonville, In._

Is your father living? _yes_ Is your mother living? _yes_
            (Yes or no)   (Yes or no)

Are your parents divorced? _yes_ Separated? _yes_ Have you a stepfather? _no_ stepmother? _yes_
                  (Yes or No)   (Yes or No)   (Yes or no)   (Yes or no)

Name and relationship of next of kin or legal guardian: _Charlotte B. Crowder_
                                                    (Full name)
_Mother_____ Home address of next of kin or legal guardian: ____
(Relationship)
235 E Jacob St. Louisville, Jefferson, Ky.
(Street No.) (Name of Street) (City or Town)   (County)   (State)

Do you drink intoxicating liquors? _no_ If so, to what extent? _____
                              (Yes or No)

Have you ever been arrested or in the custody of police? _no_ If so, for what? _____

_____

Have you ever been in a reform school, jail, or penitentiary, or have you ever been convicted of any crime?

_____ _no_ _____

Have you ever served in the U. S. Navy, Marine Corps, Army or Coast Guard? _U. S. Navy_
If so, how long? _2 yrs 3 mo 11 days_ What is the date of your last discharge? _6-13-27_
Character of discharge _Honorable_ Are you now or have you been a member of the National Guard, Naval Militia, Naval Reserve, or Marine Corps Reserve, or Civilian Conservation Corps? __
_yes___ If so, what company or unit? _Band 138th F.A._ Produce discharge _no_
Ky N.G. Louisville, Ky.

(Applicant sign full name here) _Samuel Warwick Crowder_

Accepted: _____ YES _____ Cause of rejection: _____

_____

Official Military Personnel File. Samuel W. Crowder, serial no. 2868801. Enlistment Paper dated 5 April 1940. National Personnel Records Center, St. Louis, Missouri.

Telegrams Reporting MIA and KIA Statuses

TELEGRAM

Mrs. Charlotte B. Cannon

235 E. Jacob Street,

Louisville, Kentucky.

December 20, 1941

THE NAVY DEPARTMENT DEEPLY REGRETS TO INFORM YOU THAT YOUR
SON, SAMUEL WARWICK CROWDER, FIREMAN FIRST CLASS, U. S. NAVY

IS MISSING FOLLOWING ACTION IN THE PERFORMANCE OF HIS DUTY AND
IN THE SERVICE OF HIS COUNTRY X THE DEPARTMENT APPRECIATES YOUR
GREAT ANXIETY AND WILL FURNISH YOU FURTHER INFORMATION PROMPTLY
WHEN RECEIVED X TO PREVENT POSSIBLE AID TO OUR ENEMIES PLEASE
DO NOT DIVULGE THE NAME OF HIS SHIP OR STATION

REAR ADMIRAL RANDALL JACOBS
CHIEF OF THE BUREAU OF NAVIGATION

TELEGRAM

MRS CHARLOTTE B CANNON

235 EAST JACOB STREET

LOUISVILLE KENTUCKY

FEB 1 2 1942

AFTER EXHAUSTIVE SEARCH IT HAS BEEN FOUND IMPOSSIBLE TO LOCATE YOUR
SON SAMUEL WARWICK CROWDER FIREMAN FIRST CLASS U S NAVY
AND HE HAS THEREFORE BEEN OFFICIALLY DECLARED TO HAVE LOST HIS LIFE
IN THE SERVICE OF HIS COUNTRY AS OF DECEMBER SEVENTH NINETEEN FORTY
ONE X THE DEPARTMENT EXPRESSES TO YOU ITS SINCEREST SYMPATHY

REAR ADMIRAL RANDALL JACOBS
CHIEF OF BUREAU OF NAVIGATION

Official Military Personnel File. Samuel W. Crowder, serial no. 2868801. Telegrams reporting Crowder's MIA and KIA statuses. National Personnel Records Center, St. Louis, Missouri.

Death Certificate

NMS-Form N
(1940)

CERTIFICATE OF DEATH

P3-1320393

From: Bureau of Medicine and Surgery, Navy Department, Washington, D. C.

To: *Bureau of Medicine and Surgery, Navy Department, Washington, D. C.*
(See Circular Letter R-6, Appendix D, Manual of the Medical Department, for instructions)

1. Name CROWDER, Samuel Warwick   Rank or rate F1c, USN

2. Born: Place Louisville, Ky.   Date 6-14-05

3. Nationality _____ (White—U. S., Colored, Samoan, etc.)   Religion _____ (Denomination)

4. Eyes _____ Hair _____ Complexion _____ Height _____ Weight _____

5. Marks, scars, etc. (noted in health record) _____

FINGERPRINT

State which finger _____
(Right index preferred)

6. Relation, name and address of next of kin or friend Mother; Charlotte E. Cannon

255 E. Jacob St.

Louisville, Kentucky.

7. Original admission: Place _____ Date _____
(Ship or station to which attached when first admitted to sick list)

8. Died: Place Pacific Area, Active Naval Service   Date 12-7-41   Hour _____

9. Cause of death { Principal KILLED IN ACTION #2545   Key Letter "X"
                   { Contributory _____

10. Death _____ the result of own misconduct and _____ in the line of duty.
       (is or is not)   (is or is not)

11. Disposition of remains Instructions have been issued to inter locally

all bodies recovered.

12. Summary of facts relative to the death:

R. R. GASSER,
Captain (MC),
U. S. Navy.

16—15556

(Continue on back of this form)

Official Military Personnel File. Samuel W. Crowder, serial no. 2868801. Death Certificate. National Personnel Records Center, St. Louis, Missouri.

Fireman 1st Class Jack Amoroso

Application for Enlistment

Physical _____

MM/P1X-1

Reproduced at the National Archives- STL

125190

_____ Company

_eM3/c_ Rating

_____ Trade

_____ Enlisted

BUREAU OF YARDS AND DOCKS

NAVY DEPARTMENT, WASHINGTON, D.C.

APPLICATION FOR ENLISTMENT

1. Name _Amoroso Jack Aloysius_ Date _Jan. 8, 1943_
(Print) (Last) (First) (Middle)

2. Present address _933 So. Hoyne Ave_, City _Chicago_ State _Ill_

3. Permanent address _____

4. Are you now employed? _I Work With my Father. (Partners)_

5. By whom? _____

6. Military service _____

7. Age _20 years & 6 mo_ Date of birth _July 27, 1922_

8. Height _5'9"_ Weight _162_

9. Nationality _ITALIAN (American born)_ Legal residence _U.S._

10. Place of birth _Chicago_

11. Are you a U. S. citizen? _Yes_ How long in U. S.? _All my Life_

12. If foreign born, when and how naturalized? _____

13. Married or single _Single_ Dependents _____

14. What physical defects have you? _None_

15. Have you ever been refused life insurance? _No_ When? _____

Why? _____

16. Are you otherwise physically sound and well? _Yes_

17. High school education: _4_ year. Where? _ST. Ignatius_

Were you graduated? _Yes_ When? _ST. Ignatius_

1-01663

Application for Enlistment

igher education:

Where	Number of years	Date of graduation	Degree received

Special study: _Aircraft Training_

Membership in what technical societies, etc. _____

_____

Have you specialized? _yes_ In what line of work? _____

Carpenter + Mason Work.

If stenographer:

Shorthand speed _____

Typing speed _____

Computing machines <u>fair-good-excellent</u>

In what lines of work are you especially interested:

First _Layout Work_

Second _Carpenter Work_

Third _Mason Work_

Fourth _____

Official Military Personnel File. Jack Amoroso, serial no. 8511936. Application for Enlistment. National Personnel Records Center, St. Louis, Missouri.

EMPLOYMENT RECORD

Give here a complete statement showing every employment you have had, and your present employment. Details may be given on supplemental sheets.

Dates (Mo. and Year) and Salary	Kind of Work Done	By Whom and Where Employed (Names of persons and Companies and Address)	Cause for Leaving
From 1934 - To 1942 $ per	Building Construction	Worked For Myself & Dad	None

Official Military Personnel File. Jack Amoroso, serial no. 8511936. Application for Enlistment. National Personnel Records Center, St. Louis, Missouri.

Navy Service Records (OMPF)

EMPLOYMENT RECORD - Continued

Dates and Salary	Kind of Work Done	By Whom and Where Employed	Cause for Leaving

REFERENCES: Persons whom we may write, preferably former employers, who are competent to judge your experience and fitness for the enlistment you seek.

Name and Relation to Applicant (Employer, Teacher, etc.)	Address	Business or Calling	Years This Person has known Applicant
City Service Lumber	8040 S. Chicago Ave	Lumberman	16
J. T. Fortin (Architect)	Suite 426 New-Era-Bldg	Architect	12
Five Point Mill + Lumber	21st + Canal Port	Millwork	10
Preskill Lumber	2030 W. Taylor	Lumber Co	12
Rockwell Lime Co	160 No La Salle St (Builders) Bldg.	Material Co	7

Add further remarks in your letter if you wish.

Official Military Personnel File. Jack Amoroso, serial no. 8511936. Application for Enlistment. National Personnel Records Center, St. Louis, Missouri.

199

Life Insurance Application

ALLOTMENT FOR $............ FOR INDEFINITE PERIOD TO PAY PREMIUM REGISTERED AT ISNCTO, NOB, NORFOLK, VA.

VETERANS ADMINISTRATION
Insurance Form 350
Rev. Sept. 1942

FIRST PAYMENT ....

Reproduced at the National Archives- STL

C E ARNOLD
ENS SC USNR

APPLICATION FOR NATIONAL SERVICE LIFE INSURANCE

87 C 1

UNDER SECTION 602 (a) NATIONAL SERVICE LIFE INSURANCE ACT OF 1940 AS AMENDED AND REGULATIONS OF THE VETERANS ADMINISTRATION
WITHOUT REPORT OF PHYSICAL EXAMINATION

For use by persons in the active service in the land or naval forces of the United States within 120 days after the date of entrance into the active service. NOTE.—Persons in the active service more than 120 days and persons who reenter the active service (including persons discharged to accept commissions), where such reentrance is a continuation of previous active service without interruption, must make application on Insurance Form 350a, which requires a complete report of physical examination. USE INK OR TYPE.

1. NAME IN FULL: (Please print or type)   JACK   *First*   ALOYSIUS   *Middle*   AMOROSO   *Last name*

2. HOME ADDRESS: Number   933   Street or rural route   Hoyne Ave.   County, city, town, or post office   Chicago   State   Illinois

3. I WAS BORN AT   City, town, or post office   Chicago,   State   Illinois   Day of month   27   Month   May   Year   1922   Age nearest birthday

4. DATE OF ENTRY INTO PRESENT TOUR OF ACTIVE DUTY   1 14 43   5. PRESENT ORGANIZATION   AS   Rank, grade, or rating.   Organization, regiment, station, ship, etc.   V-6 USNR, USNCTC, NOB, NORFOLK, VA.   6. SERIAL NUMBER   851 19 38

7. DATE OF SEPARATION FROM LAST TOUR OF ACTIVE DUTY. (If no previous active duty, state "none.")   NONE   8. ARE YOU NOW DISABLED ON ACCOUNT OF INJURY OR DISEASE? IF SO, STATE DETAILS   NO

9. I HEREBY APPLY FOR INSURANCE ON THE FIVE-YEAR LEVEL PREMIUM TERM PLAN IN THE AMOUNT OF $ 10,000

10. ARE YOU NOW CARRYING GOVERNMENT LIFE INSURANCE? (ANSWER "YES" OR "NO") NO IF "YES" GIVE AMOUNT OF INSURANCE AND POLICY NUMBER IF AVAILABLE. AMOUNT, $............ POLICY No.............
(No person may carry a combined amount of National Service Life Insurance and U. S. Government Life Insurance in excess of $10,000 at any one time)

11. COMPLETE NAME OF EACH BENEFICIARY (If married woman, her own first and middle name and husband's last name must be stated)	Relationship	Amount of insurance to be paid to each beneficiary	Post-office address (Number and street, city, town, or post office and State)
PRINCIPAL Ruby Amoroso	Mother	5,000	933 So. Hoyne, Chicago, Ill.
Benny Amoroso	Father	5,000	Same
CONTINGENT Vito Amoroso	Brother	Equally	Same
Venty Amoroso	Brother	Equally	

Permitted class of beneficiaries: Husband or wife, child, parent, brother, or sister of the insured. (For further information see reverse side, paragraph 2.)

12. I REQUEST THE POLICY BE MAILED TO—(Please print or type)   First Beneficiary   As shown above
(Full name)   (Address)

13. EFFECTIVE DATE OF INSURANCE (see reverse side, paragraph 1). I REQUEST THAT THE EFFECTIVE DATE of this policy be made the 30 day of Jan , 19 43 , and

A. I enclose herewith remittance payable to the TREASURER OF THE UNITED STATES by .... (Check, draft, or money order) in the amount of $............ in payment of the first .... (Write above whether monthly, quarterly, semiannual, or annual) premium on the insurance, or

B. I will register an allotment of pay involving advance of active service pay under the provisions of Public Law 451, 77th Congress, in payment of the first monthly premium of $ 6.50 on the insurance, or

C. I will register an allotment of pay effective in the month in which application for insurance is signed, in payment of the first monthly premium of $............ on the insurance.

If an effective date is not specified by the applicant, the insurance herein applied for shall become effective as follows:
(a) If the first premium is paid by direct remittance or by advance of active service pay under the provisions of Public Law 451, 77th Congress, the insurance shall become effective as of the date on which valid application is signed and such premium is tendered.
(b) If the first premium is paid by regular allotment of pay effective in the month in which application for insurance is signed, the insurance shall become effective as of the first day of the month following the month in which valid application and such allotment are executed, provided the applicant is then in the active service and the amount of the premium is deducted from the applicant's service pay in accordance with the allotment.
THE UNITED STATES IS NOT LIABLE IF DEATH OCCURS PRIOR TO THE EFFECTIVE DATE OF THE POLICY

14. I WILL PAY SUBSEQUENT PREMIUMS IN THE MANNER AND AMOUNT INDICATED BELOW:

A. BY ALLOTMENT OF PAY MONTHLY 6.50	B. BY DIRECT REMITTANCE TO THE VETERANS ADMINISTRATION			
	Monthly	Quarterly	Semiannually	Annually
$	X X X X X X X X	30	X X X X X X X X	Jan

SIGNED AT USNCTC, NOB, NORFOLK, VA. ON THE 30 DAY OF Jan , 19 43

WITNESSED BY: .... and the INFORMATION AS TO SERVICE CERTIFIED BY: ....

(Applicant sign here. Do not print signature)

ENS. USNR
(Rank and organization. See reverse side, paragraph 4.)

NOTE.—Penalties for fraud in securing for self or another the issue or payment of insurance: $1,000 to $5,000 fine and imprisonment. Insurance will be forfeited for mutiny, treason, spying or other specified offenses. (Sections 613, 615, and 619, National Service Life Insurance Act of 1940.)

DO NOT USE THIS SPACE

Effective Date .... Age .... Amt., $............ Premium: Mo. $............ Qr. $............ S. A. $............ A. $............

Beneficiary ....

Action taken ....

Examiner .... Reviewer ....

Certificate issued .... Policy issued ....

16—30588-1

Official Military Personnel File. Jack Amoroso, serial no. 8511936. Life Insurance Application. National Personnel Records Center, St. Louis, Missouri.

Notice of Separation (Discharge Paper)

NOTICE OF SEPARATION FROM U. S. NAVAL SERVICE
NAVPERS-553 (REV. 8-45)

83-1

1. SERIAL OR FILE NO.	2. NAME (LAST) (FIRST) (MIDDLE)	3. RATE AND CLASS/OR	5. PLACE OF SEPARATION
RANK AND CLASSIFICATION	4. PERMANENT ADDRESS FOR MAILING PURPOSES		USN PER. SEP. CEN. GREAT LAKES, ILL.

851-19-36
AMOROSO, JACK ALOYSIUS
FIREMAN 1/C SV-6 USNR
933 S. HOYNE AVE.
CHICAGO, ILL.
COOK CO.

6. CHARACTER OF SEPARATION

HONORABLE

7. ADDRESS FROM WHICH EMPLOYMENT WILL BE SOUGHT

SAME

8. RACE	9. SEX	10. MARITAL STATUS	11. U.S. CITIZEN (YES OR NO)	12. DATE AND PLACE OF BIRTH
W	M	S (D)	YES	7-27-22 CHICAGO, ILL.

13. REGISTERED [X] YES [ ] NO
14. SELECTIVE SERVICE BOARD OF REGISTRATION COOK CO., ILL.
15. HOME ADDRESS AT TIME OF ENTRY INTO SERVICE SAME

16. MEANS OF ENTRY (INDICATE BY CHECK IN APPROPRIATE BOX)
[X] ENLISTED DATE 1-14-43
[X] INDUCTED DATE
[ ] COMMISSIONED DATE

17. DATE OF ENTRY INTO ACTIVE SERVICE 1-14-43
19. PLACE OF ENTRY INTO ACTIVE SERVICE 7-27-22 CHICAGO, ILL.
18. NET SERVICE (FOR PAY PURPOSES) (YRS., MOS., DAYS) 2-10-20

20. QUALIFICATIONS, CERTIFICATES HELD, ETC.

SEE RDB FOR F1/C

21. RATINGS HELD AS, S2/C, S1/C, F1/C

22. FOREIGN AND/OR SEA SERVICE WORLD WAR II [X] YES [ ] NO

23. SERVICE SCHOOLS COMPLETED WEEKS

NONE

24. SERVICE (VESSELS AND STATIONS SERVED ON)
NRS CHICAGO, ILL.
CONST. BATT'S. US NCTC NOB, NOR., VA
" " " " WIM., VA.
69TH NAVAL C.B.
49TH NAVAL C.B.
134TH N.C.B. (T.D.)

IMPORTANT: IF PREMIUM IS NOT PAID WHEN DUE OR WITHIN THIRTY-ONE DAYS THEREAFTER, INSURANCE WILL LAPSE. MAKE CHECKS OR MONEY ORDERS PAYABLE TO THE TREASURER OF THE U. S. AND FORWARD TO COLLECTOR'S SUBDIVISION, VETERAN'S ADMINISTRATION, WASHINGTON 25, D. C

25. KIND OF INSURANCE	26. EFFECTIVE MONTH OF ALLOTMENT DISCONTINUANCE	27. MO. NEXT PREMIUM DUE	28. AMOUNT OF PREMIUM DUE EACH MONTH	29. INTENTION OF VETERAN TO CONTINUE INS.
N	Dec.	Jan	6.50	Yes

30. TOTAL PAYMENT UPON DISCHARGE	31. TRAVEL OR MILEAGE ALLOWANCE INCLUDED IN TOTAL PAYMENT	32. INITIAL MUSTERING OUT PAY	33. NAME OF DISBURSING OFFICER
$ 342.09	$ 1.60	Yes	O.E. Wale 520000

34. REMARKS
POINT SYSTEM
VICTORY RIBBON
ASIATIC-PACIFIC

35. SIGNATURE (BY DIRECTION OF COMMANDING OFFICER)

[signature]

FOR T.V. RILEY   LT. USNR

36. NAME AND ADDRESS OF LAST EMPLOYER	37. DATES OF LAST EMPL'MT.	38. MAIN CIVILIAN OCCUPATION AND D. O. T. NO.
FATHER CHICAGO, ILL.	FROM 1939 TO 1943	NONE

39. JOB PREFERENCE (LIST TYPE, LOCALITY, AND GENERAL AREA)
CONSTRUCTION BUSINESS
CHICAGO, ILL.

40. PREFERENCE FOR ADDITIONAL TRAINING (TYPE OF TRAINING)
ENGINEERING

44. VOCATIONAL OR TRADE COURSES (NATURE AND LENGTH OF COURSE)
12 WEEK AIRCRAFT ENG.

41. NON-SERVICE EDU. (YRS. SUCCESSFULLY COMPLETED) GRAM.: 8 H. S.: 4 COLL.: —
42. DEGREES —
43. MAJOR COURSE OR FIELD GEN

45. RIGHT INDEX FINGERPRINT
46. OFF DUTY EDUCATIONAL COURSES COMPLETED

NONE

47. DATE OF SEPARATION 12-4-45
48. SIGNATURE OF PERSON BEING SEPARATED *[signature]* Jack Aloysius Amoroso

C1

TO: BUR____ ___ NAVAL PERSONNEL

Official Military Personnel File. Jack Amoroso, serial no. 8511936. Separation Paper dated 4 Dec 1945. National Personnel Records Center, St. Louis, Missouri.

Navy Records Created In The Field

The creation of a sailor's story is affected by many pieces. Once you have established the basic facts on a sailor's service, it is time to move beyond only researching the individual to his unit, collaterals within his unit, and the overall organizational histories. Looking at the story from several angles will provide a greater picture of service placed in historical context.

Obtaining Records

While there are many places to obtain Naval records, only two main resources will be described here. The National Archives, College Park, Maryland, and the Naval History and Heritage Command (NHHC) located at the Washington Navy Yard.

The Naval History and Heritage Command recently re-opened to the public after a lengthy closure and limited research services. The staff still only offers limited research services to the public. For extensive research needs, researchers are encouraged to schedule time to visit the NHHC to use the records.

> For current information on the records, access, and availability of services at the Navy History and Heritage Command, visit:
> http://www.history.navy.mil/content/history/nhhc/about-us/contact/directions-and-access.html

Naval Deck Logs

Naval Deck Logs are a valuable resource because they contain rosters of naval personnel, merchant mariners, and Armed Guard units on a vessel or at a station. Logs also contain daily activities performed on the vessel or station.

Deck Logs are available for specific ship or stations and date ranges in which your sailor served. For example, my grandfather, Joseph Holik US Naval Armed Guard, served on the S/S Joshua Hendy from 5 May 1944 to 17 September 1944. Providing the ship and dates of service, I was able to obtain his deck logs for both the ship and Armed Guard.

A Deck Log of a voyage will contain a summary of the voyage, issues encountered with the vessel, convoy, air support, or personnel. A list of cargo, ports of departure and arrival, and a day by day list or full description of events. Each Commanding Officer provided similar, yet different details within the logs. I have received some handwritten and some typewritten.

Repository: RG: 24 Records of the Bureau of the Navy, National Archives, College Park, MD. Naval History and Heritage Command (See Archives then Deck Logs.)

Questions a Navy Deck Log May Answer:

1. What is the name, rank, and serial number of my sailor? What role did he play on the vessel?
2. In what ports did my sailor serve?
3. Where did my sailor go during service on this vessel?
4. What was the purpose of the vessel my sailor was on? Troop transport, cargo transport, hospital ship?
5. Did the ship encounter enemy action? If so, what occurred?
6. What problems occurred while the ship was at sea?
7. Who else served with my sailor? What information can I find for those individuals?

Deck Log SS Joshua Hendy Voyage Ending 2 May 1944

5/5/44 - 9/17/44

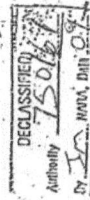

Op-23-L-2

ARMED GUARD UNIT
SS. JOSHUA HENDY
ARMED GUARD CENTER (PACIFIC)
Treasure Island
San Francisco, California

2 May, 1944

CONFIDENTIAL

From: Lieut. (jg) J. L. Brotherton, D-V(S), USNR
             Commanding Officer, Naval Armed Guard
             c/o Armed Guard Center (PACIFIC)
             S.S. JOSHUA HENDY   Gross tons: 7176

To: The Chief of Naval Operations.

Via: The Port Director
             Norfolk, Virginia.

Subject: Report of Voyage, S.S. JOSHUA HENDY
             From: Oran, Algeria. To: Norfolk, Virginia.

Reference: (a) General Instructions for Commanding Officers
                 of Naval Armed Guards on Merchant Ships, par-
                 agraph 4301.

        1.   In accordance with reference (a) the following
information is submitted:

        (a) Type of vessel: EC2(dry cargo). Type of cargo: Army.
             Owner of vessel: War Shipping Administration.
             Operator of vessel: Coastwise Pacific (Fareast) Line.
             Chartered to: United States Army.

        (b) Port of departure: Oran, Algeria. Date: 5 April, 1944.
             Convoyed or independent: convoyed. Speed (average): 8.5.
             No. of ships in convoy, no. of surface escorts and no. of
             aircraft escorts: varying, as indicated in paragraph (d).

        (c) Contacts with enemy: none. Action with enemy: none.

        (d) General resume of voyage: Vessel departed Oran, Algeria,
at 1400 hours, 5 April, 1944, under escort by two (2) PC craft, in station
assigned within column of Oran joiners. At 1510 hours, 5 April, 1944, vessel was forced to leave column station because of temporary breakdown of
telemotor system. At 1530 hours, 5 April, 1944, the telemotor system being
repaired, vessel resumed column station. At 1825 hours, 5 April, 1944, the
column of Oran joiners having taken position to the starboard of westbound
convoy, this vessel was assigned its proper column station by the convoy

(continued)

Deck Log SS Joshua Hendy, Voyage from Oran, Algeria to Norfolk, VA, 5 April 1944 - 2 May 1944. RG: 24.2.2 Logs, Records of the Bureau of Naval Personnel. National Archives, College, Park, MD.

CONFIDENTIAL
page 2

commodore. At 1830 hours, 5 April, 1944, all guns were manned at General Quarters, for a period of two (2) hours before sunset, in accordance with instructions from the United States Naval Liaison Officer, Gibraltar, for for ships steaming in Mediterranean convoys. At 1950 hours, that date, vessel took up proper distance and interval in columns of convoy. At 2030 hours, 5 April, 1944, vessels of convoy were ordered by commodore to man guns and prepare for instant action. At 2117 hours, 5 April, 1944, sea watches were posted and all hands secured from General Quarters.

The convoy joined by subject vessel on 5 April, 1944, was composed of fifty-eight (58) merchant ships, one (1) submarine, one (1) yard net-tender and an air escort varyingly composed of two (2) to four (4) aircraft.

At 0343 hours, 6 April, 1944, vessel suffered breakdown of steering apparatus, and narrowly averted collision with vessel of adjoining column, to port. Emergency signal on ship's whistle was sounded and not-under-command lights were hoisted and displayed at the bridge in good order. At 0355, 6 April, 1944, all guns were manned at battle stations for the protection of vessel as it steamed at reduced speed, falling astern of convoy. At 0425 hours, 6 April, 1944, breakdown was temporarily repaired, the ship being steered by hand gear from the auxilliary steering station, aft. Ship's telemotor system not functioning. Vessel was at this time within columns of convoy, rapidly regaining assigned station. Secure from battle stations. At 1210 hours, 6 April, 1944, vessel was ordered by flashing light signal from convoy commodore to proceed into Gibraltar to effect repairs. In reply, commodore was informed that ship's difficulty was due to an air-bound, unequalized telemotor system and repairs in convoy requested. At 1740 hours, 6 April, 1944, guns were manned for the protection of the vessel while detaching from convoy and entering harbor of Gibraltar. At 1900 hours, 6 April, 1944, anchor was dropped in Gibraltar harbor in moorings designated by pilot and an armed security watch was posted fore and aft and 'midships to port and starboard. Secure from battle stations.

On 15 April, 1944, the ship's telemotor system being satisfactorily repaired, vessel was ordered by the Routing Officer, Royal Naval Control Service Office, Gibraltar, to proceed at 2000 hours GMT that date, independently to seaward to effect rendezvous with convoy westbound through the Straits of Gibraltar. Accordingly, at 1940 hours, 15 April, 1944, guns were manned at General Quarters and at 2000 hours that date, anchor was weighed. Vessel proceeded as ordered down channel to seaward, arriving on stand-by area at 2100 hours, 15 April, 1944. Dim navigation

(continued)

Deck Log SS Joshua Hendy, Voyage from Oran, Algeria to Norfolk, VA, 5 April 1944 - 2 May 1944. RG: 24.2.2 Logs, Records of the Bureau of Naval Personnel. National Archives, College, Park, MD.

CONFIDENTIAL
page 3

lights were shown, in accordance with routing instructions. At 2345 hours, 15 April, 1944, after approximately three (3) hours steaming within the Straits of Gibraltar under conditions of total darkness and without escort, vessel was challenged vocally by advance escort of convoy which this vessel was intended to join. Upon satisfactorily responding to challenge, vessel was provided with bearing and distance of main body of convoy and ordered to take station in rear commodore's portion of convoy. With the assurance that vessel was within the scope of protection offered by the convoy escort, sea watches were posted and all hands secured from General Quarters.

Convoy joined by this vessel on 15 April, 1944, was composed of seventy-seven (77) merchant ships, twelve (12) surface escorts, and an air escort, while within the range of land-based aircraft, varyingly composed of one (1) to three (3) aircraft daily.

On 23 April, 1944, vessels of convoy were ordered to display stern blue lights during dark hours, by convoy commodore. At 2220 hours, 27 April, 1944, vessel suffered temporary breakdown due to failure of lubrication system in engine room. (Further details not provided by ship's master, when requested.) Not-under-command lights hoisted and displayed. At 2230 hours, 27 April, 1944, the vessel making steerage way, not-under-command lights were extinguished and at 2238 hours that date, the breakdown was repaired and vessel resumed column station. At 0740 hours, 28 April, 1944, the vessel was informed by flashing light signal from the convoy commodore that its destination was Hampton Roads, Virginia.

At 2000 hours, 30 April, 1944, ships bound for New York altered course to the northward and dispersed from convoy. Convoy after dispersal was composed of thirty-five ships (35) and six escorts (6).

At 1900 hours, 1 May, 1944, vessels of convoy reformed into two (2) columns for entry into Hampton Roads. At 0030 hours, 1 May, 1944, the pilot came aboard and at 0350 hours, that date, vessel dropped anchor at the Quarantine Anchorage, Norfolk, Virginia. Thereafter, vessel proceeded to berth at dock, in accordance with orders, and discharging of cargo began. Dim navigation lights were shown in accordance with instructions from the Royal Naval Control Service Office, Gibraltar, from the hour of weighing anchor within the harbor of Gibraltar until junction with convoy had been made, 15 April, 1944. Not-under-command lights were displayed as outlined above. Ship did not zig-zag, nor was it ordered to. No fog signals were used.

(e) Delays which resulted in loss of time and turn-

(continued)

Deck Log SS Joshua Hendy, Voyage from Oran, Algeria to Norfolk, VA, 5 April 1944 - 2 May 1944. RG: 24.2.2 Logs, Records of the Bureau of Naval Personnel. National Archives, College, Park, MD.

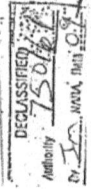

page 4

around of vessel: Vessel lay at anchor in Gibraltar harbor from 6 April, 1944 until 15 April, 1944 undergoing repairs to telemotor system which were completed by 10 April, 1944. Remainder of time in port was spent awaiting convoy.

(f) The commercial radio operator appeared to carry out wartime radio instructions for merchant vessels.

(g) Armament deficiencies or defects: 4"/50 calibre gun, Mk IX, Mod. 5, serial number 2944, installed aft, requires lifting.

(h) Instances of non-compliance with the provisions of Wartime Instructions for United States Merchant Vessels cited in Voyage Reports, this vessel, of 7 February, 1944 and 1 April, 1944 continue in effect, with the following exceptions or additions:

para. (3) Ref. art. 2210, W.I.M.S. No further examples of improper disposal of ship's refuse have been observed.

para. (4) Ref. arts. 11106 and 11107, W.I.M.S. Since departure from the port of Oran, Algeria, ship's master has maintained a file of Admiralty lettered and United States B.A.M.S. numbered messages, which is secured in the perforated metal strong-box provided for ship's classified papers. From the period 15 April until 29 April, 1944, messages decoded on subject voyage were not secured by that officer in the strong-box mentioned.

para. (6) Ref. art. 2302, W.I.M.S. While steaming in Mediterranean waters, at this officer's suggestion that a lookout be posted in the foretop, ship's master advised stationing a member of the Armed Guard Unit in the crow's nest, since the gun crew was standing doubled watches at the time. Thus, in submarine-dangerous waters, no high-level lookout was maintained.

para. (7) Ref. art. 1201, W.I.M.S. At no time since departure from the United States has a merchant marine security or gangway watch been maintained, in port. On one occasion, while vessel was at anchor in the harbor of Freetown, Sierra Leone, West Africa, (as indicated in Voyage Report, this vessel, of 1 April, 1944) no merchant marine officer was present aboard ship for a period of approximately two and one-half hours ($2\frac{1}{2}$), during which the mate on watch had been ordered by the master to take the master ashore in the ship's launch and to await, on the shoreside, the master's return to the ship. Other ship's officers were on regular liberty at the time. In the harbor of Gibraltar, the master was in-

(continued)

Deck Log SS Joshua Hendy, Voyage from Oran, Algeria to Norfolk, VA, 5 April 1944 - 2 May 1944. RG: 24.2.2 Logs, Records of the Bureau of Naval Personnel. National Archives, College, Park, MD.

CONFIDENTIAL
Page 5

sistent that the Armed Guard security watch keep all bum-boats and small craft off the ship's side, to prevent sales of liquor to his crew. All merchant marine personnel were aboard at all times in this port, but no gangway or security watch was maintained. In neither of the instances cited was the ship loading cargo, which under a strict interpretation of the Wartime Instructions would relieve the master of the necessity of posting a security watch, yet in both harbors the danger from sabotage was reported by shore authorities to be great.

para. (8) Ref. art. 1603, W.I.M.S. At all times on subject voyage, lifeboats were swung out.

(i) Recommendations tending to the improvement of the service:

Application of numbers to the 20 mm. magazines in the ready box is useful in designating which magazines are initially to be tensioned to the maximum and in providing a means for the systematic release and increase of tension on the magazine follower springs, in rotation, throughout the voyage. (This procedure suggested by ADAMS, Ernest Lynn, GM3c, 630 25 25, USNR.)

(j) Instances of improper procedure on the part of friendly aircraft: none to report.

Note: Since vessel was not engaged in action with the enemy on subject voyage, a list of Armed Guard and Communication Liaison personnel embarked has not been included in the present report.

Joseph L. Brotherton

JOSEPH L. BROTHERTON

Deck Log SS Joshua Hendy, Voyage from Oran, Algeria to Norfolk, VA, 5 April 1944 - 2 May 1944. RG: 24.2.2 Logs, Records of the Bureau of Naval Personnel. National Archives, College, Park, MD.

Navy Muster Rolls

Navy Muster Rolls are similar to Army Morning Reports and the Marine Corps Muster Rolls in that they document the comings and goings of sailors stationed on a vessel or port station. Monthly rosters were compiled to show changes in personnel while quarterly Muster Rolls were created to document the entire history of the quarter.

Muster Rolls contain the name, rank, serial number, station or vessel, enlistment date, and date the sailor or other personnel reported for duty. Muster Rolls also contain personnel other than Naval sailors, like Army personnel being transported, women in service, and personnel from other branches on Naval Hospital Transports. Combined with a sailor's OMPF, and deck logs, a researcher can compile a detailed summary of service.

Repository: RG: 24.2.3 Records of the Bureau of the Navy, National Archives, College Park, MD. Some are available on Ancestry.com but due to the way they are indexed, you may not find every roll on which your sailor should be listed. If you seek Armed Guard lists, try College Park first.

Questions a Navy Muster Roll May Answer:

1. Name, rank, service number, and unit of a Marine.
2. Casualty information.
3. Transfer information.
4. Change of duty information.

Muster Roll Report of Changes USS Antaeus 6 Dec 1943

Muster Roll USS Antaeus, 6 December 1943. RG: 24.2.2 Muster Rolls, Records of the Bureau of Naval Personnel. National Archives, College, Park, MD.

Navy Records Created in the Field

The Muster Roll shown on these two pages contains the top port on the page prior and the bottom portion shown here. The numbers correspond to the same sailor at the top. Using Muster Rolls to track change of station or vessel, you can then request Deck Logs if you did not previously know a ship on which your ancestor served.

	6 Branch of Service	7 Received, transferred, deserted, discharged, change of rating, death, or any other change of status	8 Date of Occurrence in column 7	9 Vessel or station from which received, to what vessel or station transferred, where discharged and character of discharge; where deserted, and amount due or overpaid. Where died, cause of death and where and when buried. If rated and authority for same. If disrated, give cause, if on detached duty, give place of duty. If passenger, give purpose of travel and final disposition.
1	V-6	Rec	12-6-43	From 69th NCB FFT Davisville, R.I.
2	V-6 S	do	do	do
3	V-6	do	do	do
4	V-6	do	do	do
5	V-6 S	do	do	do
6	V-6	do	do	do
7	V-6 S	do	do	do
8	V-6 S	do	do	do
9	V-6 S	do	do	do
10	V-6	do	do	do
11	V-6 S	do	do	do
12	V-6 S	do	do	do
13	V-6	do	do	do
14	V-6 S	do	do	do
15	V-6 S	do	do	do

This form to be submitted by commanding officers of all ships and stations, whenever any ship or station is commissioned or placed out of commission, on the last day of each month showing all changes for the month for which submitted; also upon sailing from one port to another, by commanding officers of point of origin of transfer and point of destination of enlisted passengers.

Muster Roll USS Antaeus, 6 December 1943. RG: 24.2.2 Muster Rolls, Records of the Bureau of Naval Personnel. National Archives, College, Park, MD.

Navy Accident Reports

Navy Accident Reports were created any time a pilot had an accident. The accident could have caused his death, or in some cases, a MIA status. The accident did not have to result in the death of the pilot, his crew, or anyone on the ground, for a report to be completed. Navy Accident Reports exist for both death accidents, and non-death accidents.

Accident Reports describe the accident which occurred, provide the vital informaiton of a pilot and his crew, if applicable, and describe damage to the aircraft. Typically pre-1950 Navy Accident Reports are one page in length. Much of the information is usually contained in the OMPF as well.

Repository: National Archives, College Park, MD. Aviation Archaeology website.
Aviation Archaeology is a company that, for a fee, will copy and send you the Navy Accident Report. Their website has many resources, including a database of pilots and crew. In some cases, there are names missing, but a quick email to the company inquiring about a name will yield a response. This company also focuses on Army Air Corps reports.

Questions a Navy Accident Report May Answer:

This section list questions, then break questions out on each page with source and answers to questions.

1. What was his full name, rank, unit, and service number?
2. When and where did the accident occur?
3. Was the pilot or crew declared KIA?
4. If pilot or crew was KIA, what were the circumstances surrounding the deaths and recovery?

| Navy Accident Report for George T. Howe Feb. 1943 |

INJURY FLYING OR LANDING CONDITIONS LOCATION OF ACCIDENT

NAME AND HOURS FLYING EXPERIENCE — PILOT

DATE OCCURRED 12 February 1943

LOCATION NAS Alameda

DETAILED CAUSE

FLYING OR LANDING CONDITIONS Normal

0805

ANALYSIS

Plane was damaged when pilot groundlooped to
left on takeoff. Pilot apparently added throttle
too fast, causing plane to swerve to left. In
addition he apparently dropped his flaps before
picking up speed and by doing so, possibly blanked
off his rudder, thus reducing effective control.

Purpose of flight: Dummy gunnery runs - F

AIRCRAFT TROUBLE ANALYSIS

NAME AND RANK HOWE, G. T., Jr., Ensign

SERVICE AND CORPS AVN, USNR

ORGANIZATION VGS-23 VC-19

DATE OF PILOT RATING 9-10-42

HRS THIS MODEL (LAST) MOS 41.1 FLYING EXPERIENCE (YEARS) 1

TOTAL HOURS 181.5

PREVIOUS ACCIDENT RECORD Clear

Injury: None

PERSONNEL

NAME AND RANK

None

43 59369

AIRPLANE CLASS VF (L)

MODEL AND NUMBER F4F-4 06291

REMARKS

Propeller badly bent. Right landing
gear broken. Right tire worn thru
and blown out. Right wing badly
wrinkled near wing tip. Right stub
wing badly wrinkled. Firewall
cracked just inboard of landing
edge of right wing.

NATURE OF ACCIDENT

PERCENTAGE EACH CAUSE

75% PE (poor technique 25% Misc.)

Navy Accident Report for George T. Howe, Jr., no. 435969, dated 12 February 1943. Aviation Archaeology.

Navy Accident Report for George T. Howe 1943

Navy Accident Report for George T. Howe, Jr., no. 448777, dated 24 September 1943. Aviation Archaeology.

Missing Air Crew Reports

Missing Air Crew Reports (MACRs) <u>are **not** Navy records</u>. These are records created by the Army Air Corps. You will not find MACRs for Navy or Marine aviators. Reports of those missing from the Navy and Marine Corps are found in Mission Reports. A MACR was created for combat losses within the Army Air Corps.

These records are helpful to researchers who had a sailor or Marine, die in an Army Air Corps plane crash, or that have a Missing In Action (MIA) status due to a combat loss, for an Army Transport aircraft or Hospital Transport aircraft.

What does this mean? If your Marine was being transported by an Army Air Corps plane, from one combat location to another, or to a different base, and the plane was lost, a MACR was created. If your sailor was a patient on an aircraft transporting patients from a combat zone or ship to a base, and the plane went down, there will be a MACR.

MACRs are explained in detail in the Army Records Created In The Field Chapter of Volume 1, but the information is repeated here for those who have a sailor or Marine who were on an Army Air Corps plane that was lost.

The Missing Air Crew Report

The main document contained in MACR is the Missing Air Crew Report. This document contains the name, rank, unit, and service number of crew members, location within the plane or bomber of each crew member, destination of the plane, and location of the crash or approximate location the plane went missing. The type of aircraft, equipment with service numbers on board, and details about the mission and crash or loss status are also included. Name, rank, and service number of those who witnessed the downing of an aircraft are listed at the bottom of the report.

Downing Report

The Downing Report contains information on the combat loss, including date and location, cause, and the fate of the crew. A combat report, sketch of the area in which the plane was lost, and witness statements are often included.

German Documents

Within European Theater MACRs, there may be German documents and translations of those documents. The Germans documented the planes they shot down, number of crew killed or captured, and credited those losses to a specific unit within the German Army. These reports may provide additional details to assist in locating buried airmen.

Maps/Diagrams

Maps or diagrams may be found within the file, showing the formation of a bomber group in relation to what happened to the lost plane(s). German documents may provide additional details, including coordinates, with a diagram or map.

Testimony on the Combat Loss and Location of Possible Graves or POW Status

Depending on the type and location of the loss, reports may exist within both the European Theater and Pacific Theater as to the fate of the crew. Testimony taken by military units during the war, or the Graves Registration Service during or after the war, may shed light on the fate of the crew.

Examine the MACR located after this section, for the 345th Bomb Group, 500th Bomb Squadron, crew of pilot James C. Buffington, dated 9 January 1945. This plane's crew took off from Tacloban Strip at Leyte, destined for Luzon. The plane was last sighted by Cpl. Myron Mauldin.

The pages following the MACR contain testimony taken after the war, when the soldier was already home in the U.S., dated 24 April 1946. His testimony describes the recovery of some crew members of a B-25 that crashed in the area. In the end, the crew was deemed unrecoverable by Graves Registration.

It is important to understand the information contained in a MACR may not always be for the airmen listed in the report. In the Pacific Theater, when planes went down in remote locations or several were downed in an area, several things could have caused the unrecoverable status of airmen.

Testimonies taken may have been months or years after the plane was lost. Memories fade or become jumbled. Airmen may have been buried, but records were either lost or not kept in the first place. Have you ever played the telephone game where a message was passed, and by the last person it barely resembles the original message? Instead of a record, information passed by word of mouth and was lost. Over time, remains may have been moved or destroyed due to war. There are numerous other reasons for information provided later to be incorrect or insufficient to recover remains. This will be discussed further in Volume 3, when I explore in greater depth, the death and associated records.

Additional Personnel Onboard – Non-Army Air Corps Personnel

Missing planes did not always carry only Air Corps personnel. Hospital planes and troop transport planes were also lost. In the following example, using MACR 13672, you will see not only airmen, but Marines, Army, and Navy personnel or patients onboard the aircraft. This aircraft was going from Mindoro to Leyte. The MACR is shown detailing the mission or flight.

Following the testimony discussed above, the following page lists all the personnel and patients missing due to the aircraft loss. Note at the bottom, the * explaining which patients were not U.S. Army Personnel or Not U.S. Personnel.

The final page shown, is the beginning of a list of each soldier on the aircraft and his next-of-kin to be notified. This page is blurry and difficult to read.

Finally, if members of a crew were captured as POWs, information concerning their capture may be contained within the MACR.

Repository: National Archives, College Park, MD. Air Force Historical Research Agency. Aviation Archaeology website. Fold3.com.

Questions a MACR May Answer:

1. For every individual listed in the MACR, what is their name, rank, unit, and service number?
2. Where was the aircraft stationed, and what was its destination?
3. When and where did the accident occur?
4. What was the fate of the crew (MIA, KIA, and POW?)
5. Was there a definitive MIA, KIA, or FOD date?
6. Were the remains buried? Where? Were they recovered?

MACR #16290

COPY

MISSING AIR CREW REPORT

1. ORGANIZATION: Location APO 72 ; Command or Air Force FEC-Fifth Group 345th Bomb ; Squadron 500th Bomb ; Detachment

2. SPECIFY: Point of Departure Tacloban Strip ; Course 300 Deg. Intended Destination Luzon ; Type of Mission Bombing & Strafi

3. WEATHER CONDITIONS AND VISIBILITY AT TIME OF CRASH OR WHEN LAST REPORTED: Weather 3/10 cu. 2000 to 4000. Visibility 10 Miles

4. GIVE: (a) Day 9 Month January Year 1945 Time 0945/I and Location Last sighted 8 mile S of Tarlac Town. of last known whereabouts of missing aircraft.
(b) Specify whether ( ) Last Sighted; ( ) Last Contacted by Radio; ( ) Forced down; ( ) Seen to Crash; or ( ) Information not Available.

5. AIRCRAFT WAS LOST, OR IS BELIEVED TO HAVE BEEN LOST, AS A RESULT OF: ( ) Enemy Aircraft; ( ) Enemy Anti-Aircraft; ( ) Other circumstances as follows: Airplane Missing

6. AIRCRAFT: Type, Model and Series B-25J ; AAF Ser. No. 43-36187

7. ENGINES: Type, Model and Series R-2600-29 ; AAF Ser. No. (a) L 43-27694
(b) R-43-277784 ; (c) ; (d)

8. INSTALLED WEAPONS (Furnish below Make, Type and Serial Number)
(a) See Attached ; (b) ; (c)
(d) Carcass. ; (f) ; (g)

9. THE PERSONS LISTED BELOW WERE REPORTED AS: (a) Battle Casualty or (b) Non Battle Casualty Missing in Action

10. NUMBER OF PERSONS ABOARD AIRCRAFT: Crew 6 ; Passengers Total 6
(Starting with Pilot, furnish the following particulars: If more than 11 persons were aboard aircraft, list similar particulars on separate sheet and attach original to this form.)

	CREW POSITION	Name in Full (Last Name First)	RANK	SERIAL NUMBER	CURRENT STATUS
1.	Pilot	BUFFINGTON, JAMES C.	2nd Lt	O-575664	
2.	Co-Pilot	THOMPSON, RICHARD T.	Capt	O-427048	
3.	Nav-Bomb	BUCHANAN, VERNON C.	2nd Lt	O-707822	
4.	Eng-Gun	DUBRAVANT, BERNARD R.	Cpl	13116888	
5.	Rad-Gun	NELSON, WALTER J.	T/Sgt	20246140	
6.	Arm-Gun	HERTZ, JOSEPH	Cpl	12794422	
7.					
8.					
9.					
10.					
11.					

11. IDENTIFY BELOW THOSE PERSONS WHO ARE BELIEVED TO HAVE LAST KNOWLEDGE OF AIRCRAFT, AND CHECK APPROPRIATE COLUMN TO INDICATE BASES FOR SAME:

Check only one Column

	Name in Full (Last Name First)	Rank	Serial Number	Contacted by Radio	Last Sighted	Saw Forced Landing
1.	MAULDIN, MYRON J	Cpl	37701833		X	
2.						
3.						

12. IF PERSONNEL ARE BELIEVED TO HAVE SURVIVED, ANSWER YES TO ONE OF THE FOLLOWING STATEMENTS: (a) Parachutes were used ; (b) Persons were seen walking away from scene of crash ; or (c) any other reason (Specify) See Attach Carcass

13. ATTACH AERIAL PHOTOGRAPH, MAP, CHART, OR SKETCH, SHOWING APPROXIMATE LOCATION WHERE AIRCRAFT WAS LAST SEEN. ATTACHED.

14. ATTACH EYEWITNESS DESCRIPTION OF CRASH, FORCED LANDING OR OTHER CIRCUMSTANCES PERTAINING TO MISSING AIRCRAFT. ATTACHED.

15. ATTACH A DESCRIPTION OF THE EXTENT OF SEARCH, IF ANY, INCLUDING DESCRIPTION AND EXTENT WITH NAME RANK AND SERIAL NO OF OFFICER IN CHARGE: GANNING, ROBERT B. 2nd Lt O-759411

Date of Report 11 January 1945

/s/ & /t/ F. F. BENTZ, 2d Lt, AC, Asst Operations Office

COPY

(Signature of Preparing Officer)

INCL #4

Missing Air Crew Report #16290, dated 11 Jan 1945. Aviation Archaeology.

April 24, 1946

Office of the Quartermaster General
Washington 25, D. C.

Attention: Memorial Division

Sir:

This is in reply to a letter from your office of April 12, 1946, reference SPQYG 704.8 in which you ask for information concerning the recovery and burial of the remains of the crew members on B-25 J 43-36187, which crashed in Angeles, Central Luzon, Philippines on January 9, 1945.

The writer, of course, has no record in this instance, but I recall that I did personally supervise the recovery of the bodies of certain crew members of a B-25 on or about February 1, 1945.

I believe that I can best impart this data to you in narrative form and the circumstances were as follows:

On or about February 1, 1945, I received information that several bodies of American airmen were buried near a church in Angeles, Luzon. I immediately contacted the Filipino Priest of this church and found that a B-25 had been disabled in the air over Clark Field (prior to our occupation of that area) and in attempting a landing had crashed through the top of the church. The roof of the church was very badly damaged and some 200 yards farther on there were parts of what Filipinos told me to be a B-25. We could not secure the numbers on the B-25, but on the vertical stabilizer there was an insignia of an Indian head, which I found later to be the insignia of a unit known as the Red Raiders or some such name. In other words, the name was Raiders, but I am not sure as to whether or not it was RED Raiders.

The Priest showed me the grave marker that the Japanese soldiers had set up over the common grave of five air crewmen from this B-25, and I immediately dispatched members of the Grave Registration Unit that was attached to my office, to disinter these bodies.

I personally saw the disinterment and know that the Grave Registration Unit made every attempt to obtain identification which was impossible due to the fact that the bodies were over 50% decomposed, and the local Filipinos told us that the Japanese had taken the identification tags and all other personal effects from the bodies before they were buried. However, we did recover sufficient of the remains to find that there were, or had been five bodies buried.

The remains were buried at Culayo Cemetery No. 1 located approximately 500 yards west of Dau Station, which is a station on the railroad near the intersection of the main highway from Manila, North, and the road that leaves this highway to Fort Stotsenberg.

21345

1 Incl. #3

Missing Air Crew Report #16290 Bombing Report dated 24 April 1945. Aviation Archaeology.

Arlington, D. C.

Page 2
April 24, 1946

The Graves Registration Unit completed GRU Form No. 1 and all other necessary data, and these were forwarded through XIV Corp Headquarters. The retained copies were turned over to the 43rd Division Quartermaster who relieved the 40th Division (of which I was the Division Quartermaster) on March 1, 1945. I do not recall the unit designation of the Graves Registration Unit, but do know that it was a XIV Corp Graves Registration Unit. All of the bodies were interred as UNIDENTIFIED.

R. B. MORGAN
1740 - 4th Avenue
Sacramento 14, California

C O P Y   C O P Y

21345

Missing Air Crew Report #16290 Bombing Report dated 24 April 1945. Aviation Archaeology.

MACR #13672 - Hospital Plane

CONFIDENTIAL

WAR DEPARTMENT
HEADQUARTERS ARMY AIR FORCES
WASHINGTON

MISSING AIR CREW REPORT

Classification changed
to **RESTRICTED**
cx .... Lt. Col., AG
by R. W. M. AN'H, Capt., AC
Date .... MAC ....

1. ORGANIZATION: Location by Name ___Tanauan___ ; Command or Air Force _5th AF_
   Group 433rd T. C. ; Squadron 69th T. C. ; Detachment _____
2. SPECIFY: Place of Departure Elmore (Mindoro) ; Course Elmore to Tanauan
   Target or Intended Destination Tanauan (Leyte) ; Type of Mission Air Evac.
3. WEATHER CONDITIONS AND VISIBILITY AT TIME OF CRASH OR WHEN LAST REPORTED:
   Unknown
4. GIVE: (a) Day 12 ; Month Mar ; Year 1945; Time 1045; and Location Elmore Strip
   of last known whereabouts of missing aircraft.
   (b) Specify whether aircraft was last sighted (X); Last contacted by
   radio ( ); Forced down ( ); Seen to Crash ( ); or Information not Available ( );
5. AIRCRAFT WAS LOST, OR IS BELIEVED TO HAVE BEEN LOST, AS A RESULT OF: (Check
   only one) Enemy Aircraft ( ); Enemy Anti-Aircraft ( ): Other Circumstances as
   follows: Weather
6. AIRCRAFT Type, Model and Series ___C-46D___ ; AAF Serial Number 44-77373
7. NICKNAME OF AIRCRAFT, If any___None___
8. ENGINES: Type, Model and Series P & W R2800-51 : AAF Serial Number
   (a) Left FP-081989 ; (b) FP-081985 ; (c)_____ ; (d)_____
9. INSTALLED WEAPONS (Furnish below Make, Type and Serial Number):
   (a) 2 Thompson Sub-Machine Guns ; (b)_____ ; (c)_____
10. THE PERSONS LISTED BELOW WERE REPORTED AS: (a) Battle Casualty _____
    or (b) Non Battle Casualty X
11. NUMBER OF PERSONS ABOARD AIRCRAFT: Crew 4 Passengers Unknown ; Total Unknown
    (Starting with Pilot, furnish the following particulars: If more than 11 persons
    were aboard aircraft, list similar particulars on separate sheet and attach ori-
    ginal to this form.)

	Crew Position	Name in Full (Last Name First)	Grade	Serial Number	Current Status
DED 1.	Pilot	Kelly, Leo J.	2nd Lt.	O-699426	Missing
DED 2.	Co-pilot	Healy, Paul A.	2nd Lt.	O-769437	Missing
DED 3.	Engineer	Oja, Theodore S.	Sgt.	17158006	Missing
DEP 4.	Radio Operator	Klester, Charles W.	S/Sgt	33080628	Missing
5.	See Attachment # 1. list of medical attendants and patients.				
6.					
7.					
8.					
9.					
10.					
11.					

Incl 1

-1-

CONFIDENTIAL

Missing Air Crew Report #13672, dated 13 Mar 1945. Aviation Archaeology.

CONFIDENTIAL

12. IDENTIFY BELOW THOSE PERSONS WHO ARE BELIEVED TO HAVE LAST KNOWLEDGE OF AIRCRAFT,
AND CHECK APPROPRIATE COLUMN TO INDICATE BASIS FOR SAME:

Check only one Column

Name in Full (Last Name First)	Grade	Serial Number	Contacted by Radio	Last Sighted	Saw Crash	Forced Landing
1. Daugherty, Robert W.	2nd Lt.	O-820962		X		
2. Operations Officer, Elmore Strip.			X			

13. IF PERSONNEL ARE BELIEVED TO HAVE SURVIVED, ANSWER YES TO ONE OF THE FOLLOWING
STATEMENTS: (a) Parachutes were used ___ ; (b) Persons were seen walking away
from scene of crash ___ ; or (c) Any other reason (Specify) Unknown
14. ATTACH AERIAL PHOTOGRAPH, MAP, CHART OR SKETCH, SHOWING APPROXIMATE LOCATION
WHERE AIRCRAFT WAS LAST SEEN OR HEARD FROM (Airplane was last seen at Elmore
Strip, Mindoro, therefore map, chart, etc. not pertinent.)
15. ATTACH EYEWITNESS DESCRIPTION OF CRASH, FORCED LANDING, OR OTHER CIRCUMSTANCES
PERTAINING TO MISSING AIRCRAFT. (See Attachment No. 1)
16. GIVE NAME, GRADE AND SERIAL NUMBER OF OFFICER IN CHARGE OF SEARCH, IF ANY,
INCLUDING DESCRIPTION AND EXTENT   No search has been made yet due to weather,
but queries have been sent out through AACS, 433rd Troop Carrier Group, and
54th Troop Carrier Wing.

Date of Report 13 March, 1945.

(Signature of Presenting Officer)
RALPH C. ALEXANDER,
Captain, Air Corps,
Commanding.

17. REMARKS OR EYEWITNESS STATEMENTS: (See attachments)

3 ATTACHMENTS:
1. Statement of 2nd Lt. Robert W. Daugherty.
2. Statement of 1st Lt. Bruce L. Marble
3. Message from 69th Sq. to Elmore Strip.
4. List of patients and medical personnel aboard X366.

Incl. 1

-2-

CONFIDENTIAL

Missing Air Crew Report #13672, dated 13 Mar 1945. Aviation Archaeology.

MACR #13672 - Additional Personnel MIA

HEADQUARTERS
54TH TROOP CARRIER WING
APO 248

MEDICAL PERSONNEL ABOARD X366, MISSING 12 MARCH 1945

STATUS		NAME	RANK	ASN	ORGN
		Medical Attendants:			
		Memler, Beatrice M.	2nd Lt.	N-788562	804th MAES
		Hudson, John H.	T/3	18216869	804th MAES
		Patients			
DNB	1.	Adamsky, Thomas (NMI)	Pfc	33395514	Hqs 21st Inf Regt
DNB	2.	Cots, Fabian T.	T/4	39842703	Hq & Sv 658 Amph Trac Bn
DNB	3.	Ingalls, Phillip	Pvt	32472946	13th Sta Hosp
DNB	4.	Sintic, Joseph E.	Pvt	35919729	21st Inf Regt
DNB	5.	Jahnke, Ray S.	Pfc	36025963	D 186th Inf Regt
DNB	6.	Meagher, Harry B.	Pvt	39328703	405 Sig Co Avn
DNB	7.	Arel, Gerald P.	Pvt	31383697	3144 Sig Sv Det
DNB	8.	Mills, Charles L.	T/4	37158737	1458 EBM
DNB	9.	Kvist, Alfred J.	Pfc	36265182	Hqs 34th Inf Regt
DNB	10.	Wells, George E.	Sgt	14097552	C 511 Para Inf
DNB	11.	Najecki, Edward J.	Pfc	32357358	A 3 Engr Bn (C)
	12.	Clarke, Matthew J.	Sgt	20229802	C 19th Inf
DNB	13.	Hankerson, John E.	Sgt	34719572	1938 Ordn Co
DNB	14.	Howard, Ralph M.	Cpl	14185538	35 Ftr Sq 5 Ftr Gp
DNB	15.	Wynn, James L.	T/5	18630578	E 543 EB & SR
DNB	16.	Anger, William F.	T/5	39142267	B 658 Amph Trac Bn
**	17.	Magboo, Maximo	Pvt		Co B 5th Phil-Amer Army
DNB	18.	Johnes, Hurtle	Pfc	34730913	K 162 Inf Regt
DNB	19.	Turner, Lytle I.	Pfc	35917725	PCAU 23 USAFFE
*	20.	Avers, William M.	Cpl	835152	MAG 32 USMC
DNB	21.	Weltick, Harold W.	Pfc	32689091	C 186 Inf Regt
DNB	22.	Bishop, Audie H.	Sgt	13036741	303 A D Sq
*	23.	Zakrzawski, Rudolph L.	S 1/c	700-92-65	USCG LST #18
DNB	24.	Twitchell, James R.	Pfc	39525522	41st Sig Corps
DNB	25.	Gilley, Paul E.	Pfc	13117368	543 EB & SR
DNB	26.	Collins, Clyde C.	T/5	36264632	Btry B 102 AAA
DNB	27.	Fredrickson, Virgil H.	Pvt	37518702	Btry A 102 AAA
DNB	28.	White, Clarence H.	Pvt	36218926	5237 Sig Co

* Not U.S. Army personnel
** Not U. S. Personnel

Missing Air Crew Report #13672, Additional Personnel on board aircraft. Aviation Archaeology.

MACR #13672 - Next-of-Kin Sample

1st Lt. Leo J. Nelly   *pilot*   Mr. Hugh J. Nelly (father)
Rising City, Nebraska

2nd Lt. Paul A. Healy   *co-pilot*   Mr. Edward C. Healy (father)
Fountain, Minnesota

2nd Lt. Beatrice M. Mahler   Mr. Isidore Mahareus (father)
Malabar Street
Los Angeles, California

T/Sgt. John R. Hudson   Mrs. Dorothy K. Hudson (wife)
Mockingbird Lane
Dallas, Texas

T/Sgt. Charles W. Kiester   *radio op.*   Mr. Paul M. Kiester (father)
Burbank Avenue
Kittanning, Pennsylvania

Sgt. Theodore S. Oja   *engineer*   Mrs. Ida Oja (mother)
Box 9
Iron, Minnesota

Sgt. George E. Wells   Mrs. Myrtle Wells (mother)
Whittington, Mississippi

Sgt. Matthew J. Clarke   Mrs. Winifred Clarke (mother)
Riverdale Avenue
Yonkers, New York

Sgt. John E. Henkerson   Mrs. Louise Henkerson (wife)
Kentucky Street
Memphis, Tennessee

Sgt. Palden T. Cote   Mrs. Donalda Cote (mother)
Roland City, Oregon

Sgt. Charles L. Mills   Mrs. Laura Mills (mother)
Route 6
Ft. Wayne, Indiana

Missing Air Crew Report #13672, next-of-kin list, dated 13 Mar 1945. Aviation Archaeology.

World War II Diaries

Naval War Diaries, also called War Diaries, were daily operational journals kept by Naval Ships, documenting personnel, enemy engagement, battles, and aircraft flown. These reports can be very detailed outlining air missions, battle engagements, and often include Marine Corps missions, particularly for pilots. Please see the chapter on Marine Corps Records in the Field for more details on these records as the Navy and Marine Corps often intertwine.

These operational journals may also contain Action Reports, which detail enemy engagement, losses, prisoners taken, and damaged equipment. The information in these journals varies from unit to unit. Some unit information may be very descriptive, while other units may provide basic facts. It is a good idea to find official Marine Corps histories written after the war to further research and document your Marine's service.

Repository: National Archives, College Park, MD. Many of these have been digitized and are available at Fold3.com.

Questions a War Diary may answer:

1. Name, rank, service number, unit in which serving at a specific time.
2. Promotions and demotions in rank.
3. Mission information – air missions or land missions.
4. Results of mission.
5. Casualty information. Status of MIA, POW, or KIA.
6. Where a ship or unit was located (you can map the locations).

Naval Unit Histories

Naval Unit Histories are similar to those written for the Army or Air Corps, Marine Corps, and Coast Guard. Histories vary in content based on the author. Some may be very detailed citing most official records created for the unit, while others may provide a less detailed record of service. As with other branch histories, depending on who wrote the history, and what was discussed, you may or may not find your sailor's name. The histories do provide historical context for your sailor and often leads to additional record sources to search.

Questions a Unit History may answer:

1. What did the overall war look like from the perspective of this unit or division?
2. How does this history help tell the story of my individual sailor?
3. What clues can I pull from this overall history to locate additional information about my sailor?
4. Are there details about the wounding, prisoner status, missing status, or death of my sailor?

Repository: Naval History and Heritage Command, Washington Navy Yard, D.C. Also search for the unit online. Some histories may have been digitized by reunion or association groups.

Correspondence

Explore the correspondence within unit records. While sailors could not outline specific things that were happening or exactly where they were, in personal correspondence, unit correspondence will provide other clues as to what was happening. These clues help provide historical context for your soldier and may lead to new research opportunities.

Repository: Naval History and Heritage Command, Washington Navy Yard, D.C. Archival collections in libraries and museum. Personal collections.

Questions Correspondence may answer:

1. Reading correspondence from another sailor's perspective, what was the war or battle like for him? How might that affect my sailor's story?
2. If this is an officer within my sailor's unit, is my soldier ever mentioned in official correspondence?
3. Does the correspondence mention other names I should research?

Photographs, Maps, and Aerial Photography

Photographs are another resource which can provide historical context, information on battles and missions, and illustrate what a sailor saw during service. Look for individual photos, miscellaneous photos, battle photos, bombing photos, and maps.

Sailor Photos. Photographs of sailors can be single person shots or group shots. Pay particular attention to any uniforms, airplanes, vehicles, stripes on the uniform, other clothing, markings on vehicles or aircraft, location of the photograph, or any piece of evidence that might identify the people and what they were doing.

Miscellaneous Photos. Some sailors carried cameras with them during training and overseas service. Often, these photos will include their buddies, scenery where they were stationed, equipment, and if on leave, tourist sites they may have visited. Even if the photos you discover are undated, comparing them against the service timeline, and possibly the country in which they were, you can piece together additional service history and experiences.

Battle Photos. Photographs which depict the battle, the weapons used, men marching or on the ships, aircraft taking off or landing, the prisoners, and the dead provide a real glimpse at war. The brutality, hunger, heat or cold, shines through and adds to your soldier's story.
Bombing and Mission Photos. If your soldier was a pilot or part of an aircrew, look for mission information, photographs of sites to bomb, both prior to and after. Just as men carried cameras into combat, your airman may have photos from the skies.

Maps. Maps are valuable because they help you trace the service locations of your soldier. They provide historical context on both large and small scale maneuvers and missions. Maps illustrate the story of your soldier.

Repository: Naval History and Heritage Command, Washington Navy Yard, D.C. Libraries and archival collections. Personal collections.

Marine Corps Records

During World War II the Marine Corps fell under the authority of the Navy. The records shown in the previous chapter have similarities to the records in this chapter. It was also not uncommon for Marines to have served in the Navy first. Many Naval Aviators transferred to the Marine Corps after earning their wings. When you receive the Marine Corps file for your Marine see if it talks about prior service. This is likely especially if the Service Record page and photograph are missing. The Marine Corps file should provide the military branch and serial number. Using this you can initiate another records search.

The Official Military Personnel File

The Official Military Personnel File (OMPF) can be a large descriptive file if the Marine had served many years or a smaller file if he was only in during part of the war. The main documents often found in an OMPF are described here. Document examples will be provided with each main record description in this chapter.

Files may also contain letters for information requests from relatives and others conducting research. The original request will be included in the file which means you may discover a relative you did not know existed.

Example records in this chapter belong to Pvt. William F. Cowart amtrac driver and Pfc. Arthur M. Pearson, rifleman. You can view entire files on my website in the book's Additional Resource section.

One of the most important things you should do when you receive the OMPF is sort it in chronological order so the reports and events make sense.

General Contents of a Marine Corps OMPF

Service Record Summary. The Service Record Summary page will contain a photograph of the Marine, vital information, and enlistment information.

Application for Reserves. The Application for Reserves was required of any man with a college-level education. These men were likely to become Officers within a short time. Each had to provide information about his life, education, job history, prior service history, and family information. Often the man had to write a letter explaining why he wished to join the service and provide proof of birth, college transcripts, and letters of recommendation.

Service Qualification Card. The Service Qualification Card contained much of the information on the service application with the inclusion of more information on hobbies and sports participation. This card may have also contained information on service. This was completed by men voluntarily enlisting in the Marine Corps. Men who were later drafted did not complete this card.

Next-of-Kin and Insurance Information. Each reservist had to complete next-of-kin contact information in case of wounds, Missing In Action, Prisoner of War, or Killed In Action status changes. Connected to this information was insurance beneficiary information.

Medical information. Some medical information will be included in an OMPF, usually regarding the physical and dental exams conducted upon induction or change in rank. Sometimes the records of Marines treated in stateside hospitals were included.

Not all medical information is contained in the OMPF. There are usually separate medical files. These files can only be requested by the veteran or his next-of-kin even if the Marine has been dead 100 years. It is important if you are the veteran or next-of-kin, you request these records. If the veteran is deceased, you must provide proof of death in the form of a death certificate, obituary, or funeral paperwork.

Professional and Conduct Record. This record contains a summary of all locations in which the Marine trained and units in which he served. This record does not specify where "In The Field" the Marine was when he was stationed overseas. You have to look at After Action Reports and unit histories to determine where the Marine unit was fighting.

Appointment for Marine Corps Reserves. The appointment document is an oath by which the individual swears to serve in the Marine Corps Reserves for the duration of the National Emergency.

Report of Dependents. The Report of Dependents lists the next-of-kin or dependents of the Marine. This form should be updated if the Marine marries and his dependents change, but this did not always happen.

Pay Records. Various pay records, family allowance documents, and insurance paperwork is found within the OMPF. These documents allow a researcher to further piece together the service history with dates, locations, changes in dependents, and status.

Appointments for Rank and Promotions

If an enlisted man rose in rank to Officer status, the commission certificate will be included in the OMPF. This record provides information on the new rank and date it is official. An Oath of Office for the Officer may also be included which contains the date of change in rank and his signature.

Temporary appointments in rank were also given when needed. This usually appears in the file as a letter or memo explaining the temporary change and duties required of the serviceman.

Training and Educational Information

The training information and any special training courses completed will be included in the OMPF. The Certificate of Completion of a course provides information on specific training, location and date your Marine received. If a man was going through flight school, those records would also be a part of his file. The documents may appear as official certificates of completion or as a letter or memo to be sent to Headquarters and placed in the man's file.

Travel Orders

Travel orders were included in the file to document every move a Marine made off base. The orders often included the name, rank, and service number of several men being transferred from one unit to another. An explanation of when to depart, how to travel, and when to arrive was included. Sometimes snippets of Marine Corps Muster Rolls will appear in the OMPF documenting the specific ship a Marine sailed on to move from the U.S. to an overseas station.

Awards and Citations Earned

The OMPF contains letters or memos providing citations to an individual or unit, and the awards issued. Sometimes the award issued was done so on an official form for that specific award. These citations and awards may provide clues to service history which includes dates and battle locations.

Miscellaneous Documents

Family Letters. Quite often, the OMPF will contain letters to the military or government, requesting information on the status of their Marine. These often appear after a Marine is declared Missing In Action (MIA) or Killed In Action (KIA.)

Vital Records of Family. Sometimes a Marine had to prove his age or provide proof of his relationship to dependents or next-of-kin. Vital records are often included in the OMPF to prove these relationships.

Death Certificate of Marine. Sometimes, but not always, if the Marine was KIA, you will find a death certificate in the OMPF.

References to Other Sources. It is important to read each letter and document carefully within the OMPF. Names and addresses of other Marines with which your Marine fought, may be included. In Pvt. William F. Cowart's OMPF, there is a letter from his mother to the military, which referenced a book in which Cowart was named.

Letters from Government Officials. Families who needed information from the military and had trouble receiving it, often went to their local VA or County Commissioner for assistance. In other cases, the family approached a higher-level government official such as their Congressman. These government officials acted as a go-between for families and the military to obtain information.

Modern Day Requests for Information. Each time an OMPF is requested, the request form or letter is included with the OMPF. The next person to request the file will receive the OMPF plus the details of all previous requests. This may lead to a new family connection.

Casualty Telegrams or Letters (MIA, POW, KIA)

Every time a Marine had a change in status, meaning he went from being a healthy, active Marine to wounded, missing, prisoner, or killed, a telegram was sent to the next-of-kin and included in his file. Often there will also be a Casualty Report explaining the change in status. Casualty did not always mean a Marine had been KIA, but included wounds, and MIA status.

Marines who were KIA in the Pacific, were sometimes buried, the family notified, only to later discover the remains could not be located. The military then followed up with a new letter explaining why the remains could not be located. Unfortunately for the family of Pvt. William F. Cowart, this occurred.

Inventory of Effects. The Inventory of Effects is always found within the IDPF, and sometimes included in the OMPF. This list documents all the personal effects of a Marine who was declared MIA or KIA, and then sent to the effects bureau in Utah for processing.

Discharge or Separation Information

The Separation and Discharge papers contain the name, rank, service number, final unit, MOS (Job) for the Marine, and enlistment and discharge or death information. Unlike other branches of the military, the Marine Corps did not list the theaters of war in which Marine served and dates of service. Dates the Marine sailed overseas, arrived, then departed overseas to return to the U.S. are also not included.

Service Record Booklet - Pvt. William F. Cowart

DIED JAN 24 1944
1. Rec'd in A. & I Dept.
   (initial and pass to next number)
2. Casualty K.A. 3. QM. Clo. E.O.
4. Mil. Hist. (FILE) M.J.H.

No. 471443

GAS MASK 2

U. S. MARINE CORPS

SERVICE-RECORD BOOK

OF

COWART,
(SURNAME)

WILLIAM FRANKLIN
(CHRISTIAN NAME)

RANK

Private.

SEP 26 1942
(DATE OF ENLISTMENT)

PREVIOUS SERVICE (ACTIVE)

None Years None Months None Days

DATE OF EXPIRATION OF EACH EXTENSION

N.M.C. 109—A & I
12-0-41—150M

15—9547-1

Official Military Personnel File. William F. Cowart, serial no. 471443. Service-Record Book. National Personnel Records Center, St. Louis, Missouri.

COWART WF.

COWART, William F.
Enl   26Sep42.
Taken   30ct42.

471443

SERVICE RECORD

OF

Name COWART, WILLIAM FRANKLIN
Citizenship U.S
Date of birth 21 FEBRUARY, 1922
Place of birth REFORM, ALA.
Legal residence STAR ROUTE, COLUMBUS, MISS.

Name, relationship, and address of person to be notified in case of emergency MRS ALICE COWART, (MOTHER), ROUTE №2, ETHELSVILLE, ALA.

Accepted for enlistment at SDHS, COLUMBUS, MISS.
Enlisted as Private,
At DHS, Jackson, Miss.
SEP 26 1942, 19 , to serve { years during minority None
Foreign shore service last enlistment (months) None
From to
Sea service last enlistment (months): None
From to

_____, U.S.M.C.,
Recruiting Officer.
EDWIN O. SCHULTZ, Major, USMCR.

William Franklin Cowart
(SIGNATURE OF RECRUIT IN FULL)

Identification tag issued _____, 19

FOR THE DURATION OF THE NATIONAL EMERGENCY.

Official Military Personnel File. William F. Cowart, serial no. 471443. Service-Record Book. National Personnel Records Center, St. Louis, Missouri.

RESERVE

471443

DURATION OF NATIONAL EMERGENCY

COWART,

William Franklin

BORN: 21 February 1922

AT: Reform, Ala.

ENLISTED: 26 September 1942
Accepted: Columbus, Miss.
AT: Jackson, Miss.
2d Recruit Bn SEP 30 1942
Rec. Depot, San Diego Cl. 3c

Active duty fr 9/26/42 11/20/43

NOV 21 1942
Jd 1 D Replacement Bn, FMF FMF TrngCenter, San Diego, Calif

For Duty in the Field. JAN 20 1943

Btry D 2nd Spl Weapons Bn
Jd 2d Mar Division FMF FEB 14 1943

Jd 2d Amphibian
Tractor Bn 2d Mar Division FMF OCT 12 1943

Killed in action **NOV 20 1943**

Died Nov. 20, 1943 at Betio Is.,
Tarawa Atoll, Gilbert Island.

FILE

Remains interred in GRAVE #33, Plot
#5, Row #1, Grave #11, at Betio
Island, Tarawa Atoll, Gilbert
Islands.

Official Military Personnel File. William F. Cowart, serial no. 471443. Service-Record Book. National Personnel Records Center, St. Louis, Missouri.

Medical Information - Pvt. Cowart

2

MARKS, SCARS, ETC.
(Marked in red ink by Medical Examiner)

3

MARKS, SCARS, ETC.
(Marked in red ink by Medical Examiner)

LEFT HAND
Rolled imprint of thumb and each finger

6. THUMB
7. INDEX
8. MIDDLE
9. RING
10. LITTLE

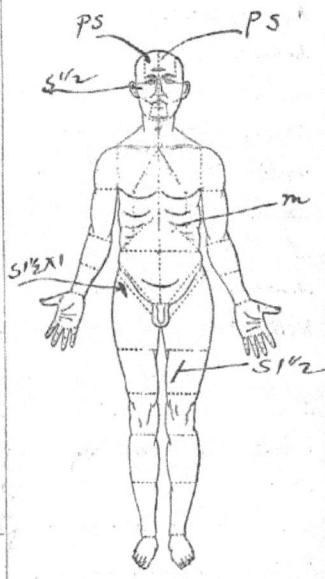

Marine Corps Base
San Diego, Calif.
Blood Kahn Negative
Blood Type _____ Inter.

LIEUT. COMDR. (MC) USNR

RIGHT HAND
Rolled imprint of thumb and each finger

5. LITTLE
4. RING
3. MIDDLE
2. INDEX
1. THUMB

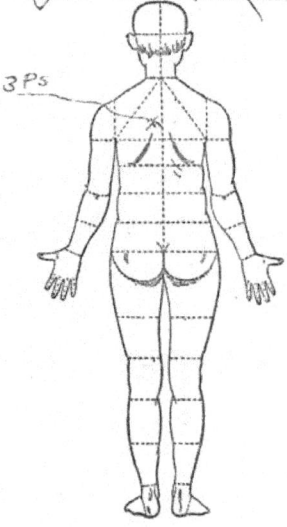

Examined SEP 26 1942 19___

Eyes BROWN

Hair BROWN

Complexion Ruddy

Height 70 3/4 inches.

Weight 129 pounds.

Date and nature of any waiver

None

JOHN A. BROWN, III
LT. MC-V(G) USNR
Surgeon.

LEFT HAND — Plain imprint of Four Fingers taken simultaneously

RIGHT HAND — Plain imprint of Four Fingers taken simultaneously

Official Military Personnel File. William F. Cowart, serial no. 471443. Medical Information. National Personnel Records Center, St. Louis, Missouri.

Professional and Conduct Record - Pvt. Cowart

PROFESSIONAL AND CONDUCT RECORD OF **COWART, WILLIAM FRANKLIN**

The following shall be executed and signed semiannually and whenever the marine is transferred, retired, discharged, deserts, or dies, or the book is closed for discharge; also (without markings) when he joins, surrenders, or is apprehended. (6 Bad; 1, Indifferent; 2, Fair; 3, Good; 3.8, Very Good; 4.3 to 5, Excellent.) Semiannual markings and markings "For Discharge" shall be entered in red ink. Military Efficiency includes all matters relating to the duties of a marine other than Neatness and Military Bearing, Intelligence, Obedience, and Sobriety.

	STATION OR VESSEL	JOINED, SURR., APP., TRANSF., SEMI-AN., FOR DIS., FINAL M., DESERTED, DISCHARGED, DIED, RETIRED, TRANSF. TO RESERVE	DATE	RANK	MILITARY EFFICIENCY	NEATNESS AND MILITARY BEARING	INTELLIGENCE	OBEDIENCE	SOBRIETY	AVERAGE STANDING	SIGNATURE OF COMMANDING OFFICER
1	DES., Jackson, Miss.	Assigned to Active Duty	SEP 26 1942	Private							EDWIN O. SCHULL, Major, U.S.M.C.R.
2	DES., Jackson, Miss.	Assigned to Active Duty	SEP 26 1942	Private							EDWIN O. SCHULL, Major, U.S.M.C.R.
3	DHS., Jackson, Miss.	Transferred	SEP 2 6 1942	Private							EDWIN O. SCHULL, Major, U.S.M.C.R.
4	R.D. 2nd RBn	Joined	SEP 3 0 1942	Private							Kpl. U.S.M.C.R.
5	R.D. 2nd RBn	Tr	NOV 2 1 1942	Private							E. R. AMES, CAPT. USMCR
6	R.D. 3rd RBn	Tr	NOV 2 1 1942	Private	3	3	3	3	3	3	E. R. AMES, CAPT. USMC
7	70th Repl Bn, F.M.F. George Elliott, Calif	Sd	21 Nov 42	Pvt	3.5	3.5	3.5	5	5		Capt USMCR
8	10th Replace Bn FMF	Semi An	31 Dec 1942	Pvt.	3.8	3.5	3.5	5	5		Major - Cmdr
9	1st H&S Bn F.M.F.	Trans.	14 Feb., 1943	Pvt.							1st Lt. USMCR
10	Btry B, 2d Sep Arbn	Jd	14 Feb 1943	Pvt.							2d Lt.
11				SEMI-AN							CAPT M.C.R.
12	D.4.SPL MPASS BN	Trans	3 0 JUN 1943	Pvt	4	4	4	5	5		K.R. Kyland
13	Co. "C", 2nd AMPH. TRACTOR Bn.	Joined	1 2 OCT 1943	Pvt.	4-4	4	4	6	5		A.P. Vildo
14											William H. Hansen, Capt. U.S.M.C.
15		KIA	DIED		5	5	5				Philip Durham
16		Final M.		Pvt.	4.2	4.2	4.2	5	5		Philip Durham, 1st Lt. USMCR
17						4.2			5	+6	Philip Durham
18		K.I.A. AT BETIO ISLAND, TARAWA ATOLL, G.I. on 20 Nov 43 by gunshot wounds									
19		LOCATION OF GRAVE UNKNOWN. CHAR. EXC.									
20											

Official Military Personnel File. William F. Cowart, serial no. 471443. Professional and Conduct Record. National Personnel Records Center, St. Louis, Missouri.

Marine Corps Reserve Application/Oath - Pvt. Cowart

N. M. C. 321 (b): A&I

MARINE CORPS RESERVE

I, William Franklin COWART , desiring
   (First name)   (Middle name, if any)   (Surname, in capitals)
to enlist in the UNITED STATES MARINE CORPS RESERVE for the DURATION OF THE NATIONAL
EMERGENCY, do declare that I was born 21 February , 1922 ,
at Reform , in the State of Alabama ; that I have
neither wife nor child and that there is nobody dependent upon me for support beyond my ability to contribute from the
pay of a private; that I know of nothing wrong with my health or body that the doctor did not find when he examined me;
that I am of good habits and character; that no judge or jury has ever found me guilty of a crime; that I have never deserted
from the United States Army, Navy, Marine Corps, Coast Guard, or Revenue Cutter Service, and have never been discharged
therefrom with a dishonorable, bad-conduct, undesirable, or inaptitude discharge, or for disability, and that I have never
served therein except as stated to the recruiting officer and recorded on the reverse side of this contract; that I am by present
occupation a Student ; and that I am a citizen of the United States. I agree to accept from
the United States such bounty, pay, rations, and clothing as are or may be established by law, and if discharged by sentence
of court martial or for bad conduct, undesirability, unfitness, or inaptitude, I agree to surrender my uniform in exchange
for civilian clothing.

Given at SDHS., Columbus, Miss. , this 24th day of September , 1942.
ACCEPTED AND SIGNATURE WITNESSED:*

WITNESS:* *Norman E. Goza*
Norman E. Goza

Staff Sgt. , U. S. M. C.

William Franklin Cowart
(Signature of applicant, in full)

DATE AND NATURE OF ANY WAIVER

None

Transferred 27 September , 1942 , to RD., MCB., San Diego, Calif.

I, William Franklin COWART , do hereby acknowledge
to have voluntarily enlisted as a PRIVATE in the VOLUNTEER MARINE CORPS RESERVE for the DURATION OF THE
NATIONAL EMERGENCY, unless sooner discharged by competent authority; and I do obligate myself during such
enlistment to serve in the Marine Corps in time of war or during the existence of a national emergency declared by the
President. And I do solemnly swear (or affirm) that I will bear true faith and allegiance to the United States of America;
that I will serve them honestly and faithfully against all their enemies whomsoever; and that I will obey the orders of the
President of the United States, and the orders of the officers appointed over me, according to the Rules and Articles for the
Government of the Army, Navy, and Marine Corps of the United States. And I do further swear (or affirm) that all
statements made by me, as now given in this record, are correct. *William Franklin Cowart*
(Signature of enlisted man, in full)

Subscribed and duly sworn to before me at DHS., Jackson, Miss.
this 26th day of September , A. D. 1942 , and
I CERTIFY, that I minutely inspected the above-named man previous to his enlistment, and that he was entirely sober when
enlisted; that, to the best of my judgment and belief, he fulfills all legal requirements; that, after fully informing him of the
nature of the service he is to perform, I have enlisted him into the service of the United States under this contract of enlistment
as duly qualified to perform the duties of an able-bodied marine, and in doing so have strictly observed the regulations which
govern the recruiting service; also that the prior service as shown on the reverse side has been verified by me personally from

the man's discharge certificates, and that I am satisfied that his status as to citizenship is† U. S.

RESERVE

EDWYN O. SCHULTZ, Major, USMCR U. S. M. C. , Recruiting Officer.

Name and address of person to be notified in case of emergency, giving degree of relationship; if friend, so state:
Mrs. Alice COWART, Rt. #2, Ethelsville, Alabama MOTHER.
(Name)   (Address, including name of street and number of house)   (Relationship)
Home or residence, with street and number Star Route, Columbus, Miss.
*To be signed by the officer or noncommissioned officer witnessing signature.   †Native born, use initials U. S.; naturalized, N. U. S.

16—26062-1

Official Military Personnel File. William F. Cowart, serial no. 471443. Application and Oath for Reserves. National Personnel Records Center, St. Louis, Missouri.

Travel and Movement Overseas - Pvt. Cowart

EMBARKED ABOARD THE S. S. PRESIDENT MONROE AT SAN DIEGO,
CALIFORNIA, 19 JANUARY, 1943; SAILED 20 JANUARY, 1943.
ARRIVED AT *Noumea, new Caledonia*
ON *5 Feb, 1943*_____, DISEMBARKED *6 Feb, 1943*.

A. I. SCHMULIAN,
MAJOR, U.S.M.C.R.,
COMMANDER OF TROOPS.

Embarked aboard the S.S. President Monroe at
Noumea, New Caledonia 10 February, 1943; Sailed
11 February, 1943. Arrived at *Wellington, N.Z.*
on *14 Feb, 1943*_____ Disembarked *15 Feb, 1943*.

William H. Haudenschild Jr.
WILLIAM H. HAUDENSCHILD Jr.
1St. Lt. U.S.M.C.R.
for Commander of Troops.

HEADQUARTERS MUSTER ROLLS

Feb43 through Sep43 Wellington, N.Z.
Oct43 12, trans to 2d Amph Tractor Bn.,
2d Mar Div, FMF; 16, emb aboard USS VIRGO
at Wellington, N.Z. for special temp duty
with 6th Mar, 2d Mar Div. FMF.
Nov43, 1, sailed from Wellington, N.Z.;
6, arr at Efate, N.H.; 9, emb and 12,
sailed; 19, arr and 20, disemb at Tarawa,
Gilbert Islands; 20, Killed in Action.

Official Military Personnel File. William F. Cowart, serial no. 471443. Travel and Movement Overseas. National Personnel Records Center, St. Louis, Missouri.

Death Certificate - Pvt. Cowart

NMS-Form N
(1940)

CERTIFICATE OF DEATH

From: CO"P", 2ndMedBn., 2ndMarDiv., FMF., In The Field.

To: *Bureau of Medicine and Surgery, Navy Department, Washington, D. C.*
(See Circular Letter R-6, Appendix D, Manual of the Medical Department, for instructions)

1. Name ___COWART, William Franklin___ 471443 — Rank or rate ___Pvt. USMCR.___

2. Born: Place ___Alabama___ Date ___2-21-22___

3. Nationality ___W-US___ (White—U. S., Colored, Samoan, etc.) Religion ___Protestant___ (Denomination)

4. Eyes ___Brown___ Hair ___Brown___ Complexion ___Ruddy___ Height ___72___ Weight ___128___

5. Marks, scars, etc. (noted in health record) ___cut: 2"S forehead; ¾ rt.___
___cheek; X left umbilical region; S 1½x1 rt. groin; sl½ left___
___upper leg. Pock: 2"S left scapular region.___

FINGERPRINT
NOT AVAILABLE

State which finger _____
(Right index preferred)

6. Relation, name and address of next of kin or friend ___Parents: Mr. & Mrs. L. V. COWART,___
___Rt. 2, Shelsville, Alabama.___

7. Original admission: Place ___2ndMedTrBn., 2ndMarDiv.,FMF.___ Date ___11-20-43___
(Ship or station to which attached when first admitted to sick list)

8. Died: Place ___Tarawa Atoll, Gilbert Islands___ Date ___11-20-43___ Hour ___Unknown___

9. Cause of death { Principal ___KILLED IN ACTION, DETAILS NOT KNOWN # 2545___ Key Letter ___X___
{ Contributory _____

10. Death ___is not___ (Is or is not) the result of own misconduct and ___is___ (Is or is not) in the line of duty.

11. Disposition of remains ___Unknown.___

12. Summary of facts relative to the death:
1. Within command.
2. Against organized enemy.
3. Negligence not apparent.
4. Killed in action.
While participating in action against enemy on Tarawa Atoll, Gilbert
Islands, was killed in action. Details and Disposition of remains unknown.

(Continue on back of this form)

16—15558

Official Military Personnel File. William F. Cowart, serial no. 471443. Death Certificate. National Personnel Records Center, St. Louis, Missouri.

Marriage Record Part 1 - Pvt. Cowart

NEW ZEALAND.
COPY OF REGISTER OF MARRIAGE.

Marriage in the District of WELLINGTON.

1943.

When and where married.	Names and Surnames of the Parties.	Ages.	Rank or Profession.	Condition of Parties	Birthplace.	Residence. 1. Present. 2. Usual.	Father's Name and Surname and his Rank or Profession
108 Sept. 7th 1943. S.John's Church, Johnsonville.	William Franklin Cowart	21	United States Marine	1. Bachelor 2. -------	Reform, Alabama, United States of America.	1.Titahi Bay Ethelsville, Alabama, United States 2.of America.	1. Lester Veene Cowart 2. Carpenter
	Lesley Alison Biggs	17	-------	1. Spinster 2. -------	Nelson	1.Johnsonville 2.Johnsonville	1. Mostyn Lesl] Biggs 2. Farmer

MARRIED, after the delivery to me of the Certificate required by the Marriage Act, 1908, by B.R.White, Officiating

This Marriage was solemnized between us, William Franklin Cowart / Lesley Alison Biggs

In the presence of us, M.L.Biggs, Pensioner, Burgess Rd., Johnsonville. / I.J.Aitken, Married, 76 Nairn St., Wellington.

I hereby certify that the above is a true copy of an entry of Marriage in the records of my office. Given under my hand at Wellington, this 26th day of ... Acting D...

(The fee for this certificate is 2/6.) CAUTION.—Any person who (1) falsifies any of the particulars on this certificate, or (2) uses it as true, knowing it to be false, is liable to prosecution under the Crimes Act, 1908.

Official Military Personnel File. William F. Cowart, serial no. 471443. Copy of Register of Marriage. National Personnel Records Center, St. Louis, Missouri.

Marriage Record Part 2

[R.G. 148.]

No. 24258

NEW ZEALAND.

COPY OF REGISTER OF MARRIAGE.

Marriage in the District of WELLINGTON.

Names and Surnames of the Parties.	Ages.	Rank or Profession.	Condition of Parties: 1. Bachelor or Spinster (or as case may be). If Widower or Widow; 2. Date of Decease of former Wife or Husband.	Birthplaces.	Residence. 1. Present. 2. Usual.	PARENTS. Father's Name and Surname (1), and his Rank or Profession (2).	PARENTS. Mother's Name (1), and Maiden Surname (2).
... Franklin ...	21	United States Marine	1. Bachelor 2. -------	Reform, Alabama, United States of America.	1. Titahi Bay Ethelsville, Alabama, United States 2. of America.	1. Lester Veaner Cowart 2. Carpenter	1. Mary Alice Cowart 2. Robinson
...ey Alison Biggs	17	-------	1. Spinster 2. -------	Nelson	1. Johnsonville 2. Johnsonville	1. Mostyn Leslie Biggs 2. Farmer	1. Muriel Emma Biggs 2. Pahl

to me of the Certificate required by the Marriage Act, 1908   , by   , Officiating Minister [or Registrar].

In the presence of us,   B.R.White

{ M.L.Biggs, Pensioner, Burgess Rd., Johnsonville.

between us,   { I.J.Aitken, Married, 76 Nairn So., Wellington.

...illiam Franklin Cowart

...esley Alison Biggs

Given under my hand at Wellington this   26th   day of   November   , 194 3.

a true copy of an entry of Marriage in the records of my office.

[signature] Acting Deputy Registrar-General.

CAUTION.—Any person who (1) falsifies any of the particulars on this certificate, or (2) uses it as true,
knowing it to be false, is liable to prosecution under the Crimes Act, 1908.

Official Military Personnel File. William F. Cowart, serial no. 471443. Copy of Register of Marriage. National Personnel Records Center, St. Louis, Missouri.

Letter Explaining Death and Remains - Pvt. Cowart

471443
DGU-1159-rft

10 February, 1947.

My dear Mrs. Cowart:

I wish to supplement previous correspondence regarding the disposition of the remains of your son, the late Private William F. Cowart, U. S. Marine Corps Reserve, who lost his life in the conquest of Tarawa.

During the intense four-day battle to wrest this strategically important island from the Japanese, approximately one thousand Marines made the supreme sacrifice. While that critical operation was being fought, it was essential that the remains of the dead be interred immediately in order to safeguard the health of the living and to facilitate rendering aid to the wounded. Under the fierce stress of battle on this small island, hasty burial methods could not be avoided, and, consequently, we were unable to survey and to chart the burial places with full accuracy or to record all the details of burial information.

As soon as Tarawa was captured, our battle-scarred Marine Corps units were relieved by garrison forces and were sent to other Pacific islands for recuperation. Having been supplied with all available information concerning the Marine Corps dead, these forces arranged, charted and beautified the cemeteries and furnished this Headquarters with reports of the names and grave locations of the Marines buried there. Among these reports was one stating that your son's remains were buried on Tarawa, and this information was furnished you.

Recently the American Graves Registration Service, under direction of the Quartermaster General of the U. S. Army, has been disinterring the bodies of the dead buried in various isolated plots and reburying them in a centrally located cemetery preparatory to transporting the remains to a final resting place selected by the next of kin.

I regret extremely that I must inform you that the remains of your son were not found to be beneath the marker previously reported. Subsequent investigation has revealed that in some instances well-meaning persons had erected individual commemorative markers in memory of our heroic dead.

- 1 -

Official Military Personnel File. William F. Cowart, serial no. 471443. Letter to Mrs. Cowart dated 10 Feb 1947. National Personnel Records Center, St. Louis, Missouri.

471443
DGU-1159-rft

10 February, 1947.

Since the Graves Registration Service has been unable to locate the remains of Private Cowart, it must be assumed that his body was among the unidentified dead and that the cross was erected in his honored memory rather than actually as a marker identifying the location of his grave.

Continued efforts are being made to locate unmarked graves and every scientific means known is being employed to establish the identity of our unidentified dead.

I am deeply grieved that there must now be added to your sorrow this most distressing information. It is earnestly hoped that the continuing and unremitting efforts which will be made may yet lead to the location and identification of your son's remains, in which event you will be notified immediately.

Sincerely yours,

A. A. VANDEGRIFT,
General, U.S.M.C.,
Commandant of the Marine Corps.

Mrs. Alice Cowart,
    Route #3,
        Millport, Alabama.

- 2 -

Official Military Personnel File. William F. Cowart, serial no. 471443. Letter to Mrs. Cowart dated 10 Feb 1947. National Personnel Records Center, St. Louis, Missouri.

Marine Corps Records Created in the Field

The next step in locating information on your Marine is to search for records created in the field which do not appear in the OMPF. Traces of the information in the OMPF may be discovered in some of these files, but it is a good idea to attempt to obtain every scrap of evidence you can for your Marine's story.

US Marine Corps Muster Rolls

Muster Rolls are similar to Army Morning Reports in the way they document men entering and exiting a unit, provide rank and status changes, and sometimes the location of the unit. Unlike Morning Reports, which were created daily, Muster Rolls were compiled monthly. In addition, the Muster Rolls may contain Army and Navy units attached to a Marine Corps unit.

Muster Rolls provided the specific location (camp) of Marines stationed stateside. Rolls for Marines stationed overseas do not list the specific location they are stationed. The Rolls only list the unit and, usually, "In the Field." If you read the entries in the roll for the month the unit is overseas, you may gather clues as to their location. The best way to discover where a unit was stationed or fought, is through service records and unit histories.

Marine Corps Muster Rolls do not repeat the same information for every Marine it pertains to; rather, it directs the reader to a footnote. The footnotes are usually listed at the end of the report for each unit, and provide information on MIA, POW, KIA, wounds, and transfer statuses. In some cases, you will an entry with the footnotes that reads "Sent under separate attachment." In this case, you will need to search unit records for more information.

An interesting and helpful piece of information provided by a Muster Roll is that these records often continue to list those with MIA statuses roughly every quarter. Those who remained MIA for a year and were then given a FOD are also listed on the Muster Rolls. This information is helpful if your soldier was missing, or if you are trying to locate a date of death.

If you are researching Muster Rolls through NARA online, just as with morning reports, it is important to attempt to provide the unit down to the lowest echelon possible. For example, B Co., 1st Battalion, 2nd Marines for 1945.[1]

USMC Muster Roll, 2nd MarDiv, November 1943. Historical Reference Branch, Marine Corps History Division, Quantico, VA.

Repository: Historical Reference Branch, Marine Corps History Division, Quantico, VA. Online at Ancestry.com.

Questions a Muster Roll may answer:

1. Name, rank, service number, and unit of a Marine.
2. Casualty information.
3. Transfer information.
4. Change of duty information.

World War II Diaries / Operational Journals

Marines who served aboard ships, were attached to ships for transport to battle, or as airmen are often found in Naval War Diaries in the National Archives Record Group 38. War Diaries were daily operational journals kept by the Navy documenting events of the day, enemy engagement, casualties, and mission information. Within these journals were reports created by the commanders of Marine Aircraft Groups and Marine Divisions.

Histories of the unit were written for submission to the Marine Corps Historical Division. These may be found within the War Diaries. Histories are important to read because you may discover some records are unavailable due to the loss of records from a fire, sinking of ship, or destruction of a truck carrying records. Operational journals may also contain Action Reports, which detail enemy engagement, losses, prisoners taken, and damaged equipment.

The information in these journals varies from unit to unit. Some unit information may be very descriptive, while other units may provide basic facts. It is a good idea to find official Marine Corps histories written after the war to further research and document your Marine's service.

If you are familiar with the Accident Reports or Missing Air Crew Reports (MACRs) for the Army Air Corps, you will not find those reports for the Marines. The information on downed or missing aircraft was contained in Mission Histories and Reports, often found within the War Diaries.

Repository: Marine Corps Historical Division. Online at Fold3.com. Also look at records at National Archives, College Park, MD in Record Group 127.9 Records of Marine Units 1914-1949.

Questions a War Diary may answer:

1. Name, rank, service number, unit in which serving at a specific time.
2. Promotions and demotions in rank.
3. Mission information – air missions or land missions.
4. Results of mission.
5. Casualty information. Status of MIA, POW, or KIA.
6. Where a ship or unit was located (you can map the locations).

Casualty Cards and Other Information

Casualty information may exist in several files related to the Marine Corps. To understand the records, we need to define the word casualty as used in Marine Corps records. The USMC defines a casualty for use in these cards as "The History Division's Historical Reference Branch holds casualty cards for World War II, War Dogs, Interwar Period 1946-50, Korea, Interwar Period 1955-1965, and Vietnam." Casualty cards were issued when a Marine was wounded, missing, killed or deemed a prisoner of war.[2]

Casualty Cards

Casualty Cards were created for all Marines who were deemed a casualty. These cards contain the history of every wound a Marine received and if he was ever deemed MIA, KIA, or POW.

The Casualty Card shown on the following page, belongs to Pvt. William F. Cowart, who was not wounded, but MIA, then KIA. The card has been split into two pieces, and a description of the card and explanation of abbreviations follows.[3]

Casualty Card for Pvt. William F. Cowart

Basic Service and Vital Information
At the top of the card, we see Cowart's unit. C Company, 2nd Amphibious Tractor Battalion, 2nd Marine Division, Fleet Marine Force, Gilbert Islands.

This means the final unit he served in was C Company, 2nd Amphibious Tractor Battalion, 2nd Marine Division, Fleet Marine Force. To search for information on this unit, try searches on 2nd Marine Division history, 2nd Marine Division Amphibious Tractor Battalions, 2nd Marines in Tarawa and your Marine's name.

Next we have his birth date and enlistment date. If Cowart had any prior service, there would be information in that space. We know where he was living at the time of enlistment and who is next-of-kin was. Cowart's file stated he was married and provided his wife's name and address.
The birth and enlistment dates are obvious as to the information they provide.

Prior Service
Prior service means if this Marine served in any other branch or time period prior to the current enlistment period. I do have records on a Marine Aviator who first served in the Navy to earn his wings. Then he transferred to the Marine Corps. His Casualty Card for Prior Service says "YES." Nothing further. To locate additional service information on a Marine who had prior service, you need to obtain his OMPF (service file) from the NPRC in St. Louis.

Next-of-kin
The next-of-kin is important because sometimes we do not have the official names of parents or a spouse. Cowart's case is interesting because when you read his OMPF, there are many documents and letters crisscrossing in the mail between his parents and the Marine Corps, and the spouse and Marine Corps. The parents apparently did not know, at the time he died, he was married, based on correspondence included in the record. If the name of a spouse appears and you did not know of the existence of this spouse, you can now look for documentation. In Cowart's case, the marriage certificate was in his OMPF.

The Marine's History
The History concerning his casualty status is described next. We know he was Killed In Action 20 November 1943 at Tarawa, Gilbert Islands. Confirmed by letter from CG, Headquarters, 2nd Marine Division, Fleet Marine Force, to Commandant of the Marine Corps dated 12/23/43 received 1/5/44. *** (the *** means GSWs – Gun Shot Wounds.)

Burial Information
His card goes on to state he was buried on Betio Island. Then his body was not recovered.
The Casualty Status states he was KIA on 20 November 1943 at Tarawa. A letter was sent to pass this information up the line. We know he died of gunshot wounds. The Marines initially buried their dead in several hastily built cemeteries and isolated graves on the island. Graves Registration Service was not present during the Battle, and the usual records and list of personal effects were not created. The Individual Deceased Personnel File (IDPF) would usually have many documents regarding the death, personal effects, and correspondence from family and the military. Cowart's does not.

After the Marines left Tarawa, other contingents arrived and "cleaned-up" the cemeteries. Quite often, they moved the crosses without the remains beneath them. In the end, the cross was only a Memorial Cross, not an actual burial location for the Marine listed on the cross. Due to the lack of record keeping, the changes in the cemeteries and inadequate records from that, many of the Marines buried on Tarawa were deemed UNRECOVERABLE in the late 1940s.

Additional Death Details

Additional details are provided on the second part of the card. They include:

*Date taken from S/R (Service Record) received 1/27/44.

Has government Insurance.

The date of death was taken from his Service Record (OMPF) obtained by the Marine Corps. The fact he had government insurance meant his spouse could collect his death benefit.

AIRMAILGRAM from Commanding Officer, 2nd Amphibious Tractor Battalion, 2nd Marine Division Fleet Marine Force to Secretary of the Navy received 3/3/44 reported man KIA on 20 November 43.

*Correct date of death taken from Certificate of Death received from zone 4-11-44.
Supplemental Certificate of Death received from zone 4-14-44.
The previous three statements show a paper trail to document the death of Cowart.

*Buried in Cemetery #33 (Lone Pine Cemetery), Grave #11, Row #1, Plot #5, Betio, Tarawa Atoll, Gilbert Islands, Letter from Commander, Betio to Commanding General, 2ndMarDiv, FMF (reconstruction of cemeteries dated 15 June 44 received 1 November 44).
(THIS IS A MEMORIAL GRAVE) Letter from Commanding General, Headquarters, Fleet Marine Force, Pacific to Commandant of Marine Corps, dated 24 April 1945, received 7 May 1945.

**Determined non-recoverable by field board 19 October 1949.

Pvt. William F. Cowart Casualty Card

Co.C,2ndAmphTrBn,2ndMarDiv,FMF,Gilbert Islands.

1- 5481

Born: 21 Feb 1922   at   Reform, Ala.
Enl :   26 Sep 1942   at   Jackson, Miss.
Prior Service: No.

RESIDENCE: Columbus, Miss.

KIN: Mrs. Lesley A. B. Cowart, wife, Burges Road,
Johnsonville, Wellington, New Zealand.

*20
HISTORY:, *20 Nov 43 Killed in action at Tarawa, Gilber
Islands. Conf Ltr fr CG,Hq,2ndMarDiv,FMF, to CMC dated
12/22/43 rec'd 1/5/44.***

★ Buried on Betio Island.
** Body not recovered.   See over. *

COWART, William Franklin   Pvt.   USMCR 471443

---

*Date taken fr S/R rec'd 1/27/44. (rsf)
  Has gov't Ins. (mk)
  AIRMAILGRAM fr CO,2ndAmphTrBn,2ndMarDiv,FMF to SECNAV
  rec'd 3/3/44 reported man KIA 20 Nov 43. (jeb)
*Correct date of death taken fr Cert of death rec'd fr
  zone 4-11-44.(OK WTR)(mvn)
  SupCert of death rec'd fr zone 4-14-44.(mvn)
*Buried in Cemetery#33, Grave#11, Row#1, Plot#5, Betio
  Is, Tarawa Atoll, G.I. Ltr fr Is.Comdr, Betio, to CG,
  2dMarDiv,FMF (reconstruction of cemeteries) dtd 15 Jun
  44 rec'd 1 Nov 44.(afm)
  (THIS IS A MEMORIAL GRAVE) Ltr fr CG, Hq, FMF, Pac, to
  CMC, dtd 24Apr45, rec'd 7May45.(afm)
** Determined non-recoverable by field board 19Oct49.(vah)

***GSW's.

Cowart, William F, Casualty Card, Historical Reference Branch, Marine Corps History Division, Quantico.

The cemetery in which Cowart was originally buried was called Lone Pine Cemetery. Interestingly, a list of all men buried there, are listed in Cowart's IDPF and in the IDPFs of others buried in this cemetery. The IDPFs are almost identical in contents. Again we have a paper trail of letters which may or may not still exist in official records.

The USMC Casualty Card gives us a glimpse into the death and burial of Cowart. It provides a paper trail we can attempt to follow for more documentation. Obtaining the OMPF (Service Record) and IDPF are next steps in learning more about Cowart's death and burial.

Repository: Marine Corps History Division holds the original Casualty Cards.

Questions a Casualty Card may answer:

1. Name, vital information, rank, and service number of a Marine.
2. Next-of-kin information.
3. Wounds received.
4. Missing In Action, Prisoner of War, or Killed In Action details.

Visit the Marine Corps History Division website for a searchable Casualty Card database, among additional resources.

https://www.mcu.usmc.mil/historydivision/SitePages/Home.aspx

Individual Deceased Personnel File (IDPF)

The Individual Deceased personnel File (IDPF) is similar across all the branches, but the Navy and Marine Corps often (but not always) provide a couple additional pieces of documentation to help tell your Marine's story. Often, the file will contain a photograph taken upon enlistment and a Marine Corps Casualty Report. See the chapter on Military Death Records for a lengthy discussion on the IDPF.

Casualty Reports document a change in status to wounded, missing, killed, or prisoner of war. These are not the same as the Casualty Card because Reports describe specific incidents. Casualty Cards document the Marine's entire history. The Casualty Report shown on the following page, is for 1st Lt. Robert E. Bishop.[4] The report was included in his IDPF and also as part of his overall Casualty Card history. Unfortunately, Bishop's IDPF did not contain a photograph of him. The only photograph I have of Bishop was on his Application for Aviation Training in the U.S. Naval Reserve or Marine Corps Reserve.

Repository: Army Human Resources Command at Ft. Knox.

Questions a Casualty Report may answer:

1. Name, vital information, rank, and service number of a Marine.
2. Next-of-kin information.
3. Wounding, Missing In Action, Prisoner of War, or Killed In Action details.

Additional Casualty Resources

Marine Corps casualties are often listed in the U.S. Navy Casualty books, which can be found on Ancestry.com. You can also read histories of specific battles in which the Marines participated. Often there are casualty lists. Finally, searching the American Battle Monuments Commission website may provide information you may not have acquired or are waiting to receive.

USMC Casualty Report - Robert E. Bishop

Official Military Personnel File. William F. Cowart, serial no. 471443. Letter to Marines from Hinton dated 24 Feb 1947. National Personnel Records Center, St. Louis, Missouri.

Coast Guard Records

During World War II, the Coast Guard fell under the authority of the Navy. Many of the documents you see in a Coast Guard file are similar to those of the Navy.

The Official Military Personnel File (OMPF) is the official record of service for a sailor. The file can be a large descriptive file if the sailor had served many years or a smaller file if he was only in during part of the war. The main documents often found in an OMPF are described here.

One of the most important things you should do when you receive the OMPF is sort it in chronological order so the reports and events make sense. Orders were issued, cancelled, and modified, and the dates of the documents may need to be clarified.

It is important to create a timeline of service based on the records in the file. If the sailor was an officer, there may be pages of only service dates and stations. Use those then go through the file to fill in the blanks.

Because Coast Guard personnel were moved so often, add to the timeline the addresses and stations you find. Include where his family was living, if he was married and they traveled with him. Also add to the timeline main historical events and records like census, vital record information, and other documentation to show a fuller picture of the sailor with his family. This helps put everything into context.

General Contents of a Coast Guard OMPF

Hazel Clark SPAR enlistment photo from OMPF

The contents of the OMPF may not only contain World War II service information but also Coast Guard Academy documentation. This chapter will contain OMPF examples from a Coast Guard SPAR, Hazel Clark and a Coast Guard Academy sailor who was killed during the war, Thomas Crotty.

Coast Guard Academy Documents. Applying for the Coast Guard Academy meant not only completing an application, but providing a written essay, taking an examination, and receiving a physical examination. Letters of recommendation were also required for the applicant. The OMPF may also contain the grades and final standing in the cadet's graduating class. Academy medical records or summary data cards may also be found with the OMPF.

Applications. Applications provided information about the life, education, job history, prior service history, and family information of the applicant. Letters of recommendation are often included.

Prior Service History. Sometimes, men will join the Coast Guard and be discharged after their term expires. Many rejoined during World War II. Prior service history will be included in their OMPF.

Service Qualification Card. The Service Qualification Card contained much of the information on the service application with the inclusion of more information on hobbies and sports participation. This card may have also contained information on prior service.

Next-of-Kin and Insurance Information. Each sailor had to complete next-of-kin contact information in case of wounds, Missing In Action, Prisoner of War, or Killed In Action status changes. Connected to this information was insurance beneficiary information.

Report of Dependents. The Report of Dependents lists the next-of-kin or dependents of the sailor. This form should be updated if the sailor marries and his dependents change, but this did not always happen.

Medical information. Some medical information will be included in an OMPF, usually regarding the physical and dental exams conducted upon induction or change in rank. Sometimes the records of sailors treated in stateside hospitals were included.

Not all medical information is contained in the OMPF. There are usually separate medical files. These files can only be requested by the veteran or his next-of-kin even if the sailor has been dead 100 years. It is important if you are the veteran or next-of-kin, you request these records. If the veteran is deceased, you must provide proof of death in the form of a death certificate, obituary, or funeral paperwork.

Pay Records. Various pay records, family allowance documents, and insurance paperwork is found within the OMPF. These documents allow a researcher to further piece together the service history with dates, locations, changes in dependents, and status.

Summary of Service. Similar to the records in a Navy and Marine Corps files, there will be Summary of Service forms which document the Vessel or Station, dates in which the sailor served on that Vessel or Station, and rank. These forms may be lined with a list of dates and locations or in memo format with greater description of service.

Appointments for Rank and Promotions

If an enlisted man or woman, rose in rank to Officer, the commission certificate will be included in the OMPF. This record provides information on the new rank and date it is official. An Oath of Office for the Officer may also be included which contains the date of change in rank and his signature.

Temporary appointments in rank were also given when needed. This usually appears in the file as a letter or memo explaining the temporary change and duties required of the serviceman.

Training and Educational Information

The training information and any special training courses completed will be included in the OMPF. The Certificate of Completion of a course provides information on specific training, location and date your sailor received. The documents may appear as official certificates of completion or as a letter or memo to be sent to Headquarters and placed in the man's file.

Travel and Furlough Orders

Travel and furlough documents and orders were included in the file to document every move a sailor made off his vessel or station. The orders often included the name, rank, and service number of several men or women, being transferred from one unit to another. An explanation of when to depart, how to travel, and when to arrive was included.

Awards, Citations, and Commendations

The OMPF contains letters or memos providing citations to an individual or unit, and the awards issued. Sometimes the award issued was done so on an official form for that specific award. These citations and awards may provide clues to service history which includes dates and battle locations.

Miscellaneous Documents

Family Letters. Quite often, the OMPF will contain letters to the military or government, requesting information on the status of their sailor. These often appear after a sailor is declared Missing In Action (MIA) or Killed In Action (KIA.)

Vital Records of Family. Sometimes a sailor had to prove his age or provide proof of his relationship to dependents or next-of-kin. Vital records are often included in the OMPF to prove these relationships.

Death Certificate. Sometimes, but not always, if the sailor was KIA, you will find a death certificate in the OMPF. If a Finding of Death was given after a sailor was MIA for one year plus one day, an explanation will be included in the file.

References to Other Sources. It is important to read each letter and document carefully within the OMPF. Names and addresses of other sailors with which your sailor fought, may be included.

Letters from Government Officials. Families who needed information from the military and had trouble receiving it, often went to their local VA or County Commissioner for assistance. In other cases, the family approached a higher-level government official such as their Congressman. These government officials acted as a go-between for families and the military to obtain information. This was not only the case during the war, but also up to the current day. You may find in OMPFs received today, the letters and contact information of government officials.

Modern Day Requests for Information. Each time an OMPF is requested, the request form or letter is included with the OMPF. The next person to request the file will receive the OMPF plus the details of all previous requests. This may lead to a new family connection.

Casualty Telegrams or Letters (MIA, POW, KIA)

Every time a sailor had a change in status, meaning he went from being a healthy, active sailor to wounded, missing, prisoner, or killed, a telegram was sent to the next-of-kin and included in his file.

Report of Casualty. The Report of Casualty was completed when a sailor was KIA or MIA then presumed dead and given a Finding of Death (FOD.) It contains his name, rank, serial number, unit, cause of casualty, next-of-kin, and vital information.

Inventory of Effects. The Inventory of Effects is always found within the IDPF, and sometimes included in the OMPF. This list documents all the personal effects of a sailor who was declared MIA or KIA, and then sent to the effects bureau in Utah for processing.

Discharge or Separation Information

The Separation and Discharge papers contain the name, rank, service number, final unit, MOS (Job) for the sailor, and enlistment and discharge or death information. Theaters of war in which sailor served, dates of service are included. Finally, the dates the man sailed overseas, arrived, then departed overseas to return to the U.S. are also included.

SPAR Application for Hazel Clark

NAVCG 2501
U. S. COAST GUARD

READ INSTRUCTION
SHEET CAREFULLY
BEFORE FILLING OUT
THIS APPLICATION

APPLICATION

WOMEN'S RESERVE, U. S. COAST GUARD RESERVE

SPARS

(Encircle class for which you are applying)

W–9 OFFICER CANDIDATE

W–10 ENLISTED CANDIDATE

(PRINT OR TYPE)

Date .... April 20, 1944

Married name .... (Last name) .... (First name) .... (Middle name)

Maiden name .... CLARK (Last name) .... Hazel (First name) .... Ruth (Middle name)

I hereby make application for enlistment in the Women's Reserve, U. S. Coast Guard Reserve, as Apprentice Seaman, submitting the following information:

(A) PERSONAL AND FAMILY RECORD

1. OFFICIAL RESIDENCE (Voting address) .... 725 Whitmore Road (Street)

   Detroit (City) .... Michigan (State)

   (Congressional district)

2. MAILING ADDRESS (Temporary address) 425 East Main Street (Street) .... Norwalk, Ohio (City and State)

   HOME PHONE No. .... — .... BUSINESS PHONE No. .... —

3. BIRTH DATE August (Month) 30 (Day) 1911 (Year) 4. AGE 32 5. RACE White

6. BIRTHPLACE .... Mendota, Illinois (City and State) 7. CITIZENSHIP ....

   If naturalized, indicate .... (Year) .... (Place) .... (Number of naturalization certificate)

8. Name of next of kin .... Glenn R. Clark .... Relationship .... Uncle

   Address .... 425 East Main Street (Street) .... Norwalk, Ohio (City and State)

9. If ever known by any other name(s), list .... None

10. Marital status (Encircle) (Single) Married Divorced Separated Widowed

11. Occupation and employer of husband ....

12. Do you have any children under 18? ....

13. Have you ever been arrested or in the custody of the police? .... No.

    Details ....

    ....

15—36921-1

Applicant does not fill in this box
Name of test ....
SCORE ....

Official Military Personnel File. Hazel Clark, serial no. 4008-328. SPAR Application. National Personnel Records Center, St. Louis, Missouri.

14. Have you ever served in any branch of the armed forces? ....No.... How long? ...."........

Date of discharge ...."........... Character of discharge ...."..........

15. Have you ever made an application for Military or Naval Service? ..No.. Branch ....

Where? ...."........... When? ...."..........

Have you ever been rejected? ...."..... Details ...."..........

(B) EDUCATIONAL RECORD

1. Encircle highest grade completed   8   9   10   11   (12)

Name of high school Washington High School Milwaukee, Wisconsin   Date of graduation June, 1930

Address Sherman Blvd. at Wright Street   Milwaukee, Wisconsin
             (Street)   (City and State)

2. NAME OF COLLEGE, BUSINESS, OR TECHNICAL SCHOOL	FROM—	TO—	MAJOR	MINOR	DEGREES (if any)	DATE
U. of Michigan	7/42	9/42	Literature, Arts & Sc.			
U. of Michigan Ext., Det.	1940	1942	Literature, Arts & Sc.			

(If you attended college you must submit a properly authenticated transcript of your college record with your application form and other papers)

3. Describe any specialized courses recently studied such as those offered in war training or defense programs, e. g., mathematics, navigation, etc. ....None........

4. In what extra-curricular activities did you participate in school? Girls' Club; Camera Club;

5. What positions of leadership did you hold in school?   None outstanding.

6. What percentage of college expenses did you earn? ...All.

7. What summer jobs have you held? ....None.

8. What hobbies do you regularly pursue? ..Photography, when possible.

9. In what community activities do you participate? (Civilian Defense, Social Service, etc.)

10. Of what professional, vocational or trade organizations have you been a member? ......None.

11. Have you ever traveled or resided in a foreign country? .Canada. Details .Lived near Detroit, and have taken innumerable trips through Canadian vicinity near Detroit.

2

16—36921-1

Enlistment Contract - Hazel Clark

N. C. G. 2500
(Rev. Dec. 1941)

ENLISTMENT CONTRACT

UNITED STATES { COAST GUARD
COAST GUARD RESERVE

Enlistment of CLARK, Hazel Ruth
(Full name, surname to left)

Accepted for enlistment at NOP Detroit, Michigan ; A.S. W-10
(Rating in which enlisted)

Enlisted at NOP Detroit, Michigan ; 2/11/43
(Date)

Transferred to ....

Occupation .... Citizenship* .... If naturalized, place and date

of naturalization .... Certificate No. ....

Date of birth August 30, 1911 Place of birth Mendota, Illinois

Home address 725 Whitmore Road, Apartment 403, Detroit, Wayne, Michigan
(Street and number) (Town) (County) (State)

Married or single Single Name and address of next of kin or legal guardian

Glenn R. Clark (Uncle) 425 E. Main St., Norwalk, Ohio
(Relationship) (Address)

Continuous Service Certificate .... Previous service { Coast Guard } ....
(Number) Reserve (Years) (Months) (Days)

First enlisted .... at .... and was
(Date) (Place)

last discharged .... from ....
(Date) (Unit)

with .... discharge as .... No. ....
(Character) (Rate)

Previous Navy service .... Previous Marine Corps service ....
(Years) (Months) (Days) (Years) (Months) (Days)

Previous Army service .... Age .... Years .... Months
(Years) (Months) (Days)

Height 5 feet 5½ inches. Weight 113 pounds

Eyes Blue Sex F Hair Dk.Brn. Complexion Fair Color White

Personal characteristics, "ANT.""VS.rt.arm; marks, etc. S.3" rt.cheek;S.½" rt.thumb;PS. rt. knee. "PCS." Acne, upper back.

For and in consideration of the pay or wages due to the ratings which may from time to time be assigned me during the

continuance of my service, I agree to and with C. W. MUILENBURG, Lt.(jg), D-V(S), USNR

.... of the United States Coast Guard, as follows:

FIRST: To enter the Coast Guard of the United States and to report to such station or vessel as I may be ordered to join, and to the utmost of my power and ability discharge my several services or duties and be in everything conformable and obedient to the several requirements and lawful commands of the officers who may be placed over me.

*Citizenship—Use expressions "NB" for native born ; "NZ" for naturalized ; "NPI" for native of Philippine Islands ; "NPR" for native of Puerto Rico.
16—9420-1

Official Military Personnel File. Hazel Clark, serial no. 4008-328. Enlistment Contract. National Personnel Records Center, St. Louis, Missouri.

Duration ~~years from~~ plus 6 months ____ 943

during minority until _____, 1

SECOND: I oblige and subject myself to serve

unless sooner discharged by proper authority.

In the event of war or National emergency declared by the President to exist during my term of service, I oblige and subject myself to serve until 6 months after the end of the war or National emergency if so required by the Secretary of the Navy unless I voluntarily reenlist or extend my enlistment. I understand that when so detained I am not entitled to enlistment allowance and that in time of war the addition of one-quarter pay as specified in the Act of July 11, 1941, is not applicable.

I also oblige myself, during such service, to comply with and be subject to such laws, regulations, and discipline for the government of the Coast Guard as are or shall be established by the Congress of the United States or other competent authority, and to submit to treatment for the prevention of smallpox, typhoid (typhoid prophylaxis), and to such other preventive measures as may be considered necessary by proper authorities.

THIRD: I am of the legal age to enlist; I have never deserted from the United States Coast Guard, Navy, Army, or Marine Corps; I have never been discharged from the United States Service or other service on account of disability or through sentence of either civilian or military court; and I have never been discharged from any service, civil or military, except with good character and for the reasons given by me to the recruiting officer prior to enlistment. I am not a member of the Coast Guard Reserve, Naval Reserve, Naval Militia, Marine Corps Reserve, National Guard, or Army Reserve.

FOURTH: I understand that upon enlistment in the Coast Guard Reserve, I may be ordered to active duty in time of war or when in the opinion of the President a National emergency exists, and that I may be required to perform active duty throughout the war or until the National emergency ceases to exist and for 6 months thereafter.

FIFTH: I have had this contract fully explained to me, I understand it, and certify that no promise of any kind has been made to me concerning assignment to duty, or promotion during my enlistment.

OATH OF ALLEGIANCE: I, Hazel Ruth CLARK

do solemnly swear (or affirm) that I will bear true faith and allegiance to the United States of America, and that I will serve them honestly and faithfully against all their enemies whomsoever, and that I will obey the orders of the President of the United States and the orders of the officers appointed over me, according to the laws of the United States and the regulations governing the Coast Guard.

And I do further swear (or affirm) that all statements made by me as now given in this record are correct.

Hazel Ruth Clark
(Signature in own handwriting, surname to right)

Hazel Ruth Clark

Subscribed and sworn to before me this 11th day of February _____, A. D. 19 43

(Commanding officer, notary public, or other officer qualified to administer oaths)

C.W. MUILENBURG, LT.(jg), D-V(S), USNR

_____ (Title)

Citizenship substantiated and contract perfected.

_____, U. S. C. G., Enlisting Officer.

18—64420-1

Official Military Personnel File. Hazel Clark, serial no. 4008-328. Enlistment Contract. National Personnel Records Center, St. Louis, Missouri.

258

Information Card - Hazel Clark

Official Military Personnel File. Hazel Clark, serial no. 4008-328. Information Card. National Personnel Records Center, St. Louis, Missouri.

Letter of Recommendation - Hazel Clark

FERRIS D. STONE
CLEVELAND THURBER
EDWARD A. MACDONALD
JOHN C. SPAULDING
WILLIAM J. SHAW
EDWARD S. REID, JR.
FREDERICK H. ROBINSON
MAXWELL E. FEAD
LAWRENCE S. KING
EDGAR H. AILES
GEORGE D. MILLER
HARRY F. MCMASTER
FREDERIC S. GLOVER, JR.
FREDERIC B. BESIMER
EMMETT E. EAGAN
GEORGE C. TILLEY
JAMES V. BUTLER
EDGAR B. GALLOWAY
WILLIAM J. WEIPERT
WILLIAM G. BUTLER

LAW OFFICES OF
MILLER, CANFIELD, PADDOCK AND STONE
PENOBSCOT BUILDING DETROIT

LOUIS H. FEAD
COUNSEL

September 3, 1942

SIDNEY T. MILLER
1864 – 1940
GEORGE L. CANFIELD
1866 – 1928
LEWIS H. PADDOCK
1866 – 1935
SIDNEY T. MILLER, JR.
1894 – 1936

CABLE
"STEM DETROIT"

TELEPHONE
CHERRY 6420

<u>TO WHOM IT MAY CONCERN</u>

Miss Hazel Clark was employed in this office as a legal stenographer and secretary from September, 1941 into June, 1942.

She is a competent secretary, and performed her work satisfactorily while in our employ. She has a pleasing personality, and was entirely satisfactory in her relations with the other employees.

She left our employ voluntarily for the purpose of advancing her education at the University of Michigan.

We are glad to recommend her for secretarial and stenographic work.

Yours very truly,

MILLER, CANFIELD, PADDOCK and STONE

By *Edward A Reid Jr*

ESR:BW

Official Military Personnel File. Hazel Clark, serial no. 4008-328. Letter of Recommendation from Miller, Canfield, Paddock, and Stowe. National Personnel Records Center, St. Louis, Missouri.

NAVCG 2599
U. S. COAST GUARD
(Rev. June 1943)

REPORT OF CHANGE IN PERSONNEL

CLARK	Hazel	R.	4008-328	Y2c(WR)
(Surname)	(First name)	(Middle initial)	(Service No.)	(Rank or rating)

COAST GUARD
TRAINING STATION   07-131   ST. AUGUSTINE, FLA.   5 January, 1945
(Major unit)   (Unit Item No. or vessel's   (Place)   (Date)
                      assigned district)

(Minor unit)

1315, 4 January, 1945: Transferred to CG Barracks, Washington, D. C., for
assignment to duty in mutual exchange with Joan M.
Eisenlohr (4009-695) Y3c(WR).

DUTY CODE No. 45-D
AUTHORITY:
HL 12-26-44 (PEA-C)(CG-783)(W).

C. LEUPOLD, Lieut. Comdr., USCGR
(Commanding)

By direction
(Title)

CC: DCGO, 7ND

SPACE BELOW IS FOR HEADQUARTERS' USE ONLY

ENLISTED PERSONNEL

Rate	R T	Pay Grade	District	Foreign Domestic	Duty
II	III	XIV	XVII	XX	XXI

OFFICER PERSONNEL

District	Sea Shore	Foreign Domestic	Duty
XI		XV	XVIII

RECORDS	
Posting	Coding

MACHINE ACCOUNTING
Punched
Verified

U. S. GOVERNMENT PRINTING OFFICE   16—30894-2

Official Military Personnel File. Hazel Clark, serial no. 4008-328. Report of Change. National Personnel Records Center, St. Louis, Missouri.

Separation Paper - Hazel Clark

Reproduced at the National Archives- STL

NOTICE OF SEPARATION FROM   E U. S. NAVAL SERVICE - COAST GU
NAVCG-553 (Rev. 9-44)

1. NAME (LAST)	(FIRST)	(MIDDLE)	2. RATE OR RANK	3. PAY GRADE	4. C. G. SERVICE NO.
CLARK	Hazel	Ruth	#Y2c(WR)	Third	(4008-328)

5. PERMANENT ADDRESS FOR MAILING PURPOSES
425 E. Main St. - Norwalk, Ohio (Huron County)

6. RACE	7. SEX	8. DATE OF BIRTH
White	Female	30 Aug., 1911

9. ADDRESS FROM WHICH DISCHARGEE WILL SEEK WORK (IF DIFFERENT FROM ITEM #5)
Same as Item 5.

10. MARRIED: YES / NO X | 11. NO. OF DEPENDENTS: None | 12. U.S. CITIZEN: YES X / NO

RECORD OF COAST GUARD SERVICE

SELECTIVE SERVICE DATA — 13. REGISTERED: YES / NO X

14. HOME ADDRESS AT TIME OF ENTRY INTO SERVICE
725 Whitmore Road - Detroit, Michigan

15. LOCAL BOARD NO. COUNTY AND STATE

16. PLACE OF ENTRY INTO SERVICE	MO.	DAY	YR.	17. PLACE OF SEPARATION FROM SERVICE	MO.	DAY	YR.
Detroit, Mich. (Active Duty)	3	25	43	Cleveland, Ohio	7	24	45

18. CHARACTER OF DISCHARGE
UNDER HONORABLE CONDITIONS

19. LENGTH OF FOREIGN AND/OR SEA SERVICE WORLD WAR II: None — YEARS 00 MONTHS 00 DAYS 00

20. SERVICE SCHOOLS ATTENDED	COURSES	WEEKS	21. OFF DUTY EDUCATIONAL COURSES	CLASS HOURS
None			None	

EMPLOYMENT AND NON-SERVICE EDUCATIONAL DATA

22. LAST EMPLOYER BEFORE ENTRY INTO SERVICE (GIVE FIRM NAME AND ADDRESS)
Judge Chester P. O'Hara - National Bank Bldg. - Detroit, Michigan
DATE LEFT: 20 March, 194

23. USUAL CIVILIAN OCCUPATION (D.O.T. TITLE AND BRIEF DESCRIPTION)
1-33.01 - Secretary - Secretary in various law offices - typing, shorthand, filing.

24. JOB FIELD PREFERENCE: Secretary
25. JOB AID DESIRED? YES / NO X
26. LOCALITY PREFERENCE (GIVE GENERAL AREA): Middle West

27. NON-SERVICE EDUCATION — ENTER NUMBER OF YEARS COMPLETED: GRAMMAR SCHOOL 8, HIGH SCHOOL 4, COLLEGE 1

28. MAJOR COURSE OR FIELD: Commercial Course

29. VOCATIONAL OR TRADE COURSES (INDICATE NATURE AND LENGTH OF COURSES)
Wayne University - Interior Decorating, Speech, Music Appreciation - Six Months.

30. PREFERENCE FOR ADDITIONAL EDUCATIONAL TRAINING
None

31. REMARKS
#Y2c(WR) - Yeoman, Second Class (Women's Reserve).

I certify that all information on this form pertaining to the Naval Service of the above named individual is in accordance with the records of the U. S. Coast Guard and that a copy of this form has been delivered to him in person.

32. (SIGNATURE OF DISCHARGING OFFICER)
J. M. BINCKLEY, Lieut., USCGR(W)
Asst. Civil Readjustment Officer
(TYPE NAME AND RANK OF DISCHARGING OFFICER)

33. SIGNATURE OF DISCHARGED PERSON
Hazel R. Clark

DATE: 24 July, 1945

2   TO: COAST GUARD HEADQUARTERS

Official Military Personnel File. Hazel Clark, serial no. 4008-328. Separation Paper. National Personnel Records Center, St. Louis, Missouri.

Application for Cadet Examination - Thomas Crotty

Q539A
3-7-30

TREASURY DEPARTMENT
U. S. COAST GUARD
Form 9530—Dec., 1926

U. S. COAST GUARD
REC'D APR 14 1930 By
ANS.

Reproduced at the National Archives- STL

Application to take the Examination for Appointment as Cadet in the United States Coast Guard

Street and No. ___18 Milford___

City ___Buffalo___

State ___New York___

Date ___April 7, 1930___

The Commandant,
   U. S. Coast Guard,
      Washington, D. C.

SIR:

I hereby make application to take the next examination for appointment as cadet in the United States Coast Guard.

Respectfully,

(Signature) _James E Crotty_

(CONFIDENTIAL INFORMATION)

PERSONAL AND SCHOOL HISTORY SHEET

In order that your desire to be designated for examination for appointment as a cadet may be given every possible consideration, it is necessary that you fill out this blank and return the same promptly to the Commandant, U. S. Coast Guard, Washington, D. C.   Read very carefully before attempting to fill out and answer every question to the best of your ability.

1. Full name (print) ___THOMAS JAMES EUGENE CROTTY___
   (No abbreviation)

2. When were you born? ___March___ ___18___ ___1912___
   (Month)   (Day)   (Year)

3. In what State or country were you born? ___New York___

4. In what State is your legal residence? ___New York___

5. State if you are a citizen of the United States ___Yes___   (If native, so state; if not, state how citizenship was acquired) ___Native___

6. Are you, or have you ever been, married? ___No___

SCHOLASTIC QUALIFICATIONS
Time of Attendance at Schools and Studies There Pursued

7. Public high school: Name of school ___South Park High___ Yrs. _5_ Mos. _--_

Highest grade attained and studies pursued in that grade.   (State if graduate) ___

___Graduate in the Arts course of study___

2—14142

Official Military Personnel File. Thomas Crotty. Application to take Examination for Appointment as a Cadet. National Personnel Records Center, St. Louis, Missouri.

8. Private high   preparatory school: Name of school _____ -- _____

Yrs. _____ -- _____ Mos. _____ -- _____ Highest grade attained and studies pursued in that grade.   (State if graduate) _____

9. Normal school or academy: Name _____ --- _____

Yrs. _____ Mos. _____ Highest grade attained and studies pursued in that grade.   (State if graduate) _____

10. University or college: Name _____ --- _____ Yrs. _____ Mos. _____

Class reached_____ Course pursued _____

_____,- (State if graduate) _____

11. Special preparation for examination for appointment to cadetship in the U. S. Coast Guard: Where? _____ --- _____ Yrs. _____ Mos. _____

12. Have you ever taught school? _____ --- _____ Where? _____

_____ Yrs. _____ Mos. _____

13. Were you ever a cadet at the Coast Guard, Military, or Naval Academy? _____ --- _____

Which? _____ When? _____

14. Were you ever in the Army, Navy, Marine Corps, or Coast Guard? _____ --- _____

Which? _____ When? _____

15. Were you ever examined as a candidate for admission to the Military, Naval, or Coast Guard Academy? _____ --- _____ Which? _____ When? _____

16. State if you ever wholly or partially earned your own living, and if so, for how long and at what work Yes, during summer months in park department as laborer, and also two months as clerk in broker's office.

_____

17. State whether you have pursued in your studies any of the following subjects, and the most advanced point reached in each:

(a) Mathematics	Algebra	Intermediate; to quadratics and beyond
	Geometry	Plane, the usual theorems, and constructions
	Trigonometry	--
	Analytical geometry	--
	Calculus	--

3—14142

Official Military Personnel File. Thomas Crotty. Application to take Examination for Appointment as a Cadet. National Personnel Records Center, St. Louis, Missouri.

264

Coast Guard Records

Reproduced at the National Archives- STL

(b) Sciences

General science

Physics

Chemistry

Biology 1st Year, introductory physiology

Botany introductory botany

Zoology introductory zoology

(c) Modern languages and classics.

French Two years

German

Spanish

Latin Latin 111, Cicero

Greek

(d) Histories

Ancient Greek and Roman History, to death of Charlemagne

European

English

American and civil government History of U.S., and study of Federal Govt.

(e) Grammar, rhetoric, English composition and literature Principles of English grammar, rules of English Composition, and study of selected subjects in Eng.& English IV Years. American Literature

(f) Physical geography

(g) Freehand drawing, time

(h) Mechanical drawing, time

Name of school (g and h)

If in drafting office, state nature of work, name of office, and time employed

7—14149

Official Military Personnel File. Thomas Crotty. Application to take Examination for Appointment as a Cadet. National Personnel Records Center, St. Louis, Missouri.

ATHLETIC QUALIFICATIONS

18. In what sports have you engaged and for how many years? Baseball--5 years
Basket-ball--3 years   Swimming--4 years

19. Name the athletic teams of which you have been a member South Park High School
South Buffalo Post 721 and Burke Bros., American Legion Champions

20. What medals, if any, have you received for athletic records? Silver medal for runners-
up in New York State 1928. Gold medals for National Junior Champions
American Legion in 1929.

21. What school or college letters have you made, and for what sports?
Three Major letters for baseball at high school

22. What athletic records, if any, have you held or broken?

23. What positions of leadership have you held in school or college organizations?
Captain of baseball team

I certify on honor that the above statements are true to the best of my knowlege and belief.

(Signature) James E Crotty

IMPORTANT

The candidate must submit with this application at least three (3) letters of recommendation from responsible persons who have known him well for at least one year, and who can vouch for his integrity, good habits, and standing in the community.

U. S. GOVERNMENT PRINTING OFFICE: 1929   2—14142

Official Military Personnel File. Thomas Crotty. Application to take Examination for Appointment as a Cadet. National Personnel Records Center, St. Louis, Missouri.

37-30

TREASURY DEPARTMENT
U. S. COAST GUARD
Form No. 9559 A

U. S. COAST GUARD
REC'D
NS'D   APR 8   1930
BY

Certificate for Preparatory School or Public High School

(To be filled out by candidate)

Name of Candidate *Thomas James Eugene Crotty* Age *17*
                    (Full name)

Since graduating from the *South Park High* school, I have been engaged as follows:

Here give history to date of certificate, including especially subsequent educational work.

Have you previously been examined or submitted certificate for entrance to the U. S. Coast Guard Academy?_____
                                                                                        (Yes or No)

If so, give date_____

To what school or college organizations have you belonged?_____

What offices, if any, did you hold in these organizations?_____

(To be filled out by Principal of Institution)

ADVICE.—It is requested that great care be exercised in filling out this certificate. Strike out all words not applicable. Incomplete or carelessly executed certificates can not be accepted. Necessary explanations should be made on margin. CERTIFICATE ON SCHOOL FORM CAN NOT BE ACCEPTED IN LIEU OF THIS FORM.

After making out this certificate the school authorities should mail it direct to the Commandant, U. S. Coast Guard, Washington, D. C., and under no circumstances return it to the custody of the candidate. Failure to comply with this provision may invalidate this certificate.

Name of school _____ South Park High School

Location (Town, County, and State): _____ Buffalo, Erie, New York

I hereby certify that I am the Principal of _____ South Park High School
                                                                (Name of school)

and that the following statements with respect to _____ Thomas James Eugene Crotty _____ are correct.
                                                                    (Name of student)

1. He attended this school from _____ Sept. _____, 19 24, to _____ June _____, 19 29

2. He completed the full high-school course and received a diploma from this school _____ June _____, 19 29 after successfully passing the final examinations set by the school for the graduating class (or grade).

3. He has completed 3½ years of the full high-school course and will receive a diploma from this school _____

_____, 19_____, if he passes the final examinations set by the school for the graduating class (or grade).

The number in his class was (or will be) 172 His standing in his class was (or will be) No. 106

(OVER)   2—13672

Official Military Personnel File. Thomas Crotty. Application to take Examination for Appointment as a Cadet. National Personnel Records Center, St. Louis, Missouri.

Coast Guard Academy Grades - Thomas Crotty

UNITED STATES COAST GUARD ACADEMY

NEW LONDON, CONNECTICUT

25 August, 1939.

ABSTRACT OF GRADES
Lieut. (j.g.) Thomas J. E. Crotty.

Appointed cadet 28 July, 1930.
Commissioned ensign 28 May, 1934.
Graduated with a standing of 3rd. in a class of 5.

FIRST YEAR

SUBJECTS	First Term Grades	Second Term Grades
Seamanship	61.59	74.83
Navigation	67.54	80.25
Communications	88.47	69.17
Chemistry	69.50	74.25
Algebra		74.25
Trigonometry	77.25	91.50
Descriptive Geometry		78.60
English	78.50	84.66
French		94.83
Drawing	72.33	
Shop		80.67
Hygiene	81.66	
Physics	61.92	

SECOND YEAR

	Sea Term		
Seamanship	70.00		72.80
Navigation	77.00	87.20	82.66
Communications	73.00	82.00	83.15
Calculus and Analytic Geometry		72.63	
Mechanics			87.00
Physics		70.87	70.67
English		80.17	65.50
French		92.67	93.04
Heat Engines		70.00	83.17
Drawing		69.67	72.66
Physics Laboratory			70.67
Physical Education		85.00	
Engineering	73.00		
Professional Fitness	72.67		

(Continued on sheet No. 2

ABSTRACT OF GRADES - Lieut. (j.g.) T. J. E. CROTTY

THIRD YEAR

SUBJECTS	Sea Term Grades	First Term Grades	Second Term Grades
Seamanship	82.00		81.00
Navigation	75.00	86.25	64.09
Ordnance	82.50		78.16
Mechanics		84.17	
English		67.50	84.50
Thermodynamics		85.65	
Boilers			76.17
Naval Construction			82.50
Engineering	65.00		76.00
Electricity		75.56	76.44
Electrical Laboratory		77.33	
Communications	75.00		
Heat Engines			86.17
Professional Fitness	75.80		

FOURTH YEAR

SUBJECTS	Sea Term Grades	First Term Grades	Second Term Grades
Seamanship	72.50	72.00	74.17
Navigation Law	90.00		
Service Regulations and Military Law		74.00	82.17
Compass Compensation		65.00	
Surveying			73.00
Ordnance and Ballistics		75.17	81.67
Tactics		82.34	
Communications	65.00		82.50
Radio		77.50	75.67
English and History		76.00	
Steam Engineering	82.00	62.00	
Internal Combustion Engines			85.34
Turbines			78.42
Engineering Laboratory			75.00
Steam		82.09	
Shop		63.67	
Professional Fitness	66.25		

CERTIFIED TRUE AND CORRECT:

L. W. PERKINS,
Commandant of Cadets.

- 2 -

Official Military Personnel File. Thomas Crotty. Coast Guard Academy Grades. National Personnel Records Center, St. Louis, Missouri.

Letter Regarding MIA Status- Thomas Crotty

FILE-
MR. CROTTY'S FILE

Washington, D.C.,
October 28, 1942.

Vice Admiral R.R. Waesche,
 Commandant, U.S. Coast Guard,
 1300 "E" Street, N.W.,
 Washington, D.C.

FILE
A. R

Dear Admiral Waesche:-

        Following our conversation at the Hotel Waldorf-Astoria on the
evening of October 16, 1942, the following information is forwarded concerning Lieutenant T.J.E. Crotty, U.S. Coast Guard.

        Lieutenant Crotty arrived on the Asiatic station about six weeks
prior to the commencement of hostilities and was attached to the in-shore
patrol headquarters of the Sixteen Naval District, with offices at the Navy
Yard, Cavite. Lieutenant Crotty continued on these duties until the afternoon
of December 10, 1941, when the Cavite Navy Yard was bombed and destroyed by
the subsequent fire. Lieutenant Crotty continued to perform duties in the
Navy Yard area while Admiral Rockwell maintained temporary quarters at Sangley
Point. When the evacuation of Manila and the Cavite Navy Yard areas became
necessary on December 24, 1941, Lieutenant Crotty, because of his special qualifications in handling explosives, supervised the demolition of the U.S.S. SEA
LION and other naval, military, and other important civilian establishments
in order that they might not fall into the hands of the enemy. To the best of
my knowledge Lieutenant Crotty arrived at Fort Mills on Corregidor the afternoon of December 25 or 26, 1941. I recall that Lieutenant Crotty accompanied
a further expedition to Sangley Point on at least one night between December
26, 1941, and January 1, 1942, prior to the Japanese occupation of Cavite Province and Manila. This was again in connection with special demolition work.
Lieutenant Crotty, while attached to Naval units at Fort Mills, performed various duties with the guard battalion of naval headquarters. For a period of
about six weeks during February and March Lieutenant Crotty was attached to
the U.S.S. QUAIL as Executive Officer. In this capacity he assisted with the
regular sweeping of the channel through mine fields, which made the servicing
of submarines possible. The U.S.S. QUAIL at this time also bombarded the
west coast of Bataan and thereby greatly assisted the naval battalion in the
Marivales area in overcoming a strong Japanese landing force that had landed
on the flank of General Wainwright's corps area and threatened to sever the
line of supplies for this organization. To the best of my knowledge Lieutenant
Crotty returned to Fort Mills for duty with the naval units the latter part of
March, at which time he became adjutant of the headquarters guard battalion
of the Sixteenth Naval District Headquarters. The headquarters company at that
time consisted of about one thousand naval enlisted men who had been on duty in
the Manila Bay area prior to its general evacuation to Fort Mills. In this
capacity Lieutenant Crotty continued to serve until the capitulation of the
forts in the Manila Bay area on May 6 and 7.

-1-

*Official Military Personnel File. Thomas Crotty. Letter Regarding MIA Status. National Personnel Records Center, St. Louis,
Missouri.*

-2-

       Lieutenant Crotty impressed us all with his fine qualities of Naval leadership which were combined with a very pleasant personality and a willingness to assist everyone to the limit of his ability. He continued to remain very cheerful and retained a high morale until my departure from Fort Mills the evening of May 3rd. Lieutenant Crotty is worthy of commendation for the energetic and industrious manner in which he performed all his tasks. He continued to be an outstanding example of an officer and a gentleman to all hands and was a source of encouragement to many who did not possess his high qualities of courage and perseverance that he displayed. Having seen Lieutenant Crotty undergo all the trials during my five months in the Manila Bay area, I feel sure that the rigors and trials of a prisoner of war will produce little if any change, and I look forward to the return of Lieutenant Crotty to active duty, for I am sure he will continue to perform his duties in keeping with all the traditions of the Naval and Coast Guard Services.

       It is a pleasure for me to forward the above remarks concerning Lieutenant Crotty. Lieutenant Crotty in all his duties was a distinct credit to the U.S. Coast Guard and a fine example of the outstanding officers which your service possesses. I will be pleased to forward any additional information concerning the foregoing remarks if such should be necessary to complete the records. From the information that is available I feel there is no doubt that Lieutenant Crotty is now a prisoner of war at a camp near Tarlac, in northern Luzon, and that he is being treated by the Japanese in accordance with the laws of war.

                          Very Respectfully,

                          DENYS W. KNOLL,
                     Lieut. Comdr., U. S. Navy.

Official Military Personnel File. Thomas Crotty. Letter regarding MIA Status. National Personnel Records Center, St. Louis, Missouri.

Finding of Death - Thomas Crotty

3-7
File
mjm

(PMM)

CG-71

10 September, 1943

Mrs. Helen Crotty
18 Milford Street
Buffalo, New York

my dear Mrs. Crotty:

In the absence of definite information as to the date of your son's death,
the Secretary of the Navy, acting under an Act of Congress approved 7 March,
1942, presumed that death occurred on 30 September, 1942. I regret that
I have so little information to give you. Please accept my sincere sympathy.

You will find inclosed the forms necessary to effect settlement of the sums
due the estate of your son, Lieutenant Thomas J. E. Crotty, USCG. Inasmuch
as the final pay due his estate is approximately $2,119.00, it will be neces-
sary that you apply to the Court for Letters of Administration, since amounts
in excess of $500.00 may be paid only to a legally appointed executor or
administrator. As soon as you receive the appointment, please forward a copy
of the Court Order showing same, together with the completed Form No. 1055.

Veterans Administration Form No. 535 is inclosed in order that you may make
application for the pension award. It will be necessary that you furnish a
copy of the public record of birth or church record of baptism of your son to
support the application for award of pension.

All forms are to be completed in the presence of two witnesses and a notary
public, taking care to answer all questions. Upon completion, please forward
them to Coast Guard Headquarters, Washington, D. C.

By direction of the Commandant.

Very truly yours,

J. R. HINNANT
Lieutenant Commander, USCG
Chief, Military Morale Div.

Incls
1 Form No. 1055
2 Form No. 1057
3 Form No. 535

mjm

BSX:mjm return to 2-4

SEP 11 1943

Official Military Personnel File. Thomas Crotty. Finding of Death. National Personnel Records Center, St. Louis, Missouri.

128   COAST GUARD BULLETIN   12/52

LT Thomas J. E. Crotty Commended by SecNavy

The Honorable Dan A. Kimball, Secretary of the Navy, has posthumously commended LT Thomas J. E. Crotty (deceased), for outstanding service in connection with operations against the enemy Japanese forces in the Pacific war area from October 1941 to May 1942.

Some time around 6 or 7 May 1942, LT Crotty was taken a prisoner of war by the Japanese upon the capitulation of the forts in the Manila Bay area, and is now legally presumed to be dead inasmuch as no official record of his death or prison incarceration have been found.

LT Crotty, arrived on the Navy Yard, Cavite, about 6 weeks prior to the date of Pearl Harbor; he was attached then to the inshore patrol headquarters of the Sixteenth Naval District at Cavite.

He continued on these duties until the afternoon of 10 December 1941, when the Cavite Yard was bombed and destroyed by the resulting fires. However, he continued to perform duties at the Navy Yard area, but when the evacuation of Manila and Cavite areas became necessary on 24 December, he, because of his special qualifications in handling explosives, supervised the demolition of the USS *Sea Lion* and other naval, military, and important civilian establishments in order that they might not fall into the hands of the enemy.

It is believed that LT Crotty arrived at Fort Mills on Corregidor the afternoon of 25 or 26 December. He accompanied an expedition to Sangley Point shortly before the Japanese occupation of Cavite Province and Manila. It was again in connection with special demolition work that, while he was attached to the Naval units at Fort Mills he worked with the guard battalion of naval headquarters.

Then for a period of about 6 weeks during February and March, LT Crotty was attached to the USS *Quail* as executive officer. In this capacity he assisted with the regular sweeping of the channel through mine fields, which made the servicing of submarines possible. The *Quail* at this time also bombarded the west coast of Bataan, thereby greatly assisting the naval battalion in the Marivales area to overcome a strong Jap landing force that had landed on the flank of General Wainwright's corps area and threatened to sever the lines of supplies for this organization.

Later LT Crotty returned to Fort Mills for duty with the naval units in the latter part of March, at which time he became adjutant of the headquarters guard battalion of the Sixteenth Naval District headquarters. That company at the time consisted of about 1,000 naval enlisted men who had been on duty in the Manila Bay area prior to its general evacuation to Fort Mills. It was in this capacity that LT Crotty continued to serve until the capitulation of the Manila Bay Area. It is from this point in his career that LT Crotty's official record is a blank.

According to official records, LT Crotty was the only Coast Guardsman to be a Japanese prisoner of war during World War II.

Official Military Personnel File. Thomas Crotty. Article about Thomas Crotty. National Personnel Records Center, St. Louis, Missouri.

Merchant Marine Records

In February 1942, as the need for men and vessels increased to support the war effort, President Roosevelt transferred the authority of the Merchant Marine to that of the Coast Guard. These Mariners were civilians who applied to serve during the war in their current role as a Merchant Mariner. The Coast Guard established training bases on both the east and west coasts, and licensed and unlicensed merchant marine personnel enlisted. Men had to be at least 19 years old with at least one year of service on an American merchant vessel. The vessel had to be more than 500 gross tons. Each man underwent either three or six months of training based on previous experience. By September 1942, the Maritime Service was transferred to the War Shipping Administration, which oversaw the vessels and personnel for the duration of the war.

The records for a Merchant Mariner are diverse and located in many places. It can be a very confusing journey to locate and obtain information on the men who served. There are different rules regarding records and who can request and receive the records. Throughout this chapter, I will provide information on the records found in the Official Military Service File (OMPF), where those records are stored, and how to prove service during World War II. My intent is to only provide information on records created during World War II.

Additional records for the Merchant Marine are available. To adequately explain additional records available and how to access them, this chapter will contain many website links to explore, as all the information cannot be reprinted in this volume.

To begin our discussion we must first understand where the Official Military Personnel Files are stored. One of the most important things you should do when you receive the OMPF is sort it in chronological order so the reports and events make sense. The record examples used in this chapter are for 19 year old Merchant Mariner Elvis N. Spotts.

Official Military Personnel File

There are two potential locations for pieces of the Official Military Personnel Files (OMPF) for a Merchant Mariner. One or both locations may have records. It is important to contact both.

National Personnel Records Center

The National Personnel Records Center (NPRC) in St. Louis may have a file. This file may contain enlistment documents for enrollment in the United States Maritime Service, training information, medical information, pay changes, and travel orders.

Note: The records held at the NPRC are available to those other than next-of-kin if the Mariner died or was discharged prior to 1952. There are also Mariners who later joined a different branch of the military. When you request service records for the Mariner at the NPRC, you may also want to include a written request for a search of the VA Index, in case your Mariner appears in there under a different service branch.

Requesting the Service File

There are three ways to access these records.

Mail in Form 180

The least expensive way to begin a search is to fill out and mail Form 180 on the NPRC website and see if the file survived. If records are discovered, NPRC will send you a letter indicating such, as well as your fee for copies. Form 180 will ONLY search personnel records.

> NPRC Form 180
> http://www.archives.gov/research/order/standard-form-180.pdf

Visit NPRC In-Person

You can visit the NPRC in-person, but there is a procedure for doing so. Visit their website for current rules regarding making an appointment, what is allowed in the research room, and how to request files and microfilm.

Hire a Researcher

Another option is to hire an independent researcher who knows their way around the NPRC records. There are many more valuable records at the NPRC besides the service files, such as Morning Reports, that Form 180 will not search for you. NARA does have a researcher's list you can check.

> I highly recommend Norm Richards, a researcher on NARA's NPRC list, with whom I have personally worked with for several years. Mr. Richards is also one of the historians for the 90th Division and is very knowledgeable.
>
> AAA Military Research
> Email: normrichards9@gmail.com
> Please tell him I referred you.

Record Examples from a National Personnel Records Center File

Records for Merchant Mariners are similar to those of the Navy and Coast Guard. Please refer to those chapters for more details on main records in the OMPF. There are some different documents you may find within a Merchant Marine file which are located on the following pages.

Seaman's Certificate

The Seaman's Certificate is similar to the enlistment paper for the Navy and Coast Guard. This record contains the name, vital information, next-of-kin, address, social security number, proof of citizenship, fingerprints, and an oath. There is also a section for the Statement of Service, which is completed after training.

Record of Certificate of Service Cards and Certificates

A Record of Certificate of Service can come in many forms. There are cards which provide information on a specific area of training for a Merchant Mariner. Cards will vary in each file, depending on which areas of training a Seaman completed. Accompanying the cards are official certificates issued by the United States Department of Commerce.

Casualty Information

If the Seaman was Killed In Action, the file may contain insurance and next-of-kin or beneficiary information. Documentation of the cause of death may also be included. Obtain the Individual Deceased Personnel File for more complete details about the death of your Merchant Mariner.

Seaman's Certificate for Elivs Spotts

NCG 719-B 45-2-E (JHY)
(Name of Seaman—Print only)

Reproduced at the National Archives. STL

Book No.
C. I. No. Z 394396
Port of LOS ANGELES, CALIF.
Date _____, 19____

DEC 27 1943

SPOTTS	Nelson	Elvis
(Last name)	(Middle name)	(First name)

THE UNITED STATES OF AMERICA
UNITED STATES COAST GUARD

SOCIAL SECURITY NO.

SEAMAN'S CERTIFICATES
(Application to be made out in duplicate)

Number and street _____ 1223 Corona
City or town _____ Denver
State, Territory, or D. C. _____ Colorado

TO THE COMMANDANT, UNITED STATES COAST GUARD.

SIR:

I hereby apply for a Seaman's {
Continuous Discharge Book ☐
Certificate of Identification ☒
Certificate of Efficiency as Lifeboatman ☐
Certificate of Service as _____ Fireman, Oiler, Watertender, Messman ☐

Age __18__ Born _6_ _Oct._ _1925_ at _Clifton Hill_ _Missouri_
(Day) (Month) (Year) (City) (State or country)

Height _5_ ft. _9_ in. Weight _153_ lb. Color of hair _Brown_ Color of eyes _Hazel_

Complexion _Ruddy_ Sex _Male_ Color _White_

Name, relationship, and address of next of kin _Mr. D. W. Spotts (Father)_
1223 Corona
Denver, Colorado

Proof of citizenship submitted _Certified photostatic copy of Missouri_ If a naturalized citizen,
DELAYED birth certificate issued in the name of Elvin Nelson Spotts; based on affidavit of
state place and date naturalization papers were issued, together with file number _____
Mother, School Record, Life Insurance policy; supported by affidavit showing change of name
from Elvin Nelson Spotts to Elvis Nelson Spotts.

If not naturalized, and declaration of intention has been filed, state place, date, and file number of intention

papers _____

If an alien, state place and date of payment of head tax _____

Seaman's Protection Certificate, number, date, and place of issue _____

Applicant now in possession of the following certificates (Itemize all licenses, showing grade, and certificates,

such as Able Seaman, Lifeboatman, etc., giving date, place, and number of issue of each) _____

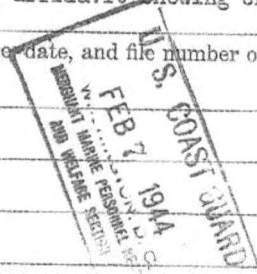

PENALTY FOR VIOLATION

Whoever receives or has in his possession with intent to unlawfully use, or uses or exhibits a certificate to which he is not lawfully entitled; or alters, changes, counterfeits, forges, or steals such a certificate, or unlawfully has in his possession any blank form thereof, or aids or abets the perpetration of any of the above, shall be liable to a fine of not more than $5,000 or imprisonment for not more than 5 years, or both.

16—39679-1

Official Military Personnel File. Elvis Spotts, serial no. Z394396. Seaman's Certificate. National Personnel Records Center, St. Louis, Missouri.

Statement of Service for Elvis Spotts

STATEMENT OF SERVICE

Record of service must be certified by official discharges or letters from masters or such other authority deemed reliable for the past 3 years, if possible

Name of Vessel	Nationality of Vessel	Service and Type of Vessel	Gross Tonnage	Rating of Seaman	Date of Shipment	Date of Discharge
		Satisfactorily completed Engine training at USMSTS, AVALON, CALIF., from 10-5-43 to 12-23-43, including four weeks aboard training vessels.				

(If more space is needed for Statement of Service the record may be stated on an additional sheet.)

OATH

(This oath must be administered by the Issuing Officer)

I hereby swear (or affirm) that all of the statements on this application are true and correct to my best knowledge and belief; that I have never received from the United States Coast Guard the document(s) for which I now make application; and I do further solemnly swear (or affirm) that I will faithfully and honestly perform all the duties required of me by law and carry out the lawful orders of my superior officers on shipboard.

Signature of seaman _Elvis Nelson Spotts_
(First name) (Middle name) (Last name)

Subscribed and sworn to (or affirmed) before me this _____ day of _____, 19___, at _Los Angeles, Calif._, County of

Los Angeles, Calif., and State (Territory or District) of _LOS ANGELES, CALIF._ I have accordingly issued the said applicant the following document(s):

DEC 27 1943

_____
(ACTG.) MERCHANT MARINE
INSPECTOR IN CHARGE

(Signature and title of issuing officer)   (SEAL)

APPLICANT WILL NOT WRITE IN THIS SPACE

1. Continuous Discharge Book No. _Z 394396_
2. Certificate of Identification No. _B. 25-29/5_
3. Certificate of Efficiency as Lifeboatman No. _____
4. Certificate of Service as Able Seaman No. _____
5. Certificate of Service as Qualified Member of Engine Department No. _162/22_
6. Certificate of Service as _Messman_ N.B. _45-52-54_
7. Certificate as Tankerman No. _____

FINGERPRINTS (Left hand)

FINGERPRINTS (Right hand)

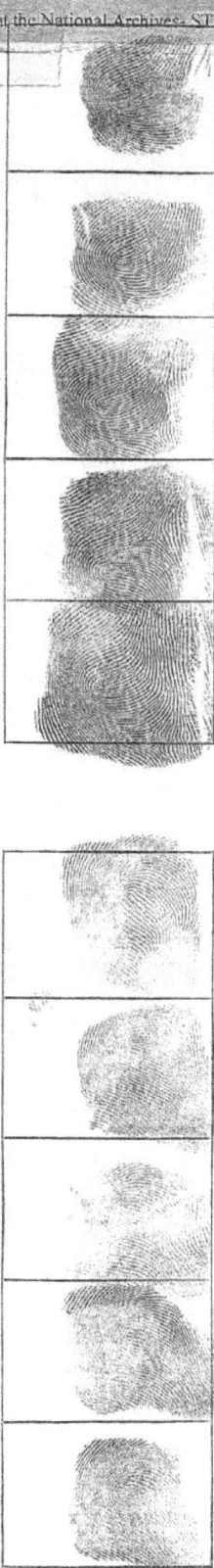

Official Military Personnel File. Elvis Spotts, serial no. Z394396. Statement of Service. National Personnel Records Center, St. Louis, Missouri.

Service Record Cards for Elvis Spotts

Form 883
Certificate of Identification Z 394 396   Book No. _____
RECORD OF CERTIFICATE OF SERVICE
ISSUED TO QUALIFIED MEMBER OF THE ENGINE DEPARTMENT
Name _Elvis N. Spotts_ Rating _Fireman_
Address _1223 Corona   Denver, Colorado_
Citizen of _U.S.A._ Native, naturalized or alien
Date of Birth _10/6/25_ Place of Birth _Missouri_
Serial number of certificate C162132   DEC 27 1943
Date of issue of certificate _____
Kind of waters for which issued _any waters_
Issued by U. S. Board of Local Inspectors at _LOS ANGELES, CALIF._
A. L. WOODRUFF
(ACTG.) MERCHANT MARINE
INSPECTOR IN CHARGE
(To be forwarded to Bureau)

Form 974 Z-394 396   Book No. _____
RECORD OF CERTIFICATE OF EFFICIENCY TO LIFEBOAT MAN
Name _Elvis N. Spotts_
Address _1223 Corona Denver, Colo._
Citizen of _U.S.A._ Native, naturalized or alien
Date of Birth _6 Oct 1925_ Place of Birth _Missouri_
Serial number of certificate B252915   DEC 27 1943
Date of issue of certificate
Issued by U. S. Board of Local Inspectors at _LOS ANGELES, CALIF._
(ACTG.) MERCHANT MARINE
U.S. Board of Local Inspectors
INSPECTOR IN CHARGE
(To be forwarded to Bureau)

Certificate of Identification Z- 394 396   Book No. _____
Form 884
RECORD OF CERTIFICATE OF SERVICE ISSUED TO SEAMAN
Rating _Messman_
Name _Elvis N. Spotts_ Department _Stewards_
Address _1223 Corona Denver Colorado_
Citizen of _U.S.A._ Native, naturalized or alien
Date of Birth _6 Oct 1925_ Place of Birth _Missouri_
Serial number of certificate E455254   DEC 27 1943
Date of issue of certificate
Issued by U. S. Board of Local Inspectors at _LOS ANGELES, CALIF._
A. L. WOODRUFF
(ACTG.) MERCHANT MARINE
U.S. Board of Local Inspectors
INSPECTOR IN CHARGE
(To be forwarded to Bureau)

Official Military Personnel File. Elvis Spotts, serial no. Z394396. Service Record Cards. National Personnel Records Center, St. Louis, Missouri.

Back of Service Cards for Elvis Spotts

Rated qualified member of the Engine Department upon examination as to his knowledge of the duties of *Fireman*

Signature of Seaman

Elvis N. Spotts

Thumb Print

Signature of Seaman

Elvis N. Spotts

Thumb Print

(If a food handler)

Examined physically and found free from communicable disease.

12-22-43

(Date)

Signature of Seaman

Elvis N. Spotts

Thumb Print

Official Military Personnel File. Elvis Spotts, serial no. Z394396. Service Record Cards. National Personnel Records Center, St. Louis, Missouri.

Certificate of Service for Elvis Spotts

Official Military Personnel File. Elvis Spotts, serial no. Z394396. Certificate of Service. National Personnel Records Center, St. Louis, Missouri.

Letter Regarding Death of Elvis Spotts

```
        C
         O
        . P
          Y
```

COPE & HADSELL
Attorneys at Law
1200 Dierks Building
Kansas City, Missouri

August 22, 1946

Chief of Merchant Marine Personnel
Records and Welfare Section
United States Coast Guard
Washington 25, D. C.

In Re: Elvis Nelson Spotts, Deceased

Dear Sir:

Under date of July 1, 1944, your file CG-MIN, R. H. Farinholt, Lieutenant (T)
U. S. C. G. R. advised by letter that his investigation had been conducted
of the circumstances incident to the electrocution and death of Elvis Nelson
Spotts, 4307-07032, United States Merchant Marine, which occurred on
February 22, 1944 in line of duty on board the SS CAPE ISABEL at Tarawa,
Gilbert Islands, L. A. Carlisle being the Master of the ship.

As Attorney for the parents of this deceased and with a view to filing suit
against the steamship company because of its negligence in causing the death
of deceased, I will appreciate it if you would furnish me with copy of the
investigation so conducted and if there is any charge for a transcript of
same, I will be glad to promptly forward check upon receipt of your statement.
We are interested in obtaining all the facts before filing a suit and will
appreciate your cooperation in the premises.

Incidentally, could you advise me the present address of Lieutenant E. C.
Potter, M. D. of the United States Coast Guard, who was called aboard ship
after the accident in question and who examined this deceased shortly after.

Again thanking you and with kindest regards, I beg to remain

                         Sincerely,

                         /Signed/ Homer A. Cope

hac/be

Original sent to Commander Storey - August 29, 1946   5472

American-Hawaiian Steamship Company Letter

UNITED STATES OF AMERICA
UNITED STATES MARITIME COMMISSION

AMERICAN-HAWAIIAN STEAMSHIP COMPANY, AGENT

215 MARKET STREET, SAN FRANCISCO 5, CALIFORNIA

October 15, 1946

FILE No. I-21-71

Quartermaster General
Memorial Division
War Department
Washington 25, D. C.

Attn: Captain Thomas F. Lewin
Assistant

Dear Sir:

Re: QMGYG 293
Spotts, Elvis N.
SN 43 07 07 032

Replying to your inquiry of October 9th, we quote
from Captain L. A. Carlisle's report as follows concerning
the burial of Elvis N. Spotts.

"On the morning of February 23, 1944 at 11:00 a.m.,
funeral services were held with military honors and
the reading of a Protestant service by Francis T. Cooke,
Chaplain, U.S.N.R. Burial was in U. S. Marine Cemetary,
Tarawa, Gilbert Islands."

We also quote communication from office of the Port
Captain, Tarawa, Gilbert Islands, dated 23 February 1944.

"Subject: Elvis N. Spotts, Wiper, S.S. CAPE ISABEL, death of,
Elvis N. Spotts was buried in the Marine Memorial Cemetary,
Betio Island, Tarawa Atoll in a marked grave. L.M. Fabien,
Lt. Cmdr., U.S.N.R."

Yours faithfully,

UNITED STATES OF AMERICA
UNITED STATES MARITIME COMMISSION
BY: AMERICAN-HAWAIIAN STEAMSHIP
COMPANY, AGENT.

W.C. WEBB
Pacific Insurance and Claims Agent

WOS:kk

By _____

Individual Deceased Personnel File. Elvis Spotts, serial no. Z394396. American-Hawaiian Steamship Company letter dated 15 Oct 1946. Army Human Resource Command, Ft. Knox, Kentucky.

Request for Disposition of Remains of Elvis Spotts

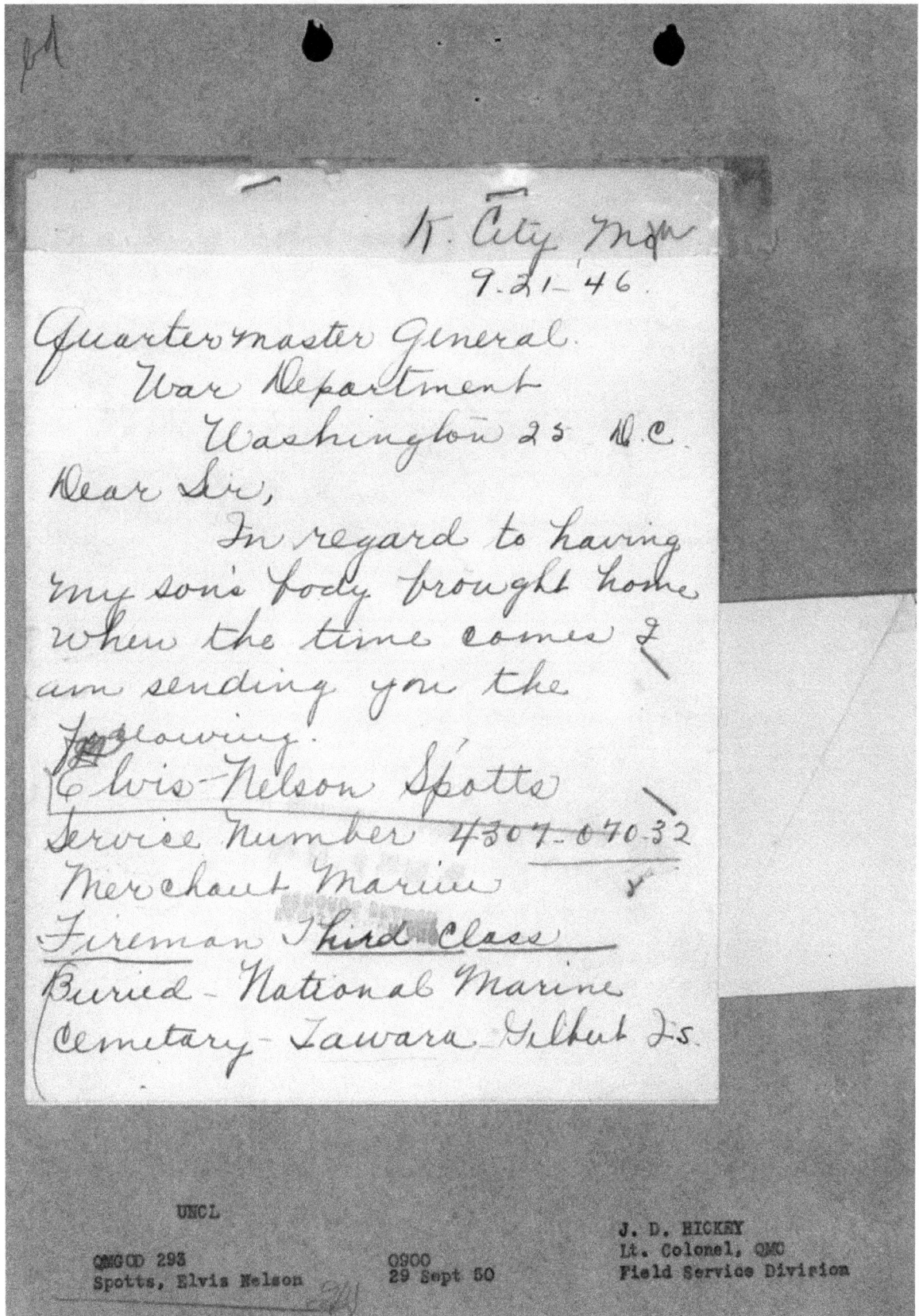

K. City Mo.
9-21-46.

Quartermaster General.
War Department
Washington 25 D.C.
Dear Sir,
In regard to having
my son's body brought home
when the time comes I
am sending you the
following.
Elvis Nelson Spotts
Service Number 4307-070-32
Merchant Marine
Fireman Third Class
Buried - National Marine
Cemetary - Tawara Gilbut Is.

UNCL

QMGOD 293
Spotts, Elvis Nelson

0900
29 Sept 50

J. D. HICKEY
Lt. Colonel, QMC
Field Service Division

Individual Deceased Personnel File. Elvis Spotts, serial no. Z394396. Request for Disposition of Remains. Army Human Resource Command, Ft. Knox, Kentucky.

Data on Remains Not Yet Recovered or Identified

DATA ON REMAINS NOT YET RECOVERED OR IDENTIFIED.

93 FILE
6-720

NAME (Last, First, Middle Initial)	GRADE	PRESENT SERIAL NUMBER
Spotts, Elvis N.	Wiper	Z-394396

ORGANIZATION	RACE	CREED	FORMER SERIAL NUMBER (If Applicable)
SS Cape Isabel	White	NR	

DATE OF DEATH/MIA: 22 Feb 1944	CAUSE OF DEATH	PLACE OF DEATH OR PLACE LAST SEEN IF MIA
DATE OF FOD	Electrocuted while closing boiler room door	Tarawa, Gilbert Islands

HEIGHT	WEIGHT	COLOR EYES	COLOR HAIR	SHOE SIZE
69"	153	Brown	Brown	NR

DENTAL CHART

UPPER RIGHT: 8 7 6 5 4 3 2 1   UPPER LEFT: 1 2 3 4 5 6 7 8

No dental information available from civilian and Marine sources

LOWER RIGHT: 16 15 14 13 12 11 10 9   LOWER LEFT: 9 10 11 12 13 14 15 16

X = Extracted   O = Cavious   1 = Cavious Non-Restorable

FRACTURES AND/OR BREAKS	TATTOOS AND/OR BIRTHMARK
None Shown	None Shown

ADDITIONAL INFORMATION

Born: 6 October 1925

Reported interred in U. S. Marine Cemetery, Tarawa, Gilbert Islands.

NOK:
Mrs. D. W. Spotts, Mother
1705 Linwood Boulevard
Kansas City, Mo.

Exhibit B

OQMG FORM 371 tno
23 SEP 46

DATE FORWARDED TO FIELD

Individual Deceased Personnel File. Elvis Spotts, serial no. Z394396. Data on remains not yet recovered or identified. Army Human Resource Command, Ft. Knox, Kentucky.

Letter to Spotts Family

UNITED STATES MARITIME COMMISSION
WASHINGTON

Operations Department

May 1, 1947

293 Spotts, Elvis N.

The Quartermaster General
War Department
Washington 25, D. C.

Attention: Colonel J. B. Colson
Memorial Division

Gentlemen:

Further reference is made to your letter of March 27,
1947, your file QMGMR 293, in which you requested information
concerning the place of burial of the remains of Elvis N. Spotts,
who formerly was employed as a member of the crew of the SS CAPE
ISABEL.

We are enclosing photostatic copy of letter from Lieut.
Commander L. M. Fabian, USNR., Port Captain at Tarawa, addressed
to American-Hawaiian Steamship Company under date of February 23,
1944; copy of letter from the Master of the SS CAPE ISABEL addressed to Mr. and Mrs. D. W. Spotts, on February 23, 1944; and
copy of certificate of death issued by the Navy Department.

It will be observed from the enclosures that burial of
the remains of this seaman was made in the Marine Memorial Cemetery,
Betio Island, Tarawa Atoll, in a marked grave. Although the plot
and grave numbers are not shown, there apparently should be no difficulty in identifying the grave, since it was marked. However,
should you require more definite information, your Division probably
could obtain the same by communicating with the Navy Department.

Very truly yours,

Act. Director, Marine Division

Enclosures

3-18-50
J. M. White
Identification Branch

Individual Deceased Personnel File. Elvis Spotts, serial no. Z394396. Letter to Spots Family dated 1 May 1947. Army Human Resource Command, Ft. Knox, Kentucky.

National Maritime Center

The records at the National Maritime Center can be used for two purposes: To prove veteran status and to obtain service record copies.

To Prove Veteran Status

The National Maritime Center's website states specific criteria which must be met to obtain veteran status. Full details are found on their website shown below. The criteria, which appear when you click the link "eligibility criteria" on that web page, are as follows[1]

Was a merchant marine serving as a crewmember of a vessel that was:

Operated by the War Shipping Administration or the Office of Defense Transportation (or an agent of the Administration or Office)

Operated in waters other than inland waters, the Great Lakes, other lakes, bays, and harbors of the United States;

Under contract or charter to, or property of, the Government of the United States; and served the Armed Forces.

While serving, was licensed or otherwise documented for service as a crewmember of such a vessel by an officer or employee of the United States authorized to license or document the person for such service.

On this page is also a link to "Reference Information Paper #77." This is a 16 page document outlining several additional records like deck logs, medical treatment records, vessel status cards, and Armed Guard reports, you may obtain and where to obtain them. This chapter will not attempt to reproduce all of this material. The National Maritime Center updates this document as needed. Please review it for the most current information on records.

> Criteria to obtain veteran status
> http://www.uscg.mil/nmc/records_request/veteran_request.asp
>
> Form DD 2168
> http://www.uscg.mil/nmc/records_request/pdfs/veteran_request_fillable.pdf

To Obtain Service Records

The National Maritime Center may also hold documentation of service and discharge. To request a search, you must complete a form, which they prefer to be submitted electronically. The form must contain the nature of the request, your contact information, name and date of birth of the Mariner, social security number, and be signed and dated.

If you choose not to submit the form electronically, you may send it to the address below.

National Maritime Center
Attn.: Correspondence (NMC-41)
100 Forbes Drive
Martinsburg, WV 25404

Note: Unlike the records held at the NPRC, according to the National Maritime Center, you must be the veteran or next-of-kin to obtain information.

National Maritime Center Requests
http://www.uscg.mil/nmc/records_request/default.asp

Casualty Information

Individual Deceased Personnel File

Casualty information is another tricky area in which you can obtain records. If your Mariner was Killed In Action, you can request a copy of their Individual Deceased Personnel File (IDPF) the same way one would request that for any other branch. Please see the chapter on Military Death Records for information on obtaining this file.

National Archives Casualty Files

There are casualty records held at the National Archives in Washington, D.C. These records are contained in Record Group 26 (Records of the US Coast Guard), entry p3 (Correspondence - Merchant Seamen, 1938-1950), boxes 1 - 8. The entire series is contained in these eight boxes. General contents of records for World War II are described here.

Boxes one through four contain files for accidental casualties, wounded men, Killed In Action, and unrecoverable Missing In Action personnel. It also contains a few files for medals and citations.

Boxes five through seven are Courts Martial proceedings case. Box eight contains information on citations, commendations, Prisoners of War, and other casualties.

Repository: National Archives Washington, D.C. RG 26 Casualty Files

After the War

It can be said the war changed the lives of everyone in the country. The men and women who served were changed at least twice. The first time, upon entry into the service from civilian to soldier. The second time, upon discharge from soldier back to civilian. The world the veterans returned to was vastly different from the one they left. For both civilian and soldier, the wait was long between the start and end of the war. Psychological stress was endured by both, yet the stress and psychological aspects of war have been studied by scholars in relation to the veterans, not those who remained at home.

The military trained men to become fighting machines, and to block out everything else but their duty to the war. When they were not in combat, relaxation and entertainment from the USO and Red Cross may have been available. They kept their fears to themselves. To do otherwise would have made them look like a coward. Many returned home psychologically damaged, and often physically damaged.

Women on the home front had to face all their fears about their soldier, new responsibilities as head of the household, and raising their children by themselves. In some cases, when their husband was Killed In Action, they became the sole supporter of the family. There was little time for relaxation or escape from their responsibilities.

In this chapter, we will explore many issues faced by the veterans and their families. These issues are explored to help you put the lives of your World War II ancestors into context. Records other than medical records may not have been created to document the changes which occurred after the war. You will likely discover these issues and changes by examining your family to see if there are any connections.

Personally, I know some of the issues explored here affected my family and the way my parents raised me, and how I raise my children. These are things I plan to explore when I write book three in my series titled Stories of the Lost.

The Waiting and Expectations of the Home Front

Women on the home front did not take up arms, but they waited. Mothers sent their sons to war with a blessing they return unharmed. Wives sent husbands to war and prayed for a quick end. Girlfriends and fiancés said goodbye to their boyfriends and future husbands, hoping they would return quickly so they could be married and start a family. They all waited for their father, brother, husband, son, nephew, or grandson (in most cases) to return home. Women waited for letters or postcards, which either came regularly or in spurts due to the location of the soldier.

The women who sent a husband off to war had to deal with the waiting to see if he would return. Each day was a new form of stress, as she waited to see if a telegram would arrive on her doorstep announcing the status, be it Missing In Action, Prisoner of War, or Killed In Action, of her spouse. Women who became widows during the war faced new challenges. Questions of where they would live, how they would support their families, would she find love again, and would her children ever know their father began to arise. Many young children grew up thinking their father was a photograph, if they even knew him at all.

Everyone suffered the effects of being separated and established alternative realities, or set expectations in their minds about what life would be like upon the return of "normal" life. Unfortunately the "normal" life they lived prior to the war was gone. A new "normal" was established when the fighting began, and another "normal" would emerge when the fighting ceased.

The Living Return from War

There were many considerations and questions for those returning from war. What would life be like? Would it return to normal? Would the soldier find a job or remain unemployed? Would anyone care where he had been and what he had done?

A New "Normal"

Returning soldiers dealt with their new "normal," which involved not killing people. Tim O'Brien, author of The Things They Carried and Vietnam Veteran, explained this well in a program I heard at the Pritzker Military Museum and Library in 2012. Tim explained he was raised to follow the 10 Commandments, especially Thou Shalt Not Kill. Yet, when he entered the military, he was trained to ignore that Commandment and kill.

O'Brien made the point that upon return, each soldier had to deal with the "normal" of war, which was the killing and death of others. The soldier did whatever it took to survive and keep his buddies alive. When he returned home, he had to deal with the guilt and remorse over actions he took in service, as well as things he was trained to do.

The fact our World War II soldiers had to face these same issues is not something we think about often. In every war, soldiers do the unthinkable and unspeakable, according to what we are taught as civilians, and carry that with them for life. Those deeds made transitioning back into civilian life more difficult.

Fitting Into Society

Fitting back into a family and society was a very real concern for veterans. They returned home to see everyone had grown and aged. While this may seem like a funny idea, for many soldiers, it was as if time stopped when they left for war, and everything and everyone remained the same until they returned. Yet when they returned home, they found parents a few years older, possibly aged from the stress of war. Siblings had grown and gone on with life, and children who had not been born or were young when the soldier left had grown. And the spouse left behind was changed, which caused an adjustment to the marriage.

Finally, the veterans themselves had matured and changed. No longer were they content being "boys" living in their mother's house. Some parents assumed life would return to pre-war normal and the child, now a full grown, mature, man or woman, would return to being told what to do by the parents. Some families could not comprehend what their soldier had gone through overseas. They also did not understand how to deal with the emotional, mental, or physical effects of war. This led to a lot of problems within families, and in some cases, the break-up of families. After the war, the veterans were ready to take life on their own terms.

Migration from families and the society they knew as a civilian occurred after the war. Some veterans were used to traveling, or dealt with restlessness, which caused them to want to move from place to place until their demons had been conquered.

The families of veterans also had to adjust to their serviceman or woman returning home. They were curious about their service, and wondered what they had seen and done.

Unemployment was a question which loomed large as to whether or not there would be any jobs available. Women had taken over the workforce while men were overseas. To help veterans transition more smoothly and deal with the unemployment situation, the federal government created the G.I. Bill.

The G.I. Bill began as the Servicemen's Readjustment Act of 1944, which was put into effect June 22, 1944. The bill gave veterans unemployment benefits, education and training, and loan guarantees for homes, farms, or businesses. Many veterans opted to attend college, as jobs were difficult to obtain just after the war, as war production ceased and fewer laborers were needed. Restrictions were in place as to how long a soldier could receive educational benefits and who could receive them. Technically, women and African Americans were allowed to take advantage of the G.I. Bill, but most women returned to the home. African Americans dealt with the issue of segregation of colleges, and many were unable to attend due to the few available colleges reaching capacity.

Finally, the issue of where to live was a big issue for those wishing to live away from their parents. Men grew up, some married, and new housing arrangements had to be made. Veterans who could not seem to fit in with their old arrangement at home found themselves looking for a place to live with friends or alone. Not only were these issues in the minds of returning veterans, but also the roles men and women would play after the war.

Roles of Men and Women

Roles for men and women changed during the war, as women joined the workforce and became more independent. Returning men were worried about finding a job if all the women remained at work. Most men preferred their wives to return to the home to resume duties as a homemaker. Returning men often had trouble adjusting to civilian life, and unconsciously may have tried to run their households like the military, with order and rules that did not exist prior to the war. For families dealing with a disabled or mentally changed soldier, the return and adjustment period was more stressful. New accommodations had to be made for the disability or psychological condition.

Psychological conditions did not always mean a soldier had to be hospitalized or committed. Many returned home to a family or group of friends who did not want to hear about their combat experiences, fears, and hopes for the future. The war was over and there was no need to talk about it. Due to this response, soldiers often held their feelings, fears, and guilt about their experience inside and suffered greatly.

What we now know as Post-Traumatic Stress Disorder, or PTSD, affected thousands of veterans. They suffered depression, anxiety, nightmares, night sweats, restlessness, emotional outbursts, and held their emotions inside. Small things civilians and pre-war soldiers took for granted, like a woman screaming or the flight of an airplane overhead, would send some veterans down to the ground looking for a foxhole to dive into. In the 1980s things changed, and it was more acceptable to talk about the war and what soldiers experienced. Many admitted even in their 70s and 80s, they still deal with nightmares and other forms of PTSD.

As you research your World War II ancestor, please keep their stories in historical context. Look at the information through the eyes of someone in that time and place. It is not for us to judge their actions through the eyes of someone in this century. Ask questions like:

- 'What was it like then?'
- 'Why did you do what you did in that situation?'
- 'How did you deal with things when you returned home?'

No judgment, just listening.

There is a book, called *To Hear Only Thunder Again*, which explains the results of a study done on the effects of soldiers returning from the war. The book also explains how the government, families, and soldiers, all worked together to bring home the veterans after World War II so the transition would be much smoother than previous wars.

The Search for the Missing

Upon cessation of hostilities, the men of the Graves Registration Service began the search for thousands of soldiers listed as Missing In Action (MIA.) They used battle maps, information from units which stated where they left soldiers or buried them. The Prisoner of War (POW) camps were emptied, and cemeteries and isolated burial sites checked whenever possible. Many of the camps kept records on the burial location of soldiers. Today, there are still thousands missing from the war. Efforts are ongoing to identify and repatriate the remains of as many as possible.

If your family had a soldier who was MIA, and you are unsure if he or she was ever recovered, visit the Defense Prisoner of War * Missing In Action Accounting Agency website (DPAA) and conduct a search. All the MIAs are listed in this website with updates on recoveries or current investigations.

The Final Disposition of the Dead

Soldiers Killed In Action (KIA) who were recovered were temporarily buried in U.S. Military Cemeteries overseas. The government did not begin giving families the option to repatriate the remains of their soldier or have them buried in a permanent American Battle Monuments Commission (ABMC) cemetery until 1947.

Letters were sent to the next-of-kin explaining the disposition options and asking for an answer to preference. The government disinterred and returned soldiers to the U.S. whose families requested their return, at government expense. Those who were to remain in foreign soil were also reburied at government expense. Each soldier was also given a military burial service upon both temporary and permanent interment.

If you have a soldier buried in an ABMC cemetery, you can email the cemetery and request a photo of the grave. The ABMC will send you a 4x6 sized photo in the corner of a large lithograph of the cemetery, free of charge.

You may also request a search of their archives for information regarding your solider. There are often burial cards, photographs, and written histories of the temporary cemeteries in the archives. You can read the most current and official histories on the ABMC website for each cemetery.

Records Created After the War

When the war ended, record creation did not cease. Separation and Discharge papers were created as soldiers exited the military. Veterans Affairs (VA) files were created for those seeking medical care. Educational records were created for those taking advantage of the G.I. Bill.

Newspapers continued to print lists of soldiers Killed In Action and Missing In Action even after the war officially ended. They also printed obituaries of soldiers as they were returned to the U.S.

Compiled Lists of the Dead

Each state compiled lists of men Killed In Action, which were organized by county. These lists contained the soldier's name, serial number, and date of death. The military also produced lists of their own. You can find most of these lists digitized online for individual states, the Army, Navy, Marine Corps, and Coast Guard.

Repository: Ancestry.com, Fold3.com, State and local archives.

World War II Bonus Applications

After the war, similar to what happened after World War I, the states authorized bonus payments to servicemen and women who served during the war years. Veterans or their beneficiaries, if deceased, had to complete applications for the bonus payment. The records contain vital information on the veteran and his family, military information, and sometimes a photograph.

There are privacy restrictions placed on these records, and not every state allows access as of the writing of this book. Illinois has a law on the books that restricts access for at least another 50 years. States like Pennsylvania and Iowa have granted access, sometimes only to immediate family members. Check with your state to find out what the rules are.

Repository: These records are usually held in the State Archives or the State Adjutant General's Office.

Military Groups and Historical Associations

Many veterans formed unit or division association groups after the war. These groups allowed them to talk amongst friends about the war, their suffering, and readjustment to life after war. Many of these groups exist today and are a valuable resource for researchers. Resources include websites, photographs, unit histories, rosters, newsletters and journals, and the opportunity to talk to a veteran.

Association Websites and Archives

Many groups and associations built websites with the latest reunion information, Taps (a list of those who died since the last newsletter or reunion), unit histories, rosters, biographies, photographs, and forums for questions and discussion. Some offer books for sale specific to the unit or battles they fought. Because members pass away and the leadership changes hands periodically, check with the association about all available resources. They may exist, but the website might not specify this.

Newsletters and Journals

Many associations produce, or did in years past, newsletters and journals. These were mailed to members, and today may exist online. These resources often contained information and stories of war, updates on soldiers today, copies of memorabilia, letters, and photographs of soldiers during war time. Many also offer a query service to reconnect with veterans or seek information.

Reunions

Reunions were one way veterans remained in touch over the years. Many groups still hold reunions today, even though the number of veterans has dwindled, in some cases, to zero. The family members of the veterans continue the organization in honor of their veteran. From personal experience, I can tell you that attending a reunion is a great way to connect with others researching the history of the unit in which your soldier served. You will make new friends for life, and many groups have historians who bring research materials to the meeting. If you have not checked to see if a reunion group exists for your veteran, I encourage you to do so.

Donating Military Materials

A lot of information has been presented in this volume regarding the location of records and many resources available to trace the history of your soldier. I have not, however, touched upon the donation process of materials, should your family wish to no longer hold onto them.

Many places will be happy to accept your materials, but it is important to ensure the materials will be properly processed, stored, and made available to the public for research. In some cases, smaller museums, libraries, and archives, with limited staff and funding, will take your materials and leave them in boxes in a closet or storage area to rot. Once the materials enter, they never again see the light of day. Think of all the materials that could be available, but are not. Perhaps that one piece of information you need is hidden away in a dusty old archive.

Before donating materials, consider the following:

• Does the facility have paid staff and an archivist, or someone specially trained to process and protect materials?

• Where are the materials stored?

• What is the policy for preparing new materials for public use?

• Does the facility provide you with a photocopy of the materials you donated?

• What happens to the materials should the facility close, or no longer choose to use them? Are you able to get them back?

• How is the public able to access the materials?

Asking these questions will help ensure your materials are stored in the best place possible.

The End of the Journey

We have reached the end of our journey discussing records and resources available to help you research your adopted soldier. I hope this volume has been helpful to you in discovering some of the history of your World War II soldier.

Please visit my website **http://wwiiresearchandwritingcenter.com** to use the Additional Resources for this volume, explore the World War II Toolbox, and to see where in the United States and Europe I will be lecturing on World War II topics.

Appendix

Abbreviations

ABMC: American Battle Monuments Commissions
Cpl: Corporal
ETO: European Theater of Operations
ETOUSA: European Theater of Operations U.S.A.
FOD: Finding Of Death
GRS: Graves Registration Service
IDPF: Individual Deceased Personnel File
KIA: Killed in Action
MCO: Main Civilian Occupation
MIA: Missing in Action
MOS: Military Occupational Specialty
POW: Prisoner of War
PTO: Pacific Theater of Operations
Sgt: Sergeant
SSN: Service Specialty Number (Not Social Security Number)
VFW: Veterans of Foreign Wars
WD: War Department

Air Force Accident Report

Visit Aviation Archaeology's website http://www.aviationarchaeology.com/src/help.htm#ACTION for an extensive list of abbreviations for Country Codes, U.S. States, Action and U.S. Navy Abbreviations

Individual Deceased Personnel File

DED: Declared Dead (Public Law 490)
DNB: Died Non-Battle
DOW: Died Of Wounds
NOK: Next Of Kin

Medical Reports

CW: Contused Wound
DOI: Died of Injuries
DOW: Died of Wounds
EW: Extensive Wound
FC: Fracture Compound
FCC: Fracture Compound Comminuted
FS: Fracture Simple
GSW: Gun Shot Wound
IW: Incised Wound
LIA: Lightly Injured in Action
LWA: Lightly Wounded in Action
LW: Lacerated Wound
MW: Multiple Wounds

NYD: Not Yet Diagnosed
Pen W: Penetrating Wound
Pun W: Punctured Wound
RTD: Returned To Duty
S: Slight
SFW: Shell Fragment Wound
SIA: Seriously Injured in Action
SV: Severe
SWA: Seriously Wounded in action

Missing Air Crew Report (MACR)

ALW: Alive And Well
ASN: Army Serial Number
CAP: Captured by enemy
DED: Declared Dead (Public Law 490)
DL: Dead List
DNB: Died Non-Battle
DIE: Died in Escape
DOW: Died Of Wounds
DOWRIA: Died Of Wounds Received In Action
EUS: Evacuated To The United States
INT: Interned as result of enemy action
KIA: Killed In Action
KNB: Killed Non Battle
LWA: Lightly Wounded In Action
MIA: Missing In Action
NOK: Next Of Kin
PDD: Presumed Date of Death
POW: Prisoner Of War
RTD: Returned To Duty
RMC: Returned To Military Control
SIU: Seriously gassed (hospitalized)
SWA: Seriously Wounded In Action
WIA: Wounded In Action

Morning Reports/Muster Rolls/Crew List Abbreviations

A: Army
A&D: Admission and Disposition
abs: Absent
Abv: Above
AGF: Allied Ground Forces
APO: Army Post Office
aptd: Appointed
ar: Arrest
AR: Army Regulation

Appendix

arr: Arrived
ASF: Army Service Forces
Asgd: Assigned
Asgmt: Assignment
Atchd: Attached
AW: Articles of War
AWOL: Absent without Leave
Bn: Battalion
Clr Sta: Clearing Station
CM: Court Martial
Comdr: Commander
Conf: Confined
DB: Daily Bulletin
DoP: Detachment of Patients
dep: Departed
det: Detached
disch: Discharged
drpd: Dropped
DS: Detached Service
dtd: Dated
dy: Duty
EDCHMR: Effective Date Concerning Morning Report
eff: Effective
EH: Evacuation Hospital
em: Enlisted Men
EPTI(S): Existing Prior to Induction
Evacd: Evacuated
FH: Field Hospital
fr: From
FR: France
fur: Furlough
GH: General Hospital
gr: Grade
Hosp: Hospital
HQ: Headquarters
IIA: Injured in Action
jd: Joined
LD: Line of Duty
Lv: Leave
NLD: Not in line of duty
NYPE: New York Port of Embarkation
opns: Operations
par: Paragraph
Pers: Personnel
Plat or Pltn: Platoon
PM: Postmaster
qrs: Quarters

Appendix

RG: Replacement Depot
regt: Regiment
reld: Relieved
repl: Replacement
RD: Reduced
RTD/U: Returned to Duty/Unit
sht: Sheet
sk: Sick
SO: Special Order
sta: Station
str: Strength
SFW: Shell Fragment Wound
TD: Temporary Duty
temp: Temporary
trfd: Transferred
unasgn: Unassigned
vic: Vicinity
WIA: Wounded in Action
Wpns: Weapons

Selected Bibliography

Selected Bibliography

90th Division Association http://www.90thdivisionassoc.org/ : 2015.

Air Force Award Cards. National Personnel Records Center, St. Louis, MO.

American Battle Monuments Commission. http://www.90thdivisionassoc.org/ : 2015.

American Battle Monuments Commission Archives. Luxembourg City, Luxembourg.

Air Force Accident Reports. Aviation Archaeology.com.

Army Mortuary Affairs History Page. http://www.qmfound.com/mortuary-affairs.htm : 2015.

Department of the Army. *Field Manual 10-63 Graves Registration.* Washington, D.C.: United States Government Printing Office, 1952.

Department of the Army. *Field Manual 10-29 Quartermaster Graves Registration Company.* Washington, D.C.: United States Government Printing Office, 1952.

Department of the Army. Technical Manual 10-240 Deceased Personnel in the United States, Excluding Alaska. Washington, D.C.: United States Government Printing Office, 1947.

Department of the Army. Technical Manual 10-285 Deceased Personnel. Washington, D.C.: United States Government Printing Office, 1947.

Department of the Army. Technical Manual 10-285 Deceased Personnel. Washington, D.C.: United States Government Printing Office, 1947.

Department of the Navy. Disposition of Navy, Marine Corps and Coast Guard World War II Dead. Washington D.C.: Navy Department, undated.

Gawne, Jonathan. *Finding Your Father's War.* Philadelphia: Casemate, 2013.

Individual Deceased Personnel Files. US Army Human Resource Command, Ft. Knox, KY.

Missing Air Crew Reports. Aviation Archaeology.com.

Official Military Personnel Files. National Personnel Records Center, St. Louis, MO.

Office of the Quartermaster General. History of the American Graves Registration Service. *Q.M.C. in Europe Volume I to September 1920, Volume II, and Volume III.* Consolidated reprint of Volumes I, II, and III. Undated.

Selective Service System. *Registration and Selective Service.* Washington: Government Printing Office, 1946.

Selected Bibliography

Shomon, Joseph James. *Crosses in the Wind.* New York: Stratford House, Inc., 1947.

Sledge, Michael. *Soldier Dead. How We Recover, Identify, Bury, and Honor Our Military Fallen.* New York: Columbia University Press, 2005.

World War II U.S. Medical Research Centre. http://www.med-dept.com/index.php : 2015.

Notes

Notes

Basics of Military Research Notes

1. Military Service File, George T. Howe, Sr. service number 8721; Record of Officers U.S. Navy, Sheets 1-10. National Personnel Records Center, St. Louis, Missouri.

2. "Illinois, Cook County Birth Certificates, 1878–1922." Index. FamilySearch, Salt Lake City, Utah, 2009. Illinois. Cook County Birth Certificates, 1878–1922. Illinois Department of Public Health. Division of Vital Records, Springfield.

3. Ancestry.com. Massachusetts, Marriage Records, 1840-1915 [database on-line]. Provo, UT, USA: Ancestry.com Operations, Inc., 2013. Original data: Massachusetts Vital Records, 1840–1911. New England Historic Genealogical Society, Boston, Massachusetts. Harry T. Howe Civil War Pension File, Declaration for Original Pension of a Widow – Child or Children under Sixteen years of age Surviving. Pension Certificate no. 578-479 Rosella J. Howe widow of Harry T. Howe.

4. Year: 1910; Census Place: Paw Paw, Van Buren, Michigan; Roll: T624_677; Page: 8B; Enumeration District: 0167; FHL microfilm: 1374690.

5. Military Service File, George T. Howe, Sr., service number 8721, Record of Officers, U.S. Navy, Sheet 1. National Personnel Records Center, St. Louis, Missouri.

6. Military Service File, George T. Howe, Sr. service number 8721; Record of Officers U.S. Navy, Sheet 1. National Personnel Records Center, St. Louis, Missouri.

7. Military Service File, George T. Howe, Sr. service number 8721; Record of Officers U.S. Navy, Sheet 1. National Personnel Records Center, St. Louis, Missouri.

8. Military Service File, George T. Howe, Sr. service number 8721; Record of Officers U.S. Navy, Sheet 1. National Personnel Records Center, St. Louis, Missouri.

9. Military Service File, George T. Howe, Sr. service number 8721; Record of Officers U.S. Navy, Sheet 3. National Personnel Records Center, St. Louis, Missouri.

10. Military Service File, George T. Howe, Sr. service number 8721; Record of Officers U.S. Navy, Sheet 3. National Personnel Records Center, St. Louis, Missouri.

Offline Military Research Notes

1. USMC Intelligence Letter dated 22 January 1945. World War II War Diaries, Other Operational Records and Histories, compiled ca. 01/01/1942 - ca. 06/01/1946, documenting the period ca. 09/01/1939 - ca. 05/30/1946; Records of the Naval Operating Forces, Record Group 313; National Archives, College Park, MD.

2. Individual Deceased Personnel File, William F. Cowart, service no. 471443; Data on Remains Not Yet Recovered or Identified, undated.

3. Individual Deceased Personnel File, Richard W. Courtleigh, service no. 364529; photo undated which includes service no.

4. Individual Deceased Personnel File, 2nd Lt. Fred A. Davis, service no. O-683416; Finding Of Death of Missing Person file stamped 18 Dec 1946.

5. CHICAGO AIRMEN DIE IN ACTION; 1 MAN MISSING: Gunner Aboard Fortress Only Crew, Chicago Daily Tribune (1923-1963); Nov 23, 1944; ProQuest Historical Newspapers: Chicago Tribune (1849-1989), pg. 26.

6. Individual Deceased Personnel File, 2nd Lt. Fred A. Davis, service no. O-683416; Letter to 2nd. Lt. Rodgers dated 14 Apr 1944 from Elsie Sherrill.

7. Individual Deceased Personnel File, PFC James Privoznik, service no. 3660529; Report of Burial dated 17 Jan 1945.

8. 29 Dec 1944, Station: Veckring, WQ 0183 Nord de Guerre. Organization: 358th Infantry Regt Co F Morning Reports Adjutant General's Office 1917-, Record Group 407; National Archives and Records Administration, Washington, D.C.

9. 18 Dec 1944, Station: Veckring, WQ 0183 Nord de Guerre. Organization: 790th Ordnance L. M. Co.; Company Morning Reports Adjutant General's Office 1917-, Record Group 407; National Archives and Records Administration, Washington, D.C.

10. Division of the Federal Register, the National Archives. Code of Federal Regulations of the United States of America. 1946 Supplement. Washington, D.C.:U.S. Government Printing Office, 1947, 5826.

11. Service Record of 1st Lt. Robert E. Bishop, serial no. 0210591, letter to the Secretary of Navy dated 17 Jan 1945. NPRC, St. Louis, Missouri.

12. Service Record of 1st Lt. Robert E. Bishop, serial no. 0210591, letter to the Robert Bishop's parents dated 22 Jan 1946. NPRC, St. Louis, Missouri.

13. Balkoski, Joseph. Beyond the Beachhead. (Mechanicsburg, PA: Stackpole Books, 1999,) 222.

Military Death Records Notes

1. Shomon, Joseph James. Crosses in the Wind,(Netherlands: Keulers, Geleen: 1947, 1991), 160.

2. History, website American Battle Monuments Commission, (http://abmc.gov/commission/history.php 6 September 2013).

3. Richardson, Eudora Ramsay, and Allan, Sherman, Quartermaster Supply in the European Theater of Operations in World War II Volume VII Graves Registration. (Camp Lee, VA: The Quartermaster School, 1948), 1.

4. Ibid.

5. Ibid.

6. Account of cemetery visit written by Patricia Holik, 29 Aug 2013.

7. Department of the Army. Field Manual 10-29 Quartermaster Graves Registration Company. (Washington, D.C.: United States Government Printing Office, 1952), 30-31.

8. Department of the Army. Field Manual 10-29 Quartermaster Graves Registration Company. (Washington, D.C.: United States Government Printing Office, 1952), 31.

9. Department of the Army. Field Manual 10-29 Quartermaster Graves Registration Company. (Washington, D.C.: United States Government Printing Office, 1952), 31-32.

10. Department of the Army. Field Manual 10-29 Quartermaster Graves Registration Company. (Washington, D.C.: United States Government Printing Office, 1952), 32.

11. Department of the Army. Field Manual 10-29 Quartermaster Graves Registration Company. (Washington, D.C.: United States Government Printing Office, 1952), 27-28.

12. Department of the Army. Field Manual 10-29 Quartermaster Graves Registration Company. (Washington, D.C.: United States Government Printing Office, 1952), 29-30.

Notes

13. Department of the Army. Field Manual 10-29 Quartermaster Graves Registration Company. (Washington, D.C.: United States Government Printing Office, 1952), 30.

14. Department of the Army. Field Manual 10-29 Quartermaster Graves Registration Company. (Washington, D.C.: United States Government Printing Office, 1952), 30.

15. Department of the Army. Field Manual 10-29 Quartermaster Graves Registration Company. (Washington, D.C.: United States Government Printing Office, 1952), 36.

16. Department of the Army. Field Manual 10-29 Quartermaster Graves Registration Company. (Washington, D.C.: United States Government Printing Office, 1952), 37.

17. Department of the Army. Field Manual 10-29 Quartermaster Graves Registration Company. (Washington, D.C.: United States Government Printing Office, 1952), 37.

18. Department of the Army. Field Manual 10-29 Quartermaster Graves Registration Company. (Washington, D.C.: United States Government Printing Office, 1952), 37-38.

19. Department of the Army. Field Manual 10-29 Quartermaster Graves Registration Company. (Washington, D.C.: United States Government Printing Office, 1952), 38.

20. Crosses at Normandy, Jun 1944, digital story, U.S. Army Quartermaster Foundation (http://www.qmfound.com/crosses.htm 6 September 2013); citing story of Colonel Elbert E. Legg.

21. Crosses at Normandy, Jun 1944, digital story, U.S. Army Quartermaster Foundation (http://www.qmfound.com/crosses.htm 6 September 2013); citing story of Colonel Elbert E. Legg.

22. Department of the Army. Field Manual 10-63 Graves Registration. (Washington, D.C.: United States Government Printing Office, 1945), 14-15.

23. Department of the Army. Field Manual 10-63 Graves Registration. (Washington, D.C.: United States Government Printing Office, 1945), 16-18.

24. Account of cemetery visit written by Patricia Holik, 29 Aug 2013.

25. Shomon, Joseph James. Crosses in the Wind,(Netherlands: Keulers, Geleen: 1947, 1991), 91.

26. Shomon, Joseph James. Crosses in the Wind,(Netherlands: Keulers, Geleen: 1947, 1991), 137-138.

27. Shomon, Joseph James. Crosses in the Wind,(Netherlands: Keulers, Geleen: 1947, 1991), 15.

28. Department of the Army. Field Manual 10-63 Graves Registration. (Washington, D.C.: United States Government Printing Office, 1945), 23-24.

29. Division of the Federal Register, the National Archives. Code of Federal Regulations of the United States of America. 1946 Supplement. Washington, D.C.:U.S. Government Printing Office, 1947, 5826.

30. Service Record of 1st Lt. Robert E. Bishop, serial no. 0210591, letter to the Secretary of Navy dated 17 Jan 1945. NPRC, St. Louis, Missouri.

31. Service Record of 1st Lt. Robert E. Bishop, serial no. 0210591, letter to the Robert Bishop's parents dated 22 Jan 1946. NPRC, St. Louis, Missouri.

32. Individual Deceased Personnel File, Samuel W. Crowder, service no. 2868801; Board Proceedings Number 1961, Proceedings of Board of Review dated 25 April 1949, p.7.

33. Department of the Army. Field Manual 10-29 Quartermaster Graves Registration Company. (Washington, D.C.: United States Government Printing Office, 1952), 52-53.

34. Shomon, Joseph James. Crosses in the Wind,(Netherlands: Keulers, Geleen: 1947, 1991), 66-67.

35. Richardson, Eudora Ramsay, and Allan, Sherman, Quartermaster Supply in the European Theater of Operations in World War II Volume VII Graves Registration. (Camp Lee, VA: The Quartermaster School, 1948), 87.

36. Richardson, Eudora Ramsay, and Allan, Sherman, Quartermaster Supply in the European Theater of Operations in World War II Volume VII Graves Registration. (Camp Lee, VA: The Quartermaster School, 1948), 88.

37. Shomon, Joseph James. Crosses in the Wind,(Netherlands: Keulers, Geleen: 1947, 1991), 147.

38. WAR-DEAD COFFINS ON WAY TO EUROPE. 1947. New York Times (1923-Current file), May 15, 1947. http://search.proquest.com/docview/107912796 by?accountid=38403 (accessed August 27, 2013).

39. Ibid.

Army, Air Corps, and National Guard Service Records (OMPF)

1. Soldiers Who Are Missing in Action: ARMY LISTS 259 YANKS MISSING ON FIVE FRONTS, Chicago Daily Tribune (1923-1963); Dec 25, 1943; ProQuest Historical Newspapers: Chicago Tribune (1849-1989), p. 4.

2. CHICAGO AIRMEN DIE IN ACTION; 1 MAN MISSING: Gunner Aboard Fortress Only Crew Chicago Daily Tribune (1923-1963); Nov 23, 1944; ProQuest Historical Newspapers: Chicago Tribune (1849-1989), p. 26.

3. American Battle Monuments Commission, Fred A. Davis, (http://abmc.gov/search-abmc-burials-and-memorializations/detail/WWII_50607#.VMunpS5Gwoo : accessed 15 Dec 2014.)

4. Missing Air Crew Report no. 42-72891, 1st Lt. Jeffries Pilot. Records of the Office of the Quartermaster General, Record Group (RG) 92. National Archives, College Park, MD.

5. 3 Nov 1943, Station: Hergla, Tunisia, Company Morning Reports for 344th Bomb Sq, 98th Bomb Group (H) AC. National Personnel Records Center, St. Louis, MO.

6. Air Force Accident Report no. 44-09-08-59. Aviation Archaeology (http://aviationarchaeology.com.)

USMC Records Created In The Field

1. USMC Muster Rolls, National Archives RG 127.3.2 Records of the United States Marine Corps, Personnel Records. William F. Cowart, serial no. 471443. National Archives, College Park, Maryland.

2. United States Marine Corps History Division, Casualty Card Database, (http://www.mcu.usmc.mil/historydivision/Pages/Frequently_Requested/Casualty-Databases.aspx : accessed 8 Jan 2015.)

3. Cowart, William F, Casualty Card, Historical Reference Branch, Marine Corps History Division, Quantico.

4. Individual Deceased Personnel File, Robert E. Bishop, service no. O-021059; USMC Casualty Report dated 18 Jan 1946.

Merchant Marine Records

1. The National Maritime Center Website, eligibility criteria link, (http://www.uscg.mil/nmc/records_request/veteran_request. asp : accessed 23 Jan 2015.)

Researching Women

1. Godson, Susan. Serving Proudly: A History of Women in the U.S. Navy. Annapolis: Naval Institute Press, 2001, 107.

2. Treadwell, Mattie E. U.S. Army in World War II Special Studies. The Women's Army Corps. Washington, D.C., Office of the Chief of Military History. Department of the Army: 1954, p.5.

3. Military Service Publishing Company. The Officer's Guide. Harrisburg: The Military Service Publishing Company, 61.

4. Military Service Publishing Company. The Officer's Guide. Harrisburg: The Military Service Publishing Company, 59-60.

5. Treadwell, Mattie E. U.S. Army in World War II Special Studies. The Women's Army Corps. Washington, D.C., Office of the Chief of Military History. Department of the Army: 1954, p.19.

6. "Women Pilots of World War II," Women in the U.S. Army, website (http://www.army.mil/women/pilots.html : accessed 7 Jan 2014.)
7. Ibid.

8. Red Cross History, website (http://www.redcross.org/about-us/history : accessed 27 Dec 2013.)

9. USO History,website (http://www.uso.org/history.aspx : accessed 27 Dec 2013.)

Acknowledgments

To Johan van Waart, who inspired this book and helped me organize my thoughts. Thank you for your unending love and constant support for my work.

I could not have written this book without the support of my three amazing boys, Andrew, Luke, and Tyler. Thank you for always believing in me and listening to me talk through research problems. I love you all.

Thank you to Nicole and Leon Spronken, Eric Bijtelaar, Ilona Boscher, and Ralph Peeters, for providing permission or sending photos I could use for the book cover.

A big thank you to the two men who help me pull records from the National Archives and answer countless questions. Norm Richards, the best independent military researcher at the National Personnel Records Center in St. Louis. And, Jonathan Webb Deiss, of Soldier Source, a most knowledgeable researcher at the National Archives in Washington, D.C., and College Park, MD. Gentlemen, I could not have written my books without your assistance.

To my editor, Logan Ausmus and cover designer, Sarah Sucansky. Thank you both for helping make this book a reality.

To the fabulous staff at Pritzker Military Museum and Library in Chicago, particularly Paul Grasmehr, Reference Coordinator for answering questions, providing resources and contacts, and brainstorming ideas with me. You make my writing much easier Paul! And to Teri Embrey, Chief Librarian. Thank you so much for your encouragement, advice, discussions on resources, and opportunities to provide this information to others.

Thank you to Annette Amerman, Senior Reference Historian, Historical Reference Branch of the Marine Corps History Division for answering all my Marine Corps questions.

Thank you Barbara Geisler, David Metherell, Danny Keay, and Robert Rumsby for sharing information and discussing the Missing, the Prisoners, the Dead, and IDFPs and X-Files with me.

Thank you to Craig Fuller of Aviation Archaeology for sharing details on Air Force and Navy Accident Reports and MACRS. Craig provided excellent explanations on each type of report and the common questions he receives when people request the files.

There are several researchers who have assisted me in the learning process by sharing their soldier's files or answering questions. They are, Mary Hoyer, Shannon Combs-Bennett, Connie Yen, Lisa Alzo, Ben Osteen, Eric Bijtelaar, Vincent Orrière, Bill Warnock, Ryan Kelly, Bill Black, Mikel Shilling, Herman Wolters, Frank van Lunteren, Norbert Morbé, Romaine Fraiture, Arthur Barie, Robert Rumsby, Yuri Beckers, Ralph Peeters, Jordan Edelstein, Peter Den Tek, Phil Rosenkrantz, and Nicole Spronken.

Index

Index

About The Author

Jennifer Holik is an international researcher, speaker, and author of numerous books, articles, and courses. She holds a BA in History from Missouri University of Science and Technology. Jennifer offers expert World War II, genealogical, and historical research services. She provides clients with detailed and fully cited reports with documents, record analysis, and suggestions for further research. She has the rare expertise to locate, analyze, and interpret World War II records across all branches, reconstruct service history, document where a soldier was throughout service, provide details on combat experience, and when necessary, document the death and burial of a soldier. Connecting the dots and piecing together multiple puzzle pieces of a soldier's story is Jennifer's specialty. Jennifer can write and publish a book about your family or soldier. In addition to research and writing, Jennifer speaks in the United States and Europe at military museums, libraries, genealogy societies, Rotary groups, corporations, and other venues. Her current program topics include beginning genealogy, youth genealogy, and World War II. Jennifer's passion is writing the stories of families, particularly men and women of World War II. She has published several books and guides on these topics.

Research Services

Jennifer offers expert research services and provides clients with detailed and fully cited reports with documents, record analysis, and suggestions for further research. She has the rare expertise to locate, analyze, and interpret World War II records across all branches, reconstruct service history, document where a soldier was throughout service, provide details on combat experience, and when necessary, document the death and burial of a soldier. Connecting the dots and piecing together multiple puzzle pieces of a soldier's story is Jennifer's specialty. In addition, she can write and publish a book about your family or soldier.

Speaking and Education

Do you need a speaker for your meeting? Jennifer speaks often at World War II reunions, European museums, genealogy societies, libraries, Rotary groups, corporations, and other venues. Her current program topics include beginning genealogy, youth genealogy, and World War II.

Writing Services

Jennifer's passion is writing the stories of families, particularly men and women of World War II. She has published several books and guides to date.

You can learn more at http:/wwiirwc.com